WITHDRAWN

before

Nations and Nationa

NATIONS AND NATIONALISM
A READER

Edited by

Philip Spencer and Howard Wollman

EDINBURGH UNIVERSITY PRESS

Selection and editorial material © Philip Spencer
and Howard Wollman, 2005. The texts are
reprinted by permission of other publishers; the
acknowledgements on pp. 349–50 constitute an
extension of this copyright page.

Edinburgh University Press Ltd
22 George Square, Edinburgh

Typeset in Sabon by
Hewer Text Ltd, Edinburgh, and
printed and bound in Great Britain by
The Cromwell Press, Trowbridge, Wilts

A CIP record for this book is available from the
British Library

ISBN 0 7486 1774 4 (hardback)
ISBN 0 7486 1775 2 (paperback)

CONTENTS

PREFACE

In editing this reader we are very appreciative of the continuing support of our families and of colleagues in the Arts and Social Sciences faculties of both Kingston and Napier Universities. We are grateful for the strong support of Nicola Carr, our editor at EUP, at various stages of the work, and for the help of all her colleagues and others involved with the process of seeing this book to completion, including Alison Bowden, Eddie Clark, Stuart Midgley and Jonathan Wadman. Thanks too to Rosa Anderson for her considerable help with the proofs. In compiling this reader, we have enjoyed the co-operation of many publishers but for reasons that will be familiar to all editors of such readers (financial and space constraints) it was sadly not possible for us to include every piece we would have wished at the outset. There is a vast literature on this topic and the keen student will, we hope, find the guide to further reading helpful.

Howard Wollman
Philip Spencer
September 2004

INTRODUCTION

There has been an enormous expansion in the literature on nationalism in recent years. Whilst it would be inaccurate to suggest that interest in the topic had ever flagged, or that it had ever become marginal, there has undoubtedly been a real revival over the past twenty or thirty years, with contributions (some from perhaps surprising quarters) which have significantly altered the terms of debate and discussion.

At one level, this renewed interest reflects the apparent success of nationalism in mobilising political support not only throughout the twentieth century but on into the new one. This mobilisation has occurred in a variety of contexts and settings across the world. The most obvious example is the seemingly unstoppable rise of national liberation movements across the globe, particularly after the Second World War, a process that continued well into the 1960s if not beyond. Then there is the re-emergence of nationalism in eastern Europe and subsequently in the former Soviet Union as the communist system disintegrated in the late 1980s and early 1990s. Even those communist regimes that have somehow survived, notably in the People's Republic of China, seem to have come to depend increasingly on nationalism rather than upon their self-evidently threadbare official ideology. The development of globalisation does not, perhaps paradoxically, appear to have halted nationalism in its tracks. In many ways one could argue the reverse, that it has fostered an increasing attachment to supposedly endangered national identities and the defence of a national sovereignty threatened by more powerful states, alliances or organisations, particularly those located in the 'West'. Even here, in what used to be seen as the more settled polities and societies of western Europe and North America, where it may have been believed that nationalism was on the wane, there is evidence of its renewed appeal, not least in some of the reactions to September 11th.

Important as each of these developments have been (and some of them are referred to in this reader), there is arguably a deeper sense in which nationalism exerts a profound and magnetic pull on citizens and subjects in and across states and regions. This has less to do with any particular set of political successes or failures and more to do with the way in which nationalism has come to shape so much of our understanding and thinking about politics and society, the way in which a belief in the primacy of the nation affects the manner in which political and social discourse is itself structured and conducted.

Some of the reasons for why this should be so, for quite how and why nationalism has become so significant at this deeper level, are the central themes of this reader. The selections here are not based on any attempt to be comprehensive (a futile if not quixotic project) but rather to bring together some of the more interesting contributions to a continually growing literature. With one or two exceptions, they are all pieces which have appeared relatively recently.

This is not in any way to minimise the significance of earlier contributions, both prior to the recent resurgence of nationalism in the latter part of the twentieth century and indeed much further back into the previous century or even earlier. Such writings are not included here for two sets of reasons. The first is a relatively straightforward one – they are both well known and widely available. The second is that, although they are undoubtedly important for a full appreciation of the subject, their significance for the contemporary debate is essentially contextual and anticipatory. They lay down important markers, identify some central issues, and provide a range of perspectives. All these have undoubtedly influenced recent contributors and left their mark in various ways, methodologically and politically. But there are also, and perhaps more importantly, critical ways in which the more recent arguments have recast the debates, changed the focus of discussion, and opened up new perspectives and lines of enquiry.

We can see this in a number of ways. Take, for instance, Johann von Herder's insistence in the eighteenth century on the significance of language, which he saw not only as a means of communication but also and more importantly as a means of differentiation. The existence of different languages, in his view, explained the division of humanity into different, discrete, identifiable nations. This differentiation was a natural phenomenon, a veritable 'law of nature'. 'Since the whole human race is not one single homogeneous group, it does not speak one and the same language. The formation of diverse national languages, therefore, is a natural corollary of human diversity' (Herder 1969: 165). Herder opposed the cosmopolitanism of much of the Enlightenment. He saw it as perverse, as destructive, as insensitive to the achievements and legacies of diverse (national) cultures. He believed that the Enlightenment's infatuation with cold, sober reason downplayed the significance of emotion, of the affective ties that bind nations together; its search for what was common blinded it to what was singular and unique, to what distinguished one nation from another. One can, certainly, trace links between these kinds of arguments and those currently taking place about the meaning and possibility of supra-national, trans-national, international and indeed cosmopolitan developments. But these take place now in a different context, *after* the apparent triumph of nationalism as a political movement, not before it. Herder, after all, might properly not even be considered a nationalist in any meaningful political sense as he was rather essentially concerned with culture; he did not know, nor could he have foreseen, the different ways in which culture itself could be politicised. How and why this has happened has been a major concern for a number of the contributors here but in new ways: in terms of debates about when and why nationalism as an ideology came to prominence; about what cultural difference does, can or should mean; about whether or not there are radically different kinds of nationalism, one 'political', the other 'cultural'.

It might be argued that others, even then, were more aware of the political power and significance of nationalism. Jean-Jacques Rousseau, writing at around the same time as Herder, is often cited as one who understood how important politically nationalism was or ought to be. There is some justice in this view – Rousseau did argue that there were important differences between peoples that needed to be taken into account in thinking about the principles that should underpin the design of political systems. He did argue that a healthy political system needed citizens who took an active pride in their polity, that a sense of patriotism is needed to sustain the ties between citizens.[1] One can certainly trace back to Rousseau, if not even earlier, the argument often advanced by nationalists that a strong sense of a shared national identity is a *sine qua non* for a viable modern state, that it alone can provide the solid basis of trust between citizens to motivate each to sacrifice herself/himself for others. This sacrifice may now take different forms of course to those imagined by Rousseau or his predecessors: it may no longer be primarily military, the demand to die for one's country, to protect one's fellow nationals. It may be a more everyday matter, of taxation for example, of payment for welfare provision for all citizens who share this identity.[2] But this is not purely a matter of shifting modes of sacrifice. The modern state, which is in one shape or form also a welfare state, exists in a different constellation of states and societies. It is no longer (if it ever was) a small-scale, cohesive, implicitly homogeneous unit of a kind that Rousseau may, in any event, have idealised, if not fabricated in his imagination. It is now a complex, large-scale unit, encompassing people who move (in large numbers) around, within and across its borders. It may seek to fortify and defend these borders from violent incursions or invasions, on or above ground; these borders are altogether more permeable with regard to population flows. It is arguable whether these borders can be used to keep people out or indeed whether they should do so at all. The cosmopolitanism of those who argue for easing or abandoning restrictions on migration is different in certain critical respects from that of some of Rousseau's eighteenth-century interlocutors. He may have scorned their lack of feeling, their emotional insensitivity, their lack of attachment to people and places. What their successors point to (as they and he did or could not) is the presence inside modern states of many (immigrants, emigrants, and especially refugees) who fit less easily into patriotism's favoured categories. Their rights are questioned and questionable, their status is uncertain and insecure, at least in part because of the difficulties they appear to pose for an unproblematic and simplistic conception of national identity. Thinking about these issues today requires us to think about how national identity is constructed, about how people have come to identify themselves with particular nations.

In many ways, it was considerations of this order which lay at the heart of the debate about the origins of nationalism, which arguably marked the beginning of the contemporary discussion, staking out key parts of the terrain and landscape. When, broadly speaking, did nationalism emerge? Was it, as some have argued, a wholly or largely new phenomenon, a product or concomitant of modernity, however understood, or does it have much deeper roots, long predating it?

THE PROBLEM OF MODERNITY

In many ways the prime movers of this debate were Anthony Smith and Ernest Gellner, each a prolific writer, and (in Gellner's case especially) not only on nationalism. Smith has argued for many years, with admirable persistence, consistency and erudition, that a major source of the appeal of nationalism lies in the way in which it draws on deep reservoirs of feeling, on a sense of identity that has a long history. This identity may not originally have been national in every sense in which we now understand the word but its broad contours have long been apparent. Nations may not have existed from time immemorial but nor did they appear suddenly or unannounced. They were preceded by what he calls *ethnie*, extensive groups whose members were already tied to each other through sharing a collective proper name, sharing beliefs about ancestry, sharing a particular history and operating within a common cultural framework, and with an enduring association with a particular place (the 'homeland'). These ties have forged over a very long time a profound sense of mutual solidarity, a sense that 'we' care for all who share this heritage, or at any rate that they have a greater and prior claim on us than on others who do not. Successful nations have been constructed on the basis of a pre-existing ethnic core, in whose absence no nationalism can mobilise effectively. Smith is careful to distinguish his argument from altogether cruder and much more instrumental arguments of a kind frequently advanced by (some) nationalists themselves that the nation (their own, at any rate) has existed from time immemorial. He rejects this primordialist or perennialist argument in favour of an altogether more nuanced and sophisticated approach, what he calls an ethno-symbolist one. This, he claims, enables him to recognise the difference between *ethnie* and nations, and thus the modern context in which nations have developed, but also to see the significance of continuities from one to the other. These continuities may involve considerable degrees of myth-making, but these myths are effective, even necessary for group cohesion and identity over time.[3]

An even stronger emphasis on continuity and the significance of the consolidation of ethnic identity can be found in the work of Adrian Hastings, with particular reference to the case of English nationalism, which he sees as going far back to the time of Alfred. So powerful was this sense that repeated invasions could not shake it. Rather, each successive invading group was 'digested' by the conquered. Through subsequent conflicts over territory and borders, but also over allegiance and beliefs, the English sense of themselves as a nation grew and developed, well in advance of modernity, whenever dated and however conceptualised. This original English experience was then replicated elsewhere, sometimes closely (as in the case of the United States), at other times with particular inflections or distortions (as in Germany and Serbia). Some of these developments and experiences may then seem quite recent and modern, but their roots are deep and profound, long predating modernity.

The modernist response is that this whole approach is fundamentally misconceived and effectively gives far too much credence, however inadvertently, to the claims of nationalists themselves. The modernists argue that the nation, in any sense that we recognise today, does not have deep roots but is an essentially modern phenomenon. It emerged at a particular point in time and space, for specific reasons. In Gellner's view, this has to do with the transition from one kind of society to another, from agrarian societies, in which literacy was confined to an elite, to modern industrial societies which require extensive communication between their mobile members. It is essentially this need to communicate in a very different kind of society that generated the need for nations. He is unsparingly critical of the claims of nationalists, insisting that 'nationalism invents nations where they do not exist' (Gellner, 1964: 169).

Not all modernists share Gellner's particular account of modernity nor are they all quite as harsh in their scepticism about nationalist claims. Benedict Anderson, who is with Gellner perhaps the most influential modernist, provides a significantly different account of the context within which nationalism first emerged. Drawing to some extent on Marxism, Anderson relates the emergence of nationalism to capitalism, to technological developments (notably the invention of printing) and to the spread of the vernacular. Anderson argues that what is novel about nationalism is how nationalists imagine the community in distinctive ways, how nationalism enables people to see themselves connected to people they have never met and will never meet. Nationalists construct and present the nation as a political community of a particular kind, at once sovereign and limited. Imagination is, however, not the same as invention. There is no one 'true' version against which other fabricated versions can be measured and found wanting. Rather, one has to think about particular nations as the products of different imaginative styles, each nationalism telling its own particular story, drawing on its own materials.

These are both sweeping and comprehensive approaches, perhaps too abstractly so in the view of John Breuilly, who locates nationalism in a conception of modernity in which politics plays a rather more central role. For Breuilly, it is the emergence of the modern state which is the key, since it is the control of its power and resources that is the prime focus of nationalist mobilisation. Nationalist ideas are important not only or primarily for their own sake but because they are used for identifiable purposes and projects. These may vary. There are nationalist movements that aim to gain control of an existing state, turning it into a nation state in the process. There are those that aim to expand the state through unifying different groups in one nation. There are those that aim to divide the state through the secession of one group from another or others.

Breuilly's focus, like that of Gellner and (to perhaps a lesser extent) Anderson, is predominantly Western. It is here that they each locate the central features of modernity. It is here where industrialisation takes off, where mass literacy becomes a major requirement. It is here where print-capitalism first develops, where it becomes possible for large numbers of people to imagine themselves as connected across time and space. It is here where what Anthony Giddens (1985) describes as the 'bordered power-container' that is the modern state emerges, with its vast array and panoply of forces, weapons, institutions and laws.

These arguments, both between modernists and their critics and within and beyond modernism, have potentially far-reaching implications. If the anti-modernists are right and nationalism has such deep and profound roots, it is not difficult to see why it has such an appeal today. Attempts to invoke alternative identifications, affiliations and loyalties are bound to be at a significant disadvantage; they are unlikely to be able to compete on an even footing with nationalism, let alone displace it, but are likely to falter and fail, in the long if not the short run. On the other hand, if nationalism is a more bounded phenomenon, a product of particular historical processes and dynamics, the future may be rather more open. It is not automatically the case that other ways of thinking, other solidarities, may not prevail, sooner or later. Within modernity, other ideologies may also have developed, before, alongside or even after and in reaction to it.

Approaches to nationalism

One way of thinking about this issue is to examine the relationship between nationalism and other ideologies, to see whether or not there is a fundamental clash between irreconcilably different ways of thinking and different sets of values, or whether nationalism can be merged in some way, integrated within other frameworks, or vice-versa.

These questions have generated considerable debate, as thinkers of various persuasions have approached nationalism in different ways, oscillating between enthusiasm and alarm, between optimism and pessimism. This has been the case, if unevenly, right across the political spectrum for the past two centuries at least. There have been liberals who have welcomed nationalism and those who have condemned it; there have been conservatives made anxious by its subversive threat to the existing order and those who have sought to harness its power; there have been socialists resolutely opposed to its divisive potential and those who have seen it as indispensable; there have been feminists who have wished to have nothing to do with it and those who have embraced it.

There have been, for example, many liberals who were enthusiastic supporters of nationalism. Perhaps its most passionate liberal advocate was the nineteenth-century Italian Giuseppe Mazzini with his generous vision of a world harmoniously divided into a federation of (selected) democratic and republican nation states. There was, in his eyes, no contradiction at all between a belief in humanity and a belief in nationality. For, 'without the nation, there can be no humanity . . . Nations are the citizens of humanity, as individuals are the citizens of the nation' (Mazzini 1891: 275). He looked forward eagerly to the day when a general rising of national movements would expel foreigners from each nation, and create a federation of democratic, republican nation states. Mazzini was by no means alone in taking such a positive view of nationalism, in seeing it as so intimately linked to fundamental liberal beliefs and values. John Stuart Mill, for instance, thought that nationalism was wholly compatible with fundamental liberal arguments for freedom and democracy, arguing that there was a strong case 'for uniting all the members of the same nationality under the same government, and a government to themselves apart . . . This is merely saying that the question of government ought to be decided by the governed'. Indeed he suggested that 'free institutions are next to impossible in a country made up of different nationalities' (Mill 1996: 41).

This optimistic view was not, however, shared by all liberals even at the time. Others saw it in a rather harsher light, as a collectivist ideology inimical to individual freedom and as an inherently authoritarian menace to both liberty and democracy. In the latter part of the nineteenth century, Lord Acton for example argued that nationalism was not a servant of liberty but a threat, that it threatened to suppress or eliminate diversity, that its homogenising drive would serve the interests of centralised state power. In the end, nationalism would not serve but become what he called 'a confutation of democracy' (Acton 1996: 41).

These two antithetical positions, one supportive of nationalism, the other opposed to it, have certainly influenced the contemporary discussion, but its tenor and focus is now different in important ways. This is not merely a reflection of the political realities to which we alluded above, although this is certainly one motivation for liberals to seek some accommodation with such a powerful force. It is also again because it is necessary to think more critically today about identity, culture and difference than earlier liberals did or could. It would be hard today for a liberal sympathetic to nationalism today to go along with Mill's assertion that 'nobody can suppose that it is not more beneficial to a

Breton or a Basque . . . to be brought into the current of the ideas and feelings of a highly civilised and cultivated people – to be a member of the French nationality . . . than to sulk on his own rocks, the half-savage relic of past times, revolving in his own little mental orbit, without participation or interest in the general movement of the world' (Mill 1996: 44). Equally, however, some of Acton's riposte to Mill rested on assumptions that would also not be accepted today. His argument for multi-national states, for example, was advanced in part on the grounds that 'inferior races are raised by living in political union with races intellectually superior' (Acton 1996: 31).

The discussion today amongst liberals is therefore more complex and more nuanced, as Andrew Vincent's careful and extensive survey makes clear. Those liberals who see liberalism and nationalism as compatible do so in part because they believe that there is no alternative, that nationalism is unchallengeable at some level, but also because they think it can reinforce liberalism in certain ways. It makes no sense, they argue, to pretend that we can ignore or do without deep attachments to a national identity which are formed very early on; the nation at some profound level helps shape who we are, our basic orientation to life. It structures our choices in some fundamental way. We cannot choose to discard this aspect of our being. Instead, we need to think about how to combine it with our other values and commitments, to celebrate, as Yael Tamir puts it, 'the particularity of [national] culture with the universality of human rights, the social and particular embeddedness of individuals together with their personal autonomy' (Tamir 1993: 79). Vincent gives full weight here to these and other arguments but also provides counters, teasing out the potential contradictions and pitfalls of such a position, offering a more sceptical view.

If there has been and still is no liberal consensus, similar oscillations can also be descried elsewhere. There has certainly been considerable uncertainty too amongst socialists and Marxists. Some of this may be due to the complexity, if not inconsistency, of Karl Marx's own writings. At one time (or better perhaps in one voice), he appeared to endorse a version of G. W. F. Hegel's distinction between historic and non-historic nations, with the former doomed to disappear and be swallowed up in larger, more economically viable units; at another to denounce nationalism as a snare and a delusion; and then to argue (as in the case of Ireland or Poland) that oppressed nations should be supported in their struggle against foreign control and domination. There certainly were clear differences of opinion amongst his immediate successors. If Rosa Luxemburg was adamant that socialists should as a matter of cardinal principle have no truck with nationalism,[4] Vladimir Lenin urged a more instrumental approach, arguing that in a capitalist world nations had a right to self-determination, although in a socialist society this was not a right that they would surely then want to exercise. Others have taken the logic of Lenin's argument still further, arguing that this is more than a matter of tactics but one itself of principle, that there is a fundamental difference between the nationalism of the oppressor and that of the oppressed, that the nationalist revolt of the periphery against the centre is inherently progressive, even if it results in the creation of small (even arguably economically unviable) units.[5]

These debates can be thought about at a number of levels. Efforts may be made to assess outcomes in any particular episode or case, to evaluate the implications of the particular strategies adopted by local communist or socialist movements, to see whether or not an attempt either to compete with or to accommodate to nationalism was successful. To what extent was the adoption of nationalism by communist parties in, for example, Cuba or Vietnam or China a major factor in their success in defeating imperialism and taking power? Conversely, how far can it be argued that nationalism came to displace communism in some or all of these cases, subverting it gradually from within? Or indeed elsewhere, did not nationalism undermine communism radically and subvert it entirely from without or from below, playing a major role in the disintegration of communist states in eastern Europe and then the Soviet Union itself at the end of the 1980s and the beginning of the 1990s?

There are detailed arguments to be had about these issues and cases which require careful and detailed empirical scrutiny. But we may also be now in a position to reconsider the overall framework within which some (if not all) of this debate has been conducted, to look back at some of the fundamental arguments in the light of these developments. This is what Erica Benner has tried to do in her effort to think now from a post-communist vantage point about what Marx and Friedrich Engels might be able to tell us about 'really existing' nationalism. She suggests that they had a greater awareness of some of the dynamics and issues we have already touched on (as well as others that also feature here) than is often recognised. They did, she claims, understand that national identity did matter to people but that what that identity might be was itself the object of debate. Different nationalists offered competing versions of this identity, as they sought to represent the nation in quite different ways. If we reconstruct their argument, we can see, she claims, that Marx and Engels, so far from either dismissing nationalism or adopting a purely external pragmatic approach, were able to discriminate between different nationalist movements. They were able to discern the logic and direction of different movements and to critique them from what she identifies as a 'normative conception of human community and self-determination' (Benner 1995: 10).

This normative position is, of course, not uncontested, its key terms not wholly self-evident. There are serious questions to be asked: for instance, about what or rather who exactly is included in such a community or ought to be. These are difficult questions which require both some serious conceptual clarification and some reconsideration of core assumptions underlying earlier arguments about nationalism. They require the development of new angles of vision, new perspectives which enable us to see not only what nationalism brings to the fore but what it obscures, not only what it presents but what it omits.

Probably the major contribution here has been from feminism. There was, after all, barely any recognition in the classic literature of the role assigned to women in the construction of the nation, little awareness of how nationalism worked to mobilise (and conversely demobilise) different sections of the 'people'. In thinking about the progressive or subversive character of nationalism, in for instance the revolutions in England, America and France, little attention was paid to the absence or marginalisation of women, an absence and marginalisation that has been only problematically and unevenly remedied in the anti-colonial struggle (Jayawardena 1986; Moghadam 1994). Thinking about this issue has, we might suggest, generated some similar uncertainties and oscillations among feminists to those we sketched above in the ranks of liberals and socialists. There have been those who have reacted with defiance to what they have seen as their exclusion from the nation. As Virginia Woolf once famously put it, 'as a woman, I have no country. As a woman, I want no country. As a woman, my country is the whole world' (Woolf 1977: 125). On the other hand, there have been those who think that women have always been central in some way to the construction of the nation, that there is no inherent flaw in nationalism but that its work is incomplete, that the inclusion of women (however unevenly) in the anti-imperialist struggle is a sign of sure if not steady progress (West 1997).

This discussion too can be conducted at a number of levels. There is a substantially empirical question of the involvement or exclusion of women from particular nationalist projects. There are important comparisons to be made over time and place, both between particular cases and within them, tracing levels of involvement and engagement as struggles have waxed and waned, as women have been drawn in and as they have been marginalised. There is also, however, the question of what implications this presence or absence has for how the nation is itself constructed, not only materially but also symbolically and for how the exclusion and selective inclusion of women on particular terms has affected what the nation was deemed to be. This shifts the focus from the specific and varied experience of women to the more general question of how the nation itself has been (en)gendered. This is the question that Joane Nagel pursues in her discussion here, not ignoring the substantial body of evidence that has been accumulated by a growing body of feminist scholarship but rather drawing on the deeper inspiration that generated these enquiries in the first place. She looks not only at how and where women have been excluded but why this might be so, at how the nation is always a gendered construct. As a result and from the outset, nationalism always addresses itself differentially to men and women, mobilises and demobilises them in different ways, both in the making of nations and in their defence.

DIFFERENTIATING NATIONALISM

But there are other questions too that need to be addressed in this context. The nation is not only a gendered construct but may also be a racialised and ethnicised one. In some respects, consideration of such questions takes us back to the debate about modernity, to the question of whether the nation is a new phenomenon, quite distinct from other group identities, or whether it grows out of them in some way. But the issue here is less *when* the nation emerged than *what* exactly the term is supposed to denote. How in particular is a nation to be distinguished, conceptually, from a 'race', how is nationality different from ethnicity?

There is of course immense debate about each of these other terms. The former term ('race') has largely been discredited scientifically, there being no serious evidence for significant biological differences between supposed 'races' at all, although many people continue of course to believe the opposite. The question of ethnicity is more complex, since it refers not so much to purported actual biological differences between people as to cultural ones, to beliefs (particularly about the past, about ancestry, about place of origin), to values and norms.

A major difficulty here is that many of the features so used to identify an ethnic group are also used to define nations. This is one of the problems with Smith's influential argument, where at least three of the six elements he uses to identity an ethnic identity reappear in his definition of a national one. But Smith's difficulty is not his alone, as Thomas Eriksen's careful discussion here makes clear. Both ethnic identities and national identities are developed in relation to others, and those who prioritise such identities have to pay considerable attention to how the necessary boundaries that distinguish one from another are constructed and maintained. It may be possible analytically to claim that what those boundaries consist of (or where they are located) differs. It can for instance be argued, as Eriksen (to some extent following Breuilly here) suggests, that nationalism seeks a state, that the boundaries are essentially political but, as he then immediately goes on to note, this distinction very often does not stand up in practice.

It may then be more helpful to look not so much at what the terms mean in abstraction or isolation, to look not so much at 'nation' or 'race' or 'ethnicity' but at racialisation, at the construction of ethnic identity and how each of these processes is connected (or not) to the construction and defence of national identity. Paul Gilroy argues that these processes are indeed closely linked, in part because they all involve elements of fixing, of treating identity as if it were something static or given, rather than something fluid and open to change. The shared concern with the vital significance of persistent sameness and difference, with the need to clearly demarcate who is 'us' and who is 'them', can become pathological, generating camp mentalities of various kinds, rooted in and fostering fears that the essential core of the identity will be undermined from without. This happens too often for it to be mere coincidence. Rather, as Etienne Balibar suggests, there may be some intrinsic ambiguity in nationalism that means it can easily become entangled and bound up with these other processes of identification. Nationalism is often racialised; it does often draw its strength from constructions of the nation and others in which difference is essentialised and polarised through the imputation of permanent biological and/or cultural differences.

FORMS OF NATIONALISM

A key issue then is whether or not it is not only desirable but possible for processes of nationalist identification to be divorced from such processes of racialisation or ethnicisation. Although these were not the terms he used, the nineteenth-century French writer Ernest Renan argued something along these lines in his effort to define the nation. Acknowledging that nationalists invoke a particular version of the past (in which what is left out is arguably as important as what is left in), Renan proposed a definition of the nation as the outcome of an sustained agreement between citizens, what he called a 'daily plebiscite' to see each other as inheritors of an agreed past, sharing in a common project for the present and the future (Renan 1996). Renan's argument has had a powerful influence on much of the literature on nationalism. There have been a number of efforts to develop and broaden his implicit contrast into a more general and systematic one. Perhaps the most sustained effort to do so came from Hans Kohn, an émigré himself (perhaps not coincidentally) from Nazi Germany, who devoted much of his life to arguing that there had for a long time been two quite distinct forms of nationalism. The first kind emerged in the West, and was an integral part and parcel of the English Revolution in the seventeenth century, and of the American and above all the French revolutions in the eighteenth century. It was an essentially political phenomenon, intimately linked to democratisation. The second, which emerged in and as a reaction to this in the East, in Germany and further afield, was cultural not political, not democratic and indeed even hostile to democracy. The first was about choice, about consent, about the will of citizens to constitute themselves as a nation. The second was about birth, about biological descent, and about what was inherited from the past. The nation here was not constituted by a decision of people to live together but was already a given, determined by history, a fate from which none could escape (Kohn 1965).

This distinction, reworked in various ways, has become very influential. Even Smith, who as we have seen insists on the significance of ethnic cores for the construction of successful nations, argues that we need an analytic framework which can enable us to distinguish different kinds of nations. There are, he argues, two (ideal) types – one civic, the other ethnic, even if in practice no actual nation may fit either type perfectly. In the former model, the nation is grounded to a significant extent on legal and political norms, in which all its members are equal before the law and all have equal political rights, underpinned by a civic culture and ideology. In the latter, there is a significantly different cultural and ideological underpinning, a persistent emphasis on origins, historically and geographically. One cannot, in this conception, easily (if at all) become a member of another nation and have all or some of these rights.

This distinction matters, it may be argued, in a whole host of ways, not least in the way in which citizenship is allocated. It is often claimed, for example, that there are clear differences in the ways in which state policies in this regard were developed in France and Germany, two states at the heart of Europe. In a detailed study published shortly after the reunification of Germany and which in many ways fleshed out some of Kohn's arguments, Rogers Brubaker (1992) suggested that one could clearly identify the evolution over time of two fundamentally different conceptions of nationhood and citizenship. In the French case, there was an essentially state-centred conception, open to others, seeking to assimilate them within a nation identified as a polity of a particular kind, a republic, whose broad contours were laid out by the revolution. In the German case, the conception of the nation was historically pre-political, grounded in a self-understanding of a *Volk*, preoccupied with difference. The long-term tendency here was to award citizenship differentially, to some but not others, depending on their origins and descent.

There is a weight of evidence, in both policy and intellectual debate, to support this line of argument. But there is also countervailing evidence and interpretation, and indeed Brubaker himself (1998) seems more recently to have modified his own position. For what it may have obscured is what is common to all forms of nationalism, whether in the East or the West, inside Europe or outside. Michael Billing argues that we need to pay more attention to background assumptions, to routine invocations of the nation, to the daily, repeated celebration of identity that is no less (indeed the more) effective for going so largely unrecognised. The contrast between a 'hot' nationalism, overtly invoking difference, mobilising passionate concerns about identity, and a 'cold' nationalism of secure and established nation states where such emotional engagement may be seen as destructive if not primitive, does not in Billig's view hold up to close scrutiny. Rather there is a constant 'flagging' of the nation, a persistent reminder of who 'we' are and how 'we' differ from 'them', a flagging whose function is to secure some in their identity and render others insecure, to confirm some in their beliefs and sense of entitlement and to undermine others. Billig's approach is largely that of a social psychologist, focusing on the forces and mechanisms that foster a sense of national belonging in the present. It may be complemented by an awareness of the complexities and vicissitudes of historical development across a range of actual nation states, old and new. Questioning the value-laden assumptions that underpin all efforts to distinguish between different forms of nationalism, we have ourselves suggested the distinctions are not firm. There seems to be a persistent tendency for supposedly civic conceptions of the nation to become ethnic, if they are not indeed always so at some level. It is not always easy to see where exactly to draw the line between the two types, particularly over time, or to see how a purely political or civic conception of the nation can sustain itself. Even the most supposedly civic nations seem to require from their citizens some level of emotional attachment to a sense of fixed and permanent distinctiveness, that this nation has and always has had a fundamentally different cultural identity to that one. But this emotional attachment has not only had to be fostered; it has also been used for various purposes, notably to keep some in and keep others out, to give rights to some and withhold them from others, undermining supposedly civic nations' conceptions of themselves and how they differ from ethnic ones. This slippage may be expressive of a deeper uncertainty about national identity, about what exactly it is that makes this nation different to that.

NATIONAL SELF-DETERMINATION AND NATIONALIST MOBILISATION

This has serious implications for some of the most apparently compelling nationalist arguments, notably those relating to the critical question of national self-determination. If we cannot be clear about how nations differ fundamentally from each other, we may not be able with any assurance to determine which nations have the right to self-determination at all and which do not, which are 'real' nations and which are not. In some ways this goes to the heart of the question of nationalism. For perhaps its strongest claim is not only that the world is divided into nations but that each nation has a fundamental right to determine its own future, to be master of its own fate. This claim is part, one might say, of the common sense of the age, linking beliefs in both freedom and democracy to beliefs about the nation. Just as we think that individuals ought to be free to determine their own lives, so too do we seem to think about nations, that they should be free from the control of others. The democratic principle, that a people should have the right to determine its own affairs seems to translate easily and directly into the notion that each nation should be sovereign over its own affairs.

This has certainly been amongst nationalism's most powerful appeals, particularly over the past two centuries, and shows little sign of diminishing. It was central in many ways to the anti-colonial struggle, which gave nationalism a whole new lease of life in the twentieth century, reinvigorating its appeal across the political spectrum. For was not Mazzini's argument for self-determination fulfilled far more extensively and consistently in the twentieth than in the nineteenth century? Were not the national liberation struggles of the Algerians (against the French), the Kenyans (against the British) or the Vietnamese (against the Americans) a vindication of his earlier vision, spreading it far and wide beyond a merely European or Western dimension?

In the immediate glow of the successful and long-awaited expulsion of imperialism, such popular struggles seemed to still much of the earlier ambivalence about nationalism. There was, clearly, enormous enthusiasm and support for such struggles not only within particular arenas of conflict, from those suffering imperialist control and exploitation, but globally. It was not too long, however, before doubts and uncertainties were again to resurface as, in the post-colonial era, new tensions and problems arose.

Thinking about these issues may require some reconsideration of some of the debates about the origins and deeper appeals of nationalism that we referred to earlier. For from a post-colonial perspective, many of these arguments may be criticised for being excessively Eurocentric, treating the development of nationalism outside the continent of Europe as largely and unproblematically derivative. Rather, as Partha Chatterjee argues, the development of nationalism should instead be thought about as an export which has had particular effects. In their eagerness to adopt an ideology whose roots (and perhaps reason) lay elsewhere, nationalists outside the West may have ended up embracing an ideology that has marginalised other, subaltern voices and acted to suppress an existing and fruitful diversity. They have presented the nation as modern, rational and progressive, as in some sense inevitable, when it may be none of these things. It is a particular discourse, secreting contradictions of its own. On the one hand, it has contributed to the effective mobilisation of popular forces against imperialism; on the other hand, this unity has been established within a specific, forced and perhaps unstable problematic. For it can be argued that nationalism here did not break quite as radically as may be supposed from the framework laid down by imperialism: the identity of the 'nation' here was in some critical respects 'given' by imperialist arrangements, administratively, cartographically, even culturally. The unity of the imperialist nation was, in a sense, bought at a price whose true costs were to show themselves after liberation – in the refusal to acknowledge difference within its borders, in the privileging of certain voices over others, of those who claimed to speak for the whole or real nation, its (self-appointed) guardians.

The outcome of many national liberation struggles has in any event seemed more mixed than many might have predicted or hoped, both externally and internally. Successful insurgency against imperialism has in too many cases been followed by bitter and fierce conflicts both between and within new, supposedly sovereign, nation states. (It was one such case indeed, a war between two supposedly socialist states, Vietnam and Cambodia, in the immediate aftermath of their jointly successful defeat of American imperialism, that led Anderson to write his influential work).[6] Internally many of the new regimes have suffered from something of a democratic deficit (to put it mildly), as repressive regimes have often formed and consolidated their grip on power, silencing and stamping down on dissent in sometimes extremely brutal ways. These issues are at the centre of Dominic Thomas's troubling essay on developments in sub-Saharan Francophone Africa, informed as it is by the kind of postcolonialist perspective which, as we have suggested above, has widened our lens on nationalism.

Thomas asks us to think about those who have been silenced by new elites in the pursuit and maintenance of nation state power. This silencing has been both symbolic and physical, in the effort to enforce uniformity and loyalty to the nation state or rather to those who claim to speak in its name. This is scarcely a new problem, as the denial of rights, to minorities and indeed often of the most basic human rights, has sadly accompanied the actual exercise of self-determination since it became widely accepted in the early years of the twentieth century. Repeatedly, the claim to exercise this right has clashed with others, as statesmen and politicians across the political spectrum, from the American President Woodrow Wilson to the Soviet Communist leader Lenin, have repeatedly failed to accord it consistently and without seemingly arbitrary if not self-interested restrictions, a pattern that has continued up to the present day.

Must this be so? Is there a fundamental problem with the concept itself that necessarily generates insurmountable problems with any effort to implement it? There have been those who have argued that this is so, that there can be no clear answer to the question of who the national 'self' is, about who exactly is supposed to have this right to self-determination. Efforts to claim such a right will generate, as Wilson himself was to discover, an infinite number of claims.[7] This right will clash with other rights – the right to form a state for example will clash with the right of another state to determine its own affairs. It is therefore no accident that it is a right which has to be fought for, its acceptance the outcome of violent conflict, which is itself likely to generate the suppression of other rights.

Margaret Moore argues that this is not so, insisting that a clear and coherent account can be given of what this right involves and that its application need not involve inconsistencies and contradictions of this kind. Whilst recognising that there have been a range of problems, in international law, in political practice and in philosophical coherence, she advocates a version of this right which involves the equal recognition of different national identities. This would take us beyond the narrow limits of a territorial conception and open the way to more imaginative solutions to what may have hitherto seemed intractable problems.

It can be argued that something like this is already happening in some places. The re-emergence of nationalism in for instance parts of western Europe or in North America has not been a simple repetition of the demand for secession, pitting one right against another or others. Rather, this revived nationalism has involved a simultaneous reassertion of national identity alongside a recognition of the existence and value of other identities, including regional, supra-national and international ones. Thus one can claim at the same time a Scottish or a Catalonian identity but also a British one and a European one, or claim a Quebecois identity alongside a Canadian and a North American one (Keating 2001). This argument would suggest that we are beginning to find ways of reconciling rights through a more flexible notion of national identity. It presumes that nationalism can still be a progressive not divisive force, aiming to include rather than exclude, acting as a bridge between peoples inside and across states, and within (if not perhaps yet across) continents.

The evidence for this is inconclusive in many ways, at least at this stage. This is in part because, within these particular arenas, there is also evidence of other more familiar dynamics, of the assertion of the primacy of national identity over others, which may well culminate precisely in the emergence of separate states and corresponding demands for demarcation and exclusion. It is also because there are a number of other cases on the other side of Europe and beyond where the reassertion of national identity has led to such outcomes. In the Baltic region, the relatively peaceful reconstitution of for instance Latvia and Estonia as sovereign states led to the withdrawal of citizenship from substantial Russian minorities, or a serious threat of such action (Kionka and Vetik 1996; Nørgaard et al. 1996). Elsewhere in the former Soviet Union, this reassertion involved extensive mobilisation by nationalist elites seeking to reorder the state's human and cultural boundaries in their own interests. Mark Beissinger insists that nationalism has to be understood as a form of contentious politics, in which elites play a critical role in developing and projecting 'master-frames'. Indeed he suggests that they were helped to do so in this particular case precisely by the fluidity (or what he calls the 'mercurial character') of identity in this region. Nationalist success was not the result of a simple reassertion of old, repressed national identity but the re-imagining of political community by determined elites with specific strategic aims in mind.

GLOBALISATION, CITIZENSHIP AND NATIONALISM

Those aims have to do above all with the control of resources that independent statehood promises. In an increasingly globalised world, it is sometimes suggested that such sovereign power is becoming increasingly tenuous and that the nation state is losing its capacity to act independently or to resolve any of the major problems besetting a world where global interconnectedness leaves nation states far less scope for autonomous action. Michael Mann disputes the simplicity of this view, arguing that the forces that are often claimed to be weakening nation states – global capitalism, environmental threats, identity politics and 'post-nuclear geopolitics' – have differential effects on states in different regions of the world. Indeed he argues that, whilst some aspects of the powers of nation states might be weakening, others are strengthening. Against the trend of many analysts (especially postmodernists) he argues that 'local interaction networks' may actually be weakening more than national ones, and that while 'global interaction networks' are strengthening, these do not necessarily entail the ending of nation state influences in the areas where they operate. Rather, nation states still crucially mediate many global forces and interactions.

If nation states do still in fact control crucial resources and do still maintain effective sovereignty, the normative basis on which they do so is arguably less clear. There are a whole host of issues that could be discussed here but proper consideration of many of them would take us far beyond the scope of this particular reader. There is clearly a major debate in international relations about the continuing validity of the Westphalian framework laid down in the seventeenth century; there are serious arguments about the resources and interests of different states in the current world order, and about the role of international, supra-national and trans-national bodies and the interests they serve; there are significant controversies over whether or not other states or bodies have the right to intervene in the internal affairs of other nation states. In this last section of this reader, we highlight only one set of issues but it is one that in many ways goes to the heart of current debates about nationalism. Over what populations do national elites now rule? Who are or ought to be members of their states and what rights do they have or ought they to have?

For it is clear that there is now very substantial global mobility, that large numbers of people do move across the borders of nation states, whether nationalists like this or not. It can of course be argued that they have always done so, but the scale and volume of migration does now seem to be of a different order and magnitude (Castles and Miller 2003). This is for a variety of reasons, which may be hard to disentangle. Economic and political factors, push-and-pull dynamics, are difficult to identify with any certainty. It can be difficult to ascertain with any precision whether migration is chosen or forced, although there are very clearly large numbers of refugees now in flight from all too many zones of conflict across the globe. What seems clear is that as they move, migrants create new communities, new identities. There are now a number of global diasporas; there are now many people with hybrid identities, composed of different historic and contemporary elements.

Stephen Castles argues that this epoch of migration poses a major challenge to prevailing conceptions of citizenship, exposing fundamental fault-lines and contradictions between image and reality, between supposed norms and their consistent application. Examining a range of issues raised by such global migration – ethnicity, racialisation, gender and minority rights – Castles argues that the nation state model cannot provide an adequate basis for belonging in 'the age of globalisation and migration'. Indeed the continued adherence to a nationality-based concept of citizenship is likely to provoke more social and political exclusion on racial and ethnic grounds.

On the other hand, it can be argued that the reality of large-scale migration is already forcing changes to citizenship rules, overriding such ideological barriers. Since large-scale migration cannot be wished away, some nation states individually and collectively have begun to modify their stubborn adherence to nationalist assumptions that no longer fit the reality. It has then been argued (Soysal 1994) that a new *postnational* model of citizenship is thus implicitly being developed, involving an expansion of rights and their allocation to those who would historically have been denied them.

There are two possible responses to this argument and development. One essentially nationalist response is to seek to turn back the tide, as it were, on the grounds that this process threatens fatally to strip the nation state of its most fundamental powers, undermining its sovereignty and weakening the ties that bind citizens to the state. As David Jacobson has warned, 'determining who may become a member and a citizen is the state's way of shaping the *national* community . . . if *strangers* can enter at will, the ability of the state to shape and define a nation is compromised' (Jacobson 1996: 5–6; our emphasis). The other response is to try to go beyond this nationalist frame of reference and consider alternatives.

David Held has worked hard to do just this, proposing to breach what he sees as the increasingly arbitrary and indefensible boundaries of the national political community. We live now in a more (but incompletely) globalised world which requires a new cosmopolitanism. It is not the abstract, bloodless version derided by Rousseau, since it recognises the contribution of national cultures but also of diaspora and hybridity. Politically, it aims to go beyond mediation between different nation states and to develop broader, complementary political structures that can cope with needs and problems that are generated at a global level as well as a national one, and guarantee the rights of citizens across national borders and boundaries as well as inside them.

Such arguments have gathered some momentum in recent years. It may be too much to suggest that they signal the beginning of a new era in the study of nationalism but they seem to signal at the very least a change of dimension and a shift of perspective. They raise the possibility of going beyond nationalism whilst acknowledging its real and profound impact over time. How possible any such move is remains to be seen but what is clear is that any effort to go beyond nationalism has to be grounded in a serious awareness of what this impact has been on history, on politics, on culture, on society, at so many levels and in so many dimensions. It is to give some sense of how this impact has been variously and diversely understood, across a range of disciplines and perspectives, that we have compiled this reader.

NOTES

1. Rousseau for instance suggested very different political arrangements for Corsica and for Poland. His awareness of the significance of nationalism is discussed by Cobban (1968) – see, especially, Chapter 4. Todorov (1993) argues, however, that Rousseau was actually in many ways a critic of nationalism.
2. For an extended theoretical argument along these lines, see Miller (1995).
3. For an interesting set of studies on the role and function of national myths in a number of cases, see Hosking and Schöpflin (1997).
4. Many of Luxemburg's arguments are collected in Davis (1976). For sympathetic interpretations of her often misunderstood arguments, see Shelton (1987) and more recently Cocks (2002).
5. This argument has been advanced for a number of years by Tom Nairn, originally in the context of his analysis of the British state and more latterly with broader reference to developments further afield, including those in the former Yugoslavia (Nairn 1977, 1997a).
6. See the preface to Anderson (1983). It is not entirely clear that Anderson's subsequent argument provides much grounds for thinking that conflicts of this kind can be avoided in the future.
7. As he somewhat ruefully reflected, 'when I gave utterance to those words ["that all nations had the right to self-determination"]I said them without the knowledge that nationalities existed, which are coming to us day after day . . . You do not know and cannot appreciate the anxieties that I have experienced as a result of many millions of people having their hopes raised by what I have said' (quoted in Cobban 1969: 65).

PART ONE
THE ORIGINS OF NATIONALISM

I

ETHNO-SYMBOLISM AND THE STUDY OF NATIONALISM

Anthony Smith

The *ethno-symbolic* approaches make a number of claims, which constitute a set of basic themes or motifs.

1. LA LONGUE DURÉE

The first theme is the claim that, if we want to grasp the power and understand the shape of modern nations and nationalisms, we must trace the origins and formation of nations, as well as their possible future course, over long periods of time (*la longue durée*), and not tie their existence and formation to a particular period of history or to the processes of modernization. Nations are historical phenomena, not only in the generic sense that they are embedded in particular collective pasts and emerge, sometimes over long time-spans, through specific historical processes, but also because, by definition, they embody shared memories, traditions, and hopes of the populations designated as parts of the nation. Indeed, a central theme of historical ethno-symbolism is the relationship of shared memories to collective cultural identities: memory, almost by definition, is integral to cultural identity, and the cultivation of shared memories is essential to the survival and destiny of such collective identities. That is why [. . .] historians have played so central a role in the delineation of the nation and in the rediscovery, transmission, and analysis of its ethnic heritage. It may also be the reason why historians dominated causal enquiry into the nature, course and appeal of nations and nationalism, at least in the earlier stages.

Anthony D. Smith (1999), *Myths and Memories of the Nation*, Oxford: Oxford University Press.

Historical enquiry, while it may demystify and dispel fictions, can also reinforce the shared memories and aspirations of members, their *ethno-history*, by providing material or documentary evidence for events and personages held in reverence by the community. At the same time, it may reveal the long-term processes in which the rise of nations and the spread of nationalism are embedded. For historical ethno-symbolism, this double historicity of nations and nationalism – their rootedness in shared long-term memories or *ethno-history*, and the resulting need to analyse them over long historical time-spans – constitutes an underlying methodological postulate. (See Llobera 1994, ch. 1; Smith 1986, chs 1–2.)

2. National past, present, and future

This long-term relationship between national past, present, and future constitutes a second major theme, and it can be examined under three headings: recurrence, continuity, and reappropriation.

Recurrence: For perennialists, the nation is a recurrent form of social organization and nationalism a perennial mode of cultural belonging. But this is to read the history of earlier epochs in the light of the nationalist present. [. . .] Using my own definition of the nation – *as a named human population sharing an historic territory, common myths and historical memories, a mass, public culture, a common economy and common legal rights and duties for all members* (admittedly a fairly modernist definition) – it is clear that the majority of nations, and nationalisms emerged in the modern world inaugurated by the French and American Revolutions. At the same time, as we saw, there may be some nations that predate modernity, and there are certainly some widely diffused ethnic elements that recur throughout recorded history: these include ethnic origin myths, beliefs in ethnic election, the development of ethnoscapes, the territorialization of memory, and the vernacular mobilization of communities. All of which suggests that *modern* nations may have *pre-modern* precursors and can form around recurrent ethnic antecedents.[1]

Continuity: Under this heading falls the vexed question of the 'date of commencement of nations' (Hastings 1997, ch. 1) – or how far back in time it is possible to trace the origins of particular nations. If the first heading signalled the recurring components or potential *building-blocks* of nations-in-general, the rubric of continuity points to the persistence of cultural components of particular nations, for example, elements that have been handed down through the generations – names, symbols, languages, customs, territories and rituals of national identity. [. . .] Much more work needs to be done on identifying the links between earlier ethnic components and modern national cultures, a point made forcefully and critically by John Breuilly (1996).

However, with ideas of ethnic election and their secular transformations, as with memories of golden ages, a start has been made in establishing important cultural continuities, despite the breaks often introduced by conquest, colonization, migration, and assimilation. (See also Smith 1993a.) This should help to

counteract what John Peel has called the *blocking presentism*, and construc-
tionism of so much current work on ethnicity, which views our understanding
of the ethnic past as social construction based on present needs and reflecting
the interests and preoccupations of present generations (Peel 1989).[2]

Reappropriation: If continuity signifies the forward reach of the ethnic past to
the national present, the rubric of *reappropriation* represents the converse
movement, a reaching back into the ethnic past to obtain the *authentic* materials,
and ethos for a distinct modern nation. [. . .] Nationalist intelligentsias [can be
seen as] as *political archaeologists* who aim, not to return to the past, but to
recover its pristine ethos and reconstruct a modern nation in the image of the past
ethnie. Hence, the quest for rediscovery, authentication, and reappropriation of
the ethnic past by philologists, historians, archaeologists and ethnologists.
Despite many instances of self-delusion and manipulation, it is necessary to treat
these activities of nationalist intellectuals as an essential element of the complex
interrelationship between national present (and future) and ethnic past. (See
Smith 1981a, chs 5–6; Pinard and Hamilton 1984; Anderson 1991, ch. 5.)[3]

3. THE ETHNIC BASIS OF NATIONS

The third fundamental theme, and claim, of ethno-symbolism concerns the
ethnic foundations of nations and nationalism. The ubiquity of ethnicity is its
starting-point. Ethnic groupings can be found in every epoch and continent,
wherever human beings feel that they share common ancestry and culture. Such
groupings come in various forms and display varying degrees of organization
and self-awareness. As a first step, we may distinguish *ethnic categories* from
ethnic communities, with other organizational forms such as ethnic associations
in between. *Ethnic categories* are populations distinguished by outsiders as
possessing the attributes of a common name or emblem, a shared cultural
element (usually language or religion), and a link with a particular territory,
Ethnic communities or *ethnies* (to use the French term) are human populations
distinguished by both members and outsiders as possessing the attributes of:

1. an identifying name or emblem;
2. a *myth* of common ancestry;
3. shared historical memories and traditions;
4. one or more elements of common culture;
5. a link with an historic territory or 'homeland';
6. a measure of solidarity, at least among the élites.

This allows us to define an *ethnie* as *a named human population with myths of
common ancestry, shared historical memories and one or more common elements
of culture, including an association with a homeland, and some degree of solidarity,
at least among the élites* (Smith 1986, ch. 2; cf. Horowitz 1985, chs 1–2).

There is, in most cases, a more or less powerful link between modern nations
and pre-existing, and often pre-modern, *ethnies*. Ethno-symbolism claims that

most nations, including the earliest, were based on ethnic ties and sentiments and on popular ethnic traditions, which have provided the cultural resources for later nation-formation; and that even those new *state-nations* in Africa and Asia that sought to turn ex-colonies into territorial nations must forge a cultural unity and identity of myth, symbol, value, and memory that can match that of nations built on pre-existing ethnic ties, if they are to survive and flourish as nations. It is this *ethnic model* of the nation that has proved the most influential, with its emphasis on genealogical descent, vernacular codes, popular mobilization and historical nativism in a *homeland*. Most nations, including the first nations in the West (if we leave aside the earlier cases of the Jews, Armenians and Ethiopian Amhara), have been formed around *ethnic cores* – dominant populations united by presumed ties of shared ancestry and vernacular culture – and have gradually expanded their social depth, territory, and geopolitical range around this dominant ethnic core and presumed descent group, to include other ethnic populations, as was the case with the English, the French and the Castilians.

[. . .]

A crucial part of this third theme is the popular basis of nations and nationalism. Nations may have emerged around élite groups, but even in these early stages, élites were repeatedly forced to take the cultures and interests of wider strata into account. These vernacular cultures and interests were often popular and ethnic in character; they assumed ties of affinity based on presumed common origins and shared customs, linked to *regna* or kingdoms, as Susan Reynolds has argued for early medieval Europe. Even a modernist like Eric Hobsbawm admits the importance of pre-existing (and often pre-modern) *proto-national* communities of language, religion, and region, though he refuses to allow any linkage between them and the rise of a modern, state-creating nationalism (Reynolds 1983; Hobsbawm 1990, ch. 2).

4. The cultural components of ethnies

The fourth major claim of ethno-symbolism is that the pre-existing components and long-term continuities of ethnic communities and nations are cultural and symbolic rather than demographic. The *differentia specifica* of *ethnies* and nations, as well as their continuities, appear in the myths, memories, symbols, values, and traditions of an ethnic community which regards itself as ancestrally related, culturally distinct, and linked to a particular historic homeland. For John Armstrong, following Fredrik Barth, the contents of the *myth-symbol complex* communicated by vernacular linguistic codes, tend to differentiate *ethnies* and guard the cultural border of the community against outsiders (Armstrong 1982, ch. 1). For myself, this differentiating function needs to be complemented by an analysis of the unifying role of a whole range of cultural and symbolic components – myths and symbols, but also values, memories, rituals, customs, and traditions. Distinctive clusters of these components mark out the boundaries of various *ethnies*, but they also serve to unite the members of each *ethnie* and structure their relations and activities. Hence, although in one sense the major symbolic and cultural elements of an ethno-symbolic approach are *subjective*, in that they focus on the perceptions, memories, beliefs, and values of individuals and communities, their long-term patterning produces a *structure* of relations and processes that is independent of those beliefs and perceptions, one which can provide a framework for the socialization of successive generations of ethnic and national members and for the regulation of their interests through myths of ethnic descent and symbols of territory and community. (See Smith 1998, ch. 8.)

This emphasis on culture, in the broadest sense, introduces some flexibility into ethnic membership, which in normal circumstances allows for a degree of demographic replenishment and cultural borrowing, and hence social and cultural adaptation. This suggests that, contrary to approaches that sharply distinguish between an open and flexible *civic* nation and a rigid and closed *ethnic* nation, the *ethnic* components constitute only one, albeit ever-present, set of (often contested) elements within the totality of modern nations, and they can also encourage openness and receptiveness to outside influences. The history of modern Catalan nationalism is a case in point. (See Miller 1995; Smith 1995, ch. 4.)[4]

There are, however, circumstances, internal and external, that bring to power nationalist intelligentsias who, in their quest for authenticity and cultural purity, increasingly seek to purge their cultures of foreign elements and ultimately of outsiders. Despite the very different emphases on *genealogy* or *ideology* in myths of descent, the drive for cultural homogeneity and purity is more common in the case of *ethnic* nationalisms, that is, those whose criterion of national membership is genealogical rather than territorial.

[. . .]

5. ETHNIC MYTHS AND SYMBOLS

Of particular importance among the cultural components of ethnicity are myths of ethnic origin and election, and symbols of territory and community.

Myths of origin and descent constitute the primary definers of the separate existence and character of particular *ethnies*. [. . .] They include accounts of the time and place of the community's origins, and trace the lines of descent from presumed common ancestors; thus Turks trace their ancestry to Central Asia in the first millennium, and to their founding father, Oghuz Khan, and Jews do likewise to Abraham and Canaan (or even to Ur or Haran). Equally important for the survival of *ethnies* has been the development of myths of ethnic election. These may be missionary or covenantal in character. Missionary election myths exalt their *ethnies* by assigning them god-given tasks or missions of warfare or conversion or overlordship; so the Franks or the medieval French monarchs interpreted their role as latter-day king Davids defending the new Israel (France and/or the Church), and the Russian Tsars came to see in Orthodox Russia a third Rome, the only truly Christian kingdom after the fall of Constantinople.

Covenantal election myths tend to set the chosen people apart from their profane surroundings, through a covenant between the deity and the elect, namely, a conditional promise of continued divine favour in return for constant observance of divine commands and ceaseless performance of a singular moral and ritual code, such as the Israelites were enjoined to practise in the Old Testament.

[. . .]

Symbols of territory and community take a variety of forms. They include emblems of difference (flags, totems, coins, ritual objects), hymns and anthems, special foods and costume, as well as representations of ethnic deities, monarchs and heroes – like Pharoah's double crown, the Jewish Menorah or the fleur-de-lys. Particular interest and significance attaches to the symbolism of ancestral or sacred territory and the development of *ethnoscapes* – landscapes endowed with poetic ethnic meaning through the historicization of nature and the territorialization of ethnic memories. These poetic landscapes often come to be associated with crucial events and personages in the history of the ethnic community and may be invested with sacred significance, a powerful motif of ethnic nationalism.

[. . .]

6. 'ETHNO-HISTORY'

A further major theme concerns the multiple, changing and uneven nature of *ethno-history*. By *ethno-history* is meant the ethnic members' memories and understanding of their communal past or pasts, rather than any more *objective* and dispassionate analysis by professional historians. Such a mode of historical discourse has three facets: it is multi-stranded and contested; it is always subject to change; and it is globally uneven.

Given the multiplicity of interests, needs and outlooks of members of any community, the likelihood of a single, unified version of the communal past emerging in any relatively free society must be minimal. In fact, the past is as much a zone of conflict as the present, and we can therefore expect to find, at any given point in time, two or more versions of the ethnic past, often in competition or conflict. This was the case in Greece throughout the nineteenth century, when a classical *Athenian* version of Hellenism held by westernised intelligentsia and merchants was pitted against a Greek Orthodox popular ethno-history which harked back to the medieval glories of the Byzantine empire. [. . .] A similar conflict erupted in France in the nineteenth and early twentieth centuries, and particularly during the Dreyfus Affair, when a medievalizing monarchist and Catholic vision of French ethno-history was challenged by a secular, revolutionary and classicizing interpretation of the French past. (See Campbell and Sherrard 1968, ch. 1; Gildea 1994, chs 3, 7.)

If *ethno-history* is always multi-stranded and contested, this implies a continuous process of reinterpretation of national identities. Homi Bhabha's dualism of traditional *pedagogical* and everyday practical *performative* narratives of *the people* fails to capture the complexity of a situation in which every generation fashions its own interpretations of national identity in the light of its reading of the ethnic past or pasts. The fund of ethnic elements, the ethno-historical heritage handed down through the generations, is always being reinterpreted and revised by various social groups in response to internal differences and external stimuli. Hence, British, Japanese or Egyptian *national identity* is never fixed or static: it is always being reconstructed in response to new needs, interests and perceptions, though always within certain limits. (Bhabha 1990, ch. 16)

From a comparative standpoint, the incidence of ethno-history is markedly uneven. Some communities can boast a *rich* or well-documented, and eventful, ethnic past; others can only summon up the barest memories and sketchiest traditions. (For example, Russian or Arab ethno-histories are eventful and abundantly documented, while Slovak and Estonian ethno-histories are more sketchy and poorly recorded). This *unevenness* of ethno-historical cultural resources is itself a source of national competition and conflict, as the less well-endowed communities seek to attain cultural parity with the better en-dowed. Hence, the appeal for Finns of the national epic of the *Kalevala*, edited in 1835 by Elias Lonnrot, as they strove to free themselves from Russian political and Swedish cultural domination.

[. . .]

7. Routes to nationhood

Another central ethno-symbolic concern is the manner in which nations in the modern world have come to be formed. Armstrong, indeed, presents a complex schema on the emergence of nations, showing how a variety of factors operating at broader or narrower levels combine to create the terrain and impetus for particular nations. These factors include differences in nomadic and sedentary lifestyles with associated nostalgias; the influence of great religious civilizations like Islam and Christianity; the impact of imperial administrations and *mytho-moteurs* (constitutive political myths); the differences in ecclesiastical organiza-tion; and, at the lowest and most dependant level, the role of language *faults* and of particular languages (Armstrong 1982, ch. 9).

[. . .] I have sought to identify *patterns* of nation-formation, depending on the initial ethnic starting-point. The important distinction here is between *lateral* and *vertical ethnies*. The former are aristocratic and extensive, their boundaries are ragged, and they rarely (seek to) penetrate culturally or socially the middle or lower classes. The latter are demotic and intensive, their boundaries are compact, barriers to entry are relatively high, and their culture spreads across all classes, if unevenly at times. There are also immigrant *ethnies*, or rather, part-*ethnies*, which have hived off from the main body to set up colonies and gradually form a separate new *ethnie*. We can then trace the routes by which modern nations have been formed from these three ethnic *bases*: a route of *bureaucratic incorporation* by which aristocratic *ethnies* may forge strong states and incorporate outlying regions and lower classes into their upper-class ethnic culture and symbolism; a route of *vernacular mobilization* whereby an indigenous intelligentsia uses folk culture to mobilize middle and lower strata and create ethnic nations; and finally, an *immigrant-colonist* route in which the founding immigrant part-*ethnie* is supplemented by waves of pioneering colonizers who together create a *plural* or polyethnic immigrant nation and culture. (See Smith 1989.)

8. THE LONGEVITY OF NATIONALISM

The final theme of ethno-symbolism concerns the power and durability of nations and nationalism. Nationalism is a modern ideological movement, but also the expression of aspirations by various social groups to create, defend or maintain *nations* – their autonomy, unity and identity – by drawing on the cultural resources of pre-existing ethnic communities and categories. Nationalism, defined as *an ideological movement for attaining and maintaining identity, unity and autonomy of a social group some of whose members deem it to constitute an actual or potential nation*, has proved a powerful instrument for forging a world of nations based on pre-existing ethnic ties and sentiments; and it is one that has by no means run its course.[5]

These aspirations for nationhood can be found in pre-modern epochs, but they are particularly widespread and powerful in the modern era. This suggests that nationalisms, as well as nations, are likely to be recurrent phenomena in future, as they were in past epochs (Billig 1995). However, the underlying ground of their persistence is not simply their frequency and intensity in the modern epoch. Both frequency and intensity are products of deeper causes, namely the ability of modern nationalisms to draw sustenance from the pre-existing memories, myths, symbols, and traditions of each ethnic community and region. Where such memories, myths, symbols, and traditions are either lacking or negative – conflictual, ambiguous, and disintegrative – the attempt to create new communities and cultural identities is likely to prove painfully slow and arduous, especially where the new identities lack clear boundaries and must compete with well-established and deep-rooted identities and communities. [. . . The] attempts to create a European cultural identity raise serious doubts about the possibility of transcending nations and superseding nationalism, since the very idea of 'Europe', insofar as it can be pinned down and given systematic coherence, appears as a pale reflection of the much more rooted, vivid and tangible national identities. Here, again, I have employed an ethno-symbolic approach to uncover some of the deeper, unspoken cultural myths, memories and assumptions about the 'new Europe'. (See Delanty 1995; Benda-Beckman and Verkuyten 1995.)

The ambiguities and nebulous character of European cultural identity contrast strongly with the dramatic and powerful diaspora nationalisms of the Greeks, Jews, and Armenians with their rich memories of golden ages of saints and heroes, their stark symbols of trauma and suffering, and their potent popular myths of glorious restoration in their age-old homelands. [. . .] The implication [. . .] is that the continuing power of myths, symbols, and memories of ethnic chosenness, golden ages and historic homelands has been largely responsible for the mass appeal of ethnic nationalism in the aftermath of the Cold War and the demise of the Soviet empire; and that we are therefore unlikely to witness the early transcendence of ethnicity or the supersession of nationalism.

NOTES

1. For this definition of the nation, see Smith (1991, ch. 1). For a general discussion of the problems of defining the concept of the nation, see Connor (1994, ch. 4). Though the distinction between *ethnies* and nations is crucial, it does not correspond to the chronological or the sociological divide between pre-modernity and modernity. Not only do many *ethnies* persist (or are crystallized) in late modernity and also become 'modernized'; a few nations antedate modernity (chronologically and sociologically) and owe little or nothing to the processes of 'modernization'.

2. This is very much the view put forward by the editors and most of the contributors to Tonkin *et al.* (1989); reacting against the idea that the 'past determines the present', they have opted for an equally unilateral understanding in which, for the most part, 'the present shapes the past' – or, at any rate, our understanding of it. One could equally well claim that our 'understanding' of the past is inevitably shaped by the frameworks of meaning handed down from previous generations, even when we dissent from their particular views of the past. (See also Eriksen 1993a.) The question of continuities of nations is also bedevilled by definitional problems. For Walker Connor (1994, ch. 9) we can only speak of mass nations; nations only exist when a majority of the designated population participates (indeed votes) in public life; whereas for Adrian Hastings (1997, ch. 1) nations can be said to exist when a significant minority of the population outside the ruling élite reveal a national consciousness, in which case we can speak of medieval nations.

   But are these 'nations' in the full sense of the term (a modern, and modernist, sense?), or only potential or 'pre-national' peoples? Perhaps we should avoid trying to draw too hard-and-fast lines between *ethnies* and nations in each case, but rather identify processes (of territorialization, homogenization, legal standardization, etc.) by which nations are formed, often discontinuously, out of pre-existing *ethnies*.

3. That is why cultural nationalism, as Hutchinson (1987, ch. 1) highlights, is so important for the creation of nations. This was also probably the case with premodern *ethnies*. A religious culture provided the foundation for the crystallisation and persistence of fluid ethnic categories. From this standpoint, nationalist 'political archaeology', for all its rhetoric, is not as fictive and fantastic as modernists are apt to portray.

4. The open, assimilatory character of Catalan linguistic nationalism can be contrasted with the relatively closed and more exclusive character of Basque religious and 'racial' nationalism. For a rich and illuminating study of these ethnic nationalisms, see Conversi (1997).

5. For this definition of nationalism, see A. D. Smith (1991, ch. 4). On globalization and nationalism, see Billig (1995, esp. ch. 6) and Guibernau (1996, ch. 7).

2

THE CONSTRUCTION
OF NATIONHOOD

Adrian Hastings

I will be suggesting that England presents the prototype of both a nation and a nation-state in the fullest sense, that its national development, while not wholly uncomparable with that of other Atlantic coastal societies, does precede every other – both in the date at which it can fairly be detected and in the roundness that it achieved centuries before the eighteenth. It most clearly manifests, in the pre-Enlightenment era, almost every appropriate 'national' characteristic. Indeed it does more than 'manifest' the nature of a nation, it establishes it. In the words of a very recent writer, Liah Greenfeld, 'The birth of the English nation was not the birth of a nation, it was the birth of the nations, the birth of nationalism.'[1] Moreover, its importance for us lies too both in its relationship with religion and in the precise impact of English nationalism on its neighbours and colonies. Much of this, I will be claiming, was detectable already in Saxon times by the end of the tenth century. Despite the, often exaggerated, counteraction of the Norman Conquest, an English nation-state survived 1066, grew fairly steadily in the strength of its national consciousness through the later twelfth and thirteenth centuries, but emerged still more vociferously with its vernacular literary renaissance and the pressures of the Hundred Years War by the end of the fourteenth. Nevertheless the greatest intensity of its nationalist experience together with its overseas impact must undoubtedly be located in and after the late sixteenth century.

I will argue that there appears to be no comparable case in Europe and that it

Adrian Hastings (1997), *The Construction of Nationhood: Ethnicity, Religion and Nationalism*, Cambridge: Cambridge University Press.

was this English model, wholly preceding the late eighteenth century, in which this sort of process is held by modernist theory to find its roots, which was then re-employed, remarkably little changed, in America and elsewhere. I will not suggest that English nationalism preceded an English nationhood. On the contrary. However English nationalism of a sort was present already in the fourteenth century in the long wars with France and still more in the sixteenth and seventeenth. Indeed, without the impact of English nationalism, the history of England's neighbours seems virtually unintelligible.

These claims have, of course, to be justified by the evidence. If true, they require a considerable rewrite of the standard modernist history of nationalism. To many people they will seem surprising claims. Perhaps as I am myself so very much an Englishman, they may even seem an expression less of historical enquiry than of English nationalism itself. Yet if there is such a thing as English nationalism it is surely right that an Englishman should explore it, especially as it is undoubtedly a category that many English people have denied to exist. Foreigners have nationalism, which is a bad thing; we English have patriotism, which is a good thing! I do not agree. English nationalism, partially transformed from the eighteenth century into British nationalism, has been a very powerful, and frequently damaging, historical force. Yet historians have made a habit of ignoring it. Thus it is strange that an historian so searching in other fields as Hobsbawm can simply remark in passing that 'the development of nations and nationalism within old-established states, such as Britain and France, has not been studied very intensively . . . The existence of this gap is illustrated by the neglect, in Britain, of any problems connected with English nationalism.'[2] That may be the most remarkable understatement of any Wiles lecture. It is odd that historians of nationalism have managed for long so easily to avert their eyes from what in hard reality, I believe, has been the prototype for the whole story.

It would surely be surprising if England was not in at the start of a process which has been so central to the political development of the modern world, surprising because England did so clearly provide the lead in regard to most other aspects of that development, such as the establishment of a strongly centralised state, the growth of parliamentary government, elective and repre-sentative, the early decline of villeinage, the limitation of royal power, the emergence of a powerful capital city, the formation of political parties, the ending of slavery, the emergence of industrial society and of an effective press. Britain has also led the way in the writing of political theory from the seventeenth to the nineteenth century, from Hobbes and Locke, through Burke, Hume and Adam Smith, to Bentham, Mill, Bagehot and Bosanquet. Benedict Anderson's astonishing claim that the English nation was only emerging at the heart of its empire in the later years of the nineteenth century[3] not only goes in the teeth of the evidence but is totally implausible. Only if national identity and nationalism were really marginal phenomena within the modernisation of the world over the last three centuries would it be easily imaginable that they did not affect the country, which had throughout provided the lead for modernisation, until the very eve of its decline. In fact they are central and indispensable elements within that movement and it would be hard to imagine the development of the modern world without them.

This does not mean that the nation-state is the only political form available for the modern world. Far from it. The nation-state does not inherently belong to modernity and if Britain, for long the prototype of modernity, pioneered the nation-state, it also pioneered the non-national world empire. While France's empire was conceived, if unrealistically, as an extension of its nation-state, Britain's was not. That does not make it less modern. Indeed it may be the political reality of Britain's global empire which looks in another fifty years' time more like the real prototype for the political structuring of modernity. The nation-state has always been itself to a very large extent an unrealised myth; it only too manifestly does not fit the complex reality of human society very helpfully in many places; its values have often been overplayed in the past hundred years, its dangers, until recently, foolishly belittled. Nationalism has been enormously damaging to peace, tolerance and common sense; and the model of a nation-state, which could seldom fit social reality without grave injustice to numerous minorities, may well be wisely superseded by arrangements which stress both smaller and larger units of power and administration. While nationalism's territorial form seems vastly preferable to its more ethnic or linguistic form, its ideal has relied far too heavily on simplistic concepts of the indivisibility of sovereignty – concepts which have in our time been in practice increasingly superseded by the working of the UNO, international law and the European Community. For many people the structures of a pre-nationalist Habsburg Empire, or an extra-nationalist British Empire, or a post-nationalist European Community look basically more sane than those of the nation-state. Nevertheless it has to be recognised that the Habsburg or British Empires were only tolerable, for most of their parts, because of relative underdevelopment. Once the dominance of Latin as the one language of civilisation in the West fell before the literary advance of French, English, German and Spanish, it came to seem inevitable that any kind of Holy Roman Empire model, whose legacy survived in the Habsburg Empire, would need to be replaced by one of 'national' states reflecting the more advanced and stable of ethnic/linguistic identities.

[. . .]

What needs explaining may be less why England, followed by Spain, France, the Netherlands, Denmark, Sweden and Portugal, moved steadily towards the creation of nation-states, than why Germany and Italy, caught more deeply in medieval structure, imperial, commercial and ecclesiastical, failed for so long to do the same. To this crucially important question we will return. For the moment it is sufficient to recognise that the attractiveness and apparent power of the nation-state, manifest above all in England and then in Britain by the eighteenth century, guaranteed that sooner or later its pursuit would be taken up across the rest of Europe. The heady shock waves of the French Revolution and Napoleonic Wars, followed by a huge increase in printing in many languages, ensured that central, southern and eastern Europe in the nineteenth century, and much of the rest of the world in the twentieth, would endeavour to imitate the political model provided by the apparently most advanced and successful countries of the world.

At this point it is appropriate to set out as clearly as possible the principal lines of disagreement with the 'modernist' view of nations and nationalism as represented by Hobsbawm, Gellner, Breuilly and Anderson. I may repeat, before I do this, that I am not alone in disagreeing. On the one hand one senses a renewed conviction among medieval historians that these are categories fully appropriate for the understanding of pre-sixteenth, let alone much pre-late eighteenth century, history.[4] On the other hand is the school of nationalist studies of a more sociological kind, led by Anthony Smith and John Hutchinson who, however much they acknowledge the inspiration of the masters of 'modernism', appear decidedly unconvinced by its central theses. Smith's most important work, *The Ethnic Origins of Nations*,[5] represents the strongest critique of modernism hitherto presented though it still accepts far too many modernist presuppositions. Equally encouraging, so far as I am concerned, is Liah Greenfeld's 1992 *Nationalism: Five Roads to Modernity*, already quoted, with its explicit recognition that England was 'the first nation in the world, and the only one, with the possible exception of Holland, for about two hundred years'.[6]

Greenfeld's work is a truly major, and originally constructed, contribution to a subject now being heavily overloaded with often repetitive studies. Nevertheless her thesis remains, in my opinion, seriously misleading on several counts. First, it is still in principle within the enterprise of the modernists. Nationalism remains the 'road to modernity', a road which still opens in the late eighteenth century apart from the one privileged exception of England. I am not convinced by the great divide between the pre-modern and the modern and I certainly do not think that nationalism is, as such, a door, let alone the main door, from the former to the latter. It can often be a road in quite the opposite direction, but the recognisable nationalism of, say, early fourteenth-century Scotland cannot usefully be described as either modernising or anti-modernising. Understanding nations and nationalism will only be advanced when any inseparable bonding of them to the modernisation of society is abandoned.

Secondly, she still does not get England right. For Greenfeld, 'the emergence of national sentiment in England' is to be located in 'the first third of the sixteenth century'.[7] I find this decidedly unlikely. For one thing there is really no obvious reason why it should emerge at that point, prior to the Reformation and in a period of peace. For another she, like all other modernists, totally avoids consideration of the medieval evidence. For that very distinguished American medievalist, Joseph R. Strayer, 'England was clearly a nation-state in the fifteenth century.'[8] Yet it would be highly implausible to claim that it was the fifteenth century when this came to be. What happened to English nationalism in the sixteenth century can only be understood, I am convinced, if the pre-

Reformation history of the English nation is fully recognised. If Greenfeld is right to claim that England was 'the first nation in the world', it requires demonstration in medieval terms.

The key issue at the heart of our schism lies in the date of commencement. For the modernists, following in this Elie Kedourie's highly influential *Nationalism* of 1960,[9] nationalism is a very modern phenomenon about which you cannot reasonably speak before the late eighteenth century; nationalism, moreover, precedes the nation. 'It is nationalism which engenders nations,' declared Gellner.[10] Again, 'Nationalism is not the awakening of nations to self-consciousness: it invents nations where they do not exist.'[11] Hobsbawm agrees. 'Nations do not make states and nationalisms, but the other way round.'[12] 'The nation', he adds, is 'a very recent newcomer in human history . . . it belongs exclusively to a particular, and historically recent, period. It is a social entity only in so far as it relates to a certain kind of modern territorial state, the "nation-state" and it is pointless to discuss nation and nationality except in so far as both relate to it.'[13] 'The basic characteristic of the modern nation and everything connected with it is its modernity.'[14] That is why, of course, Hobsbawm puts 'since 1780' into his title. For him it is 'pointless' to discuss the subject in pre-1780 terms. 'Nations', Gellner agrees, 'can be defined only in terms of the age of nationalism.'[15] For Breuilly too nation-states appear in principle inadmissible before the nineteenth century, anything prior to that being dismissed with remarkably little investigation, as 'prelude' only in a period when anything 'nationalist' is considered by him to be necessarily in opposition to the state.[16] Anderson wholly agrees and his conclusion, faced with the national reality of the American War of Independence, is that it must all have begun there: 'The large cluster of new political entities that sprang up in the western hemisphere between 1778 and 1838, all of which self-consciously defined themselves as nations . . . were historically the first such states to emerge on the world stage, and therefore inevitably provided the first real model of what such states should "look like".'[17] The French Revolution quickly followed in the American wake and in consequence this new entity, the nation, Anderson continues, was 'a complex composite of French and American elements'[18] which became 'available for pirating' by the second decade of the nineteenth century. All our authors follow Kedourie in insisting on this late eighteenth-century date for the start of the whole process (even though Gellner does at one point, self-contradictorily, admit that England somehow became a nation in a much earlier age). On why or where it all began they are not so united. Anderson claims that it was really all a great American invention – 'Nationalism emerged first in the New World not the Old . . . it is an astonishing sign of the depth of Eurocentrism that so many European scholars persist, in the face of all the evidence, in regarding nationalism as a European invention.'[19] For Kedourie, it was Kant and the Enlightenment that must accept responsibility; for others, the political, military and intellectual impact of the French Revolution was the precipitating factor. For Gellner and Hobsbawm it appears to be more an inevitable consequence of capitalism and industrialisation. The problem with that is twofold. First, much of the nationalist explosion in central and eastern Europe has not been in areas noted for industrialisation; second, it does not well explain why the process should begin in America. Anderson has a point in claiming that the first example of this new wave of nation-making was the American; what he does not at all explain is why that should be so.[20] The general explanation given by both Anderson and Breuilly of the rise of nationalism in terms of the decline of dynasties and of religion and the growth in printed literature implies an extraordinarily over-simple picture of both the state and religion in Europe before the late eighteenth century, while Anderson offers no explanation as to why the growth in books did not have in the sixteenth century the effect he postulates for the late eighteenth.

I do not wish to dispute the rapid spread of nationalist ideology and nation-creating movements from that time, nor do I question the sort of Hobsbawmian analysis of why in the nineteenth century this took hold of central and eastern Europe in the way that it did. Gellner and Hobsbawm are in their roots central Europeans and the view from Vienna or Prague is naturally somewhat different from that from London or Edinburgh. But a balanced history of nationalism in its entirety must not be allowed to belittle the primacy of experience of the Atlantic coastal states. The basic question remains whether 1789 or thereabouts is a reasonable starting date for a study of this subject. Hobsbawm wrote a history of nineteenth- and twentieth-century nationalism, but not a history of nationalism, and denial of the first half of the story has inevitably skewed the whole. In particular it impairs an understanding of the nation-nationalism relationship because while in the later period nationalisms may often have preceded nations rather than the reverse, in the earlier period it is far truer to say that nations as they grew more self-conscious, or came under threat, produced nationalisms.

Where, then, did these nations come from? The answer can only be, I argue, out of certain ethnicities, affected by the literary development of a vernacular and the pressures of the state. The second area in which Hobsbawm and Gellner are quite unconvincingly negative is that of the relationship between ethnicity and nationhood. Clearly enough, as they so strongly insist, every ethnicity did not become a nation, but many have done so. What has to be asserted counter to modernism is not any kind of primordialism – a claim that every nation existent today, and just those nations, all existed in embryo a thousand or fifteen hundred years ago – but, rather, a finely constructed analysis of why some ethnicities do become nations while others do not. The defining origin of the nation, like that of every other great reality of modern western experience, whether it be the university, the bureaucratic state or individualism, needs to be located in an age a good deal further back than most modernist historians feel safe to handle, that of the shaping of medieval society. I will argue that ethnicities naturally turn into nations or integral elements within nations at the point when their specific vernacular moves from an oral to written usage to the extent that it is being regularly employed for the production of a literature, and particularly for the translation of the Bible. Once an ethnicity's vernacular becomes a language with an extensive living literature of its own, the Rubicon on the road to nationhood appears to have been crossed. If it fails to pass that point – and most spoken vernaculars do fail that hurdle – then transformation to nationhood is almost certain never to take place.

NOTES

1. Liah Greenfeld, *Nationalism: Five Roads to Modernity* (Harvard University Press, 1992), p. 23. This constitutes, of course, a precise denial of Renan's claim for France: 'Le principe des nations est le nôtre', *Qu'est-ce qu'une nation?* (Paris, 1882), p. 10.
2. Hobsbawm, *Nations and Nationalism since 1780*, p. 11.
3. Anderson, *Imagined Communities*, p. 111.
4. R. R. Davies's presidential addresses to the Royal Historical Society for 1993 and 1994: 'The Peoples of Britain and Ireland 1100–1400: I Identities', *Transactions of the Royal Historical Society*, 6th series, vol. 4 (1994), pp. 1–20, and 'The Peoples of Britain and Ireland 1100–1400: II Names, Boundaries and Regnal Solidarities', *Transactions of the Royal Historical Society*, vol. 5 (1995), pp. 1–20; Susan Reynolds, *Kingdoms and Communities in Western Europe 900–1300* (Oxford: Clarendon Press, 1984); Claus Bjørn, Alexander Grant and Keith J. Stringer (eds), *Nations, Nationalism and Patriotism in the European Past* (Copenhagen: Academic Press, 1994), Simon Forde, Lesley Johnson and Alan V. Murray (eds), *Concepts of National Identity in the Middle Ages* (Leeds Texts and Monographs, 1995); Thorlac Turville-Petre, *England the Nation: Language, Literature and National Identity 1200–1340* (Oxford: Clarendon Press, 1996).
5. Anthony D. Smith, *The Ethnic Origins of Nations* (Oxford: Blackwell, 1986); see also *National Identity* (Harmondsworth: Penguin, 1991), and John Hutchinson, *Modern Nationalism* (London: Fontana, 1994).
6. Liah Greenfeld, *Nationalism: Five Roads to Modernity* (Cambridge, MA: Harvard University Press), p. 14. Another wide-ranging American study which significantly deviates from full modernist orthodoxy is John A. Armstrong, *Nations before Nationalism*. (Chapel Hill: University of North Carolina Press, 1982). Despite its title it has nevertheless little to say about nations, being rather a discussion of the construction of ethnicity. Verbally at least the author appears to accept the modernist thesis that there are no nations before nationalism and no nationalism before the eighteenth century. He also strangely avoids serious consideration of almost any of the older nations of western Europe. Furthermore while claiming to 'provide an overview of Eastern and Western Christendom and Islamic civilisation' (p. 3) he does not appear to realise how profound is the difference between Christianity and Islam in relation to nationhood. Despite its richness of material, it is in consequence a confused and confusing book.
7. Greenfeld, *Nationalism: Five Roads to Modernity*, p. 42.
8. Joseph R. Strayer, *Medieval Statecraft and the Perspectives of History* (Princeton, NJ: Princeton University Press, 1971), p. 347 (the essay in question first appeared in 1963).
9. Elie Kedourie, *Nationalism* (London: Hutchinson, 1960).
10. Ernest Gellner, *Nations and Nationalism* (Oxford: Blackwell, 1983), p. 55.
11. Ernest Gellner, *Thought and Change* (London: Weidenfeld and Nicolson, 1964), p. 168.
12. E. J. Hobsbawm, *Nations and Nationalism since 1780* (Cambridge: Cambridge University Press, 1990), p. 10.
13. *Ibid.*, pp. 5 and 9–10.

14. *Ibid.*, p. 14.
15. Gellner, *Nations and Nationalism*, p. 55.
16. Yet he has to admit in his far too brief analysis of the English experience of the sixteenth and seventeenth centuries that 'the idea of the nation was not radically distinct from the idea of the state'. John Breuilly, *Nationalism and the State*, 2nd edn (Manchester: Manchester University Press, 1993), p. 85.
17. Benedict Anderson, *Imagined Communities: Reflections on the Origin and Spread of Nationalism* (London: Verso, 1983), p. 46.
18. *Ibid.*, p. 81, n. 34.
19. *Ibid.*, p. 191 and n. 9.
20. Liah Greenfeld provides the explanation: in essence it was not new at all – 'the story of the emergence of the American nation' represents a realisation of 'the promise of original English nationalism', *Nationalism: Five Roads to Modernity*, p. 401.

3

NATIONALISM AND MODERNITY

Ernest Gellner

Do nations have navels?

Perhaps the major debate which has arisen in the theory of nationalism of late occurs between primordialists and modernists. The issue is simple: is the sense of ethnicity, the identification with a 'nation', and the political expression of this passionate identification, something old and present throughout history, or is it, on the contrary, something modern and a corollary of the distinctive feature of our recent world? The present book is, of course, firmly on the latter side, but this does not prevent it, one hopes, from presenting the issues in a clear and unprejudical manner.

As so often, not one, but several overlapping questions are involved. At the most abstract level, one is dealing with the metaphysical question of the reality of the past and the present. It was Bertrand Russell, I think, who once played with the following conundrum: how do we know the world was not created five minutes ago, complete with memories and, naturally, the whole complement of historical, archeological and geological records? What conceivable difference would there be, *now*, between such a world, and the world which in fact we think we inhabit: that is, a world which has been here for quite some time? The question poses a problem for any radical empiricist, who would maintain that two propositions only have distinct meanings if evidence is conceivable which would support the one, but contradict the other. *Ex hypothesi*, there is no piece of evidence, at any rate in the present or the future, which could distinguish

---

Ernest Gellner (1997), *Nationalism*, London: Weidenfeld and Nicolson.

between the hypothesis of a world created complete with memories and records, and the hypothesis of a long-established world, which had 'genuinely' accumulated the record and the memories. As we only have access to evidence in the present or the future, it follows that we cannot possess evidence on the basis of which we could rationally choose between the two hypotheses, which are consequently identical by extreme empiricist criteria, but profoundly different intuitively and to common sense.

There is a certain similarity between this question and the extreme version of the opposition between Evolutionists and 'Creationists', as the confrontation developed under the impact of Darwinism. One suggestion made was that the issue could be decided by finding out whether or not Adam had a navel: if, as the Biblical account affirms, he was directly created by God, clearly there was no reason why he should have a navel. However, not all Creationists accepted this argument: if God created the world at a given moment, things could only function if they had the structure *they would have had*, had they existed for some time. For instance, rivers would already be flowing, as opposed to having to wait to be filled by wholly new springs. So God would create riverbeds already filled, as if they had been flowing for ages, and similarly, Adam would be endowed with a perfectly pointless navel. This argument can then be, quite logically, extended: God would also create geological strata, fossils, etc. *as if* the world had existed for a long time, and so permit geologists and others to reconstruct a non-existent, but internally coherent past.

On this issue, which divides fundamentalist believers from Darwinists, it is the adherents of traditional common sense who uphold Creation, and the upholders of the authority of Science who defend the evolutionist view. In the debate concerning nationalism, it is the other way round: common-sense popular belief is on the side of the antiquity of nation and nationalist sentiment, whereas it is we rather modernist thinkers, eager to practise science in the social sphere, who are Creationists. We believe in the Creation of Nations, not in a week, but in a couple of centuries or so. The alignments are inversed, but the logic of the debate is similar. Hence my question: do nations have navels?

There is an artificiality about the very general formulation of the question ('can the past *ever* be real?') which inclines one to dismiss it as 'metaphysical' in a pejorative sense, implying that the issue is simultaneously difficult and trivial. Yet there is an element of just this issue in the debate between primordialists and modernists. The modernist is, at least in part, motivated by this very general consideration: after all, only the present can be operative in the present. The past is dead, gone, unreal: no past force can act *now*, because it is, indeed, *past*; it has 'passed'. It is not present here and now, so it cannot make any difference here and now.

This argument is quite often present in the human and social sciences and is liable to influence research and explanatory strategies: for instance, in economics, anthropology or psychoanalysis. In economics, it takes the form of stressing the relevance of *present* supply and demand (never mind 'historic' costs). In anthropology it is known as 'functionalism' and the recommendation to explain societies in terms of the synchronic interaction of institutions rather than in terms of the past. In psychoanalysis the same argument emerges as the stress on the actual therapeutic situation and interaction, as opposed to the alleged influence of distant traumata.

This very general consideration is involved, but clearly it is not the whole story. A 'modernist' theorist of nationalism, such as myself, considers *nationalism* to be an inherently modern phenomenon, but he does not consider all social phenomena to be modern, or everything to be made over new in the modern age. On the contrary, he believes both culture and power to be perennial, but to be related to each other in a new way in the modern age, a way which then engenders nationalism. So what else is involved?

It is a question of continuity or, rather, a whole set of related continui*ties*: do cultures, power structures, the recognition of a given culture as a thing, an entity (as an object of love, loyalty and identification), and the *political* use of cultural identification and differentiation – do all these persist across the boundary, wherever exactly it is to be drawn, between the traditional and the modern? A primordialist is a man who repudiates the suggestion that 'nations', and the idea that they are at the root of political obligation, have been invented (even if not consciously) in modern times. The primordialist refuses to accept that the attribution of an immemorial antiquity to nations is a illusion. Whether or not the primordialist is himself a nationalist, whether he reveres some particular culture/nation and believes it to be hallowed by age, at any rate he sympathises with the nationalist who insists on the genuine antiquity (never mind the periods of somnolence induced by enemies) of his nation. By contrast, the modernist considers this antiquity to be either an illusion or an irrelevance.

What evidence could decide this issue? Here we are no longer in the realm of two hypotheses, intuitively incompatible with each other, but, both of them, equally compatible with all available evidence.

As stated, what is at issue is *continuity*. Are cultures continuous and, often, continuous right across historical watersheds between one form of social organisation and another? The answer is, unquestionably, *yes*. Culture *is* something transmitted over time. Yet the very diversity of cultures which is of the essence of humanity also includes diversity over time: cultures can change fast, and sometimes do so. It is precisely the shift from genetic to cultural transmission which makes possible, on a shared genetic base, the astonishing diversity of cultures and the possibility of very rapid change. So there is no general answer: cultures persist and cultures change. The striking empirical evidence points *both* ways. On the one hand, the historians and social scientists who have focused on the *Invention of Tradition* (Hobsbawm and Ranger 1983) have cogently demonstrated that what passes for ('continuous', 'immemorial') tradition is frequently invented (sometimes consciously) and of recent date, and that its validating antiquity is often spurious. At the same time, the experience of 'modernisers' who attempt to reorganise the structure of a given society is often that, not-withstanding organisational changes, a certain style of doing things may have an astonishing tenacity, and survive radical reorganisation. So, both these points are valid. Cultures are both tenacious and volatile. It is neither true that they are virtually immutable, like some slow-moving glacier which only shifts a few metres every year, preserving continuity while changing, nor is it the case that they are ever reinvented, ever spurious in their pretence of continuity. *Both* things happen, and if there are any laws concerning which predominates, we do not know them.

Cultures are sometimes invisible to their bearers, who look through them like the air they breathe, and sometimes heavily underscored and objects of great reverence and passion. There is, it seems to me, no valid general rule affirming either the volatility or the fidelity of men *vis-à-vis* their cultures. This is something which needs to be explored, by concrete historical and ethnographic research: abstract argument can and does provide us with plausible, sometimes persuasive models, but it cannot on its own clinch the matter.

In anthropology and the social sciences more generally, there has of late been a certain vogue for exclusive preoccupation with 'culture', its diversity and ultimacy. This vogue has various roots, which it would not be appropriate to explore here. What is relevant here is to stress the damage this vogue does to the advancement of understanding in the field which concerns us: by seeking primarily or exclusively 'cultural' rather than organisational explanations, this trend prejudges, unjustifiably, a most important question concerning the relative importance of structural and cultural factors. (It is quite possible that there is no *general* answer to this question, that the relative importance of the two types of cause varies from case to case and situation to situation.) The exclusive culturalism or hermeneuticism or interpretivism, to mention some of the available appellations for this trend, makes it hard or impossible even to ask the most important question, let alone to seek the evidence for answering it.

Nationalists claim to love their own culture in virtue of its particular qualities: it is, they claim, exceedingly beautiful. When they contemplate it, their feelings are deeply moved, and it is for this reason that they are patriots. Well and good: but if nationalism is a general phenomenon, covering a whole variety of nations, quite obviously it cannot be explained by the reasons operating internally within each national movement: these reasons must be specifically related to each nation and its culture; they cannot apply generally, otherwise there could hardly be *rival* nationalisms. So the general explanation cannot be internal to the cultures concerned: it must stand outside them and explain why, in general, cultures have become a political principle, a principle of the delimitation of political units. Whether cultures themselves are continuous or not is another question.

If the continuity of cultures is an open question, which probably has a diversity of specific answers rather than a single general one, what of the issue of the political sex-appeal of cultures, whether permanent or ephemeral? Here again, it is not clear that there is an exceptionless *general* answer. Some cultures have in the past inspired political action, but on the whole, this has been exceptional. In our modern world, nationalism is not the only force, nor is it always victorious. All we can say is this: we are in possession (and have offered) an inherently plausible and persuasive argument which purports to show (a) that homogeneity of culture is an unlikely determinant of political boundaries in the agrarian world, and a very probable one in the modern, industrial/scientific world, and (b) that the transition from Agraria to Industria is also the transition from a world in which high (literacy and education-linked) cultures are a minority accomplishment and privilege (if they exist at all), to a world in which they become the pervasive culture of society as a whole. We have linked these general observations to the emergence of nationalism.

The available evidence fits *on the whole*, at any rate in Europe, but it doesn't fit perfectly and everywhere. There the matter rests, until further evidence is marshalled or further arguments presented. The counter-evidence and counter-arguments provided certainly do not warrant a repudiation of the theory, but equally, they do not justify the theory being treated as firmly established. If true, and that remains to be seen, it does link nationalism to the modern world, without prejudice to the occasional persistence of cultures over time, or the occasional power of cultures to inspire political action and loyalty in the past. For all that, if we are to understand nationalism, it seems to me that we must look above all at what is distinctive in the modern world, rather than at what it shares with the past. My own view is that some nations possess genuine ancient navels, some have navels invented for them by their own nationalist propaganda, and some are altogether navel-less. My belief is also that the middle category is by far the largest, but I stand open to correction by genuine research. At any rate, this is how the question should be formulated.

[. . .]

The industrial and industrialising world

In various very fundamental ways, the industrial world in which we live (and much of this applies to the industrial*ising* world) is different from the agrarian one. First of all, industrial civilisation is based on economic (and scientific) growth, rather than on a stable technology. This growth is capable of being faster than population growth and frequently is such, especially as the social consequences of industrialism eventually diminish population growth, sometimes reducing it to zero or a minus quantity. In brief, the industrial world is no longer Malthusian.

One of the industrial world's two main principles of political legitimacy – of the assessment of the acceptability of regimes – is indeed economic growth. (The other principle is *nationalism*, which is our theme.) Regimes are acceptable if they can, over a period, engender growth, and they lose their authority if they do not. What had been called, by Sidney and Beatrice Webb, a 'New Civilisation' collapsed ignominiously, and without the slightest external impulsion or even internal violence, simply because it visibly failed to provide growth. Thus ended the world's first and greatest Cold War in a uniquely and unexpectedly clear manner: it never needed to become hot in order to be terminated, which had been a perfectly reasonable, and exceedingly frightening, expectation.

This modern growth-orientation has one immediate consequence: pervasive social mobility. Throughout history, as societies became larger and more complex – more 'developed' – they also tended to become more inegalitarian. Then, suddenly, with the coming of modernity, this trend is reversed, and we appear to be living in an age of ever increasing equalisation of conditions. Tocqueville even made this into the prime and dominant trend of European history since the Middle Ages. Why this astonishing reversal of direction? Were we converted to the ideal of equality by its luminous attractiveness?

We are not mobile because we are egalitarians, we are egalitarians because we are mobile. The mobility in turn is imposed on us by social circumstance. Growth entails innovation, the use of new techniques, hence the creation of new jobs and the relinquishing of old ones. A society which lives by growth, which bribes its members into acquiescing by giving them a confident and justified expectation of moral improvement, rather than by the old method of terror and superstition, cannot conceivably have a stable occupational structure. This may once have had a certain charm, by allowing people to become habituated to their social station, to identify with it, to love it; but the option is no longer available. With a rapidly changing technology and its associated occupational structure, the latter simply cannot be stable. Hence there is no way of running a modern society with a system of castes or estates. The one attempt to do so openly, in South Africa, also failed ignominiously.

Apart from its instability, a modern occupational structure must, in some measure at least, be meritocratic: it must fill some posts at least in terms of the talents and qualifications of available candidates. The proportion of such qualification-related posts to others is probably much higher in industrial society than in agrarian society, though the matter has not, to my knowledge, been formally documented. The qualifications required for performing adequately as a medieval baron are probably not very great: he needs to ride well, shout, impose his authority, possess some political cunning. Consequently, these positions, provided the recruits are trained long enough, can be filled by any random method, and heredity is the simplest and most widely used one. Feudal society can be inegalitarian in that it turns the dominant warrior stratum into a distinct and hereditary estate. It was not open to haggling: as Tocqueville put it, membership was beyond price.

You simply cannot do this in a modern society for professors of physics. (In the social sciences and humanities, this is not quite so obvious.) Mathematico-physical ability may in fact be more gene-linked than horsemanship (which is probably open to a very broad category of able-bodied person, given the training), but nonetheless, a society which turned its Association of Physics Teachers into a caste would rapidly find itself internationally ostracised, and would find its standards rapidly falling.

Innovation and the talent-specificity of many tasks leads to the replacement of rigidly stratified societies by formally egalitarian ones. The placement of members of lower strata over members of higher strata would lead to constant friction: far better to embrace a theory of a kind of baseline equality. All men are equals: differences linked to their occupancy of posts in given bureaucratic hierarchies, or to their bank balances, do not enter their souls, or not too much, and do not officially turn them into radically different kinds of human being. A man cannot take his professional status with him and invoke it outside the workplace. Status operates in office hours, so to speak.

Modern society is not, of course, egalitarian in the sense that it is free of tremendous differences in wealth and power. It is egalitarian in the sense that the differences are arranged along a kind of continuum, so that there is not, at any one point, a major break, ratified by law, ritual or deep custom. The differences are gradual and continuous, and not hallowed. Where there is a deep chasm, such as the one which threatens to surround an identifiable under-class, this is recognised as a scandal, and one questionably compatible with the principles or the functioning of the society. In other cases, there is the belief in, and in some measure the reality of, significant social mobility.

The mobility and anonymity of modern society are very marked features of it. Members relate to the total society directly, without mediation, rather than by belonging first of all to one of its sub-groups. Associations which exist within the total society, though effective and important, are ephemeral and optional, and have no important legal powers over their members. Adherence is not dictated by birth or fortified by awesome ritual; nor does it commit members to irreversible loyalties.

This characteristic of modern society – anonymity, mobility, atomisation – is complemented by another one which is even more important: the semantic nature of work. In the agrarian world, most men worked with their muscle. In industrial society, physical work is virtually unknown, and there is simply no market for human brawn. What passes for manual work generally presupposes the capacity to read instructions and manuals. The garage mechanic, who may lose social standing because his work involves dirtying his hands, is in fact paid not for the use of his physical strength, but for his understanding and handling of quite complex machinery. In brief, what passes for manual work presupposes a level of literacy and sophistication which must often be well above that of the professional scholar of the agrarian age.

When work is semantic it involves the manipulation of messages and contact with a large number of anonymous, frequently invisible partners, at the other end of telephones and faxes, and so forth. The anonymity and invisibility of the partners in communication has an important consequence: context cannot be used in the determination of meaning. In the stable, intimate, restricted communication of agrarian sub-communities, context – status of the participants, their tone, expression, body-posture – was probably the most important constituent in the determination of meaning. Context was, so to speak, the principal phoneme. Only a small number of specialists – lawyers, theologians, bureaucrats – were able, willing or allowed to take part in context-free communication. For the rest, context was everything. Now, it is eliminated from a large part of the communication process which makes up the working lives of men.

The capacity either to articulate or to comprehend context-free messages is not an easy one to acquire. It requires schooling, prolonged schooling. And modern society, given that work is semantic in this manner, requires *everyone* to possess this skill. It is the first society in history in which literacy is near universal; to put it another way, it is also the first society ever in which a high culture becomes the pervasive culture of the entire society, displacing folk or low culture. This is not due, as some educational enthusiasts might suppose, to a miraculous diffusion of commitment to the finer pleasures of the mind. It is a corollary of the manner in which society functions: precision of articulation, such as enables a message to transmit meaning by its own internal resources, without making use of context – a skill possessed in the past by at most a few specialised scribes – is now a precondition of employability and social participation and acceptability. And the communication must take place not merely in a 'high' (i.e. codified, script-linked, educationally transmitted) code, but in some one definite code, say Mandarin Chinese or Oxford English.

That is all. It is this which explains nationalism: the principle – so strange and eccentric in the age of agrarian cultural diversity and of the 'ethnic' division of labour – that homogeneity of culture is *the* political bond, that mastery of (and, one should add, acceptability in) a given high culture (the one used by the surrounding bureaucracies) is the precondition of political, economic and social citizenship. If you satisfy this condition, you can enjoy your *droit de cité*. If you do not, you must accept second-class and subservient status, or you must assimilate, or migrate, or migrate, or seek to change the situation through irredentist nationalist activity. This principle does not operate in other social conditions and is not a permanent part of the human psyche or social order; it is not an ideological invention, or a political device at the service of other interests; nor is it the expression of dark, blind, atavistic forces. But it operates powerfully in our type of social condition, it has a strong hold over the hearts and minds of men, and it is not transparent to those under its sway, who generally do not understand its genuine mainsprings.

4

IMAGINED COMMUNITIES

Benedict Anderson

Introduction

My point of departure is that nationality, or, as one might prefer to put it in view of that word's multiple significations, nation-ness, as well as nationalism, are cultural artefacts of a particular kind. To understand them properly we need to consider carefully how they have come into historical being, in what ways their meanings have changed over time, and why, today, they command such profound emotional legitimacy. I will be trying to argue that the creation of these artefacts towards the end of the eighteenth century[1] was the spontaneous distillation of a complex 'crossing' of discrete historical forces; but that, once created, they became 'modular', capable of being transplanted, with varying degrees of self-consciousness, to a great variety of social terrains, to merge and be merged with a correspondingly wide variety of political and ideological constellations. I will also attempt to show why these particular cultural artefacts have aroused such deep attachments.

Concepts and Definitions

Before addressing the questions raised above, it seems advisable to consider briefly the concept of 'nation' and offer a workable definition. Theorists of nationalism have often been perplexed, not to say irritated, by these three paradoxes: (1) The objective modernity of nations to the historians' eye vs. their subjective antiquity in the eyes of nationalists. (2) The formal universality of

Benedict Anderson (1983), *Imagined Communities: Reflections on the Origin and Spread of Nationalism*, London: Verso.

nationality as a socio-cultural concept – in the modern world everyone can, should, will 'have' a nationality, as he or she 'has' a gender – vs. the irremediable particularity of its concrete manifestations, such that, by definition, 'Greek' nationality is sui generis. (3) The 'political' power of nationalisms vs. their philosophical poverty and even incoherence. In other words, unlike most other isms, nationalism has never produced its own grand thinkers: no Hobbeses, Tocquevilles, Marxes, or Webers. This 'emptiness' easily gives rise, among cosmopolitan and polylingual intellectuals, to a certain condescension. Like Gertrude Stein in the face of Oakland, one can rather quickly conclude that there is 'no there there'. It is characteristic that even so sympathetic a student of nationalism as Tom Nairn can nonetheless write that: ' "Nationalism" is the pathology of modern developmental history, as inescapable as "neurosis" in the individual, with much the same essential ambiguity attaching to it, a similar built-in capacity for descent into dementia, rooted in the dilemmas of help-lessness thrust upon most of the world (the equivalent of infantilism for societies) and largely incurable.'[2]

Part of the difficulty is that one tends unconsciously to hypostasize the existence of Nationalism-with-a-big-N (rather as one might Age-with-a-capi-tal-A) and then to classify 'it' as *an* ideology. (Note that if everyone has an age, Age is merely an analytical expression.) It would, I think, make things easier if one treated it as if it belonged with 'kinship' and 'religion', rather than with 'liberalism' or 'fascism'.

In an anthropological spirit, then, I propose the following definition of the nation: it is an imagined political community – and imagined as both inherently limited and sovereign.

It is *imagined* because the members of even the smallest nation will never know most of their fellow-members, meet them, or even hear of them, yet in the minds of each lives the image of their communion.[3] Renan referred to this imagining in his suavely back-handed way when he wrote that 'Or l'essence d'une nation est que tous les individus aient beaucoup de choses en commun, et aussi que tous aient oublié bien des choses.'[4] With a certain ferocity Gellner makes a comparable point when he rules that 'Nationalism is not the awakening of nations to self-consciousness: it *invents* nations where they do not exist.'[5] The drawback to this formulation, however, is that Gellner is so anxious to show that nationalism masquerades under false pretences that he assimilates 'inven-tion' to 'fabrication' and 'falsity', rather than to 'imagining' and 'creation'. In this way he implies that 'true' communities exist which can be advantageously juxtaposed to nations. In fact, all communities larger than primordial villages of face-to-face contact (and perhaps even these) are imagined. Communities are to be distinguished, not by their falsity/genuineness, but by the style in which they are imagined. Javanese villagers have always known that they are connected to people they have never seen, but these ties were once imagined particularistically – as indefinitely stretchable nets of kinship and clientship. Until quite recently, the Javanese language had no word meaning the abstraction 'society'. We may today think of the French aristocracy of the *ancien régime* as a class; but surely it was imagined this way only very late.[6] To the question 'Who is the Comte de X?' the normal answer would have been, not 'a member of the aristocracy', but 'the lord of X', 'the uncle of the Baronne de Y', or 'a client of the Duc de Z'.

The nation is imagined as *limited* because even the largest of them, encompassing perhaps a billion living human beings, has finite, if elastic, boundaries, beyond which lie other nations. No nation imagines itself coterminous with mankind. The most messianic nationalists do not dream of a day when all the members of the human race will join their nation in the way that it was possible, in certain epochs, for, say, Christians to dream of a wholly Christian planet.

It is imagined as *sovereign* because the concept was born in an age in which Enlightenment and Revolution were destroying the legitimacy of the divinely-ordained, hierarchical dynastic realm. Coming to maturity at a stage of human history when even the most devout adherents of any universal religion were inescapably confronted with the living *pluralism* of such religions, and the allomorphism between each faith's ontological claims and territorial stretch, nations dream of being free, and, if under God, directly so. The gage and emblem of this freedom is the sovereign state.

Finally, it is imagined as a *community*, because, regardless of the actual inequality and exploitation that may prevail in each, the nation is always conceived as a deep, horizontal comradeship. Ultimately it is this fraternity that makes it possible, over the past two centuries, for so many millions of people, not so much to kill, as willingly to die for such limited imaginings.

These deaths bring us abruptly face to face with the central problem posed by nationalism: what makes the shrunken imaginings of recent history (scarcely more than two centuries) generate such colossal sacrifices? I believe that the beginnings of an answer lie in the cultural roots of nationalism.

Cultural roots

No more arresting emblems of the modern culture of nationalism exist than cenotaphs and tombs of Unknown Soldiers. The public ceremonial reverence accorded these monuments precisely *because* they are either deliberately empty or no one knows who lies inside them, has no true precedents in earlier times. To feel the force of this modernity one has only to imagine the general reaction to the busy-body who 'discovered' the Unknown Soldier's name or insisted on filling the cenotaph with some real bones. Sacrilege of a strange, contemporary kind! Yet void as these tombs are of identifiable mortal remains or immortal souls, they are nonetheless saturated with ghostly *national* imaginings. (This is why so many different nations have such tombs without feeling any need to specify the nationality of their absent occupants. What else could they be *but* Germans, Americans, Argentinians . . .?)

The cultural significance of such monuments becomes even clearer if one tries to imagine, say, a Tomb of the Unknown Marxist or a cenotaph for fallen Liberals. Is a sense of absurdity avoidable? The reason is that neither Marxism nor Liberalism are much concerned with death and immortality. If the nation-alist imagining is so concerned, this suggests a strong affinity with religious imaginings. As this affinity is by no means fortuitous, it may be useful to begin a consideration of the cultural roots of nationalism with death, as the last of a whole gamut of fatalities.

If the manner of a man's dying usually seems arbitrary, his mortality is inescapable. Human lives are full of such combinations of necessity and chance. We are all aware of the contingency and ineluctability of our particular genetic heritage, our gender, our life-era, our physical capabilities, our mother-tongue, and so forth. The great merit of traditional religious world-views (which naturally must be distinguished from their role in the legitimation of specific systems of domination and exploitation) has been their concern with man-in-the-cosmos, man as species being, and the contingency of life. The extraordinary survival over thousands of years of Buddhism, Christianity or Islam in dozens of different social formations attests to their imaginative response to the over-whelming burden of human suffering – disease, mutilation, grief, age, and death. Why was I born blind? Why is my best friend paralysed? Why is my daughter retarded? The religions attempt to explain. The great weakness of all evolutionary/progressive styles of thought, not excluding Marxism, is that such questions are answered with impatient silence. At the same time, in different ways, religious thought also responds to obscure intimations of immortality, generally by transforming fatality into continuity (karma, original sin, etc.) In this way, it concerns itself with the links between the dead and the yet unborn, the mystery of re-generation. Who experiences *their* child's conception and birth without dimly apprehending a combined connectedness, fortuity, and fatality in a language of 'continuity'? (Again, the disadvantage of evolutionary/progressive thought is an almost Heraclitean hostility to any idea of continuity.)

I bring up these perhaps simpleminded observations primarily because in Western Europe the eighteenth century marks not only the dawn of the age of nationalism but the dusk of religious modes of thought. The century of the Enlightenment, of rationalist secularism, brought with it its own modern darkness. With the ebbing of religious belief, the suffering which belief in part composed did not disappear. Disintegration of paradise: nothing makes fatality more arbitrary. Absurdity of salvation: nothing makes another style of con-tinuity more necessary. What then was required was a secular transformation of fatality into continuity, contingency into meaning. As we shall see, few things were (are) better suited to this end than an idea of nation. If nation-states are widely conceded to be 'new' and 'historical', the nations to which they give political expression always loom out of an immemorial past,[7] and, still more important, glide into a limitless future. It is the magic of nationalism to turn chance into destiny. With Debray we might say, 'Yes, it is quite accidental that I am born French; but after all, France is eternal.'

Needless to say, I am not claiming that the appearance of nationalism towards the end of the eighteenth century was 'produced' by the erosion of religious certainties, or that this erosion does not itself require a complex explanation. Nor am I suggesting that somehow nationalism historically 'supersedes' religion. What I am proposing is that nationalism has to be understood by aligning it, not with self-consciously held political ideologies, but with the large cultural systems that preceded it, out of which – as well as against which – it came into being.

[. . .]

Before proceeding to a discussion of the specific origins of nationalism, it may be useful to recapitulate the main propositions put forward thus far. Essentially, I have been arguing that the very possibility of imagining the nation only arose historically when, and where, three fundamental cultural conceptions, all of great antiquity, lost their axiomatic grip on men's minds. The first of these was the idea that a particular script-language offered privileged access to ontological truth, precisely because it was an inseparable part of that truth. It was this idea that called into being the great transcontinental sodalities of Christendom, the Islamic Ummah, and the rest. Second was the belief that society was naturally organized around and under high centres – monarchs who were persons apart from other human beings and who ruled by some form of cosmological (divine) dispensation. Human loyalties were necessarily hierarchical and centripetal because the ruler, like the sacred script, was a node of access to being and inherent in it. Third was a conception of temporality in which cosmology and history were indistinguishable, the origins of the world and of men essentially identical. Combined, these ideas rooted human lives firmly in the very nature of things, giving certain meaning to the everyday fatalities of existence (above all death, loss, and servitude) and offering, in various ways, redemption from them.

The slow, uneven decline of these interlinked certainties, first in Western Europe, later elsewhere, under the impact of economic change, 'discoveries' (social and scientific), and the development of increasingly rapid communications, drove a harsh wedge between cosmology and history. No surprise then that the search was on, so to speak, for a new way of linking fraternity, power and time meaningfully together. Nothing perhaps more precipitated this search, nor made it more fruitful, than print-capitalism, which made it possible for rapidly growing numbers of people to think about themselves, and to relate themselves to others, in profoundly new ways.

THE ORIGINS OF NATIONAL CONSCIOUSNESS

If the development of print-as-commodity is the key to the generation of wholly new ideas of simultaneity, still, we are simply at the point where communities of the type 'horizontal-secular, transverse-time' become possible. Why, within that type, did the nation become so popular? The factors involved are obviously complex and various. But a strong case can be made for the primacy of capitalism.

As already noted, at least 20,000,000 books had already been printed by

1500,[8] signalling the onset of Benjamin's 'age of mechanical reproduction'. If manuscript knowledge was scarce and arcane lore, print knowledge lived by reproducibility and dissemination.[9] If, as Febvre and Martin believe, possibly as many as 200,000,000 volumes had been manufactured by 1600, it is no wonder that Francis Bacon believed that print had changed 'the appearance and state of the world'.[10]

One of the earlier forms of capitalist enterprise, book-publishing felt all of capitalism's restless search for markets. The early printers established branches all over Europe: 'in this way a veritable "international" of publishing houses, which ignored national [sic] frontiers, was created.'[11] And since the years 1500–1550 were a period of exceptional European prosperity, publishing shared in the general boom. 'More than at any other time' it was 'a great industry under the control of wealthy capitalists.'[12] Naturally, 'book-sellers were primarily concerned to make a profit and to sell their products, and consequently they sought out first and foremost those works which were of interest to the largest possible number of their contemporaries.'[13]

The initial market was literate Europe, a wide but thin stratum of Latin-readers. Saturation of this market took about a hundred and fifty years. The determinative fact about Latin – aside from its sacrality – was that it was a language of bilinguals. Relatively few were born to speak it and even fewer, one imagines, dreamed in it. In the sixteenth century the proportion of bilinguals within the total population of Europe was quite small; very likely no larger than the proportion in the world's population today, and – proletarian internationalism notwithstanding – in the centuries to come. Then and now the bulk of mankind is monoglot. The logic of capitalism thus meant that once the elite Latin market was saturated, the potentially huge markets represented by the monoglot masses would beckon. To be sure, the Counter-Reformation encouraged a temporary resurgence of Latin-publishing, but by the mid-seventeenth century the movement was in decay, and fervently Catholic libraries replete. Meantime, a Europe-wide shortage of money made printers think more and more of peddling cheap editions in the vernaculars.[14]

The revolutionary vernacularizing thrust of capitalism was given further impetus by three extraneous factors, two of which contributed directly to the rise of national consciousness. The first, and ultimately the least important, was a change in the character of Latin itself. Thanks to the labours of the Humanists in reviving the broad literature of pre-Christian antiquity and spreading it through the print-market, a new appreciation of the sophisticated stylistic achievements of the ancients was apparent among the trans-European intelligentsia. The Latin they now aspired to write became more and more Ciceronian, and, by the same token, increasingly removed from ecclesiastical and everyday life. In this way it acquired an esoteric quality quite different from that of Church Latin in mediaeval times. For the older Latin was not arcane because of its subject matter or style, but simply because it was written at all, i.e. because of its status as *text*. Now it became arcane because of what was written, because of the language-in-itself.

Second was the impact of the Reformation, which, at the same time, owed much of its success to print-capitalism. Before the age of print, Rome easily won every war against heresy in Western Europe because it always had better internal lines of communication than its challengers. But when in 1517 Martin Luther nailed his theses to the chapel-door in Wittenberg, they were printed up in German translation, and 'within 15 days [had been] seen in every part of the country.'[15] In the two decades 1520–1540 three times as many books were published in German as in the period 1500–1520, an astonishing transformation to which Luther was absolutely central. His works represented no less than one third of *all* German-language books sold between 1518 and 1525. Between 1522 and 1546, a total of 430 editions (whole or partial) of his Biblical translations appeared. 'We have here for the first time a truly mass readership and a popular literature within everybody's reach.'[16] In effect, Luther became the first best-selling author *so known*. Or, to put it another way, the first writer who could 'sell' his *new* books on the basis of his name.[17]

Where Luther led, others quickly followed, opening the colossal religious propaganda war that raged across Europe for the next century. In this titanic 'battle for men's minds', Protestantism was always fundamentally on the offensive, precisely because it knew how to make use of the expanding vernacular print-market being created by capitalism, while the Counter-Reformation defended the citadel of Latin. The emblem for this is the Vatican's *Index Librorum Prohibitorum* – to which there was no Protestant counterpart – a novel catalogue made necessary by the sheer volume of printed subversion. Nothing gives a better sense of this siege mentality than François I's panicked 1535 ban on the printing of *any* books in his realm – on pain of death by hanging! The reason for both the ban and its unenforceability was that by then his realm's eastern borders were ringed with Protestant states and cities producing a massive stream of smugglable print. To take Calvin's Geneva alone: between 1533 and 1540 only 42 editions were published there, but the numbers swelled to 527 between 1550 and 1564, by which latter date no less than 40 separate printing-presses were working overtime.[18]

The coalition between Protestantism and print-capitalism, exploiting cheap popular editions, quickly created large new reading publics – not least among merchants and women, who typically knew little or no Latin – and simultaneously mobilized them for politico-religious purposes. Inevitably, it was not merely the Church that was shaken to its core. The same earthquake produced Europe's first important non-dynastic, non-city states in the Dutch Republic and the Commonwealth of the Puritans. (François I's panic was as much political as religious.)

Third was the slow, geographically uneven, spread of particular vernaculars as instruments of administrative centralization by certain well-positioned would-be absolutist monarchs. Here it is useful to remember that the universality of Latin in mediaeval Western Europe never corresponded to a universal political system. The contrast with Imperial China, where the reach of the mandarinal bureaucracy and of painted characters largely coincided, is instructive. In effect, the political fragmentation of Western Europe after the collapse of the Western Empire meant that no sovereign could monopolize Latin and make it his-and-only-his language-of-state, and thus Latin's religious authority never had a true political analogue.

The birth of administrative vernaculars predated both print and the religious upheaval of the sixteenth century, and must therefore be regarded (at least initially) as an independent factor in the erosion of the sacred imagined community. At the same time, nothing suggests that any deep-seated ideological, let alone proto-national, impulses underlay this vernacularization where it occurred. The case of 'England' – on the northwestern periphery of Latin Europe – is here especially enlightening. Prior to the Norman Conquest, the language of the court, literary and administrative, was Anglo-Saxon. For the next century and a half virtually all royal documents were composed in Latin. Between about 1200 and 1350 this state-Latin was superseded by Norman French. In the meantime, a slow fusion between this language of a foreign ruling class and the Anglo-Saxon of the subject population produced Early English. The fusion made it possible for the new language to take its turn, after 1362, as the language of the courts – and for the opening of Parliament. Wycliffe's vernacular *manuscript* Bible followed in 1382.[19] It is essential to bear in mind that this sequence was a series of 'state', not 'national', languages; and that the state concerned covered at various times not only today's England and Wales, but also portions of Ireland, Scotland *and France*. Obviously, huge elements of the subject populations knew little or nothing of Latin, Norman French, or Early English.[20] Not till almost a century *after*. Early English's political enthronement was London's power swept out of 'France'.

On the Seine, a similar movement took place, if at a slower pace. As Bloch wrily puts it, 'French, that is to say a language which, since it was regarded as merely a corrupt form of Latin, took several centuries to raise itself to literary dignity',[21] only became the official language of the courts of justice in 1539, when François I issued the Edict of Villers-Cotterêts.[22] In other dynastic realms Latin survived much longer – under the Habsburgs well into the nineteenth century. In still others, 'foreign' vernaculars took over: in the eighteenth century the languages of the Romanov court were French and German.[23]

In every instance, the 'choice' of language appears as a gradual, unselfconscious, pragmatic, not to say haphazard development. As such, it was utterly different form the selfconscious language policies pursued by nineteenth-century dynasts confronted with the rise of hostile popular linguistic-nationalisms. One clear sign of the difference is that the old administrative languages were *just that*: languages used by and for officialdoms for their own inner convenience. There was no idea of systematically imposing the language on the dynasts' various subject populations.[24] Nonetheless, the elevation of these vernaculars to the status of languages-of-power, where, in one sense, they were competitors with Latin (French in Paris, [Early] English in London), made its own contribution to the decline of the imagined community of Christendom.

At bottom, it is likely that the esotericization of Latin, the Reformation, and the haphazard development of administrative vernaculars are significant, in the present context, primarily in a negative sense – in their contributions to the dethronement of Latin. It is quite possible to conceive of the emergence of the new imagined national communities without any one, perhaps all, of them being present. What, in a positive sense, made the new communities imaginable was a half-fortuitous, but explosive, interaction between a system of production and productive relations (capitalism), a technology of communications (print), and the fatality of human linguistic diversity.[25]

The element of fatality is essential. For whatever superhuman feats capitalism was capable of, it found in death and languages two tenacious adversaries.[26] Particular languages can die or be wiped out, but there was and is no possibility of humankind's general linguistic unification. Yet this mutual incomprehensibility was historically of only slight importance until capitalism and print created monoglot mass reading publics.

While it is essential to keep in mind an idea of fatality, in the sense of a *general* condition of irremediable linguistic diversity, it would be a mistake to equate this fatality with that common element in nationalist ideologies which stresses the primordial fatality of *particular* languages and their association with *particular* territorial units. The essential thing is the *interplay* between fatality, technology, and capitalism. In pre-print Europe, and, of course, elsewhere in the world, the diversity of spoken languages, those languages that for their speakers were (and are) the warp and woof of their lives, was immense; so immense, indeed, that had print-capitalism sought to exploit each potential oral vernacular market, it would have remained a capitalism of petty proportions. But these varied idiolects were capable of being assembled, within definite limits, into print-languages far fewer in number. The very arbitrariness of any system of signs for sounds facilitated the assembling process.[27] (At the same time, the more ideographic the signs, the vaster the potential assembling zone. One can detect a sort of descending hierarchy here from algebra through Chinese and English, to the regular syllabaries of French of Indonesian.) Nothing served to 'assemble' related vernaculars more than capitalism, which, within the limits imposed by grammars and syntaxes, created mechanically reproduced print-languages capable of dissemination through the market.[28]

These print-languages laid the bases for national consciousnesses in three distinct ways. First and foremost, they created unified fields of exchange and communication below Latin and above the spoken vernaculars. Speakers of the huge variety of Frenches, Englishes, or Spanishes, who might find it difficult or even impossible to understand one another in conversation, became capable of comprehending one another via print and paper. In the process, they gradually became aware of the hundreds of thousands, even millions, of people in their particular language-field, and at the same time that *only those* hundreds of thousands, or millions, so belonged. These fellow-readers, to whom they were connected through print, formed, in their secular, particular, visible invisibility, the embryo of the nationally imagined community.

Second, print-capitalism gave a new fixity to language, which in the long run helped to build that image of antiquity so central to the subjective idea of the nation. As Febvre and Martin remind us, the printed book kept a permanent form, capable of virtually infinite reproduction, temporally and spatially. It was no longer subject to the individualizing and 'unconsciously modernizing' habits of monastic scribes. Thus, while twelfth-century French differed markedly from that written by Villon in the fifteenth, the rate of change slowed decisively in the sixteenth. 'By the 17th century languages in Europe had generally assumed their modern forms.'[29] To put it another way, for three centuries now these stabilized print-languages have been gathering a darkening varnish; the words of our seventeenth-century forebears are accessible to us in a way that to Villon his twelfth-century ancestors were not.

Third, print-capitalism created languages-of-power of a kind different from the older administrative vernaculars. Certain dialects inevitably were 'closer' to each print-language and dominated their final forms. Their disadvantaged cousins, still assimilable to the emerging print-language, lost caste, above all because they were unsuccessful (or only relatively successful) in insisting on their own print-form. 'Northwestern German' became Platt Deutsch, a largely spoken, thus sub-standard, German, because it was assimilable to print-German in a way that Bohemian spoken-Czech was not. High German, the King's English, and, later, Central Thai, were correspondingly elevated to a new politico-cultural eminence. (Hence the struggles in late-twentieth-century Europe by certain 'sub-'nationalities to change their subordinate status by breaking firmly into print – and radio.)

It remains only to emphasize that in their origins, the fixing of print-languages and the differentiation of status between them were largely unselfconscious processes resulting from the explosive interaction between capitalism, technology and human linguistic diversity. But as with so much else in the history of nationalism, once 'there', they could become formal models to be imitated, and, where expedient, consciously exploited in a Machiavellian spirit. Today, the Thai government actively discourages attempts by foreign missionaries to provide its hill-tribe minorities with their own transcription-systems and to develop publications in their own languages: the same government is largely indifferent to what these minorities *speak*. The fate of the Turkic-speaking peoples in the zones incorporated into today's Turkey, Iran, Iraq, and the USSR is especially exemplary. A family of spoken languages, once everywhere assemblable, thus comprehensible, within an Arabic orthography, has lost that unity as a result of conscious manipulations. To heighten Turkish-Turkey's national consciousness at the expense of any wider Islamic identification, Atatürk imposed compulsory romanization.[30] The Soviet authorities followed suit, first with an anti-Islamic, anti-Persian compulsory romanization, then, in Stalin's 1930s, with a Russifying compulsory Cyrillicization.[31]

We can summarize the conclusions to be drawn from the argument thus far by saying that the convergence of capitalism and print technology on the fatal diversity of human language created the possibility of a new form of imagined community, which in its basic morphology set the stage for the modern nation. The potential stretch of these communities was inherently limited, and, at the same time, bore none but the most fortuitous relationship to existing political boundaries (which were, on the whole, the highwater marks of dynastic expansionisms).

Yet it is obvious that while today almost all modern self-conceived nations – and also nation-states – have 'national print-languages', many of them have these languages in common, and in others only a tiny fraction of the population 'uses' the national language in conversation or on paper. The nation-states of Spanish America or those of the 'Anglo-Saxon family' are conspicuous examples of the first outcome; many ex-colonial states, particularly in Africa, of the second. In other words, the concrete formation of contemporary nation-states is by no means isomorphic with the determinate reach of particular print-languages. To account for the discontinuity-in-connectedness between print-languages, national consciousness, and nation-states, it is necessary to turn to the large cluster of new political entities that sprang up in the Western hemisphere between 1776 and 1838, all of which self-consciously defined themselves as nations, and, with the interesting exception of Brazil, as (non-dynastic) republics. For not only were they historically the first such states to emerge on the world stage, and therefore inevitably provided the first real models of what such states should 'look like', but their numbers and contemporary births offer fruitful ground for comparative enquiry.

NOTES

1. As Aira Kemiläinen notes, the twin 'founding fathers' of academic scholarship on nationalism, Hans Kohn and Carleton Hayes, argued persuasively for this dating. Their conclusions have, I think, not been seriously disputed except by nationalist ideologues in particular countries. Kemiläinen also observes that the word 'nationalism' did not come into wide general use until the end of the nineteenth century. It did not occur, for example, in many standard nineteenth century lexicons. If Adam Smith conjured with the wealth of 'nations', he meant by the term no more than 'societies' or 'states'. Kemiläinen, *Nationalism*, pp. 10, 33, and 48–9.
2. Nairn, *Break-up of Britain*, p. 359.
3. Cf. Seton-Watson, *Nations and States*, p. 5: 'All that I can find to say is that a nation exists when a significant number of people in a community consider themselves to form a nation, or behave as if they formed one.' We may translate 'consider themselves' as 'imagine themselves.'
4. Renan, 'Qu'est-ce qu'une nation?', p. 892. He adds: 'Tout citoyen français doit avoir oublié la Saint-Barthélemy, les massacres du Midi au XIIIe siècle. Il n'y a pas en France dix familles qui puissent fournir la preuve d'une origine franque . . .'
5. Gellner, *Thought and Change*, p. 169. Emphasis added.

6. Hobsbawm, for example, 'fixes' it by saying that in 1789 it numbered about 400,000 in a population of 23,000,000. (See his *The Age of Revolution*, p. 78). But would this statistical picture of the noblesse have been imaginable under the *ancien régime*?

7. The late President Sukarno always spoke with complete sincerity of the 350 years of colonialism that his 'Indonesia' had endured, although the very concept 'Indonesia' is a twentieth-century invention, and most of today's Indonesia was only conquered by the Dutch between 1850 and 1910. Preeminent among contemporary Indonesia's national heroes is the early nineteenth-century Javanese Prince Diponegoro, although the Prince's own memoirs show that he intended to 'conquer [not liberate!] *Java*', rather than expel 'the Dutch'. Indeed, he clearly had no concept of 'the Dutch' as a collectivity. See Benda and Larkin, *World of Southeast Asia*, p. 158; and Kumar, 'Diponegoro (1778?–1855)', p. 103. Emphasis added. Similarly, Kemal Atatürk named one of his state banks the Eti Banka (Hittite Bank) and another the Sumerian Bank. (Seton – Watson, *Nations and States*, p. 259). These banks flourish today, and there is no reason to doubt that many Turks, possibly not excluding Kemal himself, seriously saw, and see, in the Hittites and Sumerians their Turkish forebears. Before laughing too hard, we should remind ourselves of Arthur and Boadicea, and ponder the commercial success of Tolkien's mythographies.

8. The population of that Europe where print was then known was about 100,000,000. Febvre and Martin, *The Coming of the Book*, pp. 248–9.

9. Emblematic is Marco Polo's *Travels*, which remained largely unknown till its first printing in 1559. Polo, *Travels*, p. xiii.

10. Quoted in Eisenstein, 'Some Conjectures,' p. 56.

11. Febvre and Martin, *The Coming of the Book*, p. 122. (The original text, however, speaks simply of 'par-dessus les frontières.' *L'Apparition*, p. 184.)

12. Ibid., p. 187. The original text speaks of 'puissants' (powerful) rather than 'wealthy' capitalists. *L'Apparition*, p. 281.

13. 'Hence the introduction of printing was in this respect a stage on the road to our present society of mass consumption and standardisation.' Ibid., pp. 259–60. (The original text has 'une civilisation de masse et de standardisation', which may be better rendered 'standardised, mass civilization'. *L'Apparition*, p. 394).

14. Ibid., p. 195.

15. Ibid., pp. 289–90.

16. Ibid., pp. 291–5.

17. From this point it was only a step to the situation in seventeenth-century France where Corneille, Molière, and La Fontaine could sell their manuscript tragedies and comedies directly to publishers, who bought them as excellent investments in view of their authors' market reputations. Ibid., p. 161.

18. Ibid., pp. 310–15.

19. Seton-Watson, *Nations and States*, pp. 28–9; Bloch, *Feudal Society*, I, p. 75.

20. We should not assume that administrative vernacular unification was immediately or fully achieved. It is unlikely that the Guyenne ruled from London was ever primarily administered in Early English.

21. Bloch, *Feudal Society*, I, p. 98.

22. Seton-Watson, *Nations and States*, p. 48.

23. Ibid., p. 83.

24. An agreeable confirmation of this point is provided by François I, who, as we have seen, banned all printing of books in 1535 and made French the language of his courts four years later!

25. It was not the first 'accident' of its kind. Febvre and Martin note that while a visible bourgeoisie already existed in Europe by the late thirteenth century, paper did not come into general use until the end of the fourteenth. Only paper's smooth plane surface made the mass reproduction of texts and pictures possible – and this did not occur for still another seventy-five years. But paper was not a European invention. It

floated in from another history – China's – through the Islamic world. *The Coming of the Book*, pp. 22, 30, and 45.

26. We still have no giant multinationals in the world of publishing.

27. For a useful discussion of this point, see S. H. Steinberg, *Five Hundred Years of Printing*, chapter 5. That the sign *ough* is pronounced differently in the words although, bough, lough, rough, cough, and hiccough, shows both the idiolectic variety out of which the now-standard spelling of English emerged, and the ideographic quality of the final product.

28. I say 'nothing served . . . more than capitalism' advisedly. Both Steinberg and Eisenstein come close to theomorphizing 'print' *qua* print as the genius of modern history. Febvre and Martin never forget that behind print stand printers and publishing firms. It is worth remembering in this context that although printing was invented first in China, possibly 500 years before its appearance in Europe, it had no major, let alone revolutionary impact – precisely because of the absence of capitalism there.

29. Febvre and Martin, *The Coming of the Book*, p. 319. Cf. *L'Apparition*, p. 477: 'Au XVIIe siècle, les langues nationales apparaissent un peu partout cristallisées.'

30. Kohn, *The Age of Nationalism*, p. 108. It is probably only fair to add that Kemal also hoped thereby to align Turkish nationalism with the modern, romanized civilization of Western Europe.

31. Seton-Watson, *Nations and States*, p. 317.

5

NATIONALISM AND THE STATE

John Breuilly

The modern state is the possessor of sovereignty over a given territory. Sovereignty resides in a specific institution such as monarchy or parliament, and is considered to be, by its very nature, indivisible. The state possesses an elaborate institutional structure which delimits, justifies and exercises the claims attached to sovereignty. The activity of the state is devoted to the maintenance and exercise of its sovereignty against both external and internal threats. Externally the limit upon sovereignty is set by the sovereignty of other states. The political world is made up of a plurality of sovereign territorial states. It has no order other than that created out of the rational pursuit of self-interest which states follow in their dealings with one another. Internally the sovereignty of the state is limited – or, more precisely, divided – by the distinction between the public and the private spheres. In the public sphere the state exercises sovereignty directly; in the private sphere it does no more than provide ground rules for dealings between individuals and groups, rules which can, if necessary, be enforced when broken.

This idea of the state is marked by internal tensions between universality and particularity and between boundlessness and limitation. These tensions are perhaps most apparent in liberal thought in nineteenth-century Europe, when this idea of the state reached its most complete expression both in theory and practice.

The state is universal in that what is envisaged is a world made up wholly of a number of such states. There should be no area or person not subject to the rule of a state. Given that the sovereignty of a state is externally bound only by that

John Breuilly (1993), *Nationalism and the State*, 2nd ed., Manchester: Manchester University Press.

of other states, such a situation would be seen as a vacuum which would have to be filled. Someone unfortunate enough to be excluded from the rule of a state, a stateless person, becomes both in theory and in practice a sort of non-person. Yet at the same time there can be no universal state. The very notion of the sovereign territorial state entails the existence of other such states. Without other such states it is impossible to imagine how the state could be bounded or its sovereignty defined. At most a state could defend its existence (rather than its sovereignty) against external forces which were not themselves states. In the absence of the need to defend sovereignty it is difficult to see why the state itself, at least in terms of its external relationships, should continue to exist. So the world is made up wholly of sovereign states with sharply defined boundaries and where the claim to sovereignty is made with the same force throughout the territory so bounded.[1]

This idea of the state is boundless in that it asserts ultimate claims over the lives of those within it. The state is the highest form of human existence in the sense that all other forms of existence are subordinate to it. Yet to define it as a form of existence requires that it be limited and set off against other forms. In liberal theory this is something which can be done only by means of abstractions. Liberals attacked, both in theory and in practice, the concentration of certain powers in particular non-state institutions such as guilds or churches or estates. If such powers were an essential part of public life they should be vested in the state; if not they should be dissolved or extended as rights to all private individuals. So the internal limitations upon the state were not those imposed by the concrete powers of particular groups or institutions – that is privilege. Rather they were limitations within the lives of those who were both citizens and private individuals. The distinction was drawn not between ruler and ruled but between state and society.

To give substance to such limits and distinctions it was necessary to define what was public and what private and to outline the position of the state in relation to these two spheres. To carry through an exhaustive classification in this way was always very difficult but some things could clearly be assigned to one or the other category. Family life, economic dealings, cultural and religious preferences were private matters; forcible attacks on persons and property were public ones. Liberals faced the problem of whether their distinctions were a convenience, confined to a particular historical situation, or a principle, founded upon natural rights or human nature. They also faced the problem of how such distinctions could be defined by any body other than the state and, therefore, how the state could be both sovereign and self-limiting. All manner of devices were set in hand to impose limitation. Certain things were defined as freedoms from the state, though how justified and defended remained a thorny problem. Equally important were the attempts to build freedom and limitation within the state itself. The state was regarded as the association of the citizens. Sovereignty was (usually) vested in parliament, which by means of representation converted the will of the citizens into state power. The successful working of representation was regarded as dependent upon certain freedoms, and on this basis various political rights were outlined which the state could not, or only with great difficulty, breach. Frequently the institutions of the state were structured through written constitutions designed to limit the way in which sovereignty was exercised. Finally, the state was regarded as being bound to observe stringent rules of procedure in the way it operated. The problem of what bound the state remained. Having accepted the absolute nature of sovereignty and vested it in the state, liberals faced an impossible theoretical task in seeking to limit state power. If the limitations were the product of utility and/or particular historical circumstances, they could not be defended in principle and were liable to be undone once utilitarian calculation or circumstances changed. If, on the other hand, limitation was a matter of principle, there was the problem of how the principles could be defined and enforced against the state without calling its sovereignty into question.

For the most part liberals did not need to face up to these questions because reality seemed to conform to their ideas. For example, the distinction between public and private was reinforced, if not actually created, by the development of capitalism as the dominant economic system in Europe and subsequently the world. This development was accompanied by a body of thought which elaborated on the internal order of the market economy and argued that non-economic interference in it should be reduced to the minimum. The idea that the market economy operated through the exchange of resources between free and rational individuals, each seeking to maximise his satisfactions in a competitive situation, suggested that political power had no part to play in these relationships the way it did in societies where resources were obtained from others by command.

The notion of privacy was not confined to economic relations. Indeed, historically it was the attempt to define other matters as private that first contributed to the notion of the limited public state. The demand for freedom of conscience in matters of religion began by defending itself against the Catholic Church but could easily be turned against the state if and when that came to be seen as the major threat to religious choice. In this way the state could come to be defined as both public and secular, although there is no need to equate these attributes with one another. Equally the notion of the 'private' family whose affairs are beyond the reach of the state cannot be reduced to one aspect of the development of capitalism, although in various ways capitalism has shaped this notion in its more modern forms. Nor can the concern with the cultivation of the 'private' personality and of 'private' friendships which has become so important in the modern period be ignored as another independent source of the notion of a private sphere from which the state should be excluded. One must remember that as much liberal energy in nineteenth-century Europe went into the defence of religious belief or family affairs such as the education of children as private matters as went into the defence of the free market economy.

Nevertheless it would be difficult to argue against the claim that by the nineteenth century capitalism provided the most important element in the notion of a 'civil society'. This had important implications for international relations as well. While political relationships internationally were seen as threatening relationships of power where individuals were represented through their state, economic relationships were regarded as non-coercive dealings between individuals which could operate across state boundaries. The market economy was international and could operate independently of the political system of competing states. In this way it was possible to envisage an international economic order which was not matched by an international political order.[2]

Even where state institutions remained highly authoritarian it is noteworthy that those states also acknowledged the necessity of retreating from economic interference. Indeed, some have argued that such states could more easily do this as well as promoting the appropriate policies than could more participatory states. Prussia, for example, led the way in Germany in state attacks on restrictions on geographical and job mobility and promoted greater freedom of trade through the German Customs Union. Emperor Napoleon III pushed through free trade agreements with Britain and the German Customs Union. Some economic liberals, noting this, assumed that the move towards democracy would also begin the move away from economic liberalism.

Clearly this ideal end-state of a constitutionally defined and bounded state which merely held the ring in activities which were not in the narrowly defined public domain was never actually reached and could only be approximated under certain special conditions. But it provides us with a notion of the ideal form of the modern state as it was being envisaged and pursued in the nineteenth century. It is necessary now to see in what ways these ideas were distinctively modern and how, historically, something approximating to the modern state developed.

The abstract notion of sovereignty long antedates the modern state. The general distinction between public and private found expression in the Roman law division between criminal and civil law. The idea of bounded and competing states was clearly important for the city-states of northern Italy in the Middle Ages. But it was the way in which various ideas were taken from these different sources and used to underpin the claims of territorial monarchs in western Europe that gave rise to the recognisably modern idea of the state. The legacy of Roman law and of papal governmental theory and of city-state methods of diplomacy all helped provide the medieval monarchs of western Europe with the intellectual capacity to define their powers as public ones. The disputes between monarchy and Catholic Church (disputes which it would be anachronistic to describe as church-state conflict) helped shift authority towards monarchs. But still monarchs could hardly enforce sovereign claims over their subjects. Indeed, in a feudal society it was impossible to make the distinctions between public and private or to crush the privileges of various groups in a way which would give some meaning to the notion of a sovereign state. In a few countries, notably France and England, the monarchy was able to press home claims to raise general taxes and to dispense justice, although these were hedged about with numerous practical and theoretical limitations. This was important in the way in which the modern state developed because it meant that the state came to be defined not by means of fiat from above but through negotiations between monarchs and the political community within which their rule operated. This meant that the concept of sovereignty that did develop was always related to notions of rights and liberties. Yet at the same time the forms of collaboration which this negotiation made possible produced more powerful states than had been achieved by conquest alone. So the idea of the sovereign state emerged gradually through a process of negotiation in western Europe.

Significantly this was not the pattern in eastern Europe. There did not develop there either a powerful and privileged class of landowners or autonomous towns with which monarchs had to bargain in order to increase their authority. Indeed, very often privileges were gifts of those rulers in their attempt to help extend their authority downwards and outwards. Privileges so granted could easily be revoked. As a consequence power was detached from social relationships; it had a 'despotic' rather than an 'infra-structural' character.[3] This meant that the extension of state power was not accompanied by a process of negotiations which created political 'liberties'. The lack of autonomy for the political community from the central state was carried over, in a different form, from tsarist to communist governments, and has meant that nationalism developed in a rather different way than was the case in western Europe.

The idea of the territorial state also emerged gradually, as for a long time monarchs did not govern bounded and continuous territories but rather possessed different bundles of powers over different areas and groups. Neither sovereignty nor boundaries were sharply defined attributes of 'public' authority until the eighteenth century. It is significant that it was the 'modern' French state of 1791–92 which objected strongly to enclaves and mixed forms of authority that were associated with *anciens régimes*, and this contributed to unleashing what was in many ways the first national war.[4]

By the early modern period a few monarchies had acquired enough control over matters such as taxation, the church and justice as to be able to conceive of themselves as sovereign in something like the modern sense. Their powers were embodied in specific institutions, and were justified and symbolised by various elaborate means. Such powers had only been achieved through a process of negotiation between the ruler and the political community of the core territory under his sway. As a consequence the monarch's rule was bound up with the institutions of this political community. Only on the basis of some consent from that community, to which various rights and liberties were conceded, was the monarch able to establish and enforce some kind of sovereign power. One of the reasons why consent was forthcoming was the need to defend the territory against the rise of similar states.

In this way the kingdoms of western Europe came to take on the form of national states. The concept of the nation, a concept which related principally to the institutions of the political community that sustained the monarchy, could be turned against the monarchy itself under certain conditions. In this way the process which created the modern idea of the state in its earliest form also gave rise to the political concept of the nation.

This represented the first step towards nationalism. Because the process was confined to a small political community that had developed along with the state, where there was little idea about wider political participation, it could give rise to only very limited national oppositions. However, when the monarchy made more and more claims to represent the public interest the scope for conflict widened. This was reinforced from the eighteenth century by the rapid spread of a market economy which helped clarify the public/private distinction and also provided civil society with new energies and solidarities that could be fed into political conflict. It was now possible for elements within the political community to go beyond their previous forms of opposition and claim to enforce the needs and interests of 'society' upon an unrepresentative state. National ideology began to acquire a mobilising as well as co-ordinating role and a more radical set of political objectives. This was not yet nationalism. New claims were grounded on historic or natural rights, and not the peculiar cultural identity of the ruled society. But the foundations for making that claim had been laid. The modern state was now regarded as deriving its sovereignty from the people, not from God. At the same time the 'people' were a particular set of people, often seen as the members of the civil society which the state ruled, and also as the occupants of the clearly defined territory the state claimed as its own.

Once the claim to sovereignty was made on behalf of a particular, territorially defined unit of humanity, it was natural to relate the claim to the particular attributes of that unit. At first this was confined to certain political characteristics and did not extend, at least explicitly, to cultural characteristics which did not already have some explicit political meaning. But when opposition came from outside the core political community the claim to sovereignty had to shift to new ground. To claim to alter the territory as well as the institutions of the state required some notion of a particular human group with a different territory. Such a notion could be sustained in three different ways. One could appeal to universal principles which were not being observed in a particular part of the state; to particular political rights which applied to only one area of the state; and to a distinctive cultural identity. At first most appeals were couched in largely political terms. The stronger the political opposition the less attractive, by and large, was the need to appeal to cultural identity. Thus American revolutionaries could couch their claims in the universal terms of natural rights, and Magyar opponents of the Habsburg emperor in terms of historic political rights. Where the political opposition was much weaker the situation was rather different. Frequently to establish a political identity and to justify political claims it was necessary to move beyond universal or purely political criteria. It was often necessary to seek support from groups hitherto excluded from political life. Given the existence of certain cultural differences within various regions of the state, it was possible to appeal to cultural identity. At that point politics took on a properly nationalist form.

So the development of the modern state shaped nationalism in various ways. Only under the modern state system could a political opposition see its objective as possession of sovereign, territorial state power and justify that objective in the name of the society ruled by the public state. Only in the context of competing territorial sovereign states could this objective be seen as the possession of a state like other states on the basis of representing a nation like other nations. Yet this claim was also particular: the state concerned had its own special characteristics, so the particular nation concerned also had special characteristics. The idea of the ruled society which might only be definable in terms of its private character, that is, in terms of its 'culture'; of the sovereign territorial state; of a world made up of such states in competition with one another – these are the essential premises upon which nationalist ideology and nationalist politics build. Their objectives may look beyond that situation, above all when they believe they can abolish the distinction between state and society, but they could arise only in that situation and in many ways are tied to it.

These represent the general conditions for the emergence of nationalism. It is the shift of political conflict away from the core political community of the state and also towards sections of society hitherto excluded from political life which provides the particular conditions for nationalism to develop. Only when the existing state is held to have different boundaries from those of the nation are political oppositions liable to move beyond political justifications to arguments that explicitly appeal to cultural identity. The first real nationalist movements, therefore, were movements of either unification or separation. I have argued that separatist movements are the more important and common of the two. But not all separatist opposition to the modern state is nationalist. This means that the question as to when nationalism proper first develops can be phrased quite specifically. In what circumstances will the types of political conflict created by the growth of state power in its distinctively modern form give rise to opposition movements which seek to create separate states and which justify this objective in the name of the nation which is defined in cultural terms? There appear to be two major situations in which this happens: in Europe within the modernising state which has a decentralised political structure and a wide range of cultural distinctions between the populations of different regions; and outside Europe where the modern colonial state has been imposed on peoples of non-European origin. There is little point in recapitulating the arguments about how nationalism developed in these circumstances. Instead I will point to some very general aspects of the way nationalism developed in these types of situation and the major differences between the two types.

The European multinational state pursued a policy of political modernisation for the most part cautiously, as it had no independent basis of power apart from the population it controlled and the historical institutional relationships it had developed with various regions in the process of building up its control. Although making far-reaching theoretical claims about sovereignty and the 'public' role of the state, particularly under Joseph II, the Habsburg state could in fact enforce only limited changes upon the existing political community, which possessed many entrenched privileges and powers. But even these limited changes, along with threats of more extensive ones, could provoke opposition from elements of that political community. The changes, however, appeared necessary, given a threatening international situation. At the same time the advance of private rights in land and in matters such as religion – rights sometimes promoted by the state – helped form a civil society which could be mobilised by oppositional elements within the political community.

In these ways, therefore, the general conditions that have been already noted – international state competition, gradual formation of civil society, new claims to power by the public state, opposition from political groups with entrenched powers and privileges – could lead to the emergence of a 'national' opposition. However, in the case of the Habsburg Empire this opposition was decentralised because of the historically federated nature of the dynasty. Political oppositions in Hungary and Italy could not act together. The only route open to them was to press for greater concessions on a regional basis. The justifications of the opposition came, therefore, to focus upon particular attributes of a region which would support special political claims. Normally such oppositions would refer to the regional political rights that had been enjoyed historically. That was the pattern of early Magyar opposition and even some of the Lombard opposition which resented the introduction of 'German' practices in matters such as noble rankings.

This was similar to cases of regional oppositions which had developed in peripheral regions of France or Spain to centralising monarchy. Given the limited nature of political conflict in the early modern period, that had been all that was necessary. Where such historic liberties, privileges or rights had shallower roots, as in North America, the argument might shift to a dependence on universal values which were not properly being applied in a particular part of the state. But where the state itself claimed to represent universal values, and where it became increasingly apparent that elements of civil society could and should be mobilised in any opposition to the state, then the justification for claiming special political rights could shift towards nationalism. In the case of dominant groups this could take the form of extending the ideas associated with historic rights beyond the privileged who had hitherto been the sole beneficiaries. Thus Magyar and Italian opponents of the Habsburg empire moved only hesitantly towards cultural nationality arguments. Where, however, such dominant groups locally controlled an ethnically distinct population, this could stimulate an explicitly cultural nationalist response. Whereas dominant groups fused the defence of privilege with the claims of historic nationality, subordinate groups fused the defence of equal rights with the claims of cultural nationality.

In this way, then, the modernising multinational state could generate authentic nationalist opposition.

In the case of European empire overseas the situation was different because the modern state had an independent base of power located outside the subject population. This meant that it was possible to establish modern state forms before either the general social arrangements (market economy, private family and religious practice, etc.) or political institutional arrangements (representative assemblies, locally staffed bureaucracies) that accompanied the development of the modern state form in Europe could be established. This partly accounts for why 'traditional' patterns of political and social action continue for so long even where the colonial state has a distinctly modern form. Gradually the colonial state did establish some modern institutions through which collaboration could be practised, and it was within these institutions that a nationalist opposition could develop. Nevertheless much of the real political community remained outside these institutions, and at the same time civil society was poorly formed. An opposition that wished to possess the colonial state rather than simply to destroy foreign domination had then to construct an image of the political community and of the society which could 'match' the state it would take over. This was a formidable intellectual and political task and one which could only partially be achieved during the actual struggle for state power. Arguments about cultural nationality played only a subordinate role in the struggle because of the difficulties of matching such arguments with the political claims to take over the state. But it played an important part in the general repudiation of European pretensions to cultural superiority. But it is in the new states that such arguments will become particularly important, because the state will itself monopolise arguments about political nationality, and any nationalist case cannot be grounded upon an implicit contrast between foreigners and natives.

In these ways nationalist movements of real force could develop both within and beyond Europe. Of course it was not their force alone that brought success. The more weakly developed nationalist movements of the Ottoman empire achieved more than the stronger movements in the Habsburg empire. The nationalist movements of Germany and Italy were more effective than the rather stronger Polish nationalist movement. One cannot equate power directly with success when looking at nationalism. In particular, where the influence of major external powers was crucial and such powers favoured separatist movements, it was often to legitimise independence from a weak imperial state rather than to wrest independence from a strong one that nationalist claims were made. Nevertheless, the rise of nationalist movements in Europe by 1918 and beyond Europe, particularly after 1945, have made a major contribution towards establishing the nation-state as the basic political unit in the world.

In this process separatist nationalism has played the leading role, and in ways which permit of generalisation. The development of effective unification or reform nationalism in non-nation-states is based upon much more specific and, therefore, rarer sets of conditions. [. . .] Generally in the two major European cases [Germany and Italy] one can note the advanced form 'civil society' had taken and the advantages unity would secure for important elements within that society as well as the various ways in which political modernisation could give rise to liberal political groups with contacts extending beyond state frontiers. But it was crucial that these groups found a state or states with which they could co-operate. The leading state in this process played the dominant role in such co-operation. In this rather special way interactions between modernising states, civil society and nationalist groups could generate a nationalist movement which could at least legitimise and help run the new nation-state once it had been created.

In the Japanese case the issue was as much about political modernisation as independence. As with 'national reform' movements in Europe, it was necessary to find new social, institutional and ideological bases from which to take over and transform a state which could not be regarded as foreign. It was also essential that these new bases were derived from existing trends or features of Japanese politics rather than being a very new sort of opposition. [. . .] Japanese reformers did not have to liquidate a 'universalist' set of values such as represented by Confucianism and Islam in the Chinese and Ottoman cases. Japanese reformers possessed in the lapsed institutions of empire an alternative political tradition, peculiar to Japan, around which reform organisation and ideology could build. These conditions enabled them to provide an alternative view of the Japanese state which did not move to new universalist challenges such as those posed by Chinese communists or Turkish secular nationalists. Given that this reform movement developed in Japan in the larger context of Western superiority and threat, it was natural that the alternative tradition was presented by reformers in nationalist terms.

These three nationalist movements and the new states to which they contributed had an enormous impact beyond their own countries. German and Italian unification firmly established the nation-state as the normal political unit in Europe and initiated a new phase of instability and conflict which led to major warfare in Europe and the extension of European conflict throughout the world. Japanese nationalism provided a potent model for many other non-European societies as well as contributing directly to the weakening of European power in the Far East. Nevertheless, although of major importance, these were not typical of the bulk of nationalist movements. It is the relationship between the modern state and separatist nationalism which provides support for a general argument about how nationalism develops in a world of non-nation-states.

On the basis of the preceding argument I would conclude that the development of nationalism as a modern form of politics was closely bound up with the nature of political modernisation in nineteenth-century Europe, and then in areas of European settlement and imperial rule overseas. A number of other points should be noted in order to place this argument into a broader context and to secure it against some possible objections.

First, these political processes that I have outlined could be reinforced by certain intellectual and social-cultural changes. There are those who consider nationalism primarily as an idea and focus on the work of intellectuals in producing and spreading this idea. Clearly political modernisation was often bound up with the creation of a secular intelligentsia. In many cases where such intellectuals were placed in subordinate positions either in peripheral regions or even at the centre, their reflections on modernisation and their role in that process could take ideas of territorial identity and popular sovereignty and go on from that to 'imagine' the nation-state as the political representative of a new kind of community, the nation. Sometimes such an intelligentsia played a major role in nationalist politics.[5]

At the same time the processes of capitalist development and urban-industrial growth, along with the extension of communications, mass literacy, and increased social and georgaphical mobility all created the conditions for what Gellner has termed 'standard national cultures'.[6] This in turn can increase the significance of identity defined in terms of member-ship of such a culture for many aspects of everyday life. For those who consider nationalism primarily in terms of the growth of such a sense of national identity this is clearly the level of development to which the most attention should be paid.

However, these are distinct even if frequently interrelated processes. Nation-alist intelligentsias and populations with a broadly shared sense of national identity are not essential to the development of significant nationalist political movements and organisations. Conversely, such intelligentsias and such popu-lations can exist independently of one another and in the absence of significant nationalist politics. Furthermore, much of the development of 'standard na-tional cultures' took place after the formation of nation-states in western Europe and areas of European settlement overseas.[7] What this meant was that the term nationalism shifted from denoting political movements seeking to create nation-states to denoting either the assertive policies of the governments of nation-states and/or the formation of a popular public opinion which favoured such policies.[8]

Finally, once the most powerful and advanced states have defined the national state as the normative political unit, then this has an enormous impact on political development everywhere else. I have already pointed to the role of 'legitimacy', that is an appeal to powerful outside states, in many nationalist movements. The peace settlement of 1919 rewarded many of these appeals and 'fixed' the nation-state as the political norm for Europe. This meant that all kinds of regional or ethnic tensions within states, as well as border disputes between states, would all now express themselves in nationalist terms. This affected political change not merely in western and central Europe but also in the USSR which, although a multi-national state, structured itself on a recognition of some kind of legitimacy to national claims. Naturally, where a nationalist intelligentsia was also formed and/or where urban-industrial development helped shape a 'standard national culture', then the claims of political movements which clustered around these political institutions would have that much more elaboration and appeal. This could help reinforce the power of nationalist politics if and when central state power broke down. But it was upon state institutions which actually paid at least lip-service to some principle of nationality that these reinforcing elements crystallised. The same argument can be developed for areas of European empire overseas after 1945 and the way political oppositions crystallised around colonial state institutions as imperial power crumbled.

In these ways, therefore, the initial conditions which generated very specific forms of nationalism (that is, separatist challenges to modernising states) could, with the formation of nation-states by the most powerful and richest societies, go on to generate an ever more diverse range of 'nationalisms'. The problem is that as the word comes to span ideas, sentiments and politics, and includes state policy, international conflicts, and supportive public opinion, so there is a danger that the term will lose all specific meaning. That, of course, is an indication of its great success.

NOTES

1. This compares sharply with pre-modern states with different power claims over different territories and groups and where claims tend to decline as one moves from the territorial core to frontier zones. See Heesterman (1978); the distinction between frontiers and borders in Giddens 1985; and the highly original study of the changing meaning of boundaries over the modern period: Sahlins, 1989.
2. The novelty and importance of this is stressed in Wallerstein 1974. For the utopian significance some liberals could derive from the separation of international economic dealings from state interference see Semmel 1986.
3. The distinction is made in volume 1 of Mann 1986.
4. See Blanning 1986.
5. This idea is developed brilliantly in Anderson 1983. For a more detailed critique of this study, as well as Gellner 1983 see my review article 'Reflections on nationalism' (Breuilly 1985).
6. Gellner 1983. For a further, more systematic development of Gellner's arguments about the changing nature and meaning of culture in the modern age of urban-industrial society see Gellner 1988.
7. See, for example, Weber 1976. There is now much agreement amongst historians that the crucial period for the creation of a mass society with national identity in western Europe was 1890–1914, with the world war then creating the most intense 'national' experience to date. For a general overview for Europe see Stone 1983; and for the USA see Brogan 1986.
8. It is actually very difficult to avoid this slippage in meaning, and I have not been completely successful myself. Partly that is because of the pull of common usage of the word nationalism. Partly it is because one can never wholly leave aside the ideas and sentiments that give nationalist politics its principal objective and which can continue to exist even when the conditions for such politics do not exist, for example in the form of pressure groups or inter-ethnic conflicts or just general chauvinism.

For example, Motyl (1990, ch. 11) makes the valid point that Russian chauvinism did not take nationalist form so long as Russians had an empire to rule. Nevertheless, the rapid switch, once the empire had collapsed, into nationalist politics can only be understood against that background. We need clear definitions and distinctions, but equally we must not forget that these express our analytical needs rather than neatly reflecting the 'real' world.

FURTHER READING

Reading the longer works from which we have drawn the extracts of Smith, Hastings, Anderson and Breuilly will provide a more comprehensive account of their arguments. A more detailed version of Gellner's arguments can be found in his 1983 book, *Nations and Nationalism* (Oxford: Blackwell). Critical debate around Gellner's positions from generally sympathetic points of view can be found in John Hall (ed.) (1998), *The State of the Nation – Ernest Gellner and the Theory of Nationalism*, (Cambridge: Cambridge University Press). A very comprehensive exegesis and discussion of modernist positions is to be found in Anthony Smith (1998), *Nationalism and Modernism: A Critical Survey of Recent Theories of Nations and Nationalism*, (London: Routledge). Although Smith is a key protagonist in these debates this is a fair and judicious account. Eric Hobsbawm (1992), *Nations and Nationalism since 1780* (2nd ed.) (Cambridge: Cambridge University Press) is a masterful historical survey from within a Marxist-inspired modernist framework (and is the explicit focus of Hastings's critique). Finally an alternative view of the relationship between modernism and nationalism can be found in Liah Greenfeld (1992), *Nationalism: Five Roads to Modernity* (Cambridge: Cambridge University Press). A 'classic' postmodern perspective can be found in Homi Bhahba (ed.) (1990), *Nation and Narration* (London: Routledge).

PART TWO
APPROACHES TO NATIONALISM

6

LIBERAL NATIONALISM – AN IRRESPONSIBLE COMPOUND?

Andrew Vincent

In this century there has been a deep concern about the dangers of nationalism. Many of those who have expressed such concerns have been liberals. Yet, ironically, in the last decade, there has been a resurgence of interest in the idea of nationalism from within liberal thought – thus giving rise to the compound term 'liberal nationalism'. Having situated liberal nationalism in a broader historical context, this paper critically reviews the arguments of liberal nationalism in the work of Neil MacCormick, David Miller and Yael Tamir. It concludes by drawing a distinction between the pragmatic and ethical significance of nationalism. This distinction neither entails a denial of the role of nationalism nor a defence of liberalism. It attempts to sever the connection between nationalism and ethics. Nationalism may be inevitable for the present, but it is not a virtue to be promoted.

In the last decade, there has been a resurgence of interest in the idea of nationalism within liberal thought. This paper places the interest in liberal nationalism in a slightly longer time frame, reviews the arguments of some of the recent enthused renderings of liberal nationalism, and then unpicks them in critical vein. I conclude by drawing a distinction between the pragmatic and ethical significance of nationalism. Pragmatically, nationalism is unavoidable in contemporary world politics. If it is to exist, then it is infinitely preferable to have a relatively innocuous form which accords with liberal intuitions. We should hesitate, however, before accepting its ethical justification. Thus, my

Andrew Vincent (1997), 'Liberal nationalism: an irresponsible compound?', *Political Studies*, 45.

critique of the ethical arguments for liberal nationalism should neither be taken as a dismissal of nationalism *per se* nor as a defence of liberalism against nationalism. The argument rather tries to decouple ethics from nationalism.[1]

NATIONALISM IN CONTEXT

Let us place the debates on liberal nationalism, first, within a broader typology and, second, in a wider historical setting. There are a number of distinct typologies of nationalism. They can be premised upon *political strategies*, *historical phases* or *ideas*. *Strategies* focus on the particular methods or tactics used by nationalists. It is thus possible to distinguish 'unificatory' from secessionist' strategies, although the ideological complexion of, say, two secessionist nationalisms might be diametrically opposed. Other theorists have been attracted by the idea of categorizing *historical phases* in the growth of nationalism. Nationalism, in this context, can be charted historically in terms of characteristic features, affiliations and modes of operation.[2] Thus, one could argue that whereas early forms of nineteenth century nationalisms were integrative and cosmopolitan, early twentieth century nationalisms were aggressive elitist and xenophobic. Typologies premised on *ideas* are in many ways much less settled. Such typologies range from twofold to fivefold classifications.[3] Typologies of ideas classify forms of nationalism in terms of characteristic values and intellectual themes.[4] The focus of this article will be on this latter form of typology.

Contemporary interest in nationalism, particularly in recent liberal theory has its roots in the discovery or rediscovery of civic or liberal nationalism. The favoured typology here is a twofold 'idea-based' classification which distinguishes liberal and authoritarian types. Plamenatz was the most important popularizer of this classification, though his work drew upon Hans Kohn. For Kohn, nationalism largely stemmed from the eighteenth century and was divided into two diametrically opposed types: Western and Eastern.[5] This distinction keeps reappearing – in slightly different dress – in contemporary debate.[6] The former, premised on Enlightenment values of reason and universalist humanism, aimed at a more open, plural, outward-looking society. It was also linked to democracy, liberalism and constitutional rule and its aim was to liberate the individual. The latter was more overtly authoritarian, closed, inward-looking, particularist, pathological, bellicose and xenophobic. Plamenatz echoed this distinction. He distinguished, like Kohn, between an acceptable 'moderate' Western civic nationalism – essentially the candidate for liberal nationalism – and a more bellicose East European cultural nationalism.[7] Nationalism, in itself, should not therefore be equated with illiberalism; as Plamenatz argued: 'No doubt, nationalists have quite often not been liberals, but that, I suggest, is largely because they have so often been active in conditions unpropitious to freedom, as the liberal understands it. I see no logical repugnance between nationalism and liberalism'.[8] By and large, the brutality or unpleasantness was dependent upon the historical context. In Western European societies nationalism was more than usually liberal. However, Plamenatz was clear that this liberal form should be kept distinct from Eastern cultural nationalism. Eastern nationalism was invariably illiberal in character and also hostile to Western liberal nationalism. It is Eastern nationalism which has given nationalism a bad press in the twentieth century.

I now turn to the wider historical setting of liberal nationalism. There was indeed a surge of interest in liberal nationalism in the nineteenth century, and Mazzini (1805–72) was the key early figure. His liberal *Risorgimento* nationalism asserted most of the core liberal values. The roots of the doctrine lay largely in an Englightenment universalism. Writers who adhered to liberal nationalism from the nineteenth century to the present did not see it as in any way incompatible with cosmopolitanism. The Greek struggles against the Ottoman Empire and the Polish struggle against the Tsarist Empire in the 1830s attracted the enthusiasm of Mazzinian-inspired liberal nationalists. Thus, the heyday of this original form of liberal nationalism was largely from the Congress of Vienna (1814–15) up to the Treaty of Versailles and President Wilson's Fourteen Points. In many ways, Wilson's Fourteen Points, promulgated after the World War I, represented, if only symbolically, the high point of liberal nationalism in so far as they stressed 'the absolute sovereignty of the national state, but sought to limit the implications of this principle by stressing individual liberties – political, economic, and religious – within each national state'.[9] The key theme was the right of self-determination by nations, with the proviso that such self-determination would inevitably lead to constitutional liberal democratic rule. One of the major problems with this position was that once having promulgated the idea of the self-determining nation, it was difficult to know where to halt. As Wilson was to complain, how could one prevent every moderately sized community perceiving itself as a nation, and thus a state. In addition, how was one to resolve conflicts between liberal nation states and even more problematically, secessionist movements *within* liberal nation states.[10]

Much of the interest in nationalism in the period from 1930 to the 1950s must be understood in the context of what might be termed the 'Weimar debates'. Most of the early writers like Kohn and Karl Deutsch, and many others, who generated the academic debate over nationalism were European émigres to America in the 1930s. They had either experienced first-hand, or second-hand through teachers, or through reflections on World War II, the rise of national socialism in Germany. They were, hardly surprisingly, deeply sensitive to the dangers of nationalism. This is the historical context for the distinctions between Eastern and Western nationalism, drawn by Kohn and Plamenatz and others.[11] Thus, a large contingent of German-speaking writers took their anguished debates with them into new countries like the USA. Compared with Germany, however, nationalism was hardly a pressing problem for American citizens in the 1920s and 1930s. Some émigrés retained a profound antipathy to anything nationalist. Others, like Kohn and Karl Deutsch, wanted to save an aspect of a good cohesive nationalism for a Weimar-type constitutional liberalism. It is thus relatively easy to see why this older generation of theorists became so interested in liberal nationalism. It is, however, slightly harder to see the urgent or immediate historical context for the present interest in liberal nationalism in the 1990s.

LIBERAL NATIONALIST ARGUMENTS

Having placed liberal nationalism in a longer time frame, I next provide a brief sketch of the oddity of liberal nationalism in the context of twentieth century liberal thought, and then turn to an outline of the key arguments of contemporary liberal nationalists. The writers who will be focused on are Neil MacCormick, David Miller and Yael Tamir.

Contemporary liberal nationalists have tried to reconcile a sensible moderate national sentiment with some form of more socially-responsive liberalism. As one very recent liberal nationalist notes: 'Underlying nationalism is a range of perceptive understandings of the human situation, of what makes human life meaningful and creative . . . Liberals are challenged to accommodate those worthy elements'.[12] However, this latter view of liberalism runs up against another very common argument in the post-1945 era which asserts that liberalism is utterly incompatible with nationalism. Apart from some well-known exceptions, liberals have usually, up to the present day, been uneasy with collectivities in general. Collectivities like states, which can be juridically rationalized, are bad enough, but collectivities like nations, which often appear to play upon irrationalism, are beyond the pale. The most that liberal writers have usually been prepared to admit is that collectivities like nations are fictional aggregates of individuals or atoms (rather as David Hume suggested) which, occasionally, could be said to have some form of fictional legal or moral identity, if we strain hard.[13] Late twentieth century liberals like Karl Popper and Friedrich Hayek tended to identify all nationalism with recidivist tribalism and authoritarianism. These latter theorists have also had a powerful impact on social and political thought in the English-speaking world. Fortuitously and ironically, this liberal contingent shared with Marxism a common opposition to the particularism of nationalism. In general, therefore, for those educated in politics during the period 1950–80 it still appears slightly odd to find liberal political philosophers waxing lyrical over nations. The only exceptions to the rule are the socially acceptable liberationist and secessionist anti-colonial nationalisms which have a form of quasi-socialist imprimatur. Yet, even if one pays little attention to the Austrian liberal contingent, there is still (if we leave aside J. S. Mill's enthused nationalism) the mumbling shade of Lord Acton to warn us off nationalism from another, more Whiggish, point of the liberal continuum.

Given the oddity of the liberal nationalist position it is diverting to find Neil MacCormick, the well-respected contemporary legal philosopher whose credentials have always been impeccably (social democratically) liberal and individualistic, writing a number of essays in praise of nationalism.[14] In Mac-Cormick's case it is premised upon a deep attachment to Scotland, irritation with English hegemony, and a commitment to the SNP (Scottish National Party). Still, MacCormick himself gives the impression at times of being surprised by his own nationalism. He freely admits that nationalism has a brutal history, but he is certain that it has a 'reasonable' side.

David Miller also attempts to capture nationalism for 'market socialism'.[15] However, market socialism, in the manner that Miller describes it, might just as well be described as social democratic liberalism. This is a more statist version of liberalism. For Miller, the nation can be defended as a self-sufficient and worthy object of allegiance and 'one that is subject to rational control'.[16] Miller's arguments are directed to a moderate particularism (and moderate communitarianism), as opposed to a 'narrow-minded' nationalism.[17] This is a direct transposition of Kohn's and Plamenatz's distinction. Nations, for Miller, share common traits. The nation is 'constituted by mutual belief, extended in history, active in character, connected with a particular territory, and . . . marked off from other communities by its members' distinct traits – [these features] served to distinguish nationality from other collective sources of personal identity'.[18]

There appear to be three major elements to the liberal nationalist case which are stressed with varying intensity. First, there is the communitarian argument that we are socially contextual beings. We are constituted through the community and its values. We cannot be prior to society in any way. MacCormick consequently advocates a social, embedded or contextual individualism, as against an atomistic individualism. One can be a normative individualist whilst rejecting methodological individualism. In fact, he suggests that the more atomistic liberal concept which allows individuals to form their own sense of the good life is deeply implausible.[19] Thus, he states: 'The truth about human beings is that they can only become individuals – acquire a sense of their own individuality – as a result of their social experiences within human communities'.[20] Families, local communities, nations, education, jobs etc. have a formative effect on the individual. MacCormick feels that he is offering a supplementation and corrective to the 'apparent individualism' of some of his other work. However, he adds that 'individuality goes beyond all that – but not in any way that renders all that superfluous or meaningless; human individuality presupposes social existence'.[21] For MacCormick, though, despite the social constitution argument, 'I continue to affirm that the good society is one in which individuals – each individual – are taken seriously'.[22]

Membership of groups, including nations, lets individuals transcend the constraints of time and place; it also provides a conceptual framework which permits them to 'comprehend [their] own existence as belonging within a continuity in time and a community in space'.[23] Human beings take pride in tradition, it allows them to transcend their 'earthly existence'.[24] For MacCormick, churches, trade unions, political parties, schools, universities and even supranational groups 'can have a like significance to human beings in just the same way as can nations'.[25] MacCormick confesses that he is very much against the notion of ranking such loyalties. It is but a step from ranking nationalism against other loyalties to ranking nations themselves, which he finds intolerable.

Miller also accepts the communitarian contextual individual claim. For Miller, national communities exist through belief, not race or language. Like Tamir (and Benedict Anderson for that matter), he also accepts the artificial dimension of nationalist thought.[26] Yet there have to be some shared substantive beliefs or 'attitudes, ritual observances and so forth' for nationalism to exist.[27] It is not, however, a belief system which can be totally conjured out of thin air. There is a pre-political element to it which forms a precondition to politics. It is an active identity which embodies historical continuity.[28] Yet Miller also suggests that this national identity can be fostered through education (a point which is not stressed by MacCormick or Tamir – although oddly it does bear a close affinity with Johann Gottlieb Fichte's views).[29] Political education must 'try to shape cultural identities in the direction of common citizenship. It must try to present an interpretation of, let us say, Indian culture in Britain that makes it possible for members of the Indian community to feel at home in, and loyal to, the British state'.[30] In this sense Miller expresses unease with multicultural education, which rests on a spurious neutrality.[31]

In addition, like MacCormick and Tamir, Miller thinks that the distinction between the universalism and particularism of nationalism can be overdone. Local loyalties can be linked with universalist claims. For Miller, a 'strengthening of commitment to a smaller group is likely to increase our commitment to wider constituencies', the point being, that 'if we start out with selves already laden with particularist commitments . . . we may be able to rationalize those commitments from a universalist perspective'.[32] Put in another way, the bad nationalist is one who fails the universalizability test.[33] In general terms, for Miller, a state is more governable if it is a national community. A state (especially a welfare state with programmes of distributive justice) needs trust and voluntary cooperation to achieve its goals. It is thus, apparently, 'self-evident that ties of community are an important source of trust between individuals who are not personally known to one another'.[34]

'Need' is a crucial concept for Miller. It links to his arguments on both moderated particularism and distributive justice under market socialism: the 'universalist case for nationality . . . is that it creates communities with the widest feasible membership, and therefore with the greatest scope for redistribution in favour of the needy'.[35] Miller is deeply concerned with the necessary preconditions for redistribution. Social justice and redistributive policies will be considerably facilitated if people see themselves as conationals.[36]

A second component of the liberal nationalist argument – respect for nations – is more strongly emphasized by MacCormick. It is supposedly (for MacCormick) Kantian, although what Kant actually had to say about nations certainly does not correspond with MacCormick's views; indeed Kant's material on nations is just deeply cranky.[37] For MacCormick, nations make up a part of our identity. Identity is deserving of respect. The principle of respect obliges us to respect that 'which in others constitutes any part of their sense of their own identity'. Thus MacCormick concludes, 'I assert it as a principle that there ought to be respect for national differences, and that there ought to be an adoption of forms of government appropriate to such differences.'[38] Autonomy does not necessarily conflict with national context – 'Autonomy is . . . a fundamental good, and thus it is a great social value to uphold societies which facilitate it'.[39] A free society and free nation can be linked. If autonomous individuals require a context of freedom-enabling, 'then the collective autonomy of society itself seems a part of the necessary context'.[40] In other words, self-determination by the nations is linked to the self-determining individuals within them.[41]

The third component of liberal nationalist argument, entails recommendations for political arrangements. Nationalism can underpin liberal individuality and social democracy, although MacCormick does add that nations are not necessarily coincidental with states. National communities should have the 'political conditions hospitable to their continuance and free development . . . the whole idea of the desirability of creating the conditions for autonomous self-determination both of individuals – contextual individuals – and of the groups and collectivities constitutive of them leads back to the claim of self-determination as quite properly a claim on behalf of each nation on similar terms to any and every other'.[42] MacCormick suggests that 'any tendency toward a greater democratization of government, a greater re-inclusion of the nation in the state, would surely be welcome, and that on simply democratic grounds'.[43] He nevertheless expresses distaste for the concept of sovereignty. Sovereignty and statehood are part of the 'inept model' of nationalism derived from 1789. Yet he does still think that 'The mode of consciousness which constitutes a national identity includes a consciousness of the need for a form of common governance which recognizes and allows for the continued flourishing of the cultural and historical community in question'.[44] MacCormick sees more hopeful signs in the European Community, subsidiarity and the development of regionalism rather than in statehood or sovereignty.[45] Scotland would become an independent regional government within the European framework.

For Miller, though, state boundaries should as far as possible coincide with national boundaries.[46] National self-determination is valuable because it corresponds to the idea of nations as active communities (although he acknowledges that they act through representatives). Self-determination follows from the identity argument. If people share substantive beliefs which are reflected in their acting representatives, then the nation can be said to act and determine itself. Miller thus also suggests that nationalism and democracy might be linked.[47] The state is thus 'likely to be better able to achieve its goals where its subjects form an encompassing community and conversely national communities are better able to preserve their culture and fulfil their aspirations where they have control of the political machinery in the relevant area'.[48] Where nation and state do not coincide, Miller distinguishes ethnicity and nationalism. One can thus have a nation with multiple ethnic groups within it. For Miller, we are thus saved from the problem of giving every ethnic group a state.[49]

Another element of Miller's case is concerned with the questions: does nationalism require state sovereignty, and are there any obligations holding between nation states? Miller takes it for granted that 'each nation in asserting its claim for self-determination must respect the equal claims of others who may be affected by its actions'.[50] This is essentially the universalist element in particularism. He suggests that complete sovereignty does not follow from nation statehood; trade-offs are possible. Sovereignty should therefore not become a fetish for nationalists. Yet, nation states still, for Miller, retain a right to decide when to secede. There may be good reasons for transferring powers to a confederal body, but the most crucial elements are still rescindable. Miller is thus not interested in applying (like Charles Beitz) the Rawlsian difference principle internationally. Yet international justice can, and frequently does limit national sovereignty.[51] Miller is perfectly content with this. There can be justice across boundaries if nations choose to act reasonably.

LIBERAL NATIONALISM: A CRITIQUE

The central arguments above can thus be systematically stated as follows. Individual identity is socially 'embedded' and much of the material in which it is embedded is national culture. Individual identity is deserving of respect. Since national culture is constitutive of individual identity, national culture is therefore deserving of respect. Constituents of individual identity which are valued, like freedom, if promoted by the national culture add substance to the case of respect for national identity. Institutional or political arrangements which embody and foster national culture and maximize the conditions of individual self-development also deserve respect. If free self-determination by the individual is valuable, then free self-determination by a nation (state) is valuable, as long as the nation state is promoting individual self-determination (this latter point is not always made clear enough, but I think that it is what liberal nationalists want to say). If the individual has a *right* to self-determination and the constituents of the embedded individual are made up from elements of national culture, then the nation state also has a right of self-determination in the international sphere. There are certain additional claims – nationalism nurtures cooperation and mutual obligations, which, for Miller, for example, form the groundwork for distributive justice. Miller also suggests that the substantive beliefs which are crucial to nationalism can be cultivated through education policies.

Embedded individualism

The argument about the 'embedded' quality of nationalism encounters four objections. First, individuals have multiple and often conflicting group allegiances, including nationalism. What is the relation between these allegiances?

Individuals are also more deeply embedded in some groups than in others. The position of the nation in this context remains ambiguous. Second, group life entails responsibilities; how are these to be ranked with nationalism? Third, nations might claim some priority over other groups either through their size or through their relation to the state. However both these latter points remain suspect. There is, in fact, a general unwillingness by nationalists to consider the sheer diversity, significance and range of group life. Fourth, nationalism might seek solace in the argument that liberal beliefs are so deeply embedded already in certain polities that to be a liberal is implicitly already to be a nationalist. Again, this argument has unforeseen consequences which liberal nationalists might not be able to accept. I now examine each of these objections in more detail.

Thus, firstly, most liberal nationalist theorists recognize, within the embedded claim, that families, local communities, education, workplace, religious groups or clubs also have profound formative effects on the individual.[52] A number of issues remain obscure here. If such groups and associations are formative for individuals, it remains unclear how far and in what manner nations relate to these other groups, especially in the constitution of the self. Such primary groups (families, villages, clans) may overlap several nations or conflict in diverse ways with the nation. Individuals are quite commonly at the interstice between multiple allegiances, many of which can be deeply opposed. Some allegiances, say religious or political (Catholicism, Islam, Marxism, even cosmopolitan Liberalism), may, in fact, entail denying national commitment In addition, individuals are also usually more deeply embedded in families, workplace, churches, unions or clubs than nations. Nations are not ephemeral, but they certainly have little everyday significance for most individuals – at least for most of the time – whereas groups like families, religious affiliations, occupations and the multiple associations of everyday life press upon us all with depressing (and often joyful) regularity. Thus, the idea that the nation forms anything more than a small aspect of embedded identity appears as simple commonsense, even, ironically, from a liberal nationalist position.[53]

Secondly, and more significantly, such diverse types of group entail a complex range of duties. There are shared ways of life in each of these diverse primary associations which often create moral responsibilities. Can we rank such responsibilities? MacCormick, for one, resists ranking.[54] It is, admittedly, difficult to see, without much more elaborate argument, how such rankings could take place.[55] If one cannot easily rank priorities, then nations become no more nor less significant than other group loyalties – in fact other loyalties are often more immediate and pressing. An additional small, but significant, point is that we do tend to recognize that some groups or associations can be immensely destructive and negative in their demands. We could cite the Mafia, but family life, political parties or neighbourhood groups are at times also adequate examples. We also usually recognize that individuals can be subject to multiple, often conflicting allegiances, within and between groups. For some unaccountable reason we do not so readily recognize nations within this setting. Nations can be potentially invasive and threatening, even in their civic format.

A third ground for ranking national groups against others might be size. It may be argued that nations are larger than other groups. It is certainly true that historically the largeness of nations over tribes or clans gave some credence to their priority. The altruism of the clan was extended to the nation. But this larger aspect of nations encounters problems if even larger units are identified – co-religionists (Islam or Catholicism), social democrats or utilitarians across the world, international legal, military, trade or political organizations, international corporations, or even those who believe in Europe. If size is the determinant, then nationalism immediately loses its privilege. If feeling and everyday pressing relevance is at issue, then it also loses out to smaller associations. If one placed these observations of groups into the Burkean language of the little platoon (favoured by some conservative writers), one wonders what a lay reader would make of it all. If one explained that the little platoon meant a congeries of platoons, including the local sports club, neighbours, family, church, colleagues at work and so forth, he might be more receptive. However, he might be slightly more baffled, except when inebriated or watching the World Cup, by the notion that he belongs to a really big platoon with some twenty, fifty or eighty million members. It takes some form of inebriation and loss of commonsense to appreciate such an idea.

Yet again, it might be contended that nations gain importance and priority through their association with the state.[56] However, such a linked association is virtually meaningless; except as a figure of speech. Homogenous 'nation' states are in fact a rarity in the world. Most states contain many subnationals.[57] The link between the nation and the state is merely a transient phenomenon of the nineteenth and early twentieth centuries. As was quite clearly seen, even by President Woodrow Wilson in his later, clearer moments, if all national or ethnic groupings were granted statehood, then international mayhem would break out. The startling fact about nations is thus their ahistorical arbitrariness. In addition, the most worrying phenomenon *is* the state which claims exclusively one particular nation identity. It is this demand for exclusivity which raises most problems. Contrary to the older nineteenth century nationalist view, it is exclusive nation states which are now the prisons of peoples. Multinational states or political organizations seem to be the only way forward.

The important general point which is missed by nationalists is that they are still under the pall of an older statist dualism, which has predominated in state discussion since the early modern period of European thought. Paradoxically, this dualism also affects their critics – the more cosmopolitan-minded liberal Kantians and utilitarians – whose solution to the 'nation/individual' dichotomy is to emphasize the global significance of individualism. In the latter it turns out by logic (if not in reality) that we have no special duties to our conationals, but rather general duties to the whole of humanity.[58] This is simply the obverse of the nationalist emphasis on the particularities of the nation state. For both cosmopolitans and nationalists there are 'nations or states' and there are 'individuals' and then, as Hobbes put it, there are worms in the entrails of the body politic – namely, cellular groups which are either regarded with antagonism (because they interfere with the life of individuals or nations) or are simply ignored. Communities are always generally regarded as 'large' things, which virtually coincide with states. Yet, states have always been multicellular entities. Nationalists and liberals both neglect the *corps inter-médiares*. States are made up of diverse constituent communities, associations and corporate groups. Some groups transcend and cross many states.[59] In sum, nationalism has no particular position of privilege within our complex array of allegiances

It may be replied that one can still retain some of the cultural priority of nations without appealing to size or statehood. Nations, in this reading, would retain a special form of respect as embodying the cultural aspirations of a significantly large group, without affecting allegiance to other groups or institutions. One could thus be both a Welsh nationalist and a good European. This is a point which I examine more closely in the next section. The gist of my response is to ask why liberals or anyone else *should* see any virtue or importance in nations above other types of group loyalty? Why should there be a virtue in giving political expression to nations above other groups? It is not clear where the systematic account of the priority lies.

Yet, fourthly, perhaps liberal nationalists should not be so concerned here. If liberal values are embedded in the political and moral fabric of communities then national members can form themselves through such liberal beliefs, without even raising the question of nationalism. In this view, which implicitly asserts the universality of liberal ideas, liberals appear to be tacitly proposing the content or substance of what individuals should want or desire. They also maintain that we should realize such content through the institutional processes of an 'embedded' liberal polity. There is some commonsense truth to the argument that liberals even where they express a strong antipathy to nation-alism, nonetheless assume the background of a national unity on primary goods like justice, liberty and individual rights. Therefore they simply do not have to address the question of nationalism, *because* liberal values are so embedded within the community. There is, indeed, something rather trivial about the very notion of liberal nationalism – namely, all liberals are intrinsically nationalist anyway, whatever their stripe. In so far as liberals seek a national education system, economy, welfare system, army, police, bureaucracy or government, they could be seen to be nationalists of a type. Adam Smith, after all, wrote about the wealth of *nations*, not the wealth of the cosmopolis. Thus, as Tamir remarks, 'liberals were thereby able to circumvent such thorny issues as membership and immigration, as well as the more general question of how groups are structured . . . Except for some cosmopolitans and radical anar-chists, nowadays most liberals are liberal nationalists'.[60] Oddly, this is an argument one can find stressed by economic nationalists, like Friedrich List, in the nineteenth century.[61]

This argument is, however, elusive and problematic even for liberals. If the nature of human beings is reduced to distinct national histories, and particularly to distinct narratives, then they become simply an aspect of the distinct languages and cultures. Human nature is articulated in a fragmented form through a series of separate narratives, narratives which figure in the distinct nations. Human nature is thus 'constituted' within different narratives. We could, therefore, have no access whatsoever to any objective factors or psychology of human beings beyond the constitutive national discourses. Liberal nationalism, in this reading, would therefore have no purchase beyond a particular localized liberal narrative. The embedded sense of liberal beliefs is thus taken with full seriousness and liberalism becomes swamped by a strong communitarian thesis. However, I do not think that liberal nationalists would be totally happy with this outcome since it would leave them with no transnational grounds whatsoever to assert any preferred way of life.[62]

Respecting democratic nations

I turn now to the respect argument: for liberal nationalists, nations make up a part of human identity and identity is deserving of respect. We are, therefore, obliged to respect that 'which in others constitutes any part of their sense of their own identity'. Thus MacCormick concludes, 'I assert it as a principle that there ought to be respect for national differences, and that there ought to be an adoption of forms of government appropriate to such differences'.[63] The central idea is that national culture is constitutive of individual identity, therefore national culture is deserving of respect. There are three objections which I wish to consider here: first, the notion of constitutive identity tied straightforwardly to respect appears downright odd; second, it is not clear why respect for a nation implies separate political organization; third, the idea of self-determination, as a ground for respect, fails to translate from the individual to the national level I finally examine the assumed connection between liberal democracy and nationalism.

Thus, first, it would appear to follow from the liberal nationalist argument that anything which constitutes part of our identity deserves respect. This, in itself, would license respect for the most abominable practices and cannot be what liberal nationalists wish to assert. On the level of nation states, this might of course be tolerated by a strict legal positivist. Yet, because something constitutes 'part' of basic human identity surely does not entail automatic respect for that part. Human identity alone is a very complex and messy thing which remains subject to immense philosophical and psychological contestation. People may have neuroses, recurring odd fantasies, unpleasant or harmless habits, which may have been communally derived (even from a national culture or historical tradition – like duelling, cannibalism, genital mutilation, racial contempt or infanticide), but surely we would not automatically render them respect simply because they constitute part of an autonomous person? What if someone conceived their identity primarily in religious terms? Respect would be due to their religious beliefs as a constituent of their identity. Respecting the constituents of that person's identity would in no way link with or carry over into respect for a nation. In fact, respect for their religious beliefs might entail antagonism to nationalism and even transcendence of the nation state. Thus, although it might be granted that autonomy requires a cultural context as a precondition to choice, and that acts performed in cultural contexts are both individual acts and cultural manifestations, none the less this would not lead us necessarily to respect on principle either the substantive act or the cultural manifestation.

Secondly, does respect for nations imply separate political organization. There is another absurdity lurking in the wings here. The groups mentioned in the first arguments (families *et al.*) all have separate existences and are often central to a person's identity, but it would be odd, even on the basis of established respect, to accord them separate political recognition. If, as argued above, national allegiance cannot be established as having *any* moral or political priority, then there is no reason not to grant each family or neighbourhood association statehood or petit-sovereignty. Surely it is also doubtful that one would want to accord groups immediate respect without careful empirical assessment. Groups (including families, religious communities or nations) may perform monstrous acts which might, in fact, require guardianship of persons within them, even by international bodies or other neighbouring states. Nations are surely no different in this regard from any other groups.

Thus, respect for a person is not something we would want to carry over automatically to groups. Group identity is certainly a feasible notion, but it needs to be carefully and juridically circumscribed and justified. There is clearly a strong tradition of argument on the state and law. However, in comparison, the vagaries of national groups do not exactly evince clarity, any more than granting moral identity to a sports crowd would be viewed as immediately reasonable. For writers like Miller or Tamir, particularly, it is also important to have a substantive national public culture. The problem here is how we recognize the national identity and culture of Britain, Canada, Australia, Germany, America or Israel? Is there a central public culture or distinctive set of values acknowledged by all the citizens? Taking Britain alone, there are so many cross-cutting differences of class, age, ethnicity, belief-systems and gender that such a judgement seems simply frivolous.

One counterargument might be that respect could still be forthcoming for all groups, including nations, but such respect would be defeasible or trumped by some higher order liberal constitutional or moral principle. Thus, respect can still be integrated with the above criticisms – small groups and nations could be given political and, even legal, recognition once we have abandoned the vocabulary of sovereignty. Taking a leaf from the European Community frame-work, one could anticipate that 'subsidiarity' might provide leeway for complex allowances to group life and local loyalties within a much larger federal framework. In this context one could anticipate very small to much larger regional groups having some participatory role and having respect accorded to them. The competence of larger bodies could thus be reconciled with the competences of local or regional bodies.

While these arguments establish the point that recognition could be given to the multiple groups they still do not solve the problem of how such group loyalties can be ranked. There is certainly a suggestion in MacCormick's argument that some form of significant 'regional' political organization should be accorded to nations like Scotland. Yet my original question still holds – what is so special or what is the special virtue of a national loyalty above other group loyalties? Unless this priority can be shown, then it follows that all of the above groups should be granted some form of significant political organization, which, as I have suggested, is an odd idea.[64]

This latter point is clearly connected to the subsidiarity issue which might be seen to resolve the complex questions of recognition and political organization. We do not, of course, have to debate subsidiarity in the abstract, since it is enshrined in the recent Maastricht treaty. The principle of subsidiarity, as it has arisen in recent European Union debates, indicates that there is a presumption in favour of local decision making and the involvement of a higher authority only when lower authorities are unable to fulfil a given task.[65] *Prima facie* the competence belongs to the member states, since the Community only has those powers attributed to it by member states. As yet, though, there is very little consensus on the interpretation of subsidiarity: some view it as a cover for further centralization, others as a genuine encouragement to local autonomy (including regional autonomy).[66] Overall, though, 'people have changed its meaning to suit new needs and circumstances. Hence lawyers still see it as an essentially political concept, if not a state of mind. As such it is not susceptible of easy definition let alone effective legal enforcement'.[67]

One strong interpretation, however, is that subsidiarity was designed to slow centralization to Brussels. The competences of the Community would tend, as much as possible, to devolve to the member states or, possibly, regions. However, the opaqueness of subsidiarity, its lack of any clear statements as to who does what, and its abstract formulation (partially to avoid mentioning federalism) does not evince much confidence.[68] Not only can it be interpreted to mean restoring powers to national governments (which is the British view), but also to subnational units, which is where some regional nationalists in Europe would see leverage. However, the subnational reading is but one of many.[69] Thus, subsidiarity in practice does not seem to provide any clear insights into the subnational question or political recognition. Conversely, it introduces further obfuscations of a basically federalist impulse which, again, does not really address the position of subnational or multiple groups.

If we focus on formal self-determination and the process of willing – as the grounds for respect – then further ambiguities appear. Many of the liberal nationalist arguments focus on ideas of self-determination in both individuals and nations. In fact, they often envisage a close relation between individual and national self-determination. Nations are or ought to be self-determining, and this, like the individual's capacity for autonomous self-determination, should be respected. What we have here though is a deeply ambiguous transposition of the argument of self-determination from the individual to the collective level. The free individual is self-determining, thus the free nation ought also apparently to be self-determining. The nation becomes the self-determining higher-order individual or self. Despite its cryptic history in the twentieth century, self-determination is admittedly often identified as a strong liberal, as well as nationalist, motif. The self-determining individual and the self-determining nation are thus parallel in some liberal minds.[70] The nation usually becomes a synonym for the governed, via ideas of democracy and popular sovereignty. Apart from the ontological difficulty of speaking about the 'self' of a nation, the crucial problem here is the fact that national self-determination does not necessarily correspond with individual self-determination.[71] There is no automatic 'carry-over'. All self-determining nations would somehow be liberal nations, which is nonsensical. Yet, self-determination can imply the right of a state to its own independent and distinctive existence. The right of the German *Volk* under the national socialists, or any other such autocratic regime, also becomes legitimized by self-determination.

The salve for the above argument is internal self-determination and participation. It is here that we encounter the link between democracy and nationalism. Respect for nations translates into respect for liberal democratic nations. It is thus argued that representative democracy should be embodied in the substantive institutions of the nation. Self-determination at the individual level would therefore mean that the government would be determined by the voters. In this latter context, individuals participate or identify themselves with national policies.[72] Ironically, to insist that the substantive content of all nationalisms should be democratic contradicts an important dimension of the nationalist respect argument, which insists on tolerance and respect for difference.[73] The democracy argument appears to dictate the actual content of regulative beliefs within diverse nations. In addition, there are many civic-inclined nations, embodying both multi-ethnicity and acceptance of equal civil rights. This would include most South American states and South East Asian states like Singapore and even Indonesia. Such states are, though, not particularly democratic (or, at least, they claim to have a different understanding of democracy). It is also worth drawing attention to the fact that liberalism has not historically always been attracted to democracy. The alliance between liberalism and democracy is fortuitous, liberalism usually seeing democracy as one among many instrumental constitutional devices for limiting governments. For liberals, democracy itself should always be hedged around by what Madison called 'auxiliary precautions' to control the sway of the 'ignorant masses'. The capacity of countries like Weimar Germany in the 1930s to elect a national socialist regime bent on destroying party democracy made liberals like Hayek deeply suspicious of the reach of democracy.

It is difficult to see how pure individual self-determination could be easily reconciled with national self-determination even in the liberal democratic format. Would anyone seriously contend that representative democracy really carried individual self-determination into the realm of national self-determination?[74] The two appear to be potentially at odds, depending upon exactly how one interprets the relation of the individual to the nation. Formally nationalism as self-determination is as compatible with Fascism as with liberalism.

CONCLUSION

Nationalism is undoubtedly not going to disappear from world politics. If this is the case, then liberal nationalism is, without a shadow of doubt, the most acceptable form of nationalism. But there is a distinction to be made between pragmatic acceptance and a principled ethical acceptance of nationalism. It is a very different matter to, on the one hand, accept nationalism, with some reluctance, pragmatically, as a pervasive form of group loyalty, and, on the other hand, to bestow some ethical significance upon it. Humans are constituted by many and diverse forms of group and association. Brutal families, religious fanatics, criminal associations and large business corporations also have a constituting role. However, although realizing that it is very difficult, most of the time, to do anything but control the peripheries of such entities, we certainly would not accord them any ethical importance *per se*, simply because they are social entities which have a constitutive role. Such entities will not disappear and will not be eliminated. We have to live with them, but we do not necessarily have to like them or approve of them. Such is my response to nationalism. Pragmatically, it is, at the present moment, an inevitable form of allegiance. If it is to exist, then it is infinitely preferable to have a relatively innocuous form which accords with liberal intuitions. Nationalism, in the final analysis, is an empty husk of a word which will always resist being assimilated into liberalism alone. It will always tend to invite its brothers and sisters and thus easily collapses into the lowest common denominator – shallow expressions of blood soil and xenophobia. Nationalism is a contemporary inevitability which should be minimized. It is not a virtue to be promoted.[75]

The central arguments of recent liberal nationalism are both confusing and unpersuasive. The complex character of the social constitution of the individual is assumed as unproblematic. The arguments for transferring respect from individuals to nations appear unsatisfactory. In addition, self-determination is a profoundly difficult and elusive notion, particularly if carried over into nations and states. It is certainly not impossible to deploy the term and it may, of course, be used in a trivial sense by international relations theories, indicating that states appear to act in a unitary manner. However, liberal nationalists want the idea to work harder for them. This 'harder' application is unconvincing, if not irresponsible. Self-determination, by individuals or states, does not lead to or guarantee, *any* particular institutional arrangements. Autocracy or liberalism are equally possible outcomes. In sum, liberal nationalism still needs to explain itself.

NOTES

1. I would like to thank all my referees on this article for their liberal and open-minded responses.

2. One of the more popular theories, which is widely quoted in the recent literature, is by Miroslav Hroch. He sees three definite historical phases. First, nationalism is embodied in nineteenth-century folklore, custom and the like. This is essentially a cultural idea, fostered by the middle and upper classes, with little or no political implication. Secondly, nationalism is pursued as a political, campaign. It is usually connected with and fostered by political parties. Finally, nationalism becomes translated into mass support and mass movements. Each of these phases is linked by Hroch to economic and cultural changes, see Miroslaw Hroch, *Social Preconditions of National Revival in Europe: a Comparative Analysis of the Social Composition of Patriotic Groups among Smaller European Nations* (Cambridge, Cambridge University Press, 1985).

3. Lord Acton in the nineteenth century distinguished between two forms – French and English see Lord Acton, *Essays on Freedom and Power* (Boston, Beacon, 1948), pp. 183–4. The earliest and most influential twofold classification was Hans Kohn's Western and Eastern nationalisms, Hans Kohn, *Idea of Nationalism: a Study in its Origins and Background* (New York, Macmillan, 1945); John Plamenatz follows roughly in the same path in 'Two Types of Nationalism' in E. Kamenka (ed.), *Nationalism: the Evolution of an Idea* (London, Edward Arnold, 1976), pp. 22–36. Friedrich Meinecke distinguished, *Staatsnation* and *Kulturnation*, see Meinecke, *Cosmopolitanism and the Nation State* (Princeton NJ, Princeton University Press, 1970); see also Kenneth Minogue, *Nationalism* (London, Batsford, 1969), p. 13; Anthony D. Smith distinguishes 'territorial' from ethnic nations in *The Ethnic Origins of Nations* (Oxford, Blackwell, 1986), pp. 134–8. In many of the twofold classifications there is usually a fierce desire to keep Western, more liberal-minded nationalism distinct from the nationalism associated with Fascism and national socialism, see Kohn, *Idea of Nationalism*, p. 351; Yael Tamir, *Liberal Nationalism* (Princeton NJ, Princeton University Press, 1993), p. 90; A. D. Smith, *Theories of Nationalism* (London and New York, Torchbooks Library, 1971), p. 7 and *Nationalism in the Twentieth Century*. (Canberra, Australian National University Press, 1979), pp. 83–5. This twofold classification will form the key theme of this paper. There are threefold typologies in Kellas who distinguishes ethnic, social and official nationalism, James G. Kellas, *Politics of Nationalism and Ethnicity* (New York, St. Martin's Press, 1991) p. 52; Peter Alter's *Risorgimento*, integral and reform nationalisms, Alter, *Nationalism* (London Edward Arnold, 1989). There are fourfold classifications, see L. Snyder, *The Meaning of Nationalism* (New Brunswick NJ, Rutgers University Press, 1954), ch. 5. Carlton Haves uses a fivefold classification: Jacobin; liberal; tradionalist; economic protectionist; and integral totalitarian, see Hayes, *Essays in Nationalism* (New York, Macmillan, 1926) and *The Historical Evolution of Modern Nationalism* (New York, Macmillan, 1949).

4. My own favoured typology reflects the way in which nationalism crosses over the territory of other ideologies. The first type is liberal *Risorgimento* nationalism; secondly, there is a more traditionalist conservative nationalism – which might be more generally associated with the conservative ideological tradition; thirdly, there is integral nationalism, which is the form most closely associated with Fascism and national socialism. There are also other possible variants like socialist nationalism and anti-colonial nationalism. Romantic nationalism has strayed across all these

forms. However, in my reading, all of these latter categories either overlap or form sub-aspects within the major categories above. For expansion on these points see Andrew Vincent, *Modern Political Ideologies* (Oxford, Blackwell, 2nd ed., 1995), ch. 9.

5. See Kohn, *Idea of Nationalism*. The distinction itself is extremely questionable, but it would take a more historically based inquiry to justify this point. As Andrzej Walicki remarks, 'It would not be too difficult for a critic of Kohn's theory to demonstrate that all the characteristics which he regards as specific to Central and Eastern European nationalism could also be found in Western Europe, see Walicki, *The Enlightenment and the Birth of Modern Nationhood: Polish Political Thought from Noble Republicanism to Tadeusz Kosciuszko* (Notre Dame IN, University of Notre Dame Press, 1989), pp. 5ff. The other point to note here is that Eastern (ethnic) nationalism is occasionally also associated with the notion of cultural nationalism. Yet both the ethnic (or Eastern) nationalism and civic liberal nationalism have cultural components. Also the ethnic or Eastern nationalism is often seen to be inward-looking, excluding immigrants. Yet it is clear that groups like the Québécois or Flemish, despite their strong cultural and ethnic emphasis, are prepared to accept immigrants, as long as they learn the language and culture. Similarly, the USA requires immigrants to learn the English language and American history in schools.

6. A recent form is in terms of 'civic' and 'ethnic' nationalism, see, for example, Michael Ignatieff, *Blood and Belonging: Journeys into the New Nationalism* (New York, Farrar, Straus and Giroux, 1993).

7. Plamenatz, 'Two Types', pp. 23ff.

8. Plamenatz, 'Two Types', p. 27.

9. Hayes, *Historical Evolution*, p. 135.

10. '. . . international *Risorgimento* nationalism had no blue-print to hand for avoiding the growing number of situations in which the competing aims of different nationalisms were hopelessly at loggerheads', Alter, *Nationalism*, p. 33.

11. In fact, a similar distinction appears in many other writers of the same period like Isaiah Berlin. As one commentator remarks on Berlin. 'It is important to stress that Berlin's sympathy with nationalism is sympathy with the nationalism of the Risorgimento and with the European revolutionaries of 1848; it is sympathy with the nationalism of Verdi and Clemenceau, not with the nationalism of Treitschke and Barrès', Stuart Hampshire 'Nationalism' in Edna and Avishai Margalit (eds), *Isaiah Berlin: a Celebration* (London, Hogarth, 1991), p. 132.

12. The theme of the book contends that 'the liberal tradition, with its respect for personal autonomy, reflection and choice, and the national tradition, with its emphasis on belonging, loyalty and solidarity . . . can indeed accommodate one another', Tamir, *Liberal Nationalism*, pp. 6 and 10.

13. See David Hume, 'Of National Characters', in Knud Haakonssen's edition of *Hume's Political Essays* (Cambridge, Cambridge University Press, 1994).

14. MacCormick, despite writing about nationalism in the early 1980s, also claims to have been influenced by Yael Tamir's work (as well as Plamenatz's writings) whilst examining her doctoral thesis in 1989. Tamir's doctoral thesis was transformed into the 1993 book *Liberal Nationalism*, see Neil MacCormick, 'Of self-determination and other things', *Bulletin of the Australian Society of Legal Philosophy*, 15, nos 54–5 (1990), p. 12. Tamir's views are thus equally instructive on liberal nationalism, on very similar grounds to MacCormick.

15. Miller does have a book on nationalism about to come out. However, I have not been able to obtain it before this article went to press. I have therefore relied upon his articles.

16. David Miller, 'The ethical significance of nationalism', *Ethics*, 98 (1988), p. 658, and 'The Nation State: A Modest Defence' in Chris Brown (ed.), *Political Restructuring in Europe* (London, Routledge, 1994), p. 136.

17. Miller, 'Ethical significance', p. 648.
18. Miller, 'Nation State', p. 141.
19. N. MacCormick, 'Is Nationalism Philosophically Credible?' in W. Twining (ed.) *Issues in Self-Determination* (Aberdeen, Aberdeen University Press, 1991), p. 13. He says in another piece. 'The truth about human individuals is that they – we – are social products, not independent atoms capable of constituting society through a voluntary coming together', Neil MacCormick, 'Of self-determination', p. 14.
20. N. MacCormick, *Legal Rights and Social Democracy: Essays in Legal and Political Philosophy* (Oxford, Clarendon, 1982), p. 247.
21. MacCormick, *Legal Rights*, p. 251.
22. MacCormick, *Legal Rights*, p. 247; see also MacCormick, 'Of self-determination', pp. 14–15.
23. MacCormick, *Legal Rights*, p. 251.
24. MacCormick, *Legal Rights*, p. 252.
25. MacCormick, *Legal Rights*, p. 252.
26. For Benedict Anderson, see *Imagined Communities: Reflections on the Origin and Spread of Nationalism* (London, Verso, 1983).
27. David Miller, *Market State and Community: Theoretical Foundations of Market Socialism* (Oxford, Clarendon, 1989), p. 244.
28. As Miller states: 'a belief that belongs together with the rest; that this association is neither transitory nor merely instrumental, but stems from a long history of living together which (it is hoped and expected) will continue into the future; that the community is marked off from other communities by its members' distinctive characteristics . . .', Miller, *Market State and Community*, p. 238.
29. See J. G. Fichte, *Addresses to the German Nation* (transl. R. F. Jones and G. H. Turnbull) (Westport CT, Greenwood, 1979), see the second address.
30. Miller, 'Socialism and Toleration' in Susan Mendus (ed.), *Justifying Toleration* (Cambridge, Cambridge University Press, 1988) p. 253.
31. An unease that he shares with the conservative writer Roger Scruton. Scruton comments on multiculturalism that 'Experience ought to warn us against such a society: experience not only of Lebanon, but also of Cyprus, and India. If we are interested in the survival of the liberal state, then we should be doing our best to preserve the loyalties which sustain the liberal jurisdiction', 'In Defence of the Nation' in Scruton, *The Philosopher on Dover Beach* (London, Carcanet, 1990), p. 325. There are also some parallel sentiments without the nationalist emphasis, developed from a more classical liberal perspective by Chandran Kukathas in Kukathas (ed.), *Multicultural Citizens: the Philosophy and Politics of Identity* (Canberra, The Centre for Independent Studies Readings 9, 1993), see pp. 29–30.
32. All quotations and references 'Ethical significance', pp. 661–2.
33. As MacCormick puts it, 'A part of the *odium philosophicum* attaching to nationalism . . . lies precisely in its failure to universalize and treat essentially like claims in like manner. But this in itself can no more discredit the legitimate claims of reasonable nationalism than the rampant selfishness and non-universalism of some individualistic persons discredits of itself universalistic doctrines of political individualism', MacCormick, 'Of self-determination', p. 18.
34. Miller, 'Nation State', p. 142.
35. Miller, 'Ethical significance, p. 662.
36. 'All evidence suggests that people give greater weight to [the principle of distribution according to need as a requirement of social justice] to the extent that they see themselves as bound to the beneficiaries of the principle by common ties. The more communal the relationship, the more need displaces merit (in particular) as a criterion of justice. Thus the kind of underpinning for a welfare state that socialists will look for can only be provided through a widespread sense of common membership throughout the society in question . . . It is . . . worth stressing that

this common identity must exist at the national level', see Miller, 'Socialism and Toleration', p. 243.

37. See I. Kant's *Anthropology from a Pragmatic View* (transl. Mary J. Gregor) (The Hague Martinus Nijhoff, 1974), see Part 2, 'Anthropological Characterizations'. See MacCormick, *Legal Rights*, p. 261.

38. Quotations from MacCormick, *Legal Rights*, pp. 261–2. As in MacCormick, for Tamir the justification of national self-determination is that membership of a nation is a 'constitutive factor of personal identity'. In addition, peoples should be able to protect their identity. There should be in other words, a right to preserve national identity which would allow groups the opportunity 'to express this identity, both privately and publicly'. All such expressions of identity, for Tamir 'however restricted, merit respect and support'. There is a need for a shared public space for 'ensuring the preservation of a nation as a vital and active community'. National self-determination implies a domain for both individual interests and communal identity; thus 'The ability to conceive of certain social and political institutions as representing a particular culture and as carriers of the national identity is at the heart of the yearning for national self-determination'. Finally, the right to national self-determination 'can be fully realized only if the national group is recognized by both members and non-members as an autonomous source of human action and creativity, and if this recognition is followed by political arrangements enabling members of the nation to develop their national life with as little external interference as possible', see Tamir, *Liberal Nationalism*, pp. 73–4.

39. MacCormick, 'Nationalism Philosophically Credible', p. 14.

40. MacCormick, 'Nationalism Philosophically Credible', p. 15.

41. . . . self-determination in a dual sense meaning that there has to be scope both for individual self-determination inside a political community and for collective self-determination of the community without external domination', MacCormick, 'Of self-determination', p. 16.

42. MacCormick, 'Nationalism Philosophically Credible', p. 17. MacCormick also thinks that liberty in a free country requires schemes of redistribution, welfare provision and educational support', MacCormick, 'Of self-determination', p. 15. See also Tamir, *Liberalism Nationalism*, pp. 16–17.

43. MacCormick, 'Nationalism Philosophically Credible', p. 11. He remarks elsewhere that 'some form of democratic self-determination has to be considered both justifiable and valuable . . . Some form of collective self-constitution, some kind of active participation in shaping and sustaining the institutions of social or communal government whose aim is to advance liberty and autonomy, seems to be a necessary part of the whole ensemble of conditions in which the autonomy of the contextual individual could be genuinely constituted and upheld', MacCormick, 'Of self-determination', p. 15.

44. MacCormick, *Legal Rights*, p. 262 and 'Of self-determination', pp. 18–9. Tamir also is suspicious of sovereignty.

45. Tamir also sees some hope in Lijphart's model of consociational democracy, Tamir, *Liberal Nationalism*, p. 156.

46. Miller, 'Nation State', p. 143. This is, of course, a very traditional nationalist belief.

47. Miller, 'Nation State', p. 144.

48. Miller, 'Nation State', p. 145.

49. Miller, 'Nation State', p. 156. I find myself perplexed by Miller's somewhat easy distinction between ethnic and national allegiance. Some scholars see ethnicity as a very old idea rooted in kinship, and nationalism is just another way of speaking about such ethnic identity. In this context, even liberal nationalism would be ethnically-based. In other words, nationalism and ethnicity are virtually identical as pre-modern forms of natural allegiance. As one recent sociobiologically-influenced writer remarks, 'we have in nationalism a combination of biological ethnocentrism, psychological ingroup/outgroup hostile propensies, and cultural and

political differences', Kellas *Politics of Nationalism*, p. 13; see also V. Reynolds *et al.*, *The Sociobiology of Ethnocentrism Evolutionary Dimensions of Xenophobia, Discrimination, Racism and Nationalism* (London, Croom Helm, 1987). Other scholars (like Ernest Gellner and Benedict Anderson) are adamant modernists who see nationalism (and ethnicity to some degree) as distinctly modern inventions. Alternatively ethnicity will sometimes be seen as more 'natural' as opposed to the invented artifice of nationalism. Anthony Smith takes a *via media* position; although seeing ethnicity and nationalism as distinct, nonetheless, he argues that all nationalism is traceable back to ethnic communities. He identifies his position as intermediate between the modernists and primordialists. He remarks that 'Nationalism both as an ideology and movement, is a wholly modern phenomenon, even if, . . . the 'modern nation" in practice incorporates several features of pre-modern *ethnie* and owes much to the general model of ethnicity', Smith, *Ethnic Origins*, p. 18. Thus Miller's deployment of the distinction between nationalism and ethnicity, as though it were obvious, looks highly questionable.

50. Miller, 'Nation State', p. 145.
51. Miller, 'Nation State', pp. 150–2.
52. 'Our sense of identity arises from our experience of belonging within significant communities, such as families, schools, workplace communities, religious communities . . . and also nations, conceived as cultural communities endowed with political relevance', MacCormick, 'Of self-determination', p. 17.
53. . . . nations are quite real and quite identifiable as some among the types of community constitutive of people', MacCormick, 'Of self-determination', p. 17.
54. MacCormick, *Legal Rights*, pp. 254–5.
55. I am not denying that it is possible to make an argument for ranking, however as yet it remains undeveloped by liberal nationalist writers.
56. Admittedly MacCormick and Tamir do not favour this association. It is also important to note that my arguments are not directed at the state, but rather the compound term 'nation state'.
57. Unless, of course, one presupposed a distinction between *ethnie* and 'nationals', then one could link nationalism with the state and reduce everyone else to *ethnie*. However, such a strategy is presupposed upon a profoundly dubious distinction between ethnicity and nationalism, and also assumes that 'a' substantive nationalism can be clearly identified.
58. This argument can be found stated in Bob Goodin's notion of the 'assigned responsibility model'; see Bob Goodin, 'What is so special about our fellow countrymen?', *Ethics*, 98 (1988), pp. 678ff. Goodin's argument hangs on the Hartian distinction between general and special duties. The purportedly classical nationalist argument denies general duties and emphasizes the place of special duties to our conationals. Goodin doubts the significance of special duties in practice, arguing, alternatively, for the idea of special duties as 'distributed general duties'. Thus special duties are viewed as 'merely devices whereby the moral community's general duties get assigned to particular agents' (p. 678). Special duties thus derive their moral force from universal general duties (underpinned in Goodin's case by utilitarianism). Goodin concludes from this that special duties – read national imperatives – can be overridden by general duties. Goodin therefore suggests that our fellow countrymen 'are not so very special after all' (p. 679). It also leads him to doubt the significance of nationalism, discrete state-oriented citizenship, state boundaries and presumably state independence or sovereignty. Goodin thus remarks, somewhat alarmingly, 'If some states prove incapable of discharging their responsibilities effectively, then they should either be reconstituted or assisted' (p. 685).
59. Sovereignty has always been regarded as a tricky issue by liberals particularly, but this is primarily due to its association with the absolutist tradition on sovereignty. The idea that sovereignty could be shared has thus always been a puzzle within this

perspective, which identities sovereignty with unitary absolute power. See Andrew Vincent, *Theories of the State* (Oxford Blackwell, 4th reprint, 1994), pp. 32–7, 51–60, 109–11.

60. Tamir, *Liberal Nationalism*, p. 139.

61. For List, liberalism, as a consequence of its blindness to commercial history, neglected the fact that it rested upon the pre-existence of the nation. There was always, therefore, a residual suppressed statism and nationalism implicit in all liberal thought. States and nations formed the essential backdrop to successful liberal markets. The framework of national law, national defence, national well-being, national aims and the national state was the secure, virtually unconscious background for the market, see Friedrich List, *The National System of Political Economy* (New York, Augustus M. Kelley, 1966). As Hobsbawm more recently remarked '. . . no economist of even the most extreme liberal persuasion could overlook or fail to take account of the national economy. Only liberal economists did not like to, or quite know how to, talk about it', E. J. Hobsbawm, *Nations and Nationalism since 1870: Programme, Myth and Reality* (Cambridge, Cambridge University Press, 2nd ed., 1992), p. 28.

62. To some extent the liberal nationalist 'embedded' claim can be read, ironically, through the dimensions of Goodin's argument mentioned in footnote 58. The national culture, for liberal nationalists, is acceptable in so far as it embodies commitments to autonomy and self-determination by individuals. This allows them to demand that respect for national identity is intimately connected to the personal identity. Thus – reading this through Goodin's spectacles – the special duties that we owe and feel toward our conationals are really general duties that humanity owes to itself in totality. General duties of respect for human autonomy, for example, are embedded in the supposedly special duties of those who live in liberal nation states. Ironically, whereas Goodin uses this argument to provide succour for a denial of the significance of nationalism and particularism, the liberal nationalists use it to provide salvation for nationalism. Both, of course, ultimately desire justice across boundaries – although Goodin is undoubtedly more convinced of this than liberal nationalists, who see more obstacles. Goodin achieves his aim by emphasizing the generality of the duty and undermining the local character of circumstances. Liberal nationalists achieve it by down playing the general duties when they wish to emphasize the particularity and the converse when they wish to stress the salve of more universal commitments. If anyone is being more duplicitous here it looks like the liberal nationalist. However, it is clear from this discussion that the argument from embeddedness certainly does not necessarily aid the case for liberal nationalism. On the other hand, Goodin's position can be questioned again by reversing the argument, namely, by asking from whence the distinction between general and special duties, and the arguments for the universality of, say liberal utilitarianism derives? It would be fairly easy to show that such a distinction derives from a historically situated or embedded liberalism. Liberalism does not stand god-like with a view from nowhere assessing the political scene. Thus, liberal nationalism could easily be seen as the socially embedded premise from which such interesting distinctions (like general and special duties) derive. Special duties and nationalist concerns never have a chance of a look in from the beginning of the argument.

63. Quotations from MacCormick, *Legal Rights*, pp. 261–2. He states in another work: 'a sense of nationality is for many people constitutive in part of their sense of identity and even of selfhood, then respect for this aspect of their selfhood is as incumbent as respect for any other, up to a certain point', MacCormick, 'Of self-determination', p. 18. The 'point' that MacCormick notes is where nationalist practices become destructive of others. However there is a dilemma here, from a nationalist perspective, as to how one would recognize 'destructive' practices. What 'objective' criteria could be adopted to condemn a practice as destructive – surely nationalist argument *per se*, appears to intrinsically limit any clear judgement on this issue? It is not clear

at what point respect stops and condemnation begins. Also, does this 'destructive-ness' include internal destructiveness or does it only imply external destructiveness, i.e. if cruelty is being exercised only upon a domestic population is this cruelty to be respected, or is it only when one nationalism attempts to destroy another? This whole area appears remarkably blurred.

64. That is, unless one were to argue a Gierke 'Germanist' type of thesis about groups and associations in relation to the law and the state, see, for example, Andrew Vincent, 'Can groups be persons?', *Review of Metaphysics*, 42 (1989), 687–715.

65. The principle of subsidiarity states that in 'areas which do not fall within its exclusive competence, the Community shall take action, in accordance with the principle of subsidiarity, only if and in so far as the objectives of the proposed action cannot be sufficiently achieved by the member States and can therefore, by reason of the scale or effects of the proposed action, be better achieved by the Community'. See Art, 3b, Treaty of the European Union.

66. Some thus see subsidiarity 'as meaningless and misleading gobbledegook designed to disguise the actual increase in central powers at the expense of national rights . . . Indeed it is seen by some as a spur to "centralizing federalism" and not a barrier to it. Other Articles, like 5 and 235, are held to rob it of real effect', Clive Church and David Phinnemore, *European Union and European Community: a Handbook and Commentary on the Post-Maastricht Treaties* (New York and London, Harvester Wheatsheaf, 1994), p. 68.

67. Church and Phinnemore, *European Union*, p. 70.

68. See Church and Phinnemore, *European Union*, pp. 72–3, and R. Dehousse, 'Community Competences: are there Limits to Growth?' in S. Bronitt, F. Burns and D. Kinley (eds), *Principles of European Law: Commentary and Materials* (Sydney, Law Book, 1995), p. 126.

69. The 1992 Edinburgh agreement, among other things, more explicitly linked deci-sion-making to local subnational levels. However, it has also 'compounded [Maas-tricht's] contradictions by making [subsidiarity] a matter of democracy as well as of federal balance and execution of power'. Church and Phinnemore, *European Union*, p. 74.

70. 'National self-determination and individual self-determination were declared part of the historical self-deliverance of mankind from ignorance and tyranny', M. Keens-Sóper, 'The liberal state and nationalism in post-war Europe', *History of European Ideas*, 10, 6 (1989), p. 702.

71. Some critics find the idea of 'self' totally mythical in this sense, see Richard T. DeGeorge, The Myth of the Right of Collective Self-Determination' in Twining (ed.), *Self-Determination*, pp. 1–4. Other theorists appear quite unfussed by the moral rights of nation states to be self-determining entities, see Michael Walzer, *Just and Unjust Wars* (New York, Basic, 1977) and 'The Moral Standing of States' in Charles Beitz *et al.* (eds), *International Ethics*, (Princeton NJ, Princeton University Press, 1985).

72. Yet if one adopted arguments about self-determination by the 'higher self' or more 'communally-orientated self', then the salve of democracy might well lose its efficacy. Individuals could still identify themselves with national policies, but it would not necessarily imply representative liberal democracy. In other words, there are no necessary grounds for adopting orthodox liberal individual liberty or representative democracy.

73. Singapore, for one, in recent years has made a point of denying the significance of democracy and individual rights to the development of their nation. In fact, they have taken to lecturing other states, like Australia, on the virtues of this position for a healthy economy.

74. I should emphasize that this is not an argument against representative democracy.

75. One response to this could be that if there is no ethical argument involved in nationalism, how could one limit or criticize it in any way? Surely my argument cuts

away the ground from any rational assessment of nationalism? How could one therefore ensure that it corresponds with liberal intuitions? My response to this is to argue, firstly, that this paper is, in itself, a critical commentary on the inchoate nature of nationalist ethical arguments. It is an argument which, thus, denies that we should seriously entertain the ethical character of nationalism. It is this sceptical stance which should be taken to all ethical nationalist claims. It is accepted, though, that nationalism is a pragmatic fact. Moderate nationalism, which corresponds with liberal intuitions, is even socially tolerable. However, conversely giving an ethical gloss to nationalism should be avoided because of its inchoateness, brutal history and political unpredictability.

7

REALLY EXISTING NATIONALISMS – A POST-COMMUNIST VIEW FROM MARX AND ENGELS

Erica Benner

By declining to single out nationalism as the subject-matter for a distinct theory, Marx and Engels left ample room for doubt about the theoretical status of their writings on specific national movements. The *Communist Manifesto* provides their most comprehensive analysis of the changing role of nation-states within the 'world market', and their most concise formulation of an international strategy for the proletariat. Most of their writings on national issues, however, appear in a variety of other genres: in speeches, journalism, and personal correspondence. Some of these writings are highly polemical, while others offer on-the-ground reportage from a radical perspective. In either case, the style is often less rigorous than that employed in their theoretical works, while the content is more overtly political: the authors' attention is focused on the volatile ephemera of contemporary affairs, only occasionally shifting back towards wider historical developments and economic processes. This emphasis has induced some commentators to draw a sharp line between Marx and Engels as self-styled 'scientific' theorists of society, on the one hand, and Marx and Engels the 'pragmatic' observers of political events, on the other.[1] Their overwhelmingly journalistic discussions of national issues may convey the impression that the authors were not at all concerned to explain the appeal and development of national movements in terms consistent with their general theory, but that they took a merely opportunistic stance towards such conflicts, hoping to channel them into their revolutionary strategy.

It would be implausible to account for their apparently untheoretical

Erica Benner (1995), *Really Existing Nationalisms: A Post-Communist View from Marx and Engels*, Oxford: Clarendon Press.

treatment of national issues by suggesting that Marx and Engels regarded all politics, including nationalist politics, as mere 'superstructural' emanations, as though they did not think that such epiphenomena required further explanation once their economic foundations had been analysed. First, [. . .] it is not at all clear that Marx and Engels conceived of nations as entities which could be fully understood within a base-superstructure schema – a schema which, I should emphasize, does not exhaust the explanatory resources of 'historical materialism'. The proposition that Marx and Engels regarded all 'superstructural' phenomena unworthy of their theoretical attention cannot, moreover, be sustained in view of the numerous works in which they offered rigorous analyses of political, legal, and cultural issues. If Marx and Engels did not develop fully fledged general theories of law, politics, and nationalism, this does not mean that they saw no need to explain why these phenomena assume different forms and take on a different historical significance within the class struggles and 'modes' of production described in their socio-economic theory.[2]

The perception of a gap between Marx and Engels' general theories and their writings on nationalism has, in fact, been fostered by a misguided belief that any properly Marxian account of nationalism must be framed primarily in terms of a base-superstructure model, or an economic theory of capitalist development, or a 'ruling class' theory of ideology. In their political writings and journalism, Marx and Engels did sometimes describe nationalism as the mere residue of outmoded historical formations, or as a deliberate policy applied by leading classes to distract or divide their opponents. But they applied these descriptions to particular forms of nationalism or uses of nationalist ideology, not treating them as general explanations of nationalism as such.[. . .] The ideas which guided their analyses of national issues can be found in a strategic theory of politics centred on, but not reduced to, the analysis of class conflicts.
[. . .]

ELEMENTS OF THEORY

[. . . There is] a distinction implied, though never elaborated, in Marx and Engels' writings: namely, that between pre-existing historical, cultural, or political attributes which distinguish one national group from another, and Marx's prescriptive concept of the nation, embodying aspirations to create a genuinely democratic community out of pre-existing elements.[. . .] Marx and Engels' understanding of nationality resists straightforward assimilation by any of the economic or sociological categories of their general theory. Nations were not seen as the product of impersonal economic forces, or as weapons wielded exclusively by the bourgeoisie in ideological battle. The prescriptive concept implies that the elements of territory, history, culture, and statehood which come to embody a nation's distinctiveness are reworked and ascribed a certain significance by people, not by the inexorable logic of capitalist development. These elements, moreover, are not the monopoly of any single 'ruling class'; they furnish the building-blocks with which all social classes must work in their efforts to preserve or redesign existing communities. Marx and Engels did not posit an inherent conflict between nations and nationalism, on the one hand, and the interests of some classes on the other. They simply observed that different classes may infuse the prescriptive concept of nationhood with conflicting aspirations, and that the social significance ascribed to pre-existing elements of nationality will vary according to those aspirations.

Having differentiated this position from more familiar 'Marxist' conceptions of nationality, we can now summarize its basic explanatory implications.

1. The political or cultural *nation* cannot be abstracted from its social bases and treated as a wholly independent source of collective interests and aspirations, and hence as a stable focus of explanation.

Marx and Engels recognized that the parameters of nationalist activity are shaped by historical, cultural, and political factors to which nationalists may ascribe a major significance in their struggles over the form and control of the state. But those struggles themselves are fuelled by the pursuit of particular, often conflicting, interests within any single nation; and it is these interests which explain the aspirations directed by different social groups towards the 'nation'.

2. *Nationalism* cannot be analysed, then, as a phenomenon *sui generis*, with origins and aims that are clearly distinct from those of movements which Marx and Engels linked to the interests of conflicting classes. Not all class movements are nationalist movements; all nationalist movements are driven forwards or backwards by class struggles, and can be analysed in terms of the class interests they aim to promote or obstruct.

While recognizing that the interests of rival classes may converge in some periods on a core set of common goals – especially when confronted with external pressures or threats – Marx and Engels stressed the limited and often fragile nature of trans-class unity, denying that its occurrence proved the perennial magnetic power of national over class allegiances. The presence of class conflict, they pointed out, may fracture an apparently cohesive national movement into antagonistic movements which all claim to represent the same 'national' community. As Engels remarked in a retrospective on the failed revolutions of 1848, 'German unity was in itself a question big with disunion, discord and, in the case of certain eventualities, civil war.'[3] Observing the same phenomenon in other countries, Marx and Engels refrained from analysing national movements as relatively monolithic blocs cemented by an overarching set of common purposes. They treated them, instead, as provisional, shifting coalitions of diverse social groups, made or broken on the basis of class interests.

3. The *international* context of nationalist activity should also be examined in relation to class conflicts which arise below the level of states and nations and cut across these units.

Marx and Engels rarely insulated the analysis of domestic class conflicts from international relations. In their empirical analyses, they constantly referred to both transnational developments and the particular facts of local history which made nationalism an effective form of politics for a wide cross-section of social classes. But they also argued that different class interests produce conflicting programmes and policies in response to the same external pressures; and these internal conflicts may shape nationalist attitudes towards outsiders as much as foreign relations *per se*. Those relations can, on Marx and Engels' account, be explained largely in class terms, and do not constitute an autonomous structure which determines the incidence and intensity of national antagonisms. Social conflicts in the domestic arena tend to produce divergent definitions of a nation's foreign friends and enemies, and different strategies for dealing with national conflict or economic interdependence.

4. Nationalism's appeal to various social groups cannot, finally, be understood primarily in terms of a primordial *national identity*, or a need for self-definition as against other national groups. Questions about the distinctive identity of a nation tend to acquire political importance only where other, concrete interests are at stake; and these interests were defined, in the societies Marx and Engels observed, largely in class terms.

[. . .] Efforts to redefine group identities as 'national' may be activated by external threats or competition which affect all groups inside a given nation. But Marx argued that the specific forms of identity asserted in response to such pressures are also shaped by domestic constraints, which may obstruct the freedom and material well-being of a nation's members as much as any external impediments. Assertions of national identity can therefore operate in one of two ways: negatively, as a frustrated response to both internal and external constraints which disable people from securing their interests through practical action; or positively, as a resource defined with a view to changing the conditions that frustrate basic needs and interests. In neither case, however, is the concern to defend or develop a distinctive national identity seen as the basic activating force behind nationalist movements.

These positions do not imply that the most conspicuous political, cultural, or ideological motives for engaging in nationalist activity merit no systematic analysis. To the contrary, one of my main contentions [. . .] is that Marx and Engels' writings on specific national movements were concerned far less with the structural or economic 'preconditions' of nationalism than with the complex motivations of nationalist actors. The theoretical rationale for this emphasis can be clarified, once again, by examining how Marx and Engels' prescriptive concept of nationality came to operate as part of an explanatory theory.

That concept carries, first of all, a specific temporal emphasis: it directs attention towards the present and future rather than back to the past, focusing on the goals of current nationalist activity rather than on the origins of distinct nations or national conflicts.[4] Whereas descriptive concepts of nationality put forward the historically 'given' conditions which shape nationalist activity, the prescriptive concept invites an enquiry into the ways in which nationalist actors seek to change those conditions in line with their aspirations. This temporal emphasis, second, fosters a theoretical preoccupation with the programmes, struggles, and negotiations that occur within and among national movements. The strategic and political aspects of nationalism thereby come to attract as much explanatory attention as its economic or sociological bases. Marx and Engels' analyses of nationalism were intended, third, to provide action-guiding maps of the complex social terrains in which national aspirations were pursued. Their explanations, that is, also served a prescriptive function, and entailed explicit judgements about the merits of some national movements or policies as against others. It is sometimes assumed that Marx and Engels based such judgements solely on 'economic' criteria, supporting all nationalisms which aimed to create large-scale economic units while opposing the separatist move-ments of less developed nations. As I will argue below, however, the authors generally subordinated such criteria to a prior set of political conditions: they did not support authoritarian national movements aimed at centralizing 'from above', or oppose the separatist movements of smaller nations where these demonstrated a commitment to progressive social reforms. In each case, the decisive factors were the class identity and political intentions of nationalists; and the analysis of these factors occupied much of Marx and Engels' attention in their political writings and journalism.

Their interest in the complex, strategic dimensions of nationalism belies the assumption that a faithfully 'Marxian' treatment must give short shrift to the ideological and political aspects of nationalism, while asserting the explanatory primacy of social structures and economic processes. This assumption is based on rigid remodelling of Marx and Engels' theory which downgrades its key emphasis on praxis or human agency, so that 'such stern realities as property relations, bureaucratic authority, or the division of labour' are seen as imposing 'their own stern discipline upon the social action of incumbents', whose 'motives, values and expectations' merit scant theoretical attention.[5] Readers who scour Marx and Engels' empirical writings on national issues in search of this kind of theory are likely to come up empty-handed. For the most part, those writings offer detailed analyses of the motives, ideas, and organizational efforts of nationalist actors, while the broader social and economic developments which stimulate the rise of 'nationalism' as a general, global phenomenon are placed in the background.[6] To elucidate the two-way relationship between Marx and Engels' general theories and their strategic-political analyses of national movements, it is useful to distinguish between the general tendencies displayed by social and political development in a given 'mode' of production, and the particular, complex settings in which national and class struggles occur. Marx and Engels' statements about particular national issues should, I suggest, be understood as contextual statements which specify and supplement the applications of the general theory itself.[7] The theory guides particular observations, while those observations will extend or otherwise modify the theory, thereby clarifying its proper scope.

Our discussion so far has stressed the central explanatory role of class interests in Marx and Engels' analyses of national issues. Before moving on to concrete examples, however, I should point out some crucial differences between the interpretation offered here and other well-known varieties of 'class analysis' that have been applied to the study of nationalism, and which claim to derive from Marx and Engels' writings. Much obfuscation has resulted from attempts to devise a simple theoretical formula expressing Marx and Engels' views on the relations between class interests and specific national movements. Against one over-simplifying line of interpretation, we have already argued that the two men did not tie nationalism as such to the interests of any single class. But there is a more sophisticated candidate for entry to the ranks of 'Marxist' approaches to nationalism which deserves closer consideration. This formula allows that different national movements may have different 'leading classes'; but it does not presume an identity between the political leaders of a movement and the class whose interests dictate its actions and programmatic content. On this view, the social origins of nationalist leaders are less important as an index of a movement's class moorings than the interests served by that movement.[8] Nationalist movements that are apparently based on broad social coalitions or the esoteric activities of intellectual, professional, and bureaucratic minorities can accordingly be found, on close investigation, to serve the interests of a particular 'dominant class'.

This type of argument invites us to probe beneath complex social constituencies in search of a unitary, dominant set of class interests ostensibly served by a particular national movement. Students of the nineteenth-century nationalisms discussed by Marx and Engels are urged, more specifically, to play what one historian has called 'the game of Hunt the Bourgeoisie'.[9] The objective of that game is to identify the bourgeoisie as the effective 'leading class' in national movements which, whether inadvertently or as a matter of policy, advanced the development of capitalism and the political conditions for its flourishing. This approach has several glaring inadequacies. It exaggerates the degree of cohesion and political self-conciousness possessed by the bourgeoisie in this period, and postulates an explanatory set of interests that were not, in fact, consistently pursued by that class in any European country. The attempt to explain particular national movements in terms of a single class's interests may, moreover, discourage close enquiry into the role of other social groups who support or oppose the nominal 'leading class'.

Several features of their theory of political action enabled Marx and Engels to avoid these shortcomings. According to that theory, first of all, the concept of class interests cannot be used to assert an abstract set of nationalist aims which class actors were expected to pursue, regardless of the circumstances in which they had to manœuvre. Marx and Engels' analyses indicate two levels of any class's interests which explain patterns of support or opposition to nationalist programmes: *substantial* interests in specific economic and political arrangements, and *prudential* interests formed, through a process of reciprocal opposition, in conflicts with other classes. The first set of interests explains class action by identifying the ends that class actors hope to maximize. The second refers to negative interests in self-preservation, which become paramount when efforts to secure substantial interests are diverted or restrained by the opposition of other classes and their supportive institutions.

Marx and Engels invoked the concept of prudential interests to explain why class actors may support nationalist programmes that do not reflect their maximal interests, or refrain from advancing programmes that do. They also recognized that the members of nascent or politically unorganized classes, like the German middle classes before 1848, may lack a clear definition of their substantial collective interests. In such cases – and this brings us to a second point – the appeal of particular nationalist ideas and policies is still explained by class interests, but in a negative rather than a substantive way. When the individuals, occupational groups, and regional segments comprising a nascent class are unable to organize around a clear set of common interests, they tend to misidentify the main obstacles that prevent them from more fully realizing their narrower interests. If those obstacles lie in political conflicts in the domestic arena, as Marx and Engels believed they did in Germany, the difficulty of forming a cohesive opposition may give rise to doctrines which invert class priorities: foreign ideas or competitors are blamed for thwarting key interests, while the political and cultural strongholds of the internal ruling class are hallowed as repositories of national uniqueness. Support for such forms of nationalism was, in Marx and Engels' view, the alienated and transitory effect of domestic repression; it reflected not a positive attraction to the aims and symbolism of nationalism as such, but a practical inability to secure social interests through any other movement. Once the members of a nascent class had begun to distinguish their interests more clearly from those of classes below and above them, they would develop a new set of substantial aims in relation to national issues.

Not all the major social groupings discussed by Marx and Engels met their criteria for constituting a 'full' class. The authors suggested that quasi-class groups like the peasants and urban petty bourgeoisie were particularly susceptible to the appeal of chauvinistic nationalism, because their socio-economic conditions of life prevented them from forming effective alternatives to the programmes advanced by other classes. [. . .] Marx – though not always Engels – denied that the members of quasi-classes were congenitally xenophobic or prone to the manipulative ruses of 'false consciousness'. Their support for specific nationalist policies was seen as conditional, not wholly irrational; and the decisive conditions involved concrete interests in security and material well-being. Following this analysis, Marx was able to argue that the 'reactionary' attitudes of quasi-class groupings could be turned around by alliances with strong progressive movements, led by the bourgeoisie or proletariat, which addressed their interests more effectively than the opposition.

This third element of their strategic theory – the concept of inter-class coalitions or alliances – is central to an adequate understanding of Marx and Engels' concrete analyses of national issues. If they refrained from positing any fixed affinity between certain classes' interests and specific forms of nationalism, this was largely because they recognized that the quest for allies – both at home and abroad – may oblige a class's members to compromise or even recant some of their initial aims. [. . .] Alliances carried risks even for the socially dominant classes, often pushing their programmes beyond a restricted set of goals or truncating them beyond recognition. Since most of the national movements observed by Marx and Engels included several different class components, no form of nationalism appears in their writings as the complete realization of any single class's interests. Their analyses are theoretically interesting not because they contain a simple formula reducing national to class phenomena, but because they draw attention to the ways that social conflicts within the national 'unit' shape the content of national ideology, conceptions of national identity, and relations with other nations and transnational actors.

NOTES

1. See e.g. Jon Elster, *Making Sense of Marx* (Cambridge: Cambridge University Press, 1985), 17.
2. Marx explicitly acknowledged the need for this kind of explanation in *Capital*, where he wrote that 'It is in each case the relationship of the owners of the conditions of production to the direct producers . . . in which we find the innermost secret, the hidden basis of the entire social edifice, and hence also the political form of the relationship of sovereignty and dependence . . . This does not prevent the same economic basis . . . from displaying endless variations and gradations in its appearance, as the result of innumerable different circumstances, natural conditions, racial relations, historical influences acting from outside, etc., and these can only be understood by analysing these empirically given conditions.' *Capital*, iii, trans. David Fernbach (Harmondsworth: Penguin, 1981), 927–8.
3. Frederick Engels, 'Revolution and Counter-Revolution in Germany', in Karl Mark and Frederick Engels, *Collected Works* (London: Lawrence and Wishart, 1975–2005), 11:25.
4. In this respect, Marx and Engels' main explanatory concerns are quite different from those of the 'sociological' theories that have dominated the literature on nationalism in the last two decades, and whose proponents are mainly interested in the question whether nations (not nationalisms) are perennial entities or the novel – and hence probably transient – creations of modernity. These two positions are perhaps best represented, respectively, by Anthony D. Smith, *The Ethnic Origins of Nations* (Oxford: Blackwell, 1986), and Ernest Gellner, *Nations and Nationalism* (Oxford: Blackwell, 1983).

5. Frank Parkin, *Marxism and Class Theory: A Bourgeois Critique* (London: Tavistock, 1981), 4.

6. It is inevitable, however, that Marx and Engels' empirical writings often reflect quite different views of how their general theories should be applied to specific cases of nationalism. As we will see later, Engels' remarks on national issues were frequently framed within a speculative, highly deterministic conception of historical change. Marx was inclined towards a more activist and class-centred view of nationalism, showing less interest than his colleague in the historical and cultural aspects of contemporary national conflicts.

7. Alan Gilbert suggests a similar relationship between Marx's general theory and what he calls 'auxiliary statements' of a more specific character, in *Marx's Politics: Communists and Citizens* (Oxford: Martin Robertson, 1981).

8. Thus John Breuilly has asserted that 'within the Marxist framework the only criterion one can employ' in identifying the dominant class of a national movement 'is not direct evidence about their social origins but to note which class interests the national movement serves'. *Nationalism and the State* (Manchester: Manchester University Press, 1985), 23.

9. David Blackbourne, 'The Discreet Charm of the Bourgeoisie: Reappraising German History in the Nineteenth Century', in David Blackbourne and Geoff Eley, *The Peculiarities of German History: Bourgeois Society and Politics in Nineteenth-Century Germany* (Oxford: Oxford University Press, 1991), 167.

8

MASCULINITY AND NATIONALISM – GENDER AND SEXUALITY IN THE MAKING OF NATIONS

Joane Nagel

Abstract

This article explores the intimate historical and modern connection between manhood and nationhood: through the construction of patriotic manhood and exalted motherhood as icons of nationalist ideology; through the designation of gendered 'places' for men and women in national politics; through the domination of masculine interests and ideology in nationalist movements; through the interplay between masculine microcultures and nationalist ideology; through sexualized militarism including the construction of simultaneously over-sexed and under-sexed 'enemy' men (rapists and wimps) and promiscuous 'enemy' women (sluts and whores). Three 'puzzles' are partially solved by exposing the connection between masculinity and nationalism: why are many men so desperate to defend masculine, monoracial, and heterosexual institutional preserves, such as military organizations and academies; why do men go to war; and the 'gender gap', that is, why do men and women appear to have very different goals and agendas for the 'nation'?

Keywords: Gender; nationalism; ethnicity; masculinity; sexuality; military; race.

Joane Nagel (1998), 'Masculinity and nationalism: gender and sexuality in the making of nations', *Ethnic and Racial Studies*, 21, 2.

INTRODUCTION: POLITICAL MAN

'Political Man'. In the light of a quarter century of 'second wave' of feminist scholarship,[1] the title of Seymour Martin Lipset's classic treatise on politics seems almost quaint in its masculinist exclusiveness. The same can be said for Ted Gurr's *Why Men Rebel* or for the ungendered, presumptively male discourse of T. H. Marshall's *Class, Citizenship, and Social Development* or Karl Deutsch's *Nationalism and Social Communication* or Barrington Moore's *The Social Origins of Dictatorship and Democracy* or Samuel N. Eisenstadt and Stein Rokkan's *Building States and Nations* or Perry Anderson's *Lineages of the Absolutist State*.[2] Even Theda Skocpol's *States and Social Revolutions* is a tale of one gender: men and the making of modern France, Russia, and China.[3]

What were the titles and content of these classics of political science and sociology trying to tell us about the structure and operation of citizenship, states, nations, revolutions, empires? Feminist theorists have argued that this absence of women from the work and thinking of these authors reflects, at best, their gender blindness or, at worst, their gender chauvinism. They argue that the result of this gender exclusion has been to render invisible women's hands in the making of nations and states. The feminist scholarly response to this omission has been twofold: first, to illuminate the role of women in politics by chronicling their participation and leadership in national and opposition politics and movements;[4] second, to uncover and document the mechanisms of women's exclusion from political organizations, movements, decision-making institutions and processes.[5]

While I shall review some of these efforts to 'bring the women back in' to the study of nationalism and national politics, I should note that this necessary and important scholarship has often involved a conflation of the terms 'gender' and 'women'. That is, the critique of classical literature on the nation and state as 'gender-blind' has resulted in an almost exclusive focus on women–women revolutionists, women leaders, women's hidden labour, women's exploitation, women's resistance to domination. While this emphasis on women by gender scholars has begun to fill a critical gap in the study of nationalism and national politics, there remains an important uncharted territory to be investigated.

My primary concern here is on another significant and interesting question, what is the 'real' meaning of the masculine focus of social and political analyses of modern states catalogued above? Is it possible that, inadvertently or not, these guys (and gals) were on to something in their preoccupation with men? That is, perhaps the projects described in these titles – state power, citizenship, nationalism, militarism, revolution, political violence, dictatorship, and democracy – are all best understood as masculinist projects, involving masculine institutions, masculine processes and masculine activities (see Pateman 1989; Connell 1995).

This is not to say that women do not have roles to play in the making and unmaking of states: as citizens, as members of the nation, as activists, as leaders.

It is to say that the scripts in which these roles are embedded are written primarily by men, for men, and about men, and that women are, by design, supporting actors whose roles reflect masculinist notions of femininity and of women's proper 'place'. If nations and states are indeed gendered institutions as much recent scholarship asserts,[6] then to limit the examination of gender in politics to an investigation of women only, misses a major, perhaps *the* major way in which gender shapes politics – through men and their interests, their notions of manliness, and masculine micro and macro cultures.

In her study of gender, race and sexuality in colonialism, *Imperial Leather*, McClintock (1995) notes the 'gendered discourse' of nationalism, commenting that 'if male theorists are typically indifferent to the gendering of nations, feminist analyses of nationalism have been lamentably few and far between. White feminists, in particular, have been slow to recognise nationalism as a feminist issue' (pp. 356–7). And when feminist scholars do set about to even the gender score, Messerschmidt (1993) argues, in his analysis of *Masculinities and Crime*, the gender lens appears to focus exclusively on women. The resulting scholarship, while more gender balanced in its coverage, still fails to examine systematically what is uniquely masculine in a structural, cultural or social sense, about such clearly gendered activities and institutions as crime, nationalism, politics, or violence, among others.

I argue that nationalist politics is a masculinist enterprise not to indict men for dominating national or international arenas, though they surely do. Nor do I intend to ignore further the contributions of women, though they have been limited by historical gender restrictions. Rather, my goal is to explore the fact of men's domination of the nation-state in order to see what insights this acknowledgment of masculinity provides us in understanding contemporary national and global politics.

CONSTRUCTING MEN AND NATIONS

In her evocative book, *Bananas, Beaches, and Bases*, Cynthia Enloe (1990: 45) observes that 'nationalism has typically sprung from masculinized memory, masculinized humiliation and masculinized hope'. She argues that women are relegated to minor, often symbolic, roles in nationalist movements and conflicts, either as icons of nationhood, to be elevated and defended, or as the booty or spoils of war, to be denigrated and disgraced. In either case, the real actors are men who are defending their freedom, their honour, their homeland and their women. Enloe's insight about the connection between manhood and nationhood raises definitional questions about each: what do we mean by 'masculinity', and what do we mean by 'nationalism'?

Masculinity

Recent historical studies of the United States argue that contemporary patterns of US middle-class masculinity arose out of a renaissance of manliness in the late nineteenth and early twentieth centuries.[7] Scholars document a resurgent preoccupation with masculine ideals of physique and behaviour around the turn of the century which became institutionalized into such organizations and institutions as the modern Olympic movement which began in 1896 (MacAloon 1981, 1984), Theodore Roosevelt's 'Rough Riders' unit which fought in the Spanish American War in 1898 (Morris 1979; Rotundo 1993), a variety of boys' and men's lodges and fraternal organizations, such as the Knights of Columbus and the Improved Order of Red Men, which were established or expanded in the late nineteenth century (Preuss 1924; Kauffman 1982; Carnes 1989, 1990; Rotundo 1993; Orr 1994; Bederman 1995), and the Boy Scouts of America which were founded in 1910 two years after the publication of R. S. S. Baden-Powell's influential *Scouting for Boys* (Warren 1986, 1987; MacKenzie 1987).

These organizations embodied US and European male codes of honour (Nye 1993) which stressed a number of 'manly virtues' described by Mosse (1996) as 'normative masculinity', which included willpower, honour, courage, discipline, competitiveness, quiet strength, stoicism, sang-froid, persistence, adventurousness, independence, sexual virility tempered with restraint, and dignity, and which reflected masculine ideals as liberty, equality, and fraternity (Bederman 1995; Mosse 1996). Borrowing from Rosenberg's (1980) analysis of 'Sexuality, Class, and Role', Rotundo (1987) divided these characteristics among three late nineteenth-century 'ideals of manhood' in the middle-class northern US: the 'Masculine Achiever' (competitiveness, independence, persistence), the 'Christian Gentleman' (willpower, restraint, discipline), and the 'Masculine Primitive' (strength, virility, courage).[8]

Of course, the value of and adherence to these normative manly traits vary by time and place. While the writers cited above were describing late nineteenth- and early twentieth-century United States and Europe, there are other scholarly efforts to define masculinity in more universal terms. Gilmore's research on cross-cultural conceptions of masculinity, *Manhood in the Making* (1990) shows that there is no universal standard of masculinity. None the less Gilmore argues that

> although there may be no 'Universal Male', we may perhaps speak of a 'Ubiquitous Male' based on these criteria of performance: . . . to be a man . . . one must impregnate women, protect dependents [*sic*] from danger, and provision kith and kin . . . We might call this quasi-global personage something like 'Man-the-Impregnator-Protector-Provider' (p. 223).

Such catalogues of masculine ideals as the historical and cross-cultural undertakings listed above are examples of what Robert Connell (1995: 68) calls 'essentialist' definitions of masculinity: 'definitions [that] pick a feature that defines the core of the masculine'. The weakness of the essentialist approach is its arbitrariness and easy falsifiability. Connell (1995: 68–71) catalogues three other definitional strategies besides essentialist: positivist, normative, semiotic.

Positivist definitions of masculinity are descriptions of men in a particular place at a particular time: ethnographies of manhood. They are limited by a lack of generalizability, inevitable researcher bias, and tautology. Men are what men do, thus it is impossible for men to behave in feminine ways or for women to behave in masculine ways (ibid.: 69). Normative definitions of masculinity emphasize manly ideals, 'blueprints', or sex role stereotypes. They are limited by their cultural, historical and value assumptions, and by their emphasis on ideal types which exclude many men, that is, many (most) men do not behave according to a 'John Wayne' model of manhood (ibid.: 70). And finally, semiotic definitions of masculinity contrast masculine and feminine and deduce from the difference the meaning of masculinity (and femininity): 'The phallus is master-signifier, and femininity is symbolically defined by lack' (ibid.: 70). Semiotic definitions are limited by their emphases on discourse and symbolism which tend to overlook the material and structural dimensions of the social constitution of gender meanings.

In a manner that combines several of these definitional approaches, some researchers attempt to articulate the meaning of manhood in negative terms – what men are *not*. These definitions include a separation from and repudiation of femininity: being a man is *not* being a woman, and no man would ever want to be a woman (Freud 1923; Chodorow 1978; Adams 1990); a distancing from masculine 'countertypes', whether racial – being a (white) man is not being a 'Jew' (Green 1993: 101–13; Mosse 1996: 60ff) or an 'Asian' (Espiritu 1996, ch. 5), or a 'Bengali' (Sinha 1995), or an 'Indian' or a 'black'. (Bederman 1995: 181), or sexual – being a man is not acting 'feminine' and/or not being a homosexual (Mosse 1985, 1996; Duroche 1991; Donaldson 1993). These racial and sexual masculine 'countertypes' are examples of what Connell (1987: 186) calls 'subordinated' forms of masculinity.

Other negative, albeit somewhat essentialist, definitions of masculinity reflect a distaste for the demands of normative masculinity. In 'Being a Man', Paul Theroux (1985: 309) complains that, 'the expression "Be a Man!" strikes me as insulting and abusive. It means: Be stupid, be unfeeling, obedient, soldierly and stop thinking'. Gerzon (1982: 5) defines normative manliness as an impossible achievement: 'In comparing themselves to the dashing figure riding off into the setting sun or racing across the goal line, ordinary men in everyday life cannot help but feel overshadowed. Even in private, men no longer feel like heroes'. Horrocks catalogues the costs of 'patriarchal masculinity':

> Patriarchal masculinity cripples men. Manhood as we know it in our society requires such a self-destructive identity, a deeply masochistic self-denial, a shrinkage of the self, a turning away from whole areas of life, the man who obeys the demands of masculinity has become only half-human ... To become the man I was supposed to be, I had to destroy my most vulnerable side, my sensitivity, my femininity, my creativity, and I had to

pretend to be both more powerful and less powerful than I feel (Horrocks 1994: 25; see also Levant 1997; Messner 1997: 5–6).

Whatever the historical or comparative limits of these various definitions and depictions of masculinity, scholars argue that at any time, in any place, there is an identifiable 'normative' or 'hegemonic' masculinity that sets the standards for male demeanour, thinking and action (Bederman 1995; Connell 1995; Mosse 1996). Hegemonic masculinity is more than an 'ideal', it is assumptive, widely held, and has the quality of appearing to be 'natural' (Morgan 1992; Donaldson 1993). This is not to say there is consensus among all men and women in any national setting about the ideal man. Indeed, hegemonic masculinity often stands in contrast to other class-, race- and sexuality-based masculinities. None the less, hegemonic masculinity remains a standard – whether reviled or revered – against which other masculinities compete or define themselves.

Whether current US hegemonic masculinity is derived from a nineteenth-century renaissance of manliness and/or is rooted in earlier historical cultural conceptions of manhood, it is certainly identifiable as the dominant form among several racial, sexual and class-based masculinities in contemporary US society (see Kimmel 1995; Kimmel and Messner 1995; Pfeil 1995; Schwalbe 1995). The same can be said for other countries as well – in Europe, Latin America, Africa, Asia or the Middle East. For instance, whether the manly attitudes and rules for behaviour for Arab men described by T. E. Lawrence in *Seven Pillars of Wisdom* (1926) set the current standards of manliness for men in the modern Arab world is not so much the question, as whether some current set of masculine standards exists and can be identified as hegemonic. The answer to that question is most certainly, yes.[9]

Nationalism

Max Weber defines a nation as 'a community of sentiment which would adequately manifest itself in a state' and which holds notions of common descent, though not necessarily common blood (Gerth and Mills 1948: 172–9). Layoun (1991: 410–11) concurs: nationalism 'constructs and proffers a narrative of the 'nation' and of its relation to an already existing or potential state'. By these definitions nationalism is both a goal – to achieve statehood, and a belief – in collective commonality. Nationalists seek to accomplish both statehood and nationhood. The goal of sovereign statehood, 'state-building', often takes the form of revolutionary or anti-colonial warfare. The maintenance and exercise of statehood *vis-à-vis* other nation-states often takes the form of armed conflict. As a result, nationalism and militarism seem to go hand in hand.

The goal of nationhood, 'nation-building', involves 'imagining' a national past and present (Anderson 1991), inventing traditions (Hobsbawm and Ranger 1983), and symbolically constructing community (Cohen 1985). As Gellner (1983: 49) argues, 'it is nationalism that engenders nations, and not the other way around'. The tasks of defining community, of setting boundaries and of articulating national character, history, and a vision for the future tend to emphasize both unity and 'otherness'. The project of establishing national identity and cultural boundaries tends to foster nationalist ethnocentrism. As a result nationalism and chauvinism seem to go hand in hand. Chauvinistic nationalism is often confined to the ideational realm in the form of attitudes and beliefs about national superiority. During periods of nationalist conflict or expansion, however, such ethnocentrism becomes animated. The result in modern world history has been for nationalism to display an intolerant, sometimes murderous face. Nairn (1977) refers to the nation as 'the modern Janus' to contrast nationalism's two sides: a regressive, jingoistic, militaristic 'warfare state' visage versus a progressive community-building 'welfare state' countenance: guns versus butter.[10]

The distinction between ideology and action characterizes most discussions on the definition and operation of nationalism. Nationalist ideology, that is, beliefs about the nation – who we are, what we represent – become the basis and justification for national actions, that is to say, activities of state- and nation-building, the fight for independence, the creation of a political and legal order, the exclusion or inclusion of various categories of members, the relations with other nations. Whether manifested in action or ideology, most scholars identify the nineteenth century as the origin of nationalism as a way of understanding and organizing local and global politics. Nairn (1977) argues that 'nationalism in its most general sense is determined by certain features of the world political economy in the era between the French and Industrial Revolutions and the present day'. These features include a 'new and heightened significance accorded to factors of nationality, ethnic inheritance, customs, and speech' and 'the creation of a national market economy and a viable national bourgeois class' (p. 333). Similarly, Seton-Watson (1977) identifies the late 1700s as the dividing line between 'old' and 'new' nations in Europe, where the old nations, such as the English, Scots, Danes, French and Swedes, enjoyed relative autonomy, and the new nations, basically the rest of the world, mobilized in the form of national movements to achieve independence, either from monarchies or from colonialism, articulating a form of nationalism designed to 'implant in [their constituents] a national consciousness and a desire for political action' (p. 9).

MASCULINITY AND NATIONALISM

By definition, nationalism is political and closely linked to the state and its institutions. Like the military, most state institutions have been historically and remain dominated by men. It is therefore no surprise that the culture and ideology of hegemonic masculinity go hand in hand with the culture and ideology of hegemonic nationalism. Masculinity and nationalism articulate well with one another, and the modern form of Western masculinity emerged at about the same time and place as modern nationalism. Mosse notes that nationalism 'was a movement which began and evolved parallel to modern masculinity' in the West about a century ago. He describes modern masculinity as a centrepiece of all varieties of nationalist movements:

> The masculine stereotype was not bound to any one of the powerful political ideologies of the previous century. It supported not only conservative movements . . . but the workers' movement as well; even Bolshevik man was said to be 'firm as an oak.' Modern masculinity from the very first was co-opted by the new nationalist movements of the nineteenth century (Mosse 1996: 7).

Other political ideologies of that time, in particular colonialism and imperialism, also resonated with contemporary standards of masculinity (see MacKenzie 1987; Walvin 1987; Bologh 1990). Many scholars link the nineteenth-century renaissance in manliness in Europe to the institutions and ideology of empire (Hobsbawm 1990; Koven 1991; Sinha 1995). Springhall (1987) describes the middle-class English ideal of Christian manliness, 'muscular Christianity', with its emphasis on sport – the 'cult of games' in the public schools; he outlines how, through organizations such as the Boys' Brigade these middle-class values were communicated to 'less privileged, board-school-educated, working-class boys in the nation's large urban centres' (p. 52). Boys from both classes served throughout the Empire in British imperial armies.

In the United States, masculinity was tightly woven into two nationalist imperialist projects: manifest destiny, which justified and advocated westward expansion, and the Monroe Doctrine, which justified and extended the US sphere of influence to include the entire western hemisphere. There is no better known embodiment of this marriage of manhood and US imperialism than Theodore Roosevelt. Well-known to have been a sickly child and labelled a privileged dandy in his youth, Roosevelt was subjected to humiliating attacks on his manliness early in his political career. When, in 1882 at the age of twenty-three Theodore Roosevelt started out in politics as a New York state assemblyman,

> Daily newspapers lampooned Roosevelt as the quintessence of effeminacy. They nicknamed him 'weakling', 'Jane-Dandy', 'Punkin-Lilly', and 'the exquisite Mr. Roosevelt'. They ridiculed his high voice, tight pants, and fancy clothing. Several began referring to him by the name of the well-known homosexual, Oscar Wilde, and one actually alleged (in a less-than-veiled phallic allusion) that Roosevelt was 'given to sucking the knob of an ivory cane' (Bederman 1995: 170).

Roosevelt set out on a campaign to reinvent himself as a man's man. Two symbolic themes formed the foundation of his self-reconstruction effort: his claimed connection to the American West and his assertion of an imperial

America. His campaign was phenomenally successful, and within five years he was running for the mayor of New York as the 'Cowboy of the Dakotas', embraced by a press which now praised him for his 'virile zest for fighting and his "blizzard-seasoned" constitution' (ibid.: 171). This remarkable transformation can be traced to his writings and to a real estate purchase. In 1883 Roosevelt visited the Badlands in South Dakota and purchased a cattle ranch (Morris 1979). Following the death of his wife in 1884, he temporarily withdrew from politics and retreated to the ranch, but not before he began his public metamorphosis from a 'gilded youth' to a 'masculine cowboy' by granting the following interview printed in the *New York Tribune*:

> It would electrify some of my friends who have accused me of representing the kid-glove element in politics if they could see me galloping over the plains, day in and day out, clad in a buckskin shirt and leather chaparajos, with a big sombrero on my head. For good healthy exercise I would strongly recommend some of our gilded youth go West and try a short course of riding bucking ponies, and assist at the branding of a lot of Texas steers (Bederman 1995: 175).

Roosevelt's cowboy career lasted only six months, but his book *Hunting Trips of a Ranchman* published the next year, in 1885, followed by *Ranch Life and the Hunting Trail* (1888) and the 4-volume *The Winning of the West* (1889–1896), secured his public identity as a real man. Roosevelt continued to reinvigorate his manliness by other writings (*The Strenuous Life* (1902) and *African Game Trails: An Account of the African Wanderings of an American Hunter Naturalist* (1910)), and by his bellicose demand for and support of the Spanish-American War in which his 'Rough Riders' personified themes of the US frontier and US imperialism.

Hoganson (1995, 1996) describes the role of masculine imagery in the discourse surrounding one campaign in the Spanish-American War, the Philippine-American War which began in 1898 when the US sank the Spanish fleet in Manila Bay, and which lasted until 1902. Following the sinking of the Spanish fleet, Filipinos began a fight for national independence. This set off a debate in the US about what should be the US stance towards the former Spanish colony: should it be free or become a US colony? Theodore Roosevelt was a central actor in this debate, and his position was clearly in the imperial camp: 'We of America . . . we, the sons of a nation yet in the pride of its lusty youth . . . know its future is ours if we have the manhood to grasp it, and we enter the new century girding our loins for the contest before us' (Hoganson 1996: 3). It was not only Roosevelt who cast the debate in gendered, as well as ageist, terms. Prominent anti-imperialist, Senator George F. Hoar, was referred to by an ally of Roosevelt as a 'fossil' and was encouraged to give up his place in the Senate to 'a young man who is progressive and who lives in the present and not in the musty past' (ibid.: 3). The 'Philippine question' became a contest of young men against 'old women' (although women did not have the vote at the time), and the discourse spread to the (male only) voting constituency:

> What this country needs most at this time are patriotic Americans not a lot of old women and decrepit politicians in their dotage who pose as statesmen . . . the nation has outgrown you. Give yourself a rest in some old man's home and give the nation a chance to grow (ibid.: 3).

Theodore Roosevelt's speeches and writings, and those of many of his contemporaries, reflect a racialized, imperial masculinity, where adventurous, but civilized white men tame or defeat inferior savage men of colour, be they American Indians, Africans, Spaniards, or Filipinos. Whether conquering the US frontier or 'protecting' the western hemisphere from European colonialism, Roosevelt's masculinity depended on a chauvinistic, militaristic nationalism. Given the close association between nineteenth- and twentieth-century ideologies of masculinity, colonialism, imperialism, militarism and nationalism, given the fact that it was mainly men who adhered to and enacted them, and given the power of those movements and institutions in the making of the modern world, it is not surprising that masculinity and nationalism seem stamped from the same mould – a mould which has shaped important aspects of the structure and culture of the nations and states in the modern state system.

MEN'S AND WOMEN'S PLACES IN THE NATION

Nationalist politics is a major venue for 'accomplishing' masculinity (Connell 1987) for several reasons. First, as noted above, the national state is essentially a masculine institution. Feminist scholars point out its hierarchical authority structure, the male domination of decision-making positions, the male superordinate/female subordinate internal division of labour, and the male legal regulation of female rights, labour and sexuality (Franzway; Court and Connell 1989; Grant and Tancred 1992; Connell 1995).

Second, the culture of nationalism is constructed to emphasize and resonate with masculine cultural themes. Terms like honour, patriotism, cowardice, bravery and duty are hard to distinguish as either nationalistic or masculinist, since they seem so thoroughly tied both to the nation and to manliness. My point here is that the 'microculture' of masculinity in everyday life articulates very well with the demands of nationalism, particularly its militaristic side. When, over the years I have asked my undergraduate students to write down on a piece of paper their answer to the question: 'What is the worst name you can be called?' the gender difference in their responses is striking. The vast majority of women respond: 'slut' (or its equivalent, with 'bitch' a rather distant second); the vaster majority of men respond: 'wimp' or 'coward' or 'pussy'. Only cowards shirk the call to duty; real men are not cowards.

Patriotism is a siren call that few men can resist, particularly in the midst of a political 'crisis'; and if they do, they risk the disdain or worse of their communities and families, sometimes including their mothers. Counter to the common stereotype of mothers attempting to hold back their sons as they march off to war, Boulding (1977: 167) Reports that many mothers of conscientious objectors during World War II opposed their sons' pacifism.[11] The disdain of men for pacifists is considerably greater, as Karlen (1971) recounts in *Sexuality and Homosexuality*: 'In 1968 pacifists set up coffee houses to spread their word near military bases. A Special Force NCO said to a *Newsweek* reporter, "We aren't fighting and dying so these goddam pansies can sit around drinking coffee"' (p. 508).

Fear of accusations of cowardice is not the only magnet that pulls men towards patriotism, nationalism, or militarism. There is also the masculine allure of adventure. Men's accountings of their enlistment in wars often describe their anticipation and excitement, their sense of embarking on a great adventure, their desire not to be 'left behind' or 'left out' of the grand quest that the war represents.

> I felt the thrill of it – even I, a hard-boiled soldier of fortune – a man who was not supposed to have the slightest trace of nerves. I felt my throat tighten and several times the scene of marching columns swam in oddly elliptical circles. By God, I was shedding tears (Adams 1990: vii; see also Green 1993).[12]

Finally, women occupy a distinct, symbolic role in nationalist culture, discourse and collective action, a role that reflects a masculinist definition of femininity and of women's proper place in the nation. Yuval-Davis and Anthias (1989) have identified five ways in which women have tended to participate in ethnic, national, and state processes and practices: (a) as biological producers of members of ethnic collectivities; (b) as reproducers of the [normative] boundaries of ethnic/national groups [by enacting proper feminine behaviour]; (c) as participating centrally in the ideological reproduction of the collectivity and as transmitters of its culture; (d) as signifiers of ethnic/national differences; and (e) as participants in national, economic, political and military struggles (pp. 7–8).

While some of these roles involve action, women participating in or even leading nationalist struggles, the list is short and the same names are heard again and again. As Horrocks (1994: 25) notes when discussing the male dominance in public life: 'The exception – Margaret Thatcher – proves the rule'. Indeed, Jayawardena (1986); Walby (1989); Yuval-Davis and Anthias (1989); Tohidi (1991); Anthias and Yuval-Davis (1992), among others, note the pressure felt by women nationalists to remain in supportive, symbolic, often suppressed and traditional roles.

Faced with these constraints, sometimes women attempt to enact nationalism through traditional roles assigned to them by nationalists – by supporting their husbands, raising their (the nation's) children and serving as symbols of national honour. In these cases women can exploit both nationalist and enemy or oppressor patriarchal views of women's roles in order to aid in nationalist struggles. For instance, in situations of military occupation, male nationalists seen on the street alone or in groups are often targets of arrest or detention. Women are less likely to be seen as dangerous or 'up to something', and so can serve as escorts for men or messengers for men who are sequestered inside houses. Similarly, women are often more successful at recruiting support for nationalist efforts because they are seen as less threatening and militant (Edgerton 1987; Sayigh and Peteet 1987; Mukarker 1993). Edgerton (1987) describes Northern Irish Catholic women's use of traditional female housekeeping roles as a warning system against British army raids; the practice was called 'bin [trash can] lid bashing':

> When troops entered an area, local women would begin banging their bin lids on the pavement; the noise would carry throughout the area and alert others to follow suit . . . At the sound of the bin lids, scores of women would emerge armed with dusters and mops for a hasty spring clean (p. 65).

In addition to these 'weapons of the weak' (Scott 1985; Hart 1991), women have also participated more directly in various nationalist movements and conflicts, involving themselves, in cadres and military units (Jayawardena 1986; Nategh 1987; Sayigh and Peteet 1987; Hélie-Lucas 1988; Urdang 1989). Despite their bravery, sometimes taking on traditional male military roles, and despite the centrality of their contribution to many nationalist struggles, it is often the case that feminist nationalists find themselves once again under the thumb of institutionalized patriarchy once national independence is won. A nationalist movement that encourages women's participation in the name of national liberation often balks at feminist demands for gender equality.

Perhaps the most well-known case of a nationalist movement 'turning' on its female supporters is that of Algeria. In 1962 Algeria finally freed itself from French colonial rule. The struggle had been a long and bitter one, and the fight for Algerian independence had been notable for the involvement of Algerian women. Danièle Djamila Amrane-Minne, who interviewed women veterans of the Algerian liberation movement in *Des Femmes dans la guerre d'Algérie*, reports that 11,000 women were active participants in the national resistance movement, and that 2,000 women were in the armed wing of the movement (Kutschera 1996: 40–41). Despite this extensive involvement of women in a Muslim country's military movement, once independence was won, Algerian women found themselves 'back in the kitchen' (Boulding 1977: 179), forced to trade their combat fatigues for Islamic dress and the veil (*hijab*).[13]

Lest this discussion of Muslim nationalism lead the reader to see masculinity and nationalism as an organizing and hegemonic relationship only for Islamic societies, it is important to remember that religious nationalism, indeed all nationalism, tends to be conservative, and 'conservative' often means 'patri-

archal' (Yuval-Davis 1981; Lievesley 1996; Waylen 1996). This is partly due to
the tendency of nationalists to be 'retraditionalizers' (Nagel 1996: 193), and to
embrace tradition as a legitimating basis for nation-building and cultural
renewal. These traditions, real or invented, are often patriarchal and point
out the tenacious and entrenched nature of masculine privilege and the tight
connection between masculinity and nationalism.

FEMININE SHAME AND MASCULINE HONOUR IN THE NATIONAL FAMILY

Many theorists of nationalism have noted the tendency of nationalists to liken
the nation to a family (McClintock 1991; Skurski 1994); it is a male-headed
household in which both men and women have 'natural' roles to play. While
women may be subordinated politically in nationalist movements and politics,
as we have seen asserted above, they occupy an important symbolic place as the
mothers of the nation. As exalted 'mothers in the fatherland' (Koonz 1987),
their purity must be impeccable, and so nationalists often have a special interest
in the sexuality and sexual behaviour of their women. While traditionalist men
may be defenders of the family and the nation, women are thought by
traditionalists to embody family and national honour; women's shame is the
family's shame, the nation's shame, the man's shame.[14]

There is no clearer example of the politics of dress and demeanour than the
politics of the veil in Islamic nationalism. Outside the home many Arab and
Muslim women wear traditional dress, ranging from a modest covering of the
arms and legs in Western-style dress to which a head scarf is sometimes added,
to the Iranian chador, a body-length scarf or cape worn over street clothing, to
the full facial and body covering of Saudi women. Many of these women assert
that such dress is their preferred choice. They argue that being veiled is
liberating, since the veil shields them from the sexual gaze of men (Makhlouf
1979: 86), and allows them to be a person, not a sex object – a status
unavailable to Western women (see Tohidi 1991: 255–8). Other veiled women
have taken up the veil as a symbol of nationalism in anti-Western, anti-colonial,
or anti-imperial rebellion against Western-allied regimes who outlawed the veil
(for example, in Iran; see Nategh 1987). For other women, veiling is a means of
signifying their discontent and protesting their loss of economic and social
position as a result of urbanization and industrialization (Macleod 1991).
Finally, for other, often immigrant, Muslim women, the veil represents a barrier
against assimilation (Pfeil 1994: 214–17). Many veiled women, however,
including many once in the second category, resent their lack of choice in
wearing the veil, and bitterly complain that what was once an act of defiance
against a corrupt government or occupier, is now used by their own men to
control and oppress them. A number of the accounts in Augustin's *Palestinian
Women* (1993) express regret and outrage at enforced veiling:

> The reason why most women here in Gaza put on the shawl is that they
> are forced to. It is becoming dangerous for women not to cover their hair

when they leave home. Some Muslim fanatics have even threatened to throw chemicals at women not wearing a shawl. There are, of course, deeply religious women who wear a shawl out of commitment. Other women rationalize, and regard the shawl not as a part of fundamentalist Islam but as a symbolic sign of the struggle for liberation, the Intifada. And a lot of women are forced by their husbands to cover their heads (Berberi 1993: 53).

These women face a difficult choice in resisting enforced veiling. If they stand up for their rights as women, they appear to be disloyal to their community, traitors to the national cause. In situations where ethnic and national communities are under siege, many women are not willing to protest patriarchal impositions such as the veil, including these Palestinian women activists:

> We can't open up a second front now. Our battle is not with men. In the context of struggling against the occupation . . . we have to postpone questions of gender liberation till after liberation . . . When we have our own state, we will work on women's issues (Augustin 1993: 37–8).[15]

Questions of women's dress and demeanour are really questions of purity and, oddly, of male honour. Women's sexuality often turns out to be a matter of prime national interest for at least two reasons. First, women's role in nationalism is most often that of a mother, the symbol of the national hearth and home. Yuval-Davis (1993: 627) reminds us, 'In France, it was *La Patrie*, a figure of a women giving birth which personified the revolution'. In their discussion of Afrikaner nationalism in South Africa, Gaitskell and Unterhalter (1989) argue that Afrikaner women appear regularly in the rhetoric and imagery of the Afrikaner 'volk' (people), and that 'they have figured overwhelmingly as mothers' (p. 60).

Second, women's sexuality is of concern to nationalists, since women as wives and daughters are bearers of masculine honour. For instance, ethnographers report Afghani Muslim nationalists' conception of resource control, particularly labour, land and women, is defined as a matter of honour; 'purdah is a key element in the protection of the family's pride and honour' (Moghadam 1991b: 433). El-Solh and Mabro (1994: 8) further refine the connection between men's and family honour and women's sexual respectability as a situation where honour is men's to gain and women's to lose: 'Honour is seen more as men's responsibility and shame as women's . . . honour is seen as actively achieved while shame is seen as passively defended'.

It is not only Third World men whose honour is tied to their women's sexuality, respectability and shame. While female fecundity is valued in the mothers of the nation, unruly female sexuality threatens to discredit the nation. Mosse (1985) describes this duality in depiction of women in European nationalist history: on the one hand, 'female embodiments of the nation stood for eternal forces . . . [and] suggested innocence and chastity' (p. 98), and most of all respectability, but on the other hand, the right women needed to be sexually available to the right men: 'the maiden with the shield, the spirit that awaits a masculine leader' (p. 101) to facilitate 'the enjoyment of peace achieved by male warriors' (p. 98). These images of acceptable female sexuality stood in contrast to female 'decadents' (prostitutes or lesbians) who were seen as 'unpatriotic, weakening the nation' (Mosse 1985: 109) and dishonouring the nation's men. Both willing and unwilling sexual encounters between national women and 'alien' men can create a crisis of honour and can precipitate vengeful violence. Saunders (1995) describes the outrage of Australian men (white and aborigine) about voluntary sexual liaisons between African American servicemen and Australian women during World War II, which escalated to such a high level of 'racial and sexual hysteria' that six black GIs were executed for allegedly raping two white nurses in New Guinea (p. 186).[16]

Sexualized and militarized nationalism

Concerns about the sexual purity and activities of women is not the only way that sexuality arises as an issue in masculinity and nationalism. Enloe (1990: 56) argues, 'when a nationalist movement becomes militarized . . . male privilege in the community usually becomes more entrenched'. She is referring to the highly masculine nature of things military. The military, it turns out, is also highly sexual. I am referring here to several (masculine hetero) sexualized aspects of military institutions and activities.

First, there is the sexualized nature of warfare. Hartsock (1983, 1984) argues that all forms of political power, including military power, have an erotic component; she points particularly to a masculine eroticism embedded in notions of military strength and valour. Classical history is replete with references linking strength and valour on the battlefield with masculine sexual virility, hence Julius Caesar's (1951) admonition to men to avoid sexual intercourse before a battle (or in more modern times before that social equivalent of war, sport) so as not to sap their strength. Mosse (1985: 34) discusses debates in Germany about masturbation and homosexuality as sexual practices that endangered national military strength, and describes war as an 'invitation to manliness'.

A second way that military institutions and actions are sexualized centres on the depiction of the 'enemy' in conflicts. Accounts of many wars and nationalist conflicts include portrayals of enemy men either as sexual demons, bent on raping nationalist women, or as sexual eunuchs, incapable of manly virility. Bederman's (1995) analysis of Theodore Roosevelt's nationalist discourse provides examples of both. In *African Game Trails*, Roosevelt adopts a colonialist's superior, in dulgent attitude towards African men, whom he describes as 'strong, patient, good-humored . . . with something childlike about them that makes one really fond of them . . . Of course, like all savages and most children, they have their limits' (Bederman 1995: 210). Roosevelt's assessment of Native Americans was less patronizingly benevolent, since Indians represented a military threat to the white man whom he saw as

> not taking part in a war against a civilized foe; he was fighting in a contest where women and children suffered the fate of the strong men . . . His sweetheart or wife had been carried off, ravished, and was at the moment the slave and concubine of some dirty and brutal Indian warrior (ibid.: 181).

Mosse (1985) describes portrayals of women on the battlefield as victims of sexual aggression or exploitation along the lines depicted above. He notes, however, that 'women haunted soldiers' dreams and fantasies' (p. 127) in other roles as well, either as 'objects of sexual desire or as pure, self-sacrificing Madonnas, in other words, the field prostitute or the battlefield nurse' (p. 128). Enemy women are more uniformly characterized as sexually promiscuous and available: sluts, whores, or legitimate targets of rape. The accounts of virtually all wars contain references to and discussions of the rape, sexual enslavement, or sexual exploitation of women by not only individual or small groups of men, but by army high commands and as part of state-run national policies (see Brownmiller 1975; Enloe 1990, 1993; Sturdevant and Stoltzfus 1992). As Theweleit (1987) summarizes: 'Woman is an infinite untrodden territory of desire which at every stage of historical deterritorialization, men in search of material for utopias have inundated with their desires' (p. 294).

A third sexualized aspect of militarized conflict is the use of the masculine imagery of rape, penetration and sexual conquest to depict military weaponry and offensives. A commonly reported phrase alleged to have been written on US missiles targeted on Iraq during the 1991 Gulf War was, 'Bend over, Saddam' (Cohn 1993: 236). There is a tendency in national defence discourse to personify and sexually characterize the actions of states and armies. Cohn (1993: 236) reports that one 'well-known academic security adviser was quoted as saying that "under Jimmy Carter the United States is spreading its legs for the Soviet Union"'. She reports similar sexualized depictions by a US defence analyst of former West German politicians who were concerned about popular opposition to the deployment of nuclear Euromissiles in the 1980s: 'Those Krauts are a bunch of limp-dicked wimps' (ibid.: 236). Such sexualized military discourse is very much from a heterosexual standpoint, as is clear when we consider the imagery of rape during the 1991 Gulf War: attacks that needed to be defended or retaliated against were cast as heterosexual rapes of women ('the rape of Kuwait'); attacks that were offensive against the Iraqi enemy were phrased as homosexual rapes of men ('bend over, Saddam') (see also Cohn 1987, 1990).

CONCLUSION: DEFENDING MASCULINITY

What does this exploration of masculinity and nationalism tell us? For one thing, understanding the extensive nature of the link between nationalism, patriotism, militarism, imperialism and masculinity helps to make sense of some puzzling items in the news. It has always seemed a mystery to me why the men in military and para-military institutions – men concerned with manly demeanour and strength of character – often seemed so agitated and afraid of the entry, first of blacks, then (still) of women, and now of homosexuals into military institutions and organizations. This unseemly, sometimes hysterical resistance to a diversity that clearly exists outside military boundaries makes more sense when it is understood that these men are not only defending tradition but are defending a particular racial, gendered and sexual conception of self: a white, male, heterosexual notion of masculine identity loaded with all the burdens and privileges that go along with hegemonic masculinity. Understanding that their reactions reflect not only a defence of male privilege, but also a defence of male culture and identity, makes clearer that there are fundamental issues at stake here for men who are committed to these masculinist and nationalist institutions and lifeways.

Another puzzling issue which this study of masculinity and nationalism has illuminated for me is the question of why men go to war. In the early 1990s, US Public Television stations aired a series on the US Civil War. I listened, night after night, to the voices of men and women in both the North and the South, and their accounts of the dangers, horrors, longings, sadness, anger and despair arising from the bloodiest conflict in US history. Night after night I asked the same question – why did these men continue to fight?

I could understand the motivations of southern men – from their perspective they were defending a homeland and way of life. I understood the 'principles' on each side: states' rights, union, abolition, and I understood the power of conscription and official coercion to enlist.[17] Even given all of that, what I did not understand was why the northerners were fighting, indeed were *volunteering* to fight. For instance, there was at that time, in the mid-1800s, just as there is now, ample evidence that African Americans were not held close to the hearts of northern white men or women. And while there was an organized movement against slavery in the north, there is no reason to believe that this issue enjoyed wide and fervent enough support to generate such high levels of northern participation in the war.

I found the first clue to the solution to this puzzle not in scholarly research, but in my own family – in my husband's disinterest in my wonderings. That rank after rank of northern male cannon fodder lined up to die in massive battles such as Gettysburg and Antietam did not seem problematic to him at all. That I found this so inexplicable and that he found it so dull, suggested that the answer lay in a domain that was likely to be very gendered as well as very assumptive. Now we both know the answer: masculinity and nationalism.

Certainly there are wars that men resist, and there are men who resist all wars. However, once a war is widely defined as a matter of 'duty', 'honour', 'patriotism', a defence of 'freedom' and 'the American way of life', etc., then resistance for many men (and women) becomes a matter of cowardice and dishonour. For men confronted with this unpalatable threat of public humiliation (why isn't he at the front?), there are added some sweeteners: the allure of adventure, the promise of masculine camaraderie, the opportunity to test and prove oneself, the chance to participate in a historic, larger-than-life, generation-defining event. Given this stick and these carrots, for many men the attraction of war becomes as irresistible as it is deadly. My husband intuitively grasped this reality; I had to write this article to 'get' it.

This is not to say that all men or all women respond in the same way to 'a call to arms'. As noted above, there are racial, class and sexuality differences in men's and women's views of hegemonic masculinity and appeals made on that basis. Indeed, many women are patriotic, concerned about honour, mobilizable; many men are critical of hegemonic masculinity and nationalism, and not mobilizable. And there are historical moments when hegemony wavers: the widespread resistance to the war in Vietnam was one such moment. Further, masculinist and nationalist ideology can affect women as well as men. Take the epithet, 'wimp'. I have argued above that this is among men's most dreaded insults, but that for women this is either not on their list, or nowhere near the top of their list. Carol Cohn (1993) was called a wimp while participating in a RAND corporation war simulation. She reported being 'stung' by the name-calling despite the fact that she was 'a woman and a feminist, not only contemptuous of the mentality that measures human beings by their degree of so-called wimpishness, but also someone for whom the term *wimp* does not have a deeply resonant personal meaning' (p. 237). Cohn's explanation for her reaction centres on the power of group membership and reality-defining social context. While she was a participant in the simulation, she became 'a participant in a discourse, a shared set of words, concepts, symbols that constituted not only the linguistic possibilities available to us but also constituted *me* in that situation' (pp. 237–8). In other words, Cohn became 'masculinized'.

But why don't women who participate in masculine organizations or situations 'feminize' those institutions and settings, rather than becoming, however momentarily, masculinized themselves? Do women who join the military become 'men'? Or if enough women join the military, will they 'feminize' it? Is there a critical mass, a point at which women cease to become masculinized in masculine institutions and begin to transform the institutions according to the feminine interests and culture they bring with them to that setting? I wonder, is the gender make-up of governments why nationalism is more associated with preparing for and waging war than with building schools, museums, hospitals and health care systems, social security systems, public transportation, arts and entertainment complexes, nature preserves? While states concern themselves with these things, they never seem to become the 'moral equivalent of war'.

The answer to this question of women becoming masculinized or masculine institutions becoming feminized is an important one for making sense of national and international politics. As women enter the political realm in greater numbers around the world, will we see a shifting of state agendas and a decoupling of nationalism from masculinity? Enloe (1990) is sceptical. She notes the limited change that has resulted from the many nationalist independence movements around the world, and observes that in many post World War II states it is 'business as usual' with indigenous masculinity replacing colonialist masculinity at the helms of states:

> Given the scores of nationalist movements which have managed to topple empires and create new ones, it is surprising that the international political system hasn't been more radically altered than it has. But a nationalist movement informed by masculinist pride and holding a patriarchal vision of the new nation-state is likely to produce just one more actor in the international arena. A dozen new patriarchal nation-states may make the international bargaining table a bit more crowded, but it won't change the international game being played at that table (Enloe 1990: 64).

There is one final puzzle that this exploration of masculinity and nationalism has begun to solve for me, that is, the different way that I, as a woman, may be experiencing my citizenship compared to the citizenship experience of men. According to a Southern African Tswana proverb, 'a woman has no tribe' (Young 1993: 26). I wonder whether it might not also be true that a woman has no nation, or that for many women the nation does not 'feel' the same as it does to many men. We are not expected to defend our country, run our country, or represent our country. Of course, many women do these things, but our presence in the masculine institutions of state – the government and the military – seems unwelcome unless we occupy the familiar supporting roles: secretary, lover, wife. We are more adrift from the nation, less likely to be called to 'important' and recognized public duty, and our contributions more likely to be seen as 'private', as linked only to 'women's issues', and as such, less valued and acknowledged. Given this difference in men's and women's connection and conception of the nation and the state, it is not surprising that there is a 'gender gap' dividing men and women on so many political issues. Thus, the intimate link between masculinity and nationalism, like all hegemonic structures, shapes not only the feelings and thinking of men, it has left its stamp on the hearts and minds of women as well.

Notes

1. The 'first wave' of feminism was the suffrage movement of the late nineteenth and early twentieth centuries; the 'second wave' began in the late 1960s; see Rupp and Taylor (1987).
2. Lipset 1963; Deutsch 1966; Marshall 1963; Moore 1966; Gurr 1970; Eisenstadt and Rokkan 1973; Anderson 1974.
3. Skocpol 1979; Skocpol's most recent book, *Protecting Soldiers and Mothers* (1992), reflects an expansion of her thinking to include women and gender as issues to be addressed in political sociology.
4. See Kaplan 1982; Alvarez 1990; Kennedy, Lubelska, and Walsh 1992; Augustin 1993; Salas 1994.

5. See Hearn 1987, 1992; Brown 1988, 1992; Davis, Leijenaar, and Oldersma 1991; Witt, Paget and Matthews 1994; Nakano Glenn 1995.

6. See Eisenstein 1985; MacKinnon 1989; Walby 1989; Enloe 1990, 1993; Davis, Leijenaar, and Oldersma 1991; Brown, 1992.

7. This renaissance is generally attributed to efforts to find new answers to questions about men's roles in a rapidly changing industrial economy and the mobilization of women for entry into the economy and politics; see Mosse 1985, 1996; Carnes 1989; Rotundo 1993; Bederman 1995. Leverenz (1989) identifies the beginning of this shift in definitions of manliness, away from a preoccupation with self-restraint and gentlemanliness to a more modern emphasis on competitive individualism, a bit earlier – in the mid-1800s.

8. In her study of the reunification of the US North and South in the decades following the Civil War, Silber (1993) argues that there were distinct northern and southern notions of manhood prior to the war, and that they converged during the masculine renaissance of the late 1800s to create contemporary US normative masculinity. On the eve of the Civil War:

> Southern white men relied on a code which counseled both chivalry and violence, both deferential respect to white womanhood and the forceful passions and energies that shaped their social power. They were men who constantly had to demonstrate their superior strength and force to the surrounding community, whether through dueling, drinking, or gambling. Northern middle-class men, in contrast, lived . . . a 'culture of dignity,' in which institutions figured more prominently than notions of honour and community. These men abhorred many of the vices of southern men and committed themselves to individual self-improvement, to economic responsibility, and most of all to self-control (Silber 1993: 8; see also Adams 1990: 25–6).

This gap in notions of manliness before and during the Civil War was in contrast to a more unified notion of manhood leading up to and culminating in the 1898 Spanish-American War. In that later conflict the combined participation of both northerners and southerners reaffirmed the latter as members of the 'South's return to the patriotic fold' (Silber 1993: 195) and established a common sense of 'manhood' between the two groups of men which represented a blending of northern and southern manly ideals:

> The patriotic propaganda of the Spanish-American War rested on the foundation of the reunited, military patriotism of northerners and southerners, especially the white people of the two regions. Moreover, the new symbolism of reunion also rested on the turn-of-the-century images of invigorated masculinity (ibid.: 196).

Thus, the US marched into the twentieth century armed with a sense of both unified nationhood and unified manhood.

9. See Mernissi 1987; Kandiyoti 1991; McCleod 1991; Moghadam 1991a; Manastra 1993; Massad 1995; Mehdid 1996.

10. Hernes's (1987) analysis of 'Welfare State and Woman Power' suggests these themes represent the feminine and masculine sides of national state politics.

11. Boulding argues that women play a clear role in preparing 'children and men for lifelong combat, whether in the occupation sphere, the civic arena, or the military battlefield' (1977: 167); see also Adams 1990: 131–2 and Vickers 1993: 43–5.

12. Women's observations of men off to war are consistent with male accounts, as illustrated by Vera Brittain's description of her son, Edward's embarkation for World War I in *Testament of Youth*:

He has departed, leaving home laughing, with a delighted sense that he is not to be one of those men who will be branded for life because they have not taken part in the greatest struggle of modern times (Adams 1990: 131).

For a discussion of adventure in paramilitary organizations, see Gibson 1994.

13. Algerian women have paid a high price for their resistance in recent years. Following the suspension of the results of the 1992 elections, whose outcome would have installed a pro-Islamic government, Islamic militants have escalated their armed opposition, and women, particularly those who do not wear the *hijab*, have become targets of their violence:

> Crimes against women included abduction, torture, rape, gang rape and killing, crimes which were common by mid-1995 . . . Feminist, militants, female journalists and teachers are particularly targeted, some of them forced to lead a clandestine life, having to hide from the bullets of the killers and their knives by constantly changing addresses and covering their tracks' (Mehdid 1996: 93–4).

For new accounts of these attacks, see Youssef (1994) and Steinfels (1995). Despite these perils, Hasan (1994: xv) notes that women's interests remain an issue in nationalist debates: 'Forging community identities does not imply or guarantee that women will always identify themselves with or adhere to prevailing religious doctrines which legitimize their subordination'.

14. The seriousness of women's capacity to shame men is reflected in the legal justification for a husband's 'honour killing' of his wife in cases of alleged adultery in Brazil (Thomas 1992).

15. Enloe (1990: 60) argues that waiting is a dangerous strategy:

> Every time women succumb to the pressures to hold their tongue about problems they are having with men in nationalist organizations, nationalism becomes that much more masculinized . . . Women who have called for more genuine equality between the sexes – in the [nationalist] movement, in the home – have been told that now is not the time, the nation is too fragile, the enemy is too near. Women must be patient, they must wait until the nationalist goal is achieved, *then* relations between women and men can be addressed. 'Not now, later' is the advice that rings in the ears of many nationalist women' (ibid.: 62).

Women who press their case face challenges to their loyalty, their sexuality, or to their ethnic or national authenticity: they are either 'carrying water' for colonial oppressors, or they are lesbians, or they are unduly influenced by Western feminism. Third World feminists are quite aware of these charges and share some concerns about the need for an indigenous feminist analysis and agenda; as Delia Aguilar, a Filipino nationalist feminist comments: 'When feminist solidarity networks are today proposed and extended globally, without a firm sense of identity – national, racial and class – we are likely to yield to feminist models designed by and for white, middle-class women in the industrial West and uncritically adopt these as our own' (ibid.: 64); see also Jayawardena (1986, 'Introduction') for a discussion of Third World indigenous feminism.

16. Luszki (1991) documents the role of General Douglas MacArthur in the execution; white American men also 'agreed that black men should be forbidden access to Anglo-Australian women' (Saunders 1995: 187).

17. See Jones (1994: 122ff) for a discussion of the coercion faced by war-wary men in the former Yugoslavia during the 1990s.

FURTHER READING

A powerful case in favour of a reconciliation between liberalism and nationalism has been made by Yael Tamir (1993) in *Liberal Nationalism* (Princeton, NJ: Princeton University Press). This may be complemented by David Miller's (1995) carefully argued *On Nationality* (Oxford: Oxford University Press). Some of the central issues here are also explored by Margaret Canovan (1996) in her *Nationhood and Political Theory* (Cheltenham: Edward Elgar). Earlier studies of the complex and ambiguous Marxist tradition can be found in Ephraim Nimni (1991), *Marxism and Nationalism: Theoretical Origins of the Present Crisis* (London: Pluto) and in Ronaldo Munck (1986), *The Difficult Dialogue: Marxism and Nationalism* (London: Zed). A major contributor to feminist studies of nationalism is Nira Yuval-Davis. See especially her *Gender and Nation* (London: Sage, 1997). A collection of feminist essays across a variety of contexts can be found in *Between Woman and Nation: Nationalisms, Transnational Feminisms, and the State* edited by Caren Kaplan, Norma Alarcon, and Minoo Moallem (Durham, NC: Duke University Press) in 1999.

PART THREE
DIFFERENTIATING NATIONALISM
– NATIONALISM, RACISM,
ETHNICITY

9

ETHNICITY AND NATIONALISM

Thomas Eriksen

THE TERM [ETHNICITY] ITSELF

'Ethnicity seems to be a new term', according to Nathan Glazer and Daniel Moynihan (1975: 1), who point to the fact that the word's earliest dictionary appearance is in the *Oxford English Dictionary* in 1972. Its first usage is attributed to the American sociologist David Riesman in 1953. The word 'ethnic', however, is much older. It is derived from the Greek *ethnos* (which in turn derived from the word *ethnikos*), which originally meant heathen or pagan (Williams 1976: 119). It was used in this sense in English from the mid-fourteenth century until the mid-nineteenth century, when it gradually began to refer to 'racial' characteristics. In the United States, 'ethnics' came to be used around the Second World War as a polite term referring to Jews, Italians, Irish and other people considered inferior to the dominant group of largely British descent. None of the founding fathers of sociology and social anthropology – with the partial exception of Weber – granted ethnicity much attention. In early modern Anglophone sociocultural anthropology, fieldwork ideally took place in a single society and concentrated on particular aspects of its social organisation or culture. British anthropology in the tradition of Radcliffe-Brown or Malinowski, moreover, tended to favour synchronic 'snapshots' of the society under study. With its emphasis on intergroup dynamics, often in the context of a modern state, as well as its frequent insistence on historical depth, ethnicity studies represent a specialisation which was not considered appropriate by the early twentieth-century founders of modern anthropology.

Thomas Eriksen (2002), *Ethnicity and Nationalism*, 2nd ed., London: Pluto Press.

Since the 1960s, ethnic groups and ethnicity have become household words in Anglophone social anthropology, although, as Ronald Cohen (1978) has remarked, few of those who use the terms bother to define them. [. . .] Sometimes, however, heated argument arises as to the nature of the object of inquiry and the appropriate theoretical framework. All of the approaches of anthropology nevertheless agree that ethnicity has something to do with the *classification of people* and *group relationships*.

In everyday language the word ethnicity still has a ring of 'minority issues' and 'race relations', but in social anthropology it refers to aspects of relationships between groups which consider themselves, and are regarded by others, as being culturally distinctive. Although it is true that 'the discourse concerning ethnicity tends to concern itself with subnational units, or minorities of some kind or another' (Chapman *et al.* 1989: 17), majorities and dominant peoples are no less 'ethnic' than minorities.

[. . .]

ETHNICITY, RACE AND NATION

A few words must be said initially about the relationship between ethnicity and 'race'. The term race has deliberately been placed within inverted commas in order to stress that it has dubious descriptive value. Whereas it was for some time fashionable to divide humanity into four main races, modern genetics tends not to speak of races. There are two principal reasons for this. First, there has always been so much interbreeding between human populations that it would be meaningless to talk of fixed boundaries between races. Second, the distribution of hereditary physical traits does not follow clear boundaries (Cavalli-Sforza *et al.* 1994). In other words, there is often greater variation within a 'racial' group than there is systematic variation between two groups. Thirdly, no serious scholar today believes that hereditary characteristics explain cultural variations. The contemporary neo-Darwinist views in social science often lumped together under the heading 'evolutionary psychology' (Barkow *et al.* 1992), are with few if any exceptions strongly universalist; they argue that people everywhere have the same inborn abilities.

Concepts of race can nevertheless be relevant to the extent that they inform people's actions: at this level, race exists as a cultural construct, whether it has a 'biological' reality or not (cf. also Jenkins 1997: 22). Racism, obviously, builds on the assumption that personality is somehow linked with hereditary characteristics which differ systematically between 'races', and in this way race may assume sociological importance even if it has no 'objective' existence. Social scientists who study race relations in Great Britain and the United States need not themselves believe in the objective existence of racial difference, since their object of study is the social and cultural relevance of the *notion* that race exists, in other words the social construction of race. If influential people in a society had developed a similar theory about the hereditary personality traits of red-haired people, and if that theory gained social and cultural significance, 'redhead studies' would for similar reasons have become a field of academic research, even if the researchers themselves did not agree that redheads were different from others in a relevant way. In societies where ideas of race are important, they must therefore be studied as part of local discourses on ethnicity.

Should the study of race relations, in this meaning of the word, be distinguished from the study of ethnicity or ethnic relations? Pierre van den Berghe (1983) does not think so, but would rather regard 'race' relations as a special case of ethnicity. Others, among them Michael Banton (1967), have argued the need to distinguish between race and ethnicity. In Banton's view, race refers to the (negative) categorisation of people, while ethnicity has to do with (positive) group identification. He argues that ethnicity is generally more concerned with the identification of 'us', while racism is more oriented to the categorisation of 'them' (Banton 1983: 106; cf. Jenkins 1986: 177). This implies that race is a negative term of exclusion, while ethnic identity is a term of positive inclusion. However, ethnicity can assume many forms, and since ethnic ideologies tend to stress common descent among their members, the distinction between race and ethnicity is a problematic one, even if Banton's distinction between groups and categories can be useful. Nobody would suggest that the horrors of Yugoslavia and Rwanda in the 1990s were racial, but they were certainly ethnic – in other words, there is no inherent reason why ethnicity should be more benign than race. Besides, the boundaries between race and ethnicity tend to be blurred, since ethnic groups have a common myth of origin, which relates ethnicity to descent, which again makes it a kindred concept to race. It could moreover be argued that some 'racial' groups are ethnified, such as American blacks who have gradually come to be known as African-Americans; but also that some ethnic groups are racialised, as when immutable traits are accorded to ethnic minorities: and finally, there are strong tendencies towards the ethnification of certain religious groups, such as European Muslims. Formerly known by their ethnic origin, they are increasingly lumped together as primarily 'Muslims'. Finally, Martin Barker's notion of *new racism* (Barker 1981; cf. also Fenton 1999, chapter 2) seems to explode the analytical usefulness of the distinction. The new racism talks of cultural difference instead of inherited characteristics, but uses it for the same purposes; to justify a hierarchical ordering of groups in society.

I shall not in the following distinguish between race relations and ethnicity. Ideas of 'race' may or may not form part of ethnic ideologies, and their presence or absence does not generally seem to be a decisive factor in interethnic relations. Now, it could be argued that the main divisive mechanism of US society is race as opposed to ethnicity; but on the other hand, the main divisive mechanism of Indian society may be said to be religion as opposed to race (or, for that matter, ethnicity). Discrimination on ethnic grounds is spoken of as 'racism' in Trinidad and as 'communalism' in Mauritius (Eriksen 1992), but the forms of imputed discrimination referred to can be nearly identical. On the other hand, it is doubtless true that groups who 'look different' from majorities or dominating groups may be less liable to become assimilated into the majority than others, and that it can be difficult for them to escape from their ethnic identity if they wish to. However, this may also hold good for minority groups with, say, an inadequate command of the dominant language. In both cases, their ethnic identity becomes an imperative status, an ascribed aspect of their personhood from which they cannot escape entirely. Race or skin colour as such is not the decisive variable in every society.

The relationship between the terms ethnicity and nationality is nearly as complex as that between ethnicity and race. Like the words ethnic and race, the word nation has a long history (Williams 1976: 213–14) and has been used with a variety of different meanings in English. We shall refrain from discussing these meanings here, and will concentrate on the sense in which nation and nationalism are used analytically in academic discourse. Like ethnic ideologies, nationalism stresses the cultural similarity of its adherents and, by implication, it draws boundaries vis-à-vis others, who thereby become outsiders. The distinguishing mark of nationalism is by definition its relationship to the state. A nationalist holds that political boundaries should be coterminous with cultural boundaries, whereas many ethnic groups do not demand command over a state. When the political leaders of an ethnic movement make demands to this effect, the ethnic movement therefore by definition becomes a nationalist movement. Although nationalisms tend to be ethnic in character, this is not necessarily the case.

[. . .]

NATIONALISM AND THE OTHER

Like other ethnic identities, national identities are constituted in relation to *others*: the very idea of the nation presupposes that there are other nations, or at least other peoples, who are not members of the nation. Nationalist dichotomisation may take many forms; it could well be argued that the main structural condition for chauvinist nationalism in our day and age is competition between nation-states on the world market. Although there have been many wars between nation-states, such wars have been comparatively rare since 1945. Instead, we may perhaps regard international sports as the most important form of metaphoric war between nation-states – containing, perhaps, most of the identity-building features of warfare and few of the violent, destructive ones (cf. MacClancy 1996; Archetti 1999). Nonetheless, boundary maintenance and ethnic dichotomisation may still take violent forms in many parts of the world, and this also holds good for a number of ethnic nationalisms, for example in Sri Lanka.

In his analysis of Sinhalese national symbolism, Kapferer (1988) links state power, nationalist ideology and the Sinhalese-Tamil conflict with the role of Sinhalese myth in cosmology and in everyday life. Important myths, recorded in the ancient Sinhalese chronicle of the *Mahavamsa*, are the Vijaya and Dutu-gemunu legends. The Vijaya myth, the main Sinhalese myth of origin, tells of a prince who arrives from India and slaughters a great number of demons in order to conquer Sri Lanka. The Dutugemunu myth, set at a later historical period, tells of a Sinhalese leader under whose military guidance the people rids itself of a foreign overlord. Later, he conquers the Tamils.

In Sinhalese political discourse, these myths are frequently 'treated as historical fact or as having foundation in fact' (Kapferer 1988: 35). Sinhalese dominance in the Sri Lankan state, including dominance over the Tamil minority, is justified by referring to the *Mahavamsa*, which is so interpreted as to state that the Sinhalese and the Tamils have the same origins, but are now two nations, with the Sinhalese as the dominant one. The myths thus form an important element in the justification of Sinhalese nationalism. Tamils produce contradictory interpretations of the myths, which are thus actively used in reconstruction of the past aimed at justifying present political projects.

Kapferer is particularly concerned with violence and the interpenetration of lived experience, myth and state power. When he analyses the ethnic riots of the early 1980s, he finds that 'the demonic passions of the rioting were fuelled in a Sinhalese Buddhist nationalism that involved cosmological arguments similar to those in exorcism, particularly in the rites of sorcery' (Kapferer 1988: 29). The human-demon dualism and other – frequently violent – aspects of myth were transferred to a nationalist ideology justifying Sinhalese hegemony and violence against Tamils.

According to many nationalist myths, the nation is born, or arises, from a painful rite of passage where it has to fight its adversaries; the Other or the enemy within. Re-enactment of that violence, as in Sri Lanka, can be justified by referring to such myths, which form part of a 'cosmic logic' or ontology through which the Sinhalese experience the world (Kapferer 1988: 79). This cosmic logic, where evil plays an important part, is congruent with the current ethnic hostilities and serves as a rationalisation for the use of force.

Kapferer's argument is complex and cannot be reproduced in full here. It may not be correct that violence is a more or less universal feature of nationalist imagery, but his analysis is consistent with the perspective on ethnicity and nationalism developed in this book. He shows the importance of the Other in the formation of ethnic identity and illuminates the mediating role of symbols in ethnic ideologies. They must simultaneously justify a power structure *and* give profound meaning to people's experience in order to motivate them to give personal sacrifices for the nation. Finally, Kapferer shows how the potential power of ethnic identifications is increased manifold when an ethnic identity is linked with a modern state – when ethnicity becomes nationalism. My descriptions of nationalism as a metaphoric kinship ideology and (from peaceful Québec) the depiction of the nation as a human organism, are perhaps too weak in this context. In relation to Sinhalese nationalism, appropriate metaphors may rather be war, birth and death. However, the peaceful Québécois nationalism and the violent Sinhalese one share certain features: both refer to the past and to assumptions of shared culture in imagining their abstract communities. In other regards, of course, they may not be comparable, since the Québécois are separatist and the Sinhalese are not. In Kapferer's words:

> The organizing and integrating potential of ideology, the propensity of certain ideological formations to unify, to embrace persons of varying and perhaps opposed political and social interests, and to engage them in concerted, directed action, may owe much to the logic of an ontology that the ideology inscribes . . . Ideology can engage a person in a fundamental and what may be experienced as a 'primordial' way. And so the passions are fired and people may burn. (Kapferer 1988: 83)

Kapferer's analysis of Sri Lankan nationalism focuses on the enactment of boundary mechanisms at different interrelated levels; symbolic, practical and political. He argues that nationalisms must be studied in a truly comparative spirit, and shows that Sinhalese nationalism is qualitatively different from European nationalisms because the societies differ. Notably, he argues that it is hierarchical in nature and not inherently egalitarian. Nevertheless, Kapferer's study is consistent with the theoretical framework on ethnic organisation and identity developed [earlier] as well as the theory of nationalism which stresses the link between ethnicity and the state.

THE PROBLEM OF IDENTITY BOUNDARIES

Problems of identity and problems of boundary maintenance have usually been studied in relation to minorities or otherwise 'threatened' or 'weak' groups, or in situations of rapid social change. It seems to have been an implicit assumption that identity processes and the maintenance of identity are unproblematic in dominant groups. 'Majority identities', Diana Forsythe writes (1989: 137), '. . . appear as they are seen from without, seeming . . . to be strong and secure, if not outright aggressive. Certainly this is how Germanness is perceived in many parts of Europe.'

Forsythe's research on German identity indicates that this central and powerful identity – considered by many as *the* dominant national identity in Europe'[1] – is characterised by anomalies, fuzzy boundaries and ambiguous criteria for belongingness. First of all, it is unclear *where* Germany is. Although both the inhabitants of the Federal Republic and the GDR are clearly German (Forsythe's article was written before the reunification), they fail to unite the nation in a nation-state. Not all West Germans would include the GDR as *Inland*. Even after reunification, the distinction between *Wessies* and *Ossies* is a salient one, which refers to economic as well as to imputed cultural differences. Further, many Germans would include the areas lost to Poland and the former USSR during the Second World War as German.

Second, it is difficult to justify the existence of the German nation by referring to history. With the Nazi period (1933–45) in mind. Forsythe writes (1989: 138): 'The German past is not one that lends itself comfortably to nostalgia, nor is it well-suited to serve as a charter for nationalists' dreams for the future.'

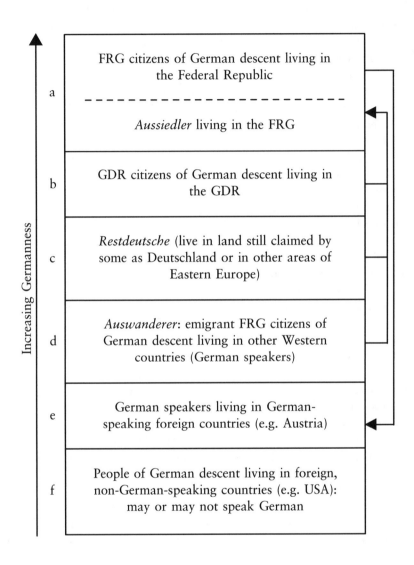

Source: Forsythe 1989: 146.

Figure 9.1: Degrees of Germanness according to emic categories

Third, more or less as a consequence, it is difficult to state what it means to be German in cultural terms. Pride in national identity has positively been discouraged since the Second World War, as many 'typical' aspects of German culture were associated with Nazism (cf. Dumont 1992, for a controversial cultural–historical analysis of German national identity).

Fourth, and this is the issue which is of particular concern here, the question of *who is German* turns out to be a complicated one. In principle, 'the universe is divided into the theoretically exhaustive and mutually exclusive categories of *Deutsche* (Germans) and *Ausländer* (foreigners)' (Forsythe 1989: 143). In practice, there are nevertheless difficult problems associated with the delineation of boundaries. The criterion for Germanness, as applied by ordinary Germans, can be either language or 'a mixture compounded of appearance, family background, country of residence, and country of origin' (*ibid.*) A certain number of foreigners are included in both definitions of Germanness, and the latter especially is quite inaccurate. Austrians and the majority of Swiss are German-speakers, but do not live in a German state. On the other hand, millions of people of German descent, who may or may not actually speak German, live in Central and Eastern Europe.[2] These, as well as other emigrants, fall into different categories (see Figure 10.1).

The category *Ausländer* (foreign) presents similar problems, and it transpires that the Dutch and Scandinavians are considered much 'less foreign' than Turks and Jews.

These anomalies, while they pose specific problems to German identity, are general and widespread. Such problems highlight the lack of congruence between ideal models or ideologies and that social reality to which they ostensibly refer. Nationalist and other ethnic ideologies hold that social and cultural boundaries should be unambiguous, clear-cut and 'digital' or binary. They should also be congruous with spatial, political boundaries. This, as we have seen, is an ideal which is very difficult to uphold in practice. Some violent nationalisms may try to eradicate the anomalies: such was the case of Nazism, where millions of members of so-called lower races occupying parts of German territory were killed or forced to emigrate; and more recently, Europeans and Africans alike have witnessed 'ethnic cleansing' in ex-Yugoslavia and Rwanda. In most cases, however, complex realities are coped with more gracefully. We should here keep in mind that there is never a perfect fit between an ideology and the social reality it is about, since an ideology is a kind of theory – like a map – which necessarily simplifies the concrete.

German identity, although ideally solid, digital and well demarcated, functions in an *analog* way on the ground: differences of degree are made relevant in the classification of others even when the classificatory system in theory requires clear dichotomisation. It is possible to be 'somewhat German' or 'not really foreign'. German identity seems to have frontiers, but no boundaries (cf. Cohen 1994). Perhaps official nationalist ideologies tend to be more concerned with clear-cut, unambiguous boundaries than other ethnic ideologies. An explanation for this could be that nations are territorial and political units with an inherent need to divide others into insiders and outsiders on the basis of citizenship. Cultural similarity among citizens becomes a political programme vested in the state. In this way, official national identities may, generally speaking, be more comprehensive and may place greater demands on the individual than ethnic identities in a polyethnic society, which are rarely sanctioned through state institutions. However, as the German example shows, popular perceptions of Germanness are more fine-grained and less unambiguous than the formal nationalism of the state would imply. The difference between dominant and popular discourses is thus evident not merely in the contrast between state nationalism and non-state ethnicity, but also in the contrast between state/formal and popular/informal nationalism (Banks 1996: 155; Baumann 1996; Eriksen 1993a).

As the above examples indicate, although it may be correct to talk of *a* general theory of nationalism, nationalisms on the ground are quite different from each other. So far, all of the nationalisms considered have been clearly ethnic in character. Sinhalese nationalism acknowledges the presence of Sri Lankan Tamils as a distinctive ethnic group, but places them in a subservient relationship to the Sinhalese. We shall therefore round off [. . .] by considering the possibility of a kind of nationalism which is *not* based on ethnicity.

NATIONALISM WITHOUT ETHNICITY?

So-called plural or polyethnic societies have often been described as deeply divided societies marked by perennial conflict and competition between discrete ethnic groups Smith 1965; Horowitz 1985). Although this view may in some cases be relevant, we have argued against it for too strongly focusing on conflict and group boundaries, at the cost of underestimating cooperation, identity formation along non-ethnic lines, and cultural integration. Mauritius is often regarded as a typical plural society (Benedict 1965); here, I shall approach it from a different perspective, focusing on shared meaning rather than group competition.

There are two complementary trends in Mauritian nationalism, and both, of them are ostensibly non-ethnic in character (Eriksen 1988, 1992, 1993b, 1998). First, the Mauritian nation may be depicted as identical with the 'mosaic of cultures' reified in the identity politics of the island. Typical expressions of this view of the nation are the cultural shows organised annually in connection with Independence Day (Republic Day as from 1992). At these shows, every main ethnic category is invited to present a 'typical' song or dance from its cultural repertoire. The Sino-Mauritians are always present with a dragon of some kind. Hindus sing Indian film songs or play sitar music, and the Creoles are always represented with a *séga* (a song form associated with the Creoles). In this way, the nation is imagined as a mosaic. This trend, which we may label 'multiculturalism', is also evident in the national mass media, where every group is represented through specific radio and TV programmes, and in the educational system, where pupils may learn their 'ancestral languages' as a foreign language.

The other main trend in Mauritian nationalism depicts the nation as a supra-ethnic or non-ethnic community, which encompasses or transcends ethnicity rather than endorsing it. The flag, the national anthem and the national language express such a nationalism. The national language of Mauritius is English, which is no one ethnic group's ancestral language or currently spoken language – and which therefore seems an appropriate choice as a supra-ethnic compromise (Eriksen 1990). Colonial symbols, which cannot be associated with a particular ethnic group, are also dominant. Formal equality and equal opportunities are emphasised.

The Mauritian situation is more complex than this outline suggests. There is some ethnic tension, and there are conflicts between national and ethnic identifications. Many post-colonial states are faced with similar problems to those of Mauritius. They are obviously constructions of recent origins. When Immanuel Wallerstein asks, rhetorically, 'Does India exist?' (Wallerstein 1991), he must therefore answer no – or at least, that it did not exist prior to colonisation. Many such states, particularly in Africa, had no pre-colonial state that could be revived, and the great majority of these states are polyethnic although it is true, as Banks (1996: 157) states, that in many cases, they are dominated by one ethnic group. Nevertheless, two points have to be made here. First, the only African state to have collapsed institutionally in the postcolonial era, Somalia, is/was also one of the few mono-ethnic ones. In other words, shared ethnic identity is not sufficient to build nationhood. Second, in most polyethnic states, some degree of compromise is needed, and some degree of supra-ethnic symbolism is required – if only to avoid riots and unrest. To depict the nation as identical with a 'mosaic of ethnic groups' could, at the same time, threaten to undermine the project of nation-building since it focuses on differences instead of similarities.

In a discussion of this section as it appeared in the first edition of this book, Banks (1996: 154–9) expresses serious doubt as to the notion of non-ethnic nations which 'bypass any local ethnicities' (ibid.: 158). Instead, he argues that 'all nationalisms, once state control is achieved, actively seeks both to enhance and reify the specifically ethnic identities of deviant others within the nation state, and at the same time to efface the idea of ethnic particularism within the national identity' (ibid.). His view is, in other words, that nations tend to be dominated by ethnic groups which deny their ethnic identity (instead presenting themselves simply as citizens or humans) and relegate others to minority status or assimilate them. This is an important argument, and symbolic domination frequently works this way. For example, male domination often expresses itself through the tacit assumption that 'humans' are 'men' (witnessed in statements, common in classic anthropology, like 'the X'es allow their women to work outside the home'). The stereotype of the 'American' is typically a white man, and so on. I am nevertheless not convinced of the general applicability of this logic. In Trinidad & Tobago, the dominant group has, since Independence, been the Afro-Trinidadians, and it could well be argued that Indo-Trinidadians have been exoticised as a minority – however, since the mid-1990s, an Indo-Trinidadian has been Prime Minister of the country, and Indo-Trinidadians are appropriating and adapting symbols of Afroness such as the steelband and even the calypso. The boundaries are becoming blurred, and the terms of discursive hegemony are becoming unclear. In the USA, the traditional hegemony of the WASPs is, if anything, being challenged from a number of directions: the anxieties and debates concerning multicultural education are a case in point; the majority of US Nobel laureates are often Jews; the current (2002) Secretary of State is black; and one of the foremost defenders of the American societal model, Francis Fukuyama, is of Japanese descent. Tony Blair's 'Cool Britannia' also tends to be much more variegated in terms of physical appearance and cultural image than its predecessors. Now, I am not saying that the ethnic element in nationhood is about to go away due to globalisation and eradication of 'radical cultural difference', only that there is no *necessary* link between national identity and ethnic identity.

Let us leave this debate for now, and instead see how some of the insights developed earlier may shed light on the Mauritian situation. From the study of ethnic processes on the interpersonal level – from the early Copperbelt studies onwards – we know that identities are negotiable and situational. From the Barthian emphasis on boundary processes and later studies of identity boundaries, we also know that the selection of boundary markers is arbitrary in the sense that only some features of culture are singled out and defined as crucial in boundary processes. Just as the potential number of nations is much larger than the actual number, the number of ethnic groups in the world is potentially infinite. From recent studies of nationalism, finally, we have learnt that the relationship between cultural practices and reified culture is not a simple one, and that ideologists always select and reinterpret aspects of culture and history which fit into the legitimation of a particular power constellation.

On the basis of these theoretical insights, it is possible to draw the conclusion that Mauritian nationalism may represent an attempt to create a nation in the conventional sense; that Mauritian society is currently at an early stage of the ethnogenesis of a nation. The invention of a shared history for all the ethnic groups of the island is under way, and it has been suggested (Eriksen 1993c) that a plausible 'myth of origin' for the nation could be the last ethnic riot, in 1967–68, the 'riot to end all riots'. The homogenisation of cultural practices has gone very far, due to rapid industrialisation and capitalist integration, and by now the vast majority of Mauritians speaks the same language at home (*Kreol*, a French-lexicon creole). As an increasing part of the individual's life is determined by his or her performance in the anonymous labour market, the supra-ethnic variety of national identity may eventually replace obsolete ethnic identities.

On the other hand, a principal lesson from ethnicity studies is that doomed ethnic categories tend to re-emerge, often with unprecedented force. An often mentioned example from Europe is that of the Celts, who have been 'perennially vanishing' for a thousand years. In the USA, occasionally mentioned as a non-ethnic nation, hyphenated identities and ethnic identity politics are perhaps more important than ever at the beginning of the twenty-first century. Referring to 'primordial' values, such identifications remain capable of mobilising people – years after the social contexts where these values were enacted had vanished. And in Mauritius itself, thirty years after 'the last ethnic riot', ethnic violence briefly erupted again in February 1999, following the unexplained death, in police custody, of a popular Creole singer. Mauritius may nonetheless remain a prosperous, stable and democratic society based on a plurality of ethnic identities which are compatible with national identity – and this is also a possible outcome of the ongoing process of transformation.

Nations are not necessarily more static than ethnic groups. Moreover, as suggested above, multi-ethnic nations may be effectively redefined historically, in order to accommodate rights claims from groups who have felt excluded from the core of the nation. In an intriguing comparison between the USA, Canada and Australia, John Hutchinson (1994) shows how the symbolism and official identities of these three 'New World' countries have been refashioned during the last decades of the twentieth century. He analyses a major com-memorative event in each country: the centenary of the federal Canadian state (1967), the Bicentenary of the Declaration of Independence in the USA (1976), and the Bicentenary of the settlement in Australia by Europeans (1988). In all three cases, the authorities had envisioned a consolidation of a homogeneous white national identity; and in all three cases, the national celebrations led to widespread contestation of the terms in which nationhood was framed. In Canada, the centenary marked the beginning of Québécois secessionism; in the USA, various minority activists demonstrated noisily; and in Australia, Abor-igines in particular were strongly against the celebrations, declaring 'a national year of mourning' (Hutchinson 1994: 170). Interestingly, all three countries have since embarked on official redefinitions of nationhood, now presenting themselves to the outside world as 'multicultural societies' rather than white ones. If one accepts that national identity does not have to be founded in common ethnic origins, the disruptions and conflicts surrounding the rituals may actually have strengthened national cohesion by making a wider participa-tion possible.

NATIONALISM AND ETHNICITY RECONSIDERED

Nationalism and ethnicity are kindred concepts, and the majority of nation-alisms are ethnic in character. The distinction between nationalism and ethnicity as analytical concepts is a simple one, if we stick to the formal level of definitions. A nationalist ideology is an ethnic ideology which demands a state on behalf of the ethnic group. However, in practice the distinction can be highly problematic.

First, nationalism may sometimes express a polyethnic or supra-ethnic ideology which stresses shared civil rights rather than shared cultural roots. That would be the case in many African countries as well as in Mauritius, where no ethnic group openly tries to turn nation-building into an ethnic project on its own behalf. A distinction between ethnic nationalisms and polyethnic or supra-ethnic nationalisms could be relevant here.

Second, certain categories of people may find themselves in a grey zone between nation and ethnic category. If some of their members want full political independence, others limit their demands to linguistic and other rights within an existing state. It depends on the interlocutor whether the category is a nation or an ethnic group. Moreover, national and ethnic membership can change situationally. A Mexican in the United States belongs to an ethnic group, but belongs to a nation when he or she returns to Mexico. Such designations are not politically innocent. Whereas the proponents of an independent Punjabi state (Khalistan) describe themselves as a nation, the Indian government sees them as ethnic rebels. Our terrorists are their freedom fighters.

Third, in the mass media and in casual conversation the terms are not used consistently. When, regarding the former Soviet Union, one spoke of the '104 nations' comprising the union, this term referred to ethnic groups. Only a handful of them were nations to the extent that their leaders wanted full independence.

In societies where nationalism above all is presented as an impartial and universalistic ideology based on bureaucratic principles of justice, ethnicity and ethnic organisation may appear as threats against national cohesion, justice and the state. This tension may appear as a conflict between *particularist* and *universalist* moralities. In these polyethnic societies, nationalism is frequently presented as a supra-ethnic ideology guaranteeing formal justice and equal rights for everybody. Typically, nationalist rhetoric stressing equality for all belongs to the political left in these societies, such as in Mauritius and South Africa.

A different kind of conflict between ethnicity and nationalism, which is perhaps more true to the conventional meaning of the term nationalism, can be described as a conflict between a dominating and a dominated ethnic group within the framework of a modern nation-state. In such contexts, the nationalist ideology of the hegemonic group will be perceived as a particularist ideology rather than a universalist one, where the mechanisms of exclusion and ethnic discrimination are more obvious than the mechanisms of inclusion and formal justice. This kind of duality, or ambiguity, is fundamental to nationalist ideology (Eriksen 1991).

This duality of nationalism has been described as 'the Janus face of nationalism' (Nairn 1977, part 3). A conflict between ethnicity and nationalism is evident, for example, in the case of the relationship between the Bretons and the French state. This kind of situation is characteristic of the contemporary world, where states tend to be dominated politically by one of the constituent ethnic groups (cf. Connor, 1978) or, more accurately, by its elites.

Notes

1. This is perhaps particularly true after reunification in 1990, when Germany suddenly became much bigger in terms of population, and geographically even more central, than the other large European countries.
2. The foreign policy spokesman for the German Social Democratic Party stated, at a public lecture in 1992, that 'there are six million Germans living in the former Soviet Union'.

10

BETWEEN CAMPS

Paul Gilroy

Modernity and infrahumanity

[. . .]

Nations, encampments, and fascism

As the example of Martinique makes clear, fascism's militarism and fraternalism changed the character of its national communities. However, the transformation of European nation-states into martial camps did not always coincide with the rise of fascism as a distinctive political and cultural technology. That process of consolidation and authoritarian reintegration should not be identified exclusively with the exceptional patterns exhibited where fascists triumphed. Colonial domination suggests that this process had a longer history and a more general significance. The nationalization, rationalization, and militarization of government communicated not only the entrance of 'race' into the operations of modern political culture but also the confluence of 'race' and nation in the service of authoritarian ends.

It should be apparent that modern nation-states have sometimes constituted camps in a straightforward descriptive sense. The organized work of disciplining and training citizens has had to coexist with less formal, involutionary complexes in which the fantastic idea of transmuting heterogeneity into homogeneity could be implemented and amplified outward as well as inward. Where 'race' and nation became closely articulated, with each order of discourse

---

Paul Gilroy (2000), *Against Race: Imagining Political Culture beyond the Color Line*, Cambridge, MA: Belknap Press.

conferring important legitimation on the other, the national principle can be recognized as having formed an important bond between different and even opposing nationalisms. The dominant varieties were bound to the subordinate by their shared notions of what nationality entailed. The forms of nationalism that invoke this mode of belonging exemplify camp-thinking. They have distinctive rules and codes, and however bitterly their various practitioners may conflict with each other, a common approach to the problem of collective solidarity is betrayed by shared patterns of thought about self and other, friend and stranger; about culture and nature as binding agents and about the technological institution of political collectivities to which one can be compelled to belong.

The recurrence of unexpected connections between avowedly sworn foes defines one axis of 'race' politics in the twentieth century. What is more properly termed the (anti-)politics of 'race' is deeply implicated in the institution of these national camps and the emergence of nationalized statecraft as an alternative to the traditional conceptions of political activity. Politics is reconceptualized and reconstituted as a dualistic conflict between friends and enemies. At its worst, citizenship degenerates into soldiery and the political imagination is entirely militarized. The exaltation of war and spontaneity, the cults of fraternity, youth, and violence, the explicitly antimodern sacralization of the political sphere, and its colonization by civil religion involving uniforms, flags, and mass spectacles, all underline that these camps are fundamentally martial phenomena. They are armed and protected spaces that offer, at best, only a temporary break in unforgiving motion toward the next demanding phase of active conflict.

Marx and Engels appropriated this idea of political solidarity in opposition to the power of nation-states when, at the start of *The Communist Manifesto*, they described the world they saw progressively divided 'into two great hostile camps . . . facing each other.' The class-based identification of the countryless proletarians was thus also a matter of camp-thinking – a mode of solidarity so powerful that it broke the historic allegiance of their universal class, industrial workers, to its respective national bourgeoisies. They saw antagonistic social forces more profound than those of the nation constituted in this distinctive arrangement. It would be foolish to deny that the internal organization of class consciousness and class struggle can also foster what Alexander Kluge and Oscar Negt, in their discussion of the history of the proletarian public sphere, call a 'camp mentality.' They contrast the oppositional but nonetheless anti-democratic moods fostered in the sealed-off space of the class-based camp with the openness that a living public culture can accumulate even in the most beleaguered circumstances. Although Kluge's and Negt's concerns differ from mine in that they are directed toward histories of class and party as sources of camp-thinking, it should be obvious that the solidarity of the camp can be constituted and fortified around dimensions of division other than class.

The camp mentalities constituted by appeals to 'race,' nation, and ethnic difference, by the lore of blood, bodies, and fantasies of absolute cultural identity, have several additional properties. They work through appeals to the value of national or ethnic purity. Their biopolitical potency immediately raises questions of prophylaxis and hygiene, 'as if the (social) body had to assure itself of its own identity by expelling waste matter.'[1] They incite the regulation of fertility even more readily than they command the labor power of their affiliates. Where the nation is a kin group supposedly composed of uniform and interchangeable family groups, the bodies of women provide the favored testing grounds for the principles of obligation, deference, and duty that the camp/nation demands. The debates about immigration and nationality that continually surface in contemporary European politics have regularly presented the intrusions of blacks, Moslems, and other interlopers as an invasion. They can be used to illustrate each of these unsavory features.

Though it may produce spectacular results, the camp mentality of the nationalists is betrayed by its crude theories of culture and might even be defined by the veneration of homogeneity, purity, and unanimity that it fosters. Inside the nation's fortifications, culture is required to assume an artificial texture and an impossibly even consistency. The national camp puts an end to any sense of cultural development. Culture as process is arrested. Petrified and sterile, it is impoverished by the national obligation not to change but to recycle the past continually in an essentially unmodified mythic form. Tradition is reduced to simple repetition.

In his unwholesome nineteenth-century raciological inquiry into the meaning of nationality, Ernst Renan famously argued that there was an active contradiction between the demands of nation-building and those of authentic historical study. The nation and its new temporal order involved, for him, socialized forms of forgetting and historical error. These can be identified as further symptoms of the camp mentality. An orchestrated and enforced amnesia supplies the best climate in which the national camp's principles of belonging and solidarity become attractive and powerful. We will see [. . .] that the national camp demands the negation of diaspora not least because the latter places a premium on commemorative work. The diaspora opposes the camp where it becomes comfortable in the in-between locations that camp-thinking deprives of any significance.

For the members of the ethnic, national, or racial camp, chronic conflict, a war in the background, latent as well as manifest hostility, can legitimize stern patterns of discipline, authority, and deference. The camp always operates under martial rules. Even if its ideologues speak the language of organic wholeness, it is stubbornly a place of seriality and mechanical solidarity. As it moves toward the totalitarian condition of permanent emergency, the camp is shaped by the terrifying sense that anything is possible.

Deliberately adopting a position between camps of this sort is not a sign of indecision or equivocation. It is a timely choice. It can [. . .] be a positive orientation against the patterns of authority, government, and conflict that characterize modernity's geometry of power. It can also promote a rich theoretical understanding of culture as a mutable and traveling phenomenon.

Of course, occupying a space between camps means also that there is danger of encountering hostility from both sides, of being caught in the pincers of camp-thinking. Responding to this perilous predicament involves rethinking the practice of politics that is always debased where the nation-state operates under camp rules. We are immediately required to move outside the frustrating binary categories we have inherited: left and right, racist and antiracist. We need analyses that are alive to the fluidity and contingency of a situation that seems to lack precedents. If we are to operate in these new circumstances, it helps to approach the problem of encampment from another angle, not as a means to comprehend the geopolitical interrelation of space, identity, and power with modern raciology, but as emblematic sociological and historical features of a volatile period.

I have already identified these national camps as locations in which particular versions of solidarity, belonging, kinship, and identity have been devised, practiced, and policed. Now I want to turn away from the camp as a *metaphor* for the pathologies of 'race' and nation and move toward reflection upon actual camps and the political and cultural logics that produced them. These camps were and are a political technology – concrete institutions of radical evil, useless suffering, and modern misery – rather than odious, if somehow routine, expressions of the bad habits of power. To identify a connection between these very different kinds of camp – in effect between levels of racism and nationalism regarded as normal and the exceptional state represented by genocidal fascisms – may be dismissed as oversimple, even far-fetched. In recent British history, nationalism has sometimes been part of the best populist responses to the menacing neo-fascisms that have been exposed as alien and unpatriotic. Many writers, including Hannah Arendt, have also counterposed the stable juridical institutions of the nation-state to the anarchy and violence of the colonies where raciology was first codified and institutionalized as a principle of government. However, I want to invoke a different case for the value of that linkage. This orientation is today supported by the bewildering tangles of recent postcolonial and postimperial history.[2] It is also a perspective that, as Aimé Césaire made clear long ago, went provocatively to the bottom of the relationship between civilization and barbarism. Its general message is certainly confirmed, for example, in the recent history of Rwanda, where, in conjunction with modern cultural technologies, the civilizing mission of colonial power hardened pre-colonial conflicts into full-fledged ethnic absolutism fueled equally by the imperatives of raciology and francophony. There, too, the emergence of camp-thinking, militaristic, camp-style nationality, and encamped ethnicity – the key features of the first kind of camps – have been implicated in the institution of camps of the second variety: first genocidal death spaces in which victims were assembled and then, bewilderingly, the refugee camps in which yesterday's killers became victims and reached out to seek aid and compassion.

Understanding this situation entails more than just seeing camps as epiphanies of catastrophic modernity and focusing on the extensive colonial precedents for genocidal killing in Europe. It necessitates recognizing our own postmodern predicament: we are caught not only between national camps but amid the uncertainties and anxieties that the condition of permanent emergency associated with the second type of camp both feeds on and creates. Drawing upon his own memories of suffering as he moved toward eloquent demands for justice, Primo Levi wisely recommended exactly this reorientation. He presents it most clearly at the conclusion of his reflections on the role of the collaborators and other victims of Nazi violence whose persecutors made them complicit in their own destruction and the destruction of their kin and their communities. Facing these recurrent abominations, Levi suggests that this stance should now be part of what it means to adopt a healthy and alert, properly ethical attitude amid chronically corrupting circumstances:

> The fever of our western civilisation that 'descends into hell with trumpets and drums,' and its miserable adornments are the distorting image of our symbols of social prestige . . . we . . . are so dazzled by power and prestige as to forget our essential fragility: willingly or not we come to terms with power, forgetting that we are all in the ghetto, that the ghetto is walled in, that outside the ghetto reign the lords of death and that close by the train is waiting.[3]

Levi's argument should not be an open license to indulge in paranoia. It loses none of its force when we appreciate that the trains are not necessarily being loaded right now in our own neighborhoods. Fascism is not permanently on the brink of assuming terroristic governmental power. His point is far more subtle. If we wish to live a good life and enjoy just relations with our fellows, our conduct must be closely guided not just by this terrible history but by the knowledge that these awful possibilities are always much closer than we like to imagine. To prevent their reappearance, we must dwell on them and with them, for they have become an essential moral resource: a compass sensitive to the demanding, individualizing, anti-ethical field of postmodernity. Levi's shocking insight is compounded by the fact that there are no more acceptable excuses for the failure to become completely familiar with the institutional life of camps. We do not have to become inmates to appreciate that their testimony calls out to us and we must answer it. This means being alive to the camps out there now and the camps around the corner, the camps that are being prepared.
[. . .]

Identity, belonging, and the critique of pure sameness

When first he opens his eyes, an infant ought to see the fatherland, and up to the day of his death he ought never to see anything else. Every true republican has drunk in love of country, that is to say love of law and liberty, along with his mother's milk. This love is his whole existence; he sees nothing but the fatherland, he lives for it alone; when he is solitary, he is nothing; when he has ceased to have a fatherland, he no longer exists; and if he is not dead, he is worse than dead.

–Rousseau

If things aren't going too well in contemporary thought, it's because there's a return . . . to abstractions, back to the problem of origins, all that sort of thing . . . Any analysis in terms of movements, vectors, is blocked. We're in a very weak phase, a period of reaction. Yet philosophy thought that it had done with the problem of origins. It was no longer a question of starting or finishing. The question was rather, what happens 'in between'?

–Gilles Deleuze

We have seen that the uncertain and divided world we inhabit has made racial identity matter in novel and powerful ways. But we should not take the concept of identity and its multiple associations with 'race' and raciology for granted. The term 'identity' has recently acquired great resonance, both inside and outside the academic world. It offers far more than an obvious, common-sense way of talking about individuality, community, and solidarity and has provided a means to understand the interplay between subjective experiences of the world and the cultural and historical settings in which those fragile, meaningful subjectivities are formed. Identity has even been taken into the viscera of postmodern commerce, where the goal of planetary marketing promotes not just the targeting of objects and services to the identities of particular consumers but the idea that any product whatsoever can be suffused with identity. Any commodity is open to being 'branded' in ways that solicit identification and try to orchestrate identity.[4]

[. . .] I want to show that there is more at stake in the current interest in identity than we often appreciate. I would also like to uncover some of the complexities that make identity a useful idea to explore if we can only leave its obviousness behind and recognize that it is far from being the simple issue that its currency in both government and marketplace makes it appear to be. Where the word becomes a concept, identity has been made central to a number of urgent theoretical and political issues, not least belonging, ethnicity, and nationality. Racialized conflicts, for example, are now understood by many commentators as a problem of the incompatible identities that mark out deeper conflicts between cultures and civilizations. This diagnosis sets up or perhaps confirms the even more widespread belief that the forms of political conflict with which racial division has been associated are somehow unreal or insubstantial, secondary or peripheral. This is something I intend to dispute. The new popularity of identity as an interpretative device is also a result of the exceptonal plurality of meanings the term can harness. These diverse inflections – some of which are adapted from highly specialized academic usage – are condensed and interwoven as the term circulates. We are constantly informed that to share an identity is to be bonded on the most fundamental levels: national, 'racial,' ethnic, regional, and local. Identity is always bounded and particular. It marks out the divisions and subsets in our social lives and helps to define the boundaries between our uneven, local attempts to make sense of the world. Nobody ever speaks of a human identity. The concept orients thinking away from any engagement with the basic, anti-anthropological sameness that is the premise of this book. As Judith Butler puts it in her thoughtful reflection on the concept: 'it seems that what we expect from the term *identity* will be cultural specificity, and that on occasion we even expect *identity* and *specificity* to work interchangeably.'[5]

The same troubling qualities are evident where the term has been employed to articulate controversial and potentially illuminating themes in modern social and political theory. It has been a core component in the scholarly vocabulary designed to promote critical reflection upon who we are and what we want. Identity helps us to comprehend the formation of that perilous pronoun 'we' and to reckon with the patterns of inclusion and exclusion that it cannot help creating. This situation is made more difficult once identity is recognized as something of a problem in itself, and thereby acquires an additional weighting. Calculating the relationship between identity and difference, sameness and otherness is an intrinsically political operation. It happens when political collectivities reflect on what makes their binding connections possible. It is a fundamental part of how they comprehend their kinship – which may be an imaginary connection, though nonetheless powerful for that.

The distinctive language of identity appears again when people seek to calculate how tacit belonging to a group or community can be transformed into more active styles of solidarity, when they debate where the boundaries around a group should be constituted and how – if at all – they should be enforced. Identity becomes a question of power and authority when a group seeks to realize itself in political form. This may be a nation, a state, a movement, a class, or some unsteady combination of them all. Writing about the need for political institutions and relationships at the dawn of our era, Rousseau drew attention to the bold and creative elements in the history of how disorganized and internally divided groups had been formed into coherent units capable of unified action and worthy of the special status that defined the nation as a political body. Reflecting on the achievements of heroic individual leaders as builders of political cultures that could 'attach citizens to the fatherland and to one another,' he noted that the provision of a unifying common identity was a significant part of this political process. Significantly for our purposes, his example was taken from the history of the Children of Israel:

> (Moses) conceived and executed the astonishing project of creating a nation out of a swarm of wretched fugitives, without arts, arms, talents, virtues or courage, who were wandering as a horde of strangers over the face of the earth without a single inch of ground to call their own. Out of this wandering and servile horde Moses had the audacity to create a body

politic, a free people . . . he gave them that durable set of institutions, proof against time, fortune and conquerors, which five thousand years have not been able to destroy or even alter . . . To prevent his people from melting away among foreign peoples, he gave them customs and usages incompatible with those of other nations; he over-burdened them with peculiar rites and ceremonies; he inconvenienced them in a thousand ways in order to keep them constantly on the alert and to make them forever strangers among other men.[6]

In outlining elements of the political technology that would eventually produce the nation as a fortified encampment, Rousseau drew attention to the old association between identity and territory. Moses' achievement is viewed as all the more impressive because it was accomplished without the binding power of shared land. Rousseau underlined that the varieties of connection to which our ideas of identity refer are historical, social, and cultural rather than natural phenomena. Even at that early point in the constitution of modernity, he recognized that work must be done to summon the particularity and feelings of identity that are so often experienced as though they are spontaneous or automatic consequences of some governing culture or tradition that specifies basic and absolute differences between people. Consciousness of identity gains additional power from the idea that it is not the end product of one great man's 'audacity' but an outcome of shared and rooted experience tied, in particular, to place, location, language, and mutuality.

When we think about the tense relationship between sameness and difference analytically, the interplay of consciousness, territory, and place becomes a major theme. It afford: insights into the core of conflicts over how democratic social and political life should be organized at the start of the twenty-first century. We should try to remember that the threshold between those two antagonistic conditions can be moved and that identity-making has a history even though its historical character is often systematically concealed. Focusing on identity helps us to ask in what sense the recognition of sameness and differentiation is a premise of the modern political culture that Rousseau affirmed and which his writings still help us to analyze.

The dizzying variety of ideas condensed into the concept of identity, and the wide range of issues to which it can be made to refer, foster analytical connections between themes and perspectives that are not conventionally associated. Links can be established between political, cultural, psychological, and psychoanalytic concerns. We need to consider, for example, how the emotional and affective bonds that form the specific basis of raciological and ethnic sameness are composed, and how they become patterned social activities with elaborate cultural features. How are they able to induce conspicuous acts of altruism, violence, and courage? How do they motivate people toward social interconnection in which individuality is renounced or dissolved into the larger whole represented by a nation, a people, a 'race,' or an ethnic group? These questions are important because, as we have seen, grave moral and political consequences have followed once the magic of identity has been engaged tactically or in manipulative, deliberately oversimple ways. Even in the most civilized circumstances, the signs of sameness have degenerated readily into emblems of supposedly essential or immutable difference. The special appeal of individuality-transcending sameness still provides an antidote to the forms of uncertainty and anxiety that have been associated with economic and political crises. The idea of fundamentally shared identity becomes a platform for the reverie of absolute and eternal division.

The use of uniforms and other symbols to effect the sameness that identity only speaks about has sometimes been symptomatic of the process in which an anxious self can be shed and its concerns conjured away by the emergence of a stronger compound whole. The uniforms worn in the 1930s by fascists (and still worn by some fascist groups today) produced a compelling illusion of sameness both for members of the group and for those who observed their spectacular activities. The British Union of Fascists, one of the less-successful black-shirted organizations from that period, argued that their garb was all the more attractive to adherents when contrasted with the conflict and bitterness created by class-based divisions that were tearing the nation apart from within:

> (The 'blackshirt') brings down one of the great barriers of class by removing differences of dress, and one of the objects of Fascism is to break the barriers of class. Already the blackshirt has achieved within our own ranks that classless unity which we will ultimately secure within the nation as a whole.[7]

We will explore below how the ultranationalist and fascist movements of the twentieth century deployed elaborate technological resources in order to generate spectacles of identity capable of unifying and coordinating inevitable, untidy diversity into an ideal and unnatural human uniformity. Their synthetic versions of fundamental identity looked most seductive where all difference had been banished or erased from the collective. Difference within was repressed in order to maximize the difference between these groups and others. Identity was celebrated extravagantly in military styles: uniforms were combined with synchronized body movement, drill, pageantry, and visible hierarchy to create and feed the comforting belief in sameness as absolute, metaphysical invariance. Men and women could then appear as interchangeable and disposable cogs in the encamped nation's military machine or as indistinguishable cells in the larger organic entity that encompassed and dissolved their individuality. Their actions may even be imagined to express the inner spirit, fate, and historicality of the national community. The citizen was manifested as a soldier, and violence – potential as well as actual – was dedicated to the furtherance of national interests. That vital community was constituted in the dynamic interaction between marchers moving together in austere time and the crowds that watched and savored the spectacle they created. In disseminating these valuable political effects, identity was mediated by cultural and communicative technologies like film, lighting, and amplified sound. These twentieth-century attributes were only partly concealed by the invocation of ancient ritual and myth.

The biblical stories of nation-building that demonstrate divine favor and the moral sanctions it supplies to worldly political purposes have been invoked by many different nationalist groups. The Afrikaners of South Africa provide one especially interesting and unwholesome example of how Rousseau's 'peculiar rites and ceremonies' need not always serve a benign purpose. Their ethnically minded ideologues systematically invented an Afrikaner identity during the period that saw the rise of fascist movements elsewhere. They provided their political community with its own version of Christianity and a repertory of myths that were the basis for the elaborate political drama that summoned their historic nation into racialized being:

> The most dramatic event in the upsurge of Afrikaner nationalism was the symbolic ox-wagon trek of 1938, which celebrated the victory of the Great Trek. Eight wagons named after voortrekker heroes such as Piet Retief, Hendrik Potgeiter and Andres Pretorius traversed South Africa by different routes . . . before they converged on a prominent hill overlooking Pretoria. There, on 16th December 1938, the centenary of the battle of Blood River, which marked the defeat of the Zulu kingdom, more than 100,000 Afrikaners – perhaps one tenth of the total Afrikaner people – attended the ceremonial laying of the foundation stone of the Voortrekker Monument. Men grew beards, women wore voortrekker dress, for the occasion . . . (they) knelt in silent prayer . . . The ceremony concluded with the singing of *Die Stem van Suid Afrika*; *God Save the King* had been excluded.[8]

Today's ubiquitous conflicts between warring constituencies that claim incompatible and exclusive identities suggest that these large-scale theatrical techniques for producing and stabilizing identity and soliciting national, 'racial,' or ethnic identification have been widely taken up. The reduction of identity to the uncomplicated, militarized, fraternal versions of pure sameness pioneered by fascism and Nazism in the 1930s is now routine, particularly where the forces of nationalism, 'tribalism,' and ethnic division are at work. Identity is thus revealed as a critical element in the distinctive vocabulary used to voice the geopolitical dilemmas of the late modern age. Where the power of absolute identity is summoned up, it is often to account for situations in which the actions of individuals and groups are being reduced to little more than the functioning of some overarching presocial mechanism. In the past, this machinery was often understood as a historical or economic process that defined the special, manifest destiny of the group in question. These days, it is more likely to be represented as a prepolitical, sociobiological, or biocultural feature, something mysterious and genetic that sanctions especially harsh varieties of deterministic thinking.

In this light, identity ceases to be an ongoing process of self-making and social interaction. It becomes instead a thing to be possessed and displayed. It is a silent sign that closes down the possibility of communication across the gulf between one heavily defended island of particularity and its equally well fortified neighbors, between one national encampment and others. When identity refers to an indelible mark or code somehow written into the bodies of its carriers, otherness can only be a threat. Identity is latent destiny. Seen or unseen, on the surface of the body or buried deep in its cells, identity forever sets one group apart from others who lack the particular, chosen traits that become the basis of typology and comparative evaluation. No longer a site for the affirmation of subjectivity and autonomy, identity mutates. Its motion reveals a deep desire for mechanical solidarity, seriality, and hypersimilarity. The scope for individual agency dwindles and then disappears. People become bearers of the differences that the rhetoric of absolute identity invents and then invites them to celebrate. Rather than communicating and making choices, individuals are seen as obedient, silent passengers moving across a flattened moral landscape toward the fixed destinies to which their essential identities, their genes, and the closed cultures they create have consigned them once and for all. And yet, the desire to fix identity in the body is inevitably frustrated by the body's refusal to disclose the required signs of absolute incompatibility people imagine to be located there.

Numerous cross-cultural examples might be used to illustrate this point. Reports from the genocide in Rwanda repeatedly revealed that identity cards issued by the political authorities were a vital source of the information necessary to classify people into the supposedly natural 'tribal' types that brought them either death or deliverance. There, as in several other well-documented instances of mass slaughter, the bodies in question did not freely disclose the secrets of identity:

> Many Tutsis have been killed either because their ID cards marked them out as a Tutsi or because they did not have their card with them at the time and were therefore unable to prove they were not a Tutsi . . . To escape the relentless discrimination they suffered, over the years many Tutsis bribed local government officials to get their ID card changed to Hutu. Unfortunately, this has not protected them . . . The Tutsi give-aways were: one, being tall and two having a straight nose. Such criteria even led hysterical militias to kill a number of Hutus whose crime was 'being too tall for a Hutu.' Where there was doubt about the person's physical characteristics or because of the complaints that too many Tutsis had changed their card, the Interahamwe called upon villagers to verify the 'tutsiship' of the quarry in question.[9]

Similar events were still being reported four years later when the genocidal assault against the Tutsis had been rearticulated into the civil war in Congo – a conflict that had already drawn in several other states and that appeared to provide the key to stability in the region. Under the presidency of Laurent Kabila, people whose physical characteristics made them suspect were still being openly murdered.[10] It is important to remember, however, that the linguistic markers of residual colonial conflict between anglophone and francophone spheres of influence were also implicated in sustaining the killing.

These fragments from a history of unspeakable barbarity underline how the notion of fixed identity operates easily on both sides of the chasm that usually divides scholarly writing from the disorderly world of political conflicts. Recently, identity has also come to constitute something of a bridge between the often discrepant approaches to understanding self and sociality found on the different sides of that widening gulf. As a theme in contemporary scholarship, identity has offered academic thinking an important route back toward the struggles and uncertainties of everyday life, where the idea of identity has become especially resonant. It has also provided the distinctive signatures of an inward, implosive turn that brings the difficult tasks of politics to an end by making them appear irrelevant in the face of deeper, more fundamental powers that regulate human conduct irrespective of governmental superficialities. If identity and difference are fundamental, then they are not amenable to being re-tooled by crude political methods that cannot possibly get to the heart of primal ontologies, destinies, and fates. When the stakes are this high, nothing can be done to offset the catastrophic consequences that result from tolerating difference and mistaken attempts at practicing democracy. Difference corrupts and compromises identity. Encounters with it are just as unwelcome and potentially destructive as they were for Houston Stewart Chamberlain. They place that most precious commodity, rooted identity, in grave jeopardy.

When national and ethnic identities are represented and projected as pure, exposure to difference threatens them with dilution and compromises their prized purities with the ever-present possibility of contamination. Crossing as mixture and movement must be guarded against. New hatreds and violence arise not, as they did in the past, from supposedly reliable anthropological knowledge of the identity and difference of the Other but from the novel problem of not being able to locate the Other's difference in the common-sense lexicon of alterity. Different people are certainly hated and feared, but the timely antipathy against them is nothing compared with the hatreds turned toward the greater menace of the half-different and the partially familiar. To have mixed is to have been party to a great betrayal. Any unsettling traces of hybridity must be excised from the tidy, bleached-out zones of impossibly pure culture. The safety of sameness can then be recovered by either of the two options that have regularly appeared at the meltdown point of this dismal logic: separation and slaughter.

Identity, solidarity, and selfhood

The political language of identity levels out distinctions between chosen connections and given particularities: between the person you choose to be and the things that determine your individuality by being thrust upon you. It is particularly important for the argument that follows that the term 'identity' has become a significant element in contemporary conflicts over cultural, ethnic, religious, 'racial,' and national differences. The idea of collective identity has emerged as an object of political thinking even if its appearance signals a sorry state of affairs in which the distinctive rules that define modern political culture are consciously set aside in favor of the pursuit of primordial feelings and mythic varieties of kinship that are mistakenly believed to be more profound. At the same time, individual identity, the counterpart to the collective, is constantly negotiated, cultivated, and protected as a source of pleasure, power, wealth, and potential danger. That identity is increasingly shaped in the marketplace, modified by the cultural industries, and managed and orchestrated in localized institutions and settings like schools, neighborhoods, and workplaces. It can be inscribed in the dull public world of official politics where issues surrounding the absence of collective identity – and the resulting disappearance of community and solidarity from social life – have also been discussed at great length by politicians on different sides of the political divide.

Other aspects of identity's foundational slipperiness can be detected in the way that the term is used to register the impact of processes that take place above and below the level at which the sovereign state and its distinctive modes of belonging are constituted. The growth of nationalisms and other absolutist religious and ethnic identities, the accentuation of regional and local divisions, and the changing relationship between supranational and subnational networks of economy, politics, and information have all endowed contemporary appeals to identity with extra significance. Identity has come to supply something of an anchor amid the turbulent waters of de-industrialization and the large-scale patterns of planetary reconstruction that are hesitantly named 'globalization.'[11] It would appear that recovering or possessing an appropriately grounded identity can provide a means to hold these historic but anxiety-inducing processes at bay. Taking pride or finding sanctuary in an exclusive identity affords a means to acquire certainty about who one is and where one fits, about the claims of community and the limits of social obligation.

The politicization of gender and sexuality has enhanced the understanding of identity by directing attention to the social, familial, historical, and cultural factors that bear upon the formation and social reproduction of masculinity and femininity. Two groups of agents are bound together by the centripetal force of the stable, gendered identities that they apparently hold in common. But the anxious, disciplinary intensity with which these ideas are entrenched seems to increase in inverse proportion to the collapse of family and household structures and the eclipse of male domestic domination. In these important areas, the concept of identity has nurtured new ways of thinking about the self, about sameness, and about solidarity. If abstract identity and its thematics are on the verge of becoming something of an obsessive preoccupation in the overdeveloped countries, this novel pattern communicates how political movements and governmental activities are being reconstituted by a change in the status and capacity of the nation-state.[12]

NOTES

1. Claude Lefort, *The Political Forms of Modern Society: Bureaucracy, Democracy, Totalitarianism*, ed. John B. Thompson (Polity Press, 1986), p. 298.
2. Chetan Bhatt, *Liberation and Purity: Race, New Religious Movements and the Ethics of Post-Modernity* (University College London Press, 1997).
3. Levi, *The Drowned and the Saved*, trans. Raymond Rosenthal (Summit Books, 1998), p. 51.
4. Mark Leonard, *Britain*[TM] (Demos, 1997).
5. Judith Butler, 'Collected and Fractured,' in *Identities*, ed. Kwame Anthony Appiah and Henry Louis Gates, Jr. (University of Chicago Press, 1995).
6. J.-J. Rousseau, 'Considerations on the Government of Poland,' in *Rousseau Political Writings*, trans. and ed: Frederick Watkins (Nelson and Sons, 1953), pp. 163–164.
7. *The Blackshirt* (November 24–30, 1933), p. 5; quoted in John Harvey, *Men in Black* (Chicago University Press, 1995), p. 242.
8. Leonard Thompson, *The Political Mythology of Apartheid* (Yale University Press, 1985), p. 39.
9. African Rights, *Rwanda: Death, Despair and Defiance* (London, 1994), pp. 347–354. See also Sander L. Gilman, *The Jew's Body* (Routledge, 1991), especially chap. 7, 'The Jewish Nose: Are Jews White or The History of the Nose Job.'
10. Arthur Malu-Malu and Thierry Oberle, *Sunday Times*, August 30, 1998.
11. William Greider, *One World, Ready or Not: The Manic Logic of Global Capitalism* (Simon and Schuster, 1997); Jerry Mander and Edward Goldsmith, eds., *The Case against the Global Economy and for a Turn toward the Local* (Sierra Books, 1996); Benjamin R. Barber, *Jihad vs. McWorld: How the Planet Is Both Falling Apart and Coming Together and What This Means for Democracy* (Random House, 1995).
12. Jean-Marie Guéhenno, *The End of the Nation State* (University of Minnesota Press, 1995).

11

RACISM AND NATIONALISM

Etienne Balibar

THE FIELD OF NATIONALISM

Let us return, then, to the connection between nationalism and racism. And let us begin by acknowledging that the very category of nationalism is intrinsically ambiguous. This has to do, first of all, with the antithetical nature of the historical situations in which nationalist movements and policies arise. Fichte or Gandhi are not Bismarck; Bismarck or De Gaulle are not Hitler. And yet we cannot, by a mere intellectual decision, suppress the effect of ideological symmetry which imposes itself here on the antagonistic forces. We have no right whatever to equate the nationalism of the dominant with that of the dominated, the nationalism of liberation with the nationalism of conquest. Yet this does not mean we can simply ignore the fact that there is a common element – if only the logic of a situation, the structural inscription in the political forms of the modern world – in the nationalism of the Algerian FLN and that of the French colonial army, or today in the nationalism of the ANC and that of the Afrikaners. Let us take this to its extreme conclusion and say that this formal symmetry is not unrelated to the painful experience we have repeatedly undergone of seeing nationalisms of liberation transformed into nationalisms of domination (just as we have seen socialist revolutions turn around to produce state dictatorships), which has compelled us at regular intervals to inquire into the oppressive potentialities contained within every nationalism. Before coming to reside in words, the contradiction resides in history itself.[1]

Etienne Balibar and Immanuel Wallerstein (1991), *Race, Nation, Class: Ambiguous Identities*, London: Verso.

Why does it prove to be so difficult to define nationalism? First, because the concept never functions alone, but is always part of a chain in which it is both the central and the weak link. This chain is constantly being enriched (the detailed modes of that enrichment varying from one language to another) with new intermediate or extreme terms: civic spirit, patriotism, populism, ethnicism, ethnocentrism, xenophobia, chauvinism, imperialism, jingoism . . . I challenge anyone to fix once and for all, unequivocally, the differential meanings of these terms. But it seems to me that the overall figure can be interpreted fairly simply.

Where the *nationalism–nation* relation is concerned, the core of meaning opposes a 'reality', the nation, to an 'ideology', nationalism. This relation is, however, perceived very differently by different people, since several obscure questions underlie it: Is nationalist ideology the (necessary or circumstantial) reflection of the existence of nations? Or do nations constitute themselves out of nationalist ideologies (though it may mean that these latter, having attained their 'goal', are subsequently transformed)? Must the 'nation' itself – and naturally this question is not independent of the preceding ones – be considered as a 'state' or as a 'society' (a social formation)? Let us leave these issues in abeyance for a moment, together with the variants to which they may give rise by the introduction of terms such as city, people, nationality and so on.

As far as the relation between *nationalism and racism* is concerned at present, the core of meaning contrasts a 'normal' ideology and politics (nationalism) with an 'excessive' ideology and behavior (racism), either to oppose the two or to offer the one as the truth of the other. Here again questions and other conceptual distinctions immediately arise. Rather than concentrating our attention upon racism, would it not be more appropriate to privilege the more 'objective' nationalism/imperialism alternative? But this confrontation brings out the other possibilities: for example, that nationalism itself may be the ideologico-political effect of the imperialist character of nations or their survival into an imperialist age and environment. One may complicate the chain further by introducing notions like fascism and Nazism with their network of attendant questions: Are these both nationalisms? Are they both imperialisms? . . .

In fact, and this is what all these questions bring out – the whole chain is inhabited by one fundamental question. As soon as 'somewhere' in this historico-political chain an intolerable, seemingly 'irrational' violence enters upon the scene, *where* are we to place that entry? Should we cut into a sequence in which only 'realities' are involved to locate it, or should we rather search among the 'ideological' conflicts? And should we consider violence as a perversion of a normal state of affairs, a deviation from the hypothetical 'straight line' of human history, or do we have to admit that it represents the truth of what has preceded it and therefore, from this point of view, the seeds of racism could be seen as lying at the heart of politics from the birth of nationalism onwards, or even indeed from the point where nations begin to exist?

Naturally, to all these questions, an extreme variety of responses are to be found, depending upon the viewpoint of the observers and the situations they reflect. In my view, however, in their very dispersion, they all revolve around a single dilemma: the notion of nationalism is constantly dividing. There is always a 'good' and a 'bad' nationalism. There is the one which ends to construct a state or a community and the one which tends to subjugate, to destroy; the one which refers to right and the one which refers to might; the one which tolerates other nationalisms and which may even argue in their defence and include them within a single historical perspective (the great dream of the 'Springtime of the Peoples') and the one which radically excludes them in an imperialist and racist perspective. There is the one which derives from love (even excessive love) and the one which derives from hate. In short, the internal split within nationalism seems as essential – and as difficult to pin down – as the step that leads from 'dying for one's fatherland' to 'killing for one's country' . . . The proliferation of 'neighbouring' terms, whether they be synonyms or antonyms, is merely an exteriorization of this split. No one, in my view, has wholly escaped this reinscription of the dilemma within the very concept of nationalism itself (and when it has been evacuated within theory, it has re-entered by the door of practice), but it is particularly visible in the liberal tradition, which is probably to be explained by the very profound ambiguity of the relations between liberalism and nationalism over at least the last two centuries.[2] We also have to say that, by displacing it one or two degrees, racist ideologies may then mimic this discussion and invade it themselves: is it not the function of notions like 'living space' to raise the question of the 'good side' of imperialism or racism? And is not the neo-racism we see proliferating today, from 'differentialist' anthropology to socio-biology, constantly concerned to distinguish what is supposed to be inevitable and, deep down, useful (a certain xenophobia which induces groups to defend their 'territories' and 'cultural identities' and to maintain the 'proper distance' between them) from what would be useless and in itself harmful (direct violence, acting out), though inevitable if one ignores the elementary exigencies of ethnicity?

How are we to break out of this circle? It is not enough simply to ask, as some recent analysts have done, that value judgements be rejected – that is, that judgement on the consequences of nationalism in different conjunctures be suspended –,[3] or, alternatively, to consider nationalism itself strictly as an ideological effect of the 'objective' process of constitution of nations (and nation states).[4] For the ambivalence of effects forms part of the very history of all nationalisms, and it is precisely this which has to be explained. From this point of view, the analysis of the place of racism in nationalism is decisive: though racism is not equally manifest in all racisms or in all the moments of their history, it none the less always represents a necessary tendency in their constitution. In the last analysis, the overlapping of the two goes back to the circumstances in which the nation states, established upon historically contested *territories*, have striven to control *population* movements, and to the very production of the 'people' as a political community taking precedence over class divisions.

At this point, however, an objection does arise regarding the very terms of the discussion. It is the objection Maxime Rodinson, among others, directs at all those – such as Colette Guillaumin – who insist upon a 'broad' definition of racism.[5] Such a definition seeks to take into account *all* forms of exclusion and depreciation, whether or not they are accompanied by biological theories. It seeks to get back beyond 'ethnic' racism to the origin of the 'race myth' and its genealogical discourse: the 'class racism' of the post-feudal aristocracy. And, most particularly, it seeks to include under the heading 'racism' all forms of minority oppression which, in a formally egalitarian society, lead in different ways to the 'racialization' of various social groups – not just ethnic groups, but women, sexual deviants, the mentally ill, subproletarians and so on – so as to be able to analyse the common mechanism of the naturalization of differences. In Rodinson's view, one ought, however, to choose: either one should make internal and external racism a tendency of nationalism and, beyond this, of ethnocentrism of which nationalism would be the modern form; or one could broaden the definition of racism in order to understand the psychological mechanisms (phobic projection, denial of the real Other overlaid with the signifiers of a phantasmatic alterity), but at the risk of dissolving its historical specificity.[6]

This objection can, however, be met. And it may even be met in such a way that the historical entanglement of nationalism and racism is made all the clearer; but on condition that one advances certain propositions which in part rectify the idea of a 'broad' definition of racism or at least make it more exact:

1. No nation, that is, no national state, has an ethnic basis, which means that nationalism cannot be defined as an ethnocentrism except precisely in the sense of the product of a *fictive* ethnicity. To reason any other way would be to forget that 'peoples' do not exist naturally any more than 'races' do, either by virtue of their ancestry, a community of culture or pre-existing interests. But they do have to institute in real (and therefore in historical) time their imaginary unity *against* other possible unities.

2. The phenomenon of 'depreciation' and 'racialization' which is directed simultaneously against different social groups which are quite different in 'nature' (particularly 'foreign' communities, 'inferior races', women and 'deviants') does not represent a juxtaposition of merely analogous behaviours and discourses applied to a potentially indefinite series of objects independent of each other, but *a historical system of complementary exclusions and dominations which are mutually interconnected*. In other words, it is not in practice simply the case that an 'ethnic racism' and a 'sexual racism' exist in parallel; racism and sexism function together and in particular, *racism always presupposes sexism*. In these conditions a general category of racism is not an abstraction which runs the risk of losing in historical precision and pertinence what it gains in universality; it is, rather, a more concrete notion of taking into account

the necessary polymorphism of racism, its overarching function, its connections with the whole set of practices of social normalization and exclusion, as we might demonstrate by reference to neo-racism whose preferred target is not the 'Arab' or the 'Black', but the 'Arab (as) junky' or 'delinquent' or 'rapist' and so on, or equally, rapists and delinquents as 'Arabs' and 'Blacks'.

3. It is this broad structure of racism, which is heterogeneous and yet tightly knit (first in a network of phantasies and, second, through discourses and behaviours), which maintains a necessary relation with *nationalism* and contributes to constituting it by producing the fictive ethnicity around which it is organized.

4. If it is necessary to include in the structural conditions (both symbolic and institutional) of modern racism the fact that the societies in which racism develops are at the same time supposed to be 'egalitarian' societies, in other words, societies which (officially) disregard status differences between individuals, this sociological thesis (advanced most notably by L. Dumont) cannot be abstracted from the national environment itself. In other words, it is not the modern state which is 'egalitarian' but the modern (nationalist) nation-state, this equality having as its internal and external limits the national community and, as its essential content, the acts which signify it directly (particularly universal suffrage and political 'citizenship'). It is, first and foremost, an equality in respect of nationality.[7]

The discussion of this controversy (as of other similar controversies to which we might refer)[8] is of considerable value to us here, since through it we begin to grasp that the connection between nationalism and racism is neither a matter of perversion (for there is no 'pure' essence of nationalism) nor a question of formal similarity, but a question of historical articulation. What we have to understand is the specific difference of racism and the way in which, in articulating itself to nationalism, it is, in its difference, necessary to nationalism. This is to say, by the very same token, that the articulation of nationalism and racism cannot be disentangled by applying classical schemas of causality, whether mechanistic (the one as the cause of the other, 'producing' the other according to the rule of the proportionality of the effects to the cause) or spiritualistic (the one 'expressing' the other, or giving it its meaning or revealing its hidden essence). It requires a dialectics of the unity of opposites.

Nowhere is this necessity more evident than in the debate, which is forever being reopened, on the 'essence of Nazism', a positive magnet for all the various forms of hermeneutics of social relations, in which the political uncertainties of the present are mirrored (and transposed).[9]

For some, Hitlerian racism is the culmination of nationalism: it derives from Bismarck, if not indeed from German Romanticism or Luther, from the defeat of 1918 and the humiliation of the Versailles *Diktat*, and provides a project of absolute imperialism with its ideology (*Lebensraum*, a German Europe). If the coherence of that ideology seems analogous to the coherence of delirium, then one should see this as precisely the explanation of its brief, but almost total hold on the 'mass' of the population, whatever their social origins, and on the 'leaders', whose blindness in the end plunged the nation to its doom. Beyond all the 'revolutionary' deception and conjunctural twists and turns, the enterprise of world domination was inherent in the nationalism shared by masses and leaders alike.

For others, such explanations are doomed always to miss the essential point, however subtly they might analyse the social forces and intellectual traditions, events and political strategies, and however skilfully they might relate the monstrous nature of Nazism to the anomalous course of German history. It was precisely by regarding Nazism as merely a nationalism analogous to their own – distinguished only by a difference of degree – that public opinion and the political leaders in the 'democratic' nations of the time deluded themselves as to its goals and thought they could come to an arrangement with it or limit the havoc it might create. Nazism is exceptional (and perhaps shows up a possibility of transgression of the political rationality inscribed in the condition of modern man) because in it the logic of racism overwhelms all other factors, and imposes itself to the detriment of 'pure' nationalist logic, because 'race war', both internal and external, ends up by depriving 'national war' (whose goals of domination remain *positive* goals) of any coherence. Nazism could thus be seen as the very embodiment of that 'nihilism' of which it spoke itself, in which the extermination of the imaginary Enemy, who is seen as the incarnation of Evil (the Jew or the Communist) and self-destruction (more the annihilation of Germany than a confession of failure on the part of its 'racial elite', the SS caste and the Nazi party) meet.

We can see that in this controversy analytic discourses and value judgements are constantly intermingling. History sets itself up as diagnosis of the normal and the pathological and ends up echoing the discourse of its own object, demonizing Nazism which itself demonized its enemies and victims. Yet it is not easy to get out of this circle, since the essential point is not to reduce the phenomenon to conventional generalities, the *practical* impotence of which it precisely revealed. We have the contradictory impression that, with Nazi racism, nationalism both plumbs the greatest depths of its latent and, to borrow Hannah Arendt's expression, tragically 'ordinary' tendencies and yet *goes beyond* itself, and the ordinary form in which it is normally realized, that is, is normally institutionalized to penetrate in a lasting way the 'common sense' of the masses. On the one hand, we can see (admittedly after the event) the irrationality of a racial mythology which ends up dislocating the nation-state whose absolute superiority it proclaims. We can see this as proof that racism, as a complex which combines the banality of daily acts of violence and the 'historical' intoxication of the masses, the bureaucratism of the forced labour and extermination camps and the delirium of the 'world' domination of the 'master race', can no longer be considered a simple aspect of nationalism. But we then have to ask ourselves immediately: How are we to avoid this irrationality becoming its own cause, the exceptional character of Nazi anti-Semitism turning into a sacred mystery, into a speculative vision of history which represents history precisely as the history of Evil (and which, correlatively, represents its victims as the true Lamb of God)? It is not, however, in any way certain that doing the opposite and deducing Nazi racism from German nationalism frees us from all irrationalism. For we have to admit that only a nationalism of an 'extreme' intensity, a nationalism exacerbated by an 'exceptional' series of internal and external conflicts was able to idealize the goals of racism to the point of making the violence wrought by the great number of torturers possible and 'normalizing' this in the eyes of the great mass of other people. The combination of this banality and this idealism tends rather to reinforce the metaphysical idea that German nationalism might itself be 'exceptional' in history: though a paradigm of nationalism in its pathological content in relation to liberalism, it would in the end be irreducible to 'ordinary' nationalism. We here fall back then into the aporias described above of 'good' and 'bad' nationalism.

Now might we not rediscover, in respect of each conjuncture in which racism and nationalism are individualized in discourses, mass movements and specific policies, what the debate on Nazism emphatically exhibits? In this internal connectedness *and* this transgression of rational interests and ends, is there not *the same contradiction*, the terms of which we believe we can see once again in our present-day reality, for example when a movement which carries within it nostalgia for a 'New European Order' and 'colonial heroism' canvasses, as successfully as it has done, the possibility of a 'solution' to the 'immigrant problem'?

Generalizing these thoughts, I shall say then, first, that in the historical 'field' of nationalism, there is always a reciprocity of determination between this and racism.

This reciprocity shows itself initially in the way in which the development of nationalism and its official utilization by the state transforms antagonisms and persecutions that have quite other origins into racism in the modern sense (and ascribes the verbal markers of ethnicity to them). This runs from the way in which, since the times of the *Reconquista* in Spain, theological anti-Judaism was transposed into genealogical exclusion based on 'purity of blood' at the same time as the *raza* was launching itself upon the conquest of the New World, down to the way in which, in modern Europe, the new 'dangerous classes' of the international proletariat tend to be subsumed under the category of 'immigration', which becomes the main name given to race within the crisis-torn nations of the post-colonial era.

This reciprocal determination shows itself again in the way in which all the 'official nationalisms' of the nineteenth and twentieth centuries, aiming to confer the political and cultural unity of a nation on the heterogeneity of a pluri-ethnic state,[10] have used anti-Semitism: as if the domination of a culture and a more or less fictively unified nationality (for example, the Russian, German or Romanian) over a hierarchically ordered diversity of 'minority' ethnicities and cultures marked down for assimilation should be 'compensated' and mirrored by the racializing persecution of an absolutely singular *pseudo-ethnic group* (without their own territory and without a 'national' language) which represents the common internal enemy of all cultures and all dominated populations.[11]

Finally, it shows itself in the history of the national liberation struggles, whether they be directed against the old empires of the first period of colonization, against the dynastic multinational states or against the modern colonial empires. There is no question of reducing these processes to a single model. And yet it cannot be by chance that the genocide of the Indians became systematic immediately after the United States – the 'first of the new nations' in Lipset's famous expression – achieved independence.[12] Just as it cannot be by chance, to follow the illuminating analysis proposed by Bipan Chandra, that 'nationalism' and 'communalism' were formed together in India, and continue into the present to be inextricable (largely because of the early historical fusion of Indian nationalism with Hindu communalism).[13] Or again that independent Algeria made assimilating the 'Berbers' to 'Arabness' the key test of the nation's will in its struggle with the multicultural heritage of colonization. Or, indeed, that the State of Israel, faced with an internal and an external enemy and the impossible gamble of forging an 'Israeli nation' developed a powerful racism directed both against the 'Eastern' Jews (called 'Blacks') and the Palestinians, who were driven out of their lands and colonized.[14]

From this accumulation of entirely individual but historically linked cases there results what might be called the cycle of historical reciprocity of nationalism and racism, which is the temporal figure of the progressive domination of the system of nation-states over other social formations. Racism is constantly emerging out of nationalism, not only towards the exterior but towards the interior. In the United States, the systematic institution of segregation, which put a halt to the first civil rights movement, coincided with America's entry into world imperialist competition and with its subscribing to the idea that the Nordic races have a hegemonic mission. In France, the elaboration of an ideology of the 'French race', rooted in the past of 'the soil and the dead', coincides with the beginning of mass immigration, the preparation for revenge against Germany and the founding of the colonial empire. And nationalism emerges out of racism, in the sense that it would not constitute itself as the ideology of a 'new' nation if the official nationalism against which it were reacting were not profoundly racist: thus Zionism comes out of anti-Semitism and Third World nationalisms come out of colonial racism. Within this grand cycle, however, there is a multitude of individual cycles. Thus to take but one example, a crucial one in French national history, the defeat suffered by anti-Semitism after the Dreyfus Affair, which was symbolically incorporated into the ideals of the republican regime, opened up to a certain extent the possibility of a colonial 'good conscience' and made it possible for many years for the notion of racism to be dissociated from that of colonization (at least in metro-politan perceptions).

Secondly, however, I argue that *the gap subsists between the representations and practices of nationalism and racism*. It is a fluctuating gap between the two poles of a contradiction and a forced identification – and it is perhaps, as the Nazi example shows, when this identification is apparently complete that the contradiction is most marked. Not a contradiction between nationalism and racism as such, but a contradiction between determinate *forms*, between the political objectives of nationalism and the crystallization of racism on a particular object, at a particular moment: for example, when nationalism undertakes to 'integrate' a dominated, potentially autonomous population, as in 'French' Algeria or 'French' New Caledonia. From this point onwards, I therefore concentrate on this gap and the paradoxical forms it may assume, the better to understand the point that was emerging from most of the examples to which I have referred: namely, that racism is not an 'expression' of nationalism, but *a supplement of nationalism* or more precisely *a supplement internal to nationalism*, always in excess of it, but always indispensable to its constitution and yet always still insufficient to achieve its project, just as nationalism is both indispensable and always insufficient to achieve the formation of the *nation* or the project of a 'nationalization' of society.

NOTES

1. For what is both a dogged and nuanced analysis of this contradiction, it would only be right to refer the reader to the whole of Maxime Rodinson's writings and, in particular, to the texts assembled in *Marxisme et monde musulman*, Editions du Seuil, Paris 1972 and *Peuple juif ou problème juif?*, Maspero, Paris 1981.
2. The primary question for liberal historians of nationalism (either as 'ideology' or as 'politics') is: 'Where and when does the transition from "liberal nationalism" to "imperialist nationalism" occur?' Cf. Hannah Arendt, 'Imperialism', Part II of *The Origins of Totalitarianism*, André Deutsch, London 1986, and Hans Kohn, *The Idea of Nationalism. A Study of Its Origins and Background*, New York 1944. Their common answer to this question is that it occurs between the 'universalist' revolutions of the eighteenth century and the 'Romanticism' of the nineteenth, which begins in Germany and then extends over the whole of Europe and finally the whole world in the twentieth century. Examining the question more closely, however, it turns out that the French Revolution could already be said to contain within itself these two contradictory aspects. It is thus the French Revolution that caused nationalism to 'go off the rails'.
3. Cf. Tom Nairn's caveats in 'The Modern Janus', *New Left Review*, no. 94, 1975 (reprinted in *The Break-Up of Britain*, New Left Books, London 1977). See the critique by Eric Hobsbawm, 'Some Reflections on The Break-Up of Britain', *New Left Review*, no. 105, 1977.
4. Which is not only a Marxist position but also the thesis of other 'economistic' thinkers in the liberal tradition. Cf. Ernest Gellner, *Nations and Nationalism*, Oxford 1983.
5. Colette Guillaumin, *L'Idéologie raciste. Genèse et langage actuel*, Mouton, Paris/ The Hague 1972; M. Rodinson, 'Quelques thèses critiques sur la démarche

poliakovienne', in M. Olender, ed., *Racisme, mythes et sciences*. See also M. Rodinson's article 'Nation: 3. Nation et idéologie', *Encyclopaedia universalis*.

6. This may usefully be compared with Erving Goffmann, *Stigma. Notes on the Management of Spoiled Identity*, Penguin, Harmondsworth 1968.

7. Cf. L. Dumont, *Essai sur l'individualisme*, Editions du Seuil, Paris 1983.

8. Cf. the debate between Tom Nairn and Benedict Anderson, in *The Break-Up of Britain* and *Imagined Communities*, on the relations between 'nationalism', 'patriotism' and 'racism'.

9. Cf. the excellent presentation by P. Ayçoberry in *La Question nazie, Essai sur les interprétations du national-socialisme, 1922–1975*, Editions du Seuil, Paris 1979.

10. Among other recent accounts, see Benedict Anderson, *Imagined Communities*, a happy parallel between the practices and discourses of Russification and Anglicization.

11. Cf. Léon Poliakov, *Histoire de l'antisémitisme*, new edn (Le Livre de Poche Pluriel), vol. II, pp. 259 *et seq*: Madeleine Rebérioux, 'L'Essor du racisme nationaliste', in P. de Comarmond and C. Duchet, eds, *Racisme et société*, Maspero, Paris 1969.

12. Cf. R. Ertel and G. Fabre and E. Marienstras, *En marge, Les minorités aux Etats-Unis*, Maspero, Paris 1974, pp. 287 *et seq*.

13. Bipan Chandra, *Nationalism and Colonialism in Modern India*, Orient Longman, New Delhi 1979, pp. 287 *et seq*.

14. Cf. Haroun Jamous, *Israël et ses juifs. Essai sur les limites du volontarisme*, Maspero, Paris 1982.

FURTHER READING

More detailed examinations of ethnicity and some discussion of its intersections with nationalism can be found in Richard Jenkins (1997), *Rethinking Ethnicity: Arguments and Explorations* (London: Sage) and Steve Fenton, (2003) *Ethnicity* (Cambridge: Polity). Both write from a sociological perspective informed by the social anthropological literature. Kenan Malik's (1996) *The Meaning of Race: Race, History and Culture in Western Society* (Basingstoke: Macmillan) traces the rise of racial thinking and the new cultural racism and its relationship historically to nationalism. A European focus on ethnicity and nationalism is provided by Hans-Rudolph Wicker's (1997) collection *Rethinking Nationalism and Ethnicity: The Struggle for Meaning and Order in Europe* (Oxford: Berg). Jyoti Puri's (2004) *Encountering Nationalism* (Oxford: Blackwell) provides a contemporary introduction that highlights issues of race, ethnicity and religion (as well as gender and sexuality).

PART FOUR
FORMS OF NATIONALISM

12

CIVIC AND ETHNIC NATIONALISM

Anthony Smith

One kind of collective identity, so important and widespread today, is barely mentioned in Sophocles' Theban plays. Though they sometimes hinge on conflict between cities, they never raise the question of 'national' identity. Oedipus' identities are multiple, but being 'foreign' (i.e. non-Greek) is never one of them. Collective conflicts are, at most, wars between Greek city-states and their rulers. Did this not, in fact, mirror the state of ancient Greece in the fifth century BC?

It was Friedrich Meinecke who in 1908 distinguished the *Kulturnation*, the largely passive cultural community, from the *Staatsnation*, the active, self-determining political nation. We may dissent from his use of these terms, indeed from the terms themselves; but the distinction itself is valid and relevant. Politically, there was no 'nation' in ancient Greece, only a collection of city-states, each jealous of its sovereignty. Culturally, however, there existed an ancient Greek community, Hellas, that could be invoked, for example by Pericles, in the political realm – usually for Athenian purposes. In other words we can speak of a Greek cultural and ethnic community but not of an ancient Greek 'nation'.[1]

This suggests that, whatever else it may be, what we mean by 'national' identity involves some sense of political community, however tenuous. A political community in turn implies at least some common institutions and a single code of rights and duties for all the members of the community. It also suggests a definite social space, a fairly well demarcated and bounded territory, with which the members identify and to which they feel they belong. This was

Anthony D. Smith (1991), *National Identity*, London: Penguin.

very much what the *philosophes* had in mind when they defined a nation as a community of people obeying the same laws and institutions within a given territory.[2]

This is, of course, a peculiarly Western conception of the nation. But then the Western experience has exerted a powerful, indeed the leading, influence on our conception of the unit we call the 'nation'. A new kind of policy – the rational state – and a new kind of community – the territorial nation – first emerged in the West, in close conjunction with each other. They left their imprint on subsequent non-Western conceptions, even when the latter diverged from their norms.

It is worth spelling out this Western or 'civic' model of the nation in more detail. It is, in the first place, a predominantly spatial or territorial conception. According to this view, nations must possess compact, well-defined territories. People and territory must, as it were, belong to each other, in the way that the early Dutch, for example, saw themselves as formed by the high seas and as forging (literally) the earth they possessed and made their own. But the earth in question cannot be just anywhere; it is not any stretch of land. It is, and must be, the 'historic' land, the 'homeland', the 'cradle' of our people, even where, as with the Turks, it is not the land of ultimate origin. A 'historic land' is one where terrain and people have exerted mutual, and beneficial, influence over several generations. The homeland becomes a repository of historic memories and associations, the place where 'our' sages, saints and heroes lived, worked, prayed and fought. All this makes the homeland unique. Its rivers, coasts, lakes, mountains and cities become 'sacred' – places of veneration and exaltation whose inner meanings can be fathomed only by the initiated, that is, the self-aware members of the nation. The land's resources also become exclusive to the people; they are not for 'alien' use and exploitation. The national territory must become self-sufficient. Autarchy is as much a defence of sacred homelands as of economic interests.[3]

A second element is the idea of a *patria*, a community of laws and institutions with a single political will. This entails as least some common regulating institutions that will give expression to common political sentiments and purposes. Sometimes, indeed, the *patria* is expressed through highly centralized and unitary institutions and laws, as in post-Revolutionary France, though even there the various regions retained their local identities into the early twentieth century. At the other extreme we find unions of separate colonies, provinces and city-states, whose federal institutions and laws are designed as much to protect local or provincial liberties as to express a common will and common political sentiments. Both the United States of America and the United Provinces of the Netherlands offer well-documented cases of such national unions. In many ways the primary purpose of the Union of Utrecht in 1579 and of the Nether-lands' States General was to protect the ancient liberties and privileges of the constituent provinces, which had been so rudely assailed by Habsburg policies of centralization under Charles V and Philip II. Nevertheless, the ferocity and duration of the war against Spain soon bred a sense of common purpose and identity (quite apart from Calvinist influence) that expressed a growing Dutch national political community, albeit incomplete.[4]

Concurrent with the growth of a sense of legal and political community we may trace a sense of legal equality among the members of that community. Its full expression is the various kinds of 'citizenship' that sociologists have enumerated, including civil and legal rights, political rights and duties, and socio-economic rights. Here it is legal and political rights that the Western conception considers integral to its model of a nation. That implies a minimum of reciprocal rights and obligations among members and the correlative exclusion of outsiders from those rights and duties. It also implies a common code of laws over and above local laws, together with agencies for their enforcement, courts of final appeal and the like. As important is the acceptance that, in principle, all members of the nation are legally equal and that the rich and powerful are bound by the laws of the *patria*.

Finally, the legal equality of members of a political community in its demarcated homeland was felt to presuppose a measure of common values and traditions among the population, or at any rate its 'core' community. In other words, nations must have a measure of common culture and a civic ideology, a set of common understandings and aspirations, sentiments and ideas, that bind the population together in their homeland. The task of ensuring a common public, mass culture has been handed over to the agencies of popular socialization, notably the public system of education and the mass media. In the Western model of national identity nations were seen as culture communities, whose members were united, if not made homogeneous, by common historical memories, myths, symbols and traditions. Even where new, immigrant communities equipped with their own historic cultures have been admitted by the state, it has taken several generations before their descendants have been admitted (in so far as they have been) into the circle of the 'nation' and its historic culture through the national agencies of mass socialization.[5]

Historic territory, legal–political community, legal–political equality of members, and common civic culture and ideology; these are the components of the standard, Western model of the nation. Given the influence of the West in the modern world, they have remained vital elements, albeit in somewhat altered form, in most non-Western conceptions of national identity. At the same time a rather different model of the nation sprang up outside the West, notably in Eastern Europe and Asia. Historically, it challenged the dominance of the Western model and added significant new elements, more attuned to the very different circumstances and trajectories of non-Western communities.

We can term this non-Western model an 'ethnic' conception of the nation. Its distinguishing feature is its emphasis on a community of birth and native culture. Whereas the Western concept laid down that an individual had to belong to some nation but could choose to which he or she belonged, the non-Western or ethnic concept allowed no such latitude. Whether you stayed in your community or emigrated to another, you remained ineluctably, organically, a member of the community of your birth and were for ever stamped by it. A nation, in other words, was first and foremost a community of common descent.

This ethnic model also has a number of facets. First, obviously, is the stress on descent – or rather, presumed descent – rather than territory. The nation is seen as a fictive 'super-family', and it boasts pedigrees and genealogies to back up its claims, often tracked down by native intellectuals, particularly in East European and Middle Eastern countries. The point here is that, in this conception, the nation can trace its roots to an imputed common ancestry and that therefore its members are brothers and sisters, or at least cousins, differentiated by family ties from outsiders.

This emphasis on presumed family ties helps to explain the strong popular or demotic element in the ethnic conception of the nation. Of course, the 'people' figure in the Western model too. But there they are seen as a political community subject to common laws and institutions. In the ethnic model the people, even where they are not actually mobilized for political action, nevertheless provide the object of nationalist aspirations and the final rhetorical court of appeal. Leaders can justify their actions and unite disparate classes and groups only through an appeal to the 'will of the people', and this makes the ethnic concept more obviously 'inter-class' and 'populist' in tone, even when the intelligentsia has little intention of summoning the masses into the political arena. Popular mobilization therefore plays an important moral and rhetorical, if not an actual, role in the ethnic conception.[6]

Similarly, the place of law in the Western civic model is taken by vernacular culture, usually languages and customs in the ethnic model. That is why lexicographers, philologists and folklorists have played a central role in the early nationalisms of Eastern Europe and Asia. Their linguistic and ethnographic research into the past and present culture of the 'folk' provided the materials for a blueprint of the 'nation-to-be', even where specific linguistic revivals failed. By creating a widespread awareness of the myths, history and linguistic traditions of the community, they succeeded in substantiating and crystallizing the idea of an ethnic nation in the minds of most members, even when, as in Ireland and Norway, the ancient languages declined.[7]

Genealogy and presumed descent ties, popular mobilization, vernacular languages, customs and traditions: these are the elements of an alternative, ethnic conception of the nation, one that mirrored the very different route of 'nation-formation' travelled by many communities in Eastern Europe and Asia and one that constituted a dynamic political challenge. It is, as we shall see, a challenge that is repeated to this day in many parts of the world, and it reflects the profound dualism at the heart of every nationalism. In fact every nationalism contains civic and ethnic elements in varying degrees and different forms. Sometimes civic and territorial elements predominate; at other times it is the ethnic and vernacular components that are emphasized. Under the Jacobins, for example, French nationalism was essentially civic and territorial; it preached the unity of the republican *patrie* and the fraternity of its citizens in a political–legal community. At the same time a linguistic nationalism emerged, reflecting pride in the purity and civilizing mission of a hegemonic French culture preached by Barère and the Abbé Gregoire. In the early nineteenth century French cultural nationalism began to reflect more ethnic conceptions of the nation, whether Frankish or Gallic; later these became validating charters for radically different ideals of France. The clerical–monarchist Right was particularly wedded to genealogical and vernacular conceptions of an 'organic' nation, which it opposed to the republican territorial and civic model, notably during the Dreyfus Affair.[8]

Nevertheless, even during the most severe conflicts mirroring opposed models of the nation certain fundamental assumptions tied the warring parties together through a common nationalist discourse. In the French example just cited both republicans and monarchists accepted the idea of France's 'natural' and historic territory (including Alsace). Similarly, there was no real dispute about the need to inculcate national ideals and history through a mass, public education system, only about some of its content (notably the Catholic dimension). Devotion to the French language was also universal. Similarly, nobody questioned the individuality of France and the French as such; differences arose only over the historical content of that uniqueness and hence the lessons to be drawn from that experience.

This suggests that behind the rival models of the nation stand certain common beliefs about what constitutes a nation as opposed to any other kind of collective, cultural identity. They include the idea that nations are territorially bounded units of population and that they must have their own homelands; that their members share a common mass culture and common historical myths and memories; that members have reciprocal legal rights and duties under a common legal system; and that nations possess a common division of labour and system of production with mobility across the territory for members. These are assumptions, and demands, common to all nationalists and widely accepted even by their critics, who may then go on to deplore the ensuing global divisions and conflicts created by the existence of such nations.

The existence of these common assumptions allows us to list the fundamental features of national identity as follows:

1. an historic territory, or homeland
2. common myths and historical memories
3. a common, mass public culture
4. common legal rights and duties for all members
5. a common economy with territorial mobility for members.

A nation can therefore be defined as *a named human population sharing an historic territory, common myths and historical memories, a mass, public culture, a common economy and common legal rights and duties for all members.*[9]

Such a provisional working definition reveals the complex and abstract nature of national identity. The nation, in fact, draws on elements of other kinds of collective identity, which accounts not only for the way in which national identity can be combined with these other types of identity – class, religious or ethnic – but also for the chameleon-like permutations of national*ism*, the ideology, with other ideologies like liberalism, fascism and communism. A national identity is fundamentally multi-dimensional; it can never be reduced to a single element, even by particular factions of nationalists, nor can it be easily or swiftly induced in a population by artificial means.

Such a definition of national identity also sets it clearly apart from any conception of the state. The latter refers exclusively to public institutions, differentiated from, and autonomous of, other social institutions and exercising a monopoly of coercion and extraction within a given territory. The nation, on the other hand, signifies a cultural and political bond, uniting in a single political community all who share an historic culture and homeland. This is not to deny some overlap between the two concepts, given their common reference to an historic territory and (in democratic states) their appeal to the sovereignty of the people. But, while modern states must legitimate themselves in national and popular terms as the states of particular nations, their content and focus are quite different.[10]

This lack of congruence between the state and the nation is exemplified in the many 'plural' states today. Indeed, Walker Connor's estimate in the early 1970s showed that only about 10 per cent of states could claim to be true 'nation-states', in the sense that the state's boundaries coincide with the nation's and that the total population of the state share a single ethnic culture. While most states aspire to become nation-states in this sense, they tend to limit their claims to legitimacy to an aspiration for political unity and popular sovereignty that, even in old-established Western states, risks being challenged by ethnic communities within their borders. These cases, and there are many of them, illustrate the profound gulf between the concepts of the state and the nation.[11]

NOTES

1. See the argument in Finley that covers Meinecke's points (1986, ch. 7); cf. Fondation Hardt (1962).
2. For early Western definitions of the nation, see Kemilainen (1964).
3. For the early Dutch case, see Schama (1987, ch. 1); for the various meanings of 'national territory', see Smith (1981b).
4. Schama (1987, ch. 2); and for persisting regionalism in late nineteenth-century France, see Weber (1979).
5. On these 'political cultures', see for example Almond and Pye (1965).
6. Nairn (1977, chs. 2, 9) emphasizes this 'inter-class', populist role. cf. also Gellner and Ionescu (1970).
7. For such linguistic revivals, see Fishman (1968); and for revivals in some Northern countries, including Ireland and Norway, see Mitchison (1980).

8. On French linguistic nationalism during the Revolution, see Lartichaux (1977); for rival myths of French descent, see Poliakov (1974, ch. 2).

9. For some of the many discussions of the problems of defining the nation and nationalism, see Deutsch (1966, ch. 1), Rustow (1967, ch. 1), Smith (1971, ch. 7) and Connor (1978).

10. See for example Tivey (1980).

11. Connor (1972) for this calculation; see also Wiberg (1983).

13

BANAL NATIONALISM

Michael Billig

Because nationalism has deeply affected contemporary ways of thinking, it is not easily studied. One cannot step outside the world of nations, nor rid oneself of the assumptions and common-sense habits which come from living within that world. Analysts must expect to be affected by what should be the object of their study. [. . .] It is easy to suppose that people 'naturally' speak different languages. The assumption is difficult to shake. What makes the problem even more complex is that there are common-sense assumptions about the nature of nationalism itself. In established nations, it seems 'natural' to suppose that nationalism is an over-heated reaction, which typically is the property of others. The assumption enables 'us' to forget 'our' nationalism. If our nationalism is to be remembered, then we must step beyond what seems to be common sense.

Roland Barthes claimed that ideology speaks with 'the Voice of Nature' (1977: 47). As others have pointed out, ideology comprises the habits of behaviour and belief which combine to make any social world appear to those, who inhabit it, as the natural world (Billig 1991; Eagleton 1991; Fairclough 1992; McLellan 1986; Ricoeur 1986). By this reckoning, ideology operates to make people forget that their world has been historically constructed. Thus, nationalism is the ideology by which the world of nations has come to seem the natural world – as if there could not possibly be a world without nations. Ernest Gellner has written that, in today's world, 'a man [sic] must have a nationality as he must have a nose and two ears' (1983: 6). It seems 'natural' to have such an identity. In the established nations, people do not generally forget their national identity. If asked 'who are you?', people may not respond by first giving their

Michael Billig (1995), *Banal Nationalism*, London: Sage.

national identity (Zavalloni 1993a, 1993b). Rarely, if asked which is their nationality, do they respond 'I've forgotten', although their answers may be not be quite straightforward (Condor 1996). National identity is not only some-thing which is thought to be natural to possess, but also something natural to remember.

This remembering, nevertheless, involves a forgetting, or rather there is a complex dialectic of remembering and forgetting. As will be seen, this dialectic is important in the banal reproduction of nationalism in established nations. Over a hundred years ago, Ernest Renan claimed that forgetting was 'a crucial element in the creation of nations' (1990: 11). Every nation must have its history, its own collective memory. This remembering is simultaneously a collective forgetting: the nation, which celebrates its antiquity, forgets its historical recency. Moreover, nations forget the violence which brought them into existence, for, as Renan pointed out, national unity 'is always effected by means of brutality' (ibid.: 11).

Renan's insight is an important one: once a nation is established, it depends for its continued existence upon a collective amnesia. The dialectic, however, is more complex than Renan implied. Not only is the past forgotten, as it is ostensibly being recalled, but so there is a parallel forgetting of the present. As will be suggested, national identity in established nations is remembered because it is embedded in routines of life, which constantly remind, or 'flag', nation-hood. However, these reminders, or 'flaggings', are so numerous and they are such a familiar part of the social environment, that they operate mindlessly, rather than mindfully (Langer 1989). The remembering, not being experienced as remembering, is, in effect, forgotten. The national flag, hanging outside a public building or decorating a filling-station forecourt, illustrates this forgotten reminding. Thousands upon thousands of such flags each day hang limply in public places. These reminders of nationhood hardly register in the flow of daily attention, as citizens rush past on their daily business.

There is a double neglect. Renan implied that intellectuals are involved in the creation of amnesia. Historians creatively remember ideologically convenient facts of the past, while overlooking what is discomfiting. Today, social scientists frequently forget the national present. The banal episodes, in which nationhood is mindlessly and countlessly flagged, tend to be ignored by sociologists. They, too, have failed to notice the flag on the forecourt. Thus, Renan's insight can be expanded: historians might forget their nation's past, whilst social scientists can forget its present reproduction.

The present chapter argues that the sociological forgetting is not fortuitous; nor is it to be blamed on the absent-mindedness of particular scholars. Instead, it fits an ideological pattern in which 'our' nationalism (that of established nations, including the United States of America) is forgotten: it ceases to appear as nationalism, disappearing into the 'natural' environment of 'socie-ties'. At the same time, nationalism is defined as something dangerously emotional and irrational: it is conceived as a problem, or a condition, which is surplus to the world of nations. The irrationality of nationalism is projected on to 'others'.

Complex habits of thought naturalize, and thereby overlook, 'our' nationalism, whilst projecting nationalism, as an irrational whole, on to others. At the core of this intellectual amnesia lies a restricted concept of 'nationalism', which confines 'nationalism' to particular social movements rather than to nation-states. Only the passionately waved flags are conventionally considered to be exemplars of nationalism. Routine flags – the flags of 'our' environment – slip from the category of 'nationalism'. And having slipped through the categorical net, they get lost. There is no other theoretical term to rescue them from oblivion.

The double neglect is critically examined in this chapter. This involves examining the rhetoric of the sociological common sense which routinely reduces nationalism to a surplus phenomenon and which forgets to analyse how established nation-states are daily reproduced as nations. If the narrowing of the concept of 'nationalism' has led to the forgetting of banal nationalism, then it is hoped that a widening of the concept will lead to a remembering. The double neglect is to be reversed by a double remembering: the banal nationalism by which nation-states are reproduced is to be remembered, as are the habits of thought which have encouraged a neglect of this reproduction.

WAVED AND UNWAVED FLAGS

The place of national flags in contemporary life bears a moment's consideration. Particular attention should be paid to the case of the United States, whose filling-station forecourts are arrayed with uncounted Stars and Stripes. The US legislature has decreed strict laws about how the flag should be displayed and what is forbidden to be done, on pain of penalty, to the precious pattern of stars and stripes. Desecration of the flag is met with reactions of outrage (Marvin 1991). Of all countries, the United States is arguably today the home of what Renan called 'the cult of the flag' (1990, p. 17).

The anthropologist, Raymond Firth (1973), in one of the few studies of the role of flags in contemporary life, distinguished between the symbolic and signalling functions of flags. The forerunners of modern national flags were often employed as signals, reducing entropy in situations of uncertainty. The mediaeval gonfanon presented a clear rallying point for soldiers in the confusion of the battleground. The *semeion*, in ancient Greece, indicated the presence of the commander to other ships of the fleet (Perrin 1922). Since the eighteenth century, a complex system of signalling with flags has been developed for vessels at sea. In all these cases, flags are a pragmatically useful means of communicating messages. By contrast argues Firth, the national flag today performs a symbolic function, being a 'condensation symbol' and 'a focus for sentiment about society' (p. 356). The national flag, according to Firth, symbolizes the sacred character of the nation; it is revered by loyal citizens and ritually defiled by those who wish to make a protest. It carries no informational message, although, as Firth points out, the manner of a flag's display can, on special occasions provide a signal. A national flag hung at half mast may communicate the death of an important figure. Notwithstanding this, the majority of national flags likely to be seen by the modern citizen in the course of a lifetime will not be signalling a particular message.

Other distinctions, besides that between symbol and signal, can be made. The signal, if it is to be effective, must pass into the conscious awareness of its recipients. However, the symbol need not have a direct emotional impact, as Firth seemed to assume. That being so, one can distinguish between the ways in which national flags are treated. Some are consciously waved and saluted symbols, often accompanied by a pageant of outward emotion. Others – probably the most numerous in the contemporary environment – remain unsaluted and unwaved. They are merely there as symbols, whether on a forecourt or flashed on to a television screen; as such they are given hardly a second glance from day to day.

The distinction between the waved and unwaved (or saluted and unsaluted) flag can be illustrated with reference to Roland Barthes' classic essay 'Myth Today'. Barthes discussed an issue of the magazine *Paris-Match*, which he was offered in a barber-shop. On its cover, 'a young Negro in French army uniform is saluting, with his eyes uplifted, probably fixed on the fold of the tricolor' (Barthes 1983: 101f.). Barthes does not make clear whether the Tricolor which the soldier was saluting was to be seen in the photograph. For the sake of illustration, let us presume it was. The three-coloured flag which the soldier actually faced was clearly a flag to be saluted in the appropriate way. However, the photographed flag on the *Paris-Match* cover was not for saluting. It could lie around the corner of the barber-shop. Eyes could flick over it, to be reminded unconsciously of the myth of imperial power, whose photographic image Barthes so brilliantly analysed. But no one stops to wave or salute this image of a symbol. The barber does not straighten up in mid-haircut, his right hand imitating that of the photographed 'young Negro'. The customer in the barber's chair, on catching sight of the cover in the mirror, does not spring to patriotic attention, risking blade and scissor in the service of the nation. The magazine is picked up and put down without ceremony. Ultimately, without risk of penalty, the *Paris-Match* flag is tossed into the rubbish bin.

The young soldier was saluting a single flag in a unique instant, which was caught by the photographer. Thousands upon thousands of the *Paris-Match* flag were distributed, gazed at and discarded. They join other flags, some of which do have recognizable, signalling functions. The French Tricolor, when displayed on loaves of bread, can indicate an approved standard of baking, or *pain de tradition française*. When the government gives such flags *lettres de noblesse*, as Monsieur Balladur's did in September 1993, the Tricolor not only signals the quality of baking; it also flags the quality of the national tradition and the quality of the national state, benevolently supervising the daily bread of its citizenry.

The uncounted millions of flags which mark the homeland of the United States do not demand immediate, obedient attention. On their flagpoles by the street and stitched on to the uniforms of public officials, they are unwaved, unsaluted and unnoticed. These are mindless flags. Perhaps if all the unwaved flags which decorate the familiar environment were to be removed, they would suddenly be noticed, rather like the clock that stops ticking. If the reds and blues were changed into greens and oranges, there would be close, scandalized scrutiny, as well as criminal charges to follow.

One can ask what are all these unwaved flags doing, not just in the USA but around the world? In an obvious sense, they are providing banal reminders of nationhood: they are 'flagging' it unflaggingly. The reminding, involved in the routine business of flagging, is not a conscious activity; it differs from the collective rememberings of a commemoration. The remembering is mindless, occurring as other activities are being consciously engaged in.

These routine flags are different from those that seem to call attention to themselves and their symbolic message. Belfast in Northern Ireland is divided into mutually suspicious Catholic and Protestant districts. In the former, the Irish tricolor is widely displayed as a gesture of defiance against British sovereignty. In the backstreets of Protestant neighbourhoods, the kerb-stones are often painted with the pattern of the Union Jack (Beattie 1993). These are not mindless symbols, for each side is consciously displaying its position and distancing itself from its neighbour. The tricolors, in this respect, differ from those hanging on public buildings south of the border. One might predict that, as a nation-state becomes established in its sovereignty, and if it faces little internal challenge, then the symbols of nationhood, which might once have been consciously displayed, do not disappear from sight, but instead become absorbed into the environment of the established homeland. There is, then, a movement from symbolic mindfulness to mindlessness.

Yassar Arafat, the leader of the Palestine Liberation Organization, declared as a peace deal with Israel was becoming a real possibility: 'The Palestine state is within our grasp. Soon the Palestine flag will fly on the walls, the minarets and the cathedrals of Jerusalem' (*Guardian*, 3 September 1993). Arafat was using the notion of the flag as a metonym: by citing the flag, he was flagging Palestine nationhood. If he was discursively waving the flag of Palestine, he was hoping that the flags would actually be waved within the recovered homeland. Yet, in a longer view, Arafat's hope was that the waving would stop. The Palestine flags, displayed routinely on walls and roofs in a Palestine state, would be barely noticed by a citizenry freely going about their business. Occasionally, on special days – an Independence Day or an Annual Arafat Thanksgiving Parade – the streets would be filled with waved, commemorating flags.

Flags are not the only symbols of modern statehood. Coins and bank notes typically bear national emblems, which remain unnoticed in daily financial transactions. Naming the unit of currency can be a highly symbolic and controversial business, especially in the early days of a nation. In 1994,

President Franjo Tudjman of Croatia decided that the dinar should be replaced by the 'kuna', which was the unit of currency used in the Nazi-backed state of Croatia between 1941 and 1945. 'Kuna' is the term for the furry marten which inhabits the forests of Croatia. The president defended his decision by claiming that 'the kuna defends our national tradition and confirms our sovereignty' (*Independent*, 15 May 1994). This tradition and sovereignty would become symbolically banalized when the citizenry exchange their kunas without a second thought for furry creatures, President Tudjman or the victims of Nazism. In this way, the tradition, including the Nazi heritage, would be neither consciously remembered, nor forgotten: it would be preserved in daily life.

Psychologically, conscious remembering and forgetting are not polar opposites which exclude all middle ground. Similarly, traditions are not either consciously remembered (or co-memorated) in flag-waving collective activity, or consigned to a collective amnesia. They can be simultaneously present and absent, in actions which preserve collective memory without the conscious activity of individuals remembering. Serge Moscovici has discussed how most social activity is itself a remembering, although it is not experienced as such: 'Social and intellectual activity is, after all, a rehearsal or recital, yet most social psychologists treat it as if it were amnesic' (1983: 10). Behaviour and thoughts are never totally created anew, but they follow, and thus repeat, familiar patterns, even when they change such patterns. To act and to speak, one must remember. Nevertheless, actors do not typically experience their actions as repetitions, and, ordinarily, speakers are not conscious of the extent to which their own words repeat, and thereby transmit, past grammars and semantics.

If banal life is to be routinely practised, then this form of remembering must occur without conscious awareness: it occurs when one is doing other things, including forgetting. Pierre Bourdieu's notion of the 'habitus' expresses well this dialectic of remembering and forgetting. The 'habitus' refers to the dispositions, practices and routines of the familiar social world. It describes 'the second nature' which people must acquire in order to pass mindlessly (and also mindfully) through the banal routines of daily life. Bourdieu emphasizes the elements of remembering and the forgetting: 'The *habitus* – embodied history, internalized as a second nature and so forgotten as history – is the active presence of the whole past of which it is the product' (1990: 56).

Patterns of social life become habitual or routine, and in so doing embody the past. One might describe this process of routine-formation as *enhabitation*: thoughts, reactions and symbols become turned into routine habits and, thus, they become *enhabited*. The result is that the past is enhabited in the present in a dialectic of forgotten remembrance. President Tudjman was hoping that the kuna (and, with it, the history of the previous Croatian republic) would become enhabited as a living, unremembered, collective memory. Once enhabited it would flag the very things which the President could only mention mindfully and controversially.

The forgetting of the national past, of which Renan wrote, is continually reproduced in nation-states. The unwaved national flag – whether literally in the form of the flag itself or [. . .] in the routine phrases of the mass media – is enhabited in contemporary daily life. These reminders of nationhood serve to turn background space into homeland space. The flag may be, as Firth suggested, a focus for sentiment, but this does not mean that each flag acts as a psychological magnet for sentiments. Far from it, mostly the flags are ignored. Their flagging and reminding are habitually overlooked in the routines of the inhabited, enhabited national homeland.

HOT AND BANAL NATIONALISM

As has been mentioned, there is a double neglect as far as the social scientific investigation of nationalism is concerned. The neglect of the unwaved flags by citizenry going about their daily business is paralleled by a theoretical neglect. The enhabitation of nationalism within established nations is largely ignored by conventional sociological common sense. Only the waved or saluted flag tends to be noticed. If sociological categories are nets for catching slices of social life, then the net, which sociologists have marked 'nationalism', is a remarkably small one: and it seems to be used primarily for catching exotic, rare and often violent specimens. The collectors of these species tend not to stand in Main Street, USA, with net poised for new varieties.

The standard definitions of nationalism tend to locate nationalism as something beyond, or prior to, the established nation-state. In this respect, the social scientific definitions follow wider patterns of thinking. For example, Ronald Rogowski (1985) defines nationalism as 'the striving' by members of nations 'for territorial autonomy, unity and independence'. He claims that this definition matches 'everyday discourse', adding that 'we routinely and properly speak of Welsh, Quebecquois and Arab nationalism' (pp. 88–9; for similar treatments of 'nationalism', see, *inter alia*, Coakley 1992; Schlesinger 1991). As will be seen, Rogowski is correct in stating that this is the way that 'nationalism' is used routinely – but whether more 'properly' is another matter. The definition, in concentrating on the striving for autonomy, unity and independence, ignores how these things are maintained once they have been achieved. No alternative term is offered for the ideological complex, which maintains the autonomous nation-state.

Nationalism, thus, is typically seen as the force which creates nation-states or which threatens the stability of existing states. In the latter case, nationalism can take the guise of separatist movements or extreme fascistic ones. Nationalism can appear as a developmental stage, which mature societies (or nations) have outgrown once they are fully established. This assumption is to be found in Karl Deutsch's (1966) classic study *Nationalism and Social Communication*. More recently, it underlies Hroch's (1985) valuable study *Social Preconditions of National Revival in Europe*. Hroch postulates three stages of nationalism. The first two stages describe how interest in the national idea is awakened by intellectuals and, then, how it is diffused; and the final stage occurs when a mass movement seeks to translate the national idea into the nation-state. There are no further stages to describe what happens to nationalism once the nation-state is established. It is as if nationalism suddenly disappears.

Nationalism, however, does not entirely disappear, according to this view: it becomes something surplus to everyday life. It threatens the established state and its established routines, or it returns when those orderly routines have broken down. Ordinary life in the normal state (the sort of state which the analysts tend to inhabit) is assumed to be banal, unexciting politically and non-nationalist. Nationalism, by contrast, is extraordinary, politically charged and emotionally driven.

Anthony Giddens describes nationalism as 'a phenomenon that is primarily psychological' (1985: 116; see also Giddens 1987: 178). Nationalist sentiments rise up when the 'sense of ontological security is put in jeopardy by the disruption of routines' (Giddens 1985: 218). In these circumstances, 'regressive forms of object-identification tend to occur', with the result that individuals invest great emotional energy in the symbols of nationhood and in the promise of strong leadership (ibid.: 218). Nationalism, according to Giddens, occurs when ordinary life is disrupted: it is the exception, rather than the rule. Nationalist feelings 'are not so much a part of regular day-to-day social life' (ibid.: 215), but 'tend to be fairly remote from most of the activities of day-to-day social life'. Ordinary life is affected by nationalist sentiments only 'in fairly unusual and often relatively transitory conditions' (ibid.: 218). Thus, the psychology of nationalism is that of an extraordinary, emotional mood striking at extraordinary times. Banal routines, far from being bearers of nationalism, are barriers against nationalism.

Analysts, such as Giddens, are reserving the term 'nationalism' for outbreaks of 'hot' nationalist passion, which arise in times of social disruption and which are reflected in extreme social movements. In so doing, they are pointing to a recognizable phenomenon – indeed, one which is all too familiar in the contemporary world. The problem is not what such theories describe as nationalist, but what they omit. If the term 'nationalism' is applied only to forceful social movements, something slips from theoretical awareness. It is as if the flags on those filling-station forecourts do not exist.

The issue is wider than that of flags. It concerns national identity and its assumed naturalness in the established nation-state. It might be argued that such identities, far from being maintained by banal routines, are, in fact, supported by extraordinary moments which psychically parallel the extraordinary moments when nationalist movements arise. A dramatic psychology of the emotions, rather than a banal psychology of routines, might be evoked to explain identity in nation-states. All nation-states have occasions when ordinary routines are suspended, as the state celebrates itself. Then, sentiments of patriotic emotion, which the rest of the year have to be kept far from the business of ordinary life, can surge forth. The yearly calendar of the modern nation would replicate in miniature its longer political history: brief moments of nationalist emotion punctuate longer periods of settled calm, during which nationalism seems to disappear from sight.

Certainly, each nation has its national days, which disrupt the normal routines. There are independence day parades, thanksgiving days and coronations, when a nation's citizenry commemorates, or jointly remembers, itself and its history (Bocock 1974; Chaney 1993; Eriksen 1993a). It could be argued that these occasions are sufficient to flag nationhood, so that it is remembered during the rest of the year, when the banal routines of private life predominate. Certainly, great national days are often experienced as being 'memorable'. The participants are aware that the day of celebration, on which the nation is collectively remembered, is itself a moment which is to be remembered (Billig 1990; Billig and Edwards 1994). Afterwards, individuals and families will have their stories to tell about what they did on the day the prince and princess married, or the queen was crowned (Billig 1992; Ziegler 1977).

These are conventional carnivals of surplus emotion, for the participants expect to have special feelings, whether of joy, sorrow or inebriation. The day has been marked as a time when normal routines are put into abeyance, and when extra emotions should be enacted. Participants may be uncertain how to mark the great national occasion in the banal setting of home, but the uncertainty itself reveals both the specialness and the conventional nature of the occasion. The Mass Observation Study asked Britons to record how they spent their time on the day in 1937 when George VI was crowned as king. A left-wing woman recalled in her diary:

> Woken by conscientious male cook stumping about in kitchen overhead. Troubled by vague necessity for waking husband with suitable greeting. Sleepily wondered whether a 'God Save the King!' would be appropriate (husband likes Happy-New-Years and Many-Happy-Returns). Finally awoke enough to realize that a shaking was sufficient. (Jennings and Madge 1987: 106)

Another routine, or conventional pattern, must be found for the special day which formally breaks the everyday routine. This special routine must enable the actor to perform the expected emotion. Thus, the woman wonders how to accomplish an appropriately patriotic greeting. In this respect, the suitable emotion is not an ineffable impulse, which mysteriously impels the social actor in unforeseeable directions. It is dependent upon, and is sustained by, social forms, which themselves can be modelled upon other familiarly conventional breaks of daily routine, such as birthdays and new year celebrations.

The great days of national celebration are patterned so that the national flag can be consciously waved both metaphorically and literally. However, these are by no means the only social forms which sustain what is loosely called national identity. In between times, citizens of the state still remain citizens and the state does not wither away. The privately waved flags may be wrapped up and put back in the attic, ready for next year's independence day, but that is not the end of flagging. All over the world, nations display their flags, day after day. Unlike the flags on the great days, these flags are largely unwaved, unsaluted, unnoticed. Indeed, it seems strange to suppose that occasional events, bracketed off from ordinary life, are sufficient to sustain a continuingly remembered national identity. It would seem more likely that the identity is part of a more banal way of life in the nation-state.

THE RETURN OF THE REPRESSED

'The repressed has returned, and its name is nationalism', writes Michael Ignatieff at the beginning of his widely publicised *Blood and Belonging*, (1993: 2). At once, nationalism is signalled as something which comes and goes. Ignatieff's book illustrates how easily – indeed, how convincingly – such a portrayal of nationalism can appear today. In this portrayal, nationalism appears as dangerous, emotional and the property of others. Ignatieff's argument is worth close attention, because of what it omits. As will be seen, his portrayal of nationalism, together with its omissions, matches themes right at the heart of sociological common sense.

Ignatieff's book expresses a common-sense view of nationalism which straddles the boundaries between academic and more general thinking. *Blood and Belonging* accompanied a television series, made by the British Broadcasting Corporation, with the rights being sold world-wide. It was also serialized in a British Sunday newspaper. Announcing the first extract, the *Independent on Sunday* declared that 'modern nationalism is as passionate and violent as ever, a call to come home and a call to arms' (24 October 1993).

Ignatieff's message is one of warning. Concentrating upon six locations – Croatia/Serbia, Germany, Ukraine, Quebec, Kurdistan and Northern Ireland – he describes how the irrational forces of ethnic nationalism are erupting to haunt the contemporary world. The collapse of communism and the growth of global communications, far from heralding a new world of cooperative rationality seem to be unleashing a primordial reaction: 'the key narrative of the new world order is the disintegration of nation states into ethnic civil war' (Ignatieff 1993: 2).

The theme of the repressed returning is easily maintained at present. Throughout Europe, the impulses of fascism are stirring again, in the form of parties which declare a politics of national regeneration. Political parties in Romania and Hungary are attracting large numbers of voters with their anti-gypsy and anti-alien messages. In Russia, the misnamed Liberal Democratic Party, campaigning for a greater, ethnically pure nation, is currently the largest party in parliament. During the 1990s the Front National has regularly attracted between 12 and 15 per cent of the French popular vote, whereas in the previous decade it could barely muster 1 per cent (Hainsworth 1992). The Vlaams Block has become the most popular party of Antwerp (Husbands 1992). The most striking example of fascism's return is Italy, where in 1994 the MSI (Italian Social Movement), having changed its name to National Alliance, entered the coalition government of Berlusconi. When this occurs, fascism is returning not on the margins of politics, but in the historical heartlands of Europe. No wonder, then, it seems as if the repressed (and the repressive) is returning.

The theme of nationalism's dangerous and irrational return is becoming commonplace in writings by academic social scientists. Majid Tehranian, like Ignatieff, tells a story of repression and return. He suggests that, during the Cold War, 'ethnicity and ethnic discourse . . . remained repressed', because, at that time, 'the universalist ideological pretensions of communism and liberalism left little room for the claims of ethnic and national loyalties' (Tehranian 1993: 193). According to Tehranian, 'the end of the Cold War . . . has unleashed the centrifugal, ethnic and tribal forces within nation states' (ibid.: 193). Now, nationalism threatens to turn the new world order into disorder (or 'dysorder', to adopt Tehranian's spelling).

One feature of these stories of repression and return can be mentioned. The claim that nationalism is returning implies that it has been away. In such comments, the world of settled nations appears as the point-zero of nationalism. The wars waged by democratic states, in contrast to the wars waged by rebel forces, are not labelled nationalist. Ignatieff hardly mentions the Vietnam or Falklands Wars, let alone the various US sorties into Korea, Panama, or Grenada. Nor does he mention the popular support given to US military actions, at least while successfully pursued. He does not label wars, occurring during nationalism's so-called quiescent period, as nationalist, despite their accompanying patriotic rhetoric. Moreover, the Cold War itself was couched in nationalist terms. Yatani and Bramel (1984), examining opinion poll evidence, concluded that the American public viewed the confrontation between two great, universalist ideologies as a conflict between two nations: communism was Russian, and capitalism was American.

To be fair, Ignatieff does not entirely forget the nationalism of established nation-states. He remembers it, only to forget it. He distinguishes between 'ethnic' and 'civic' nationalism. Ethnic nationalism is the hot, surplus variety, being based on sentiments of 'blood loyalty' (Ignatieff 1993: 6). It is the nationalism of the intolerant bigots. Ignatieff dissociates himself from ethnic nationalism, declaring 'I am a civic nationalist' (ibid.: 9). Civic nationalism, according to Ignatieff, is a political creed, which defines common citizenship and which emerged from the universalist philosophies of the Enlightenment. It is, he writes, the nationalism of established European democracies at their best. Despite Ignatieff's claim to be a civic nationalist, he personally disavows loyalty to a single nation-state. He does not describe how 'civic nationalists' create a nation-state with its own myths; how the civic nations recruit their citizenry in war-time; how they draw their own boundaries; how they demarcate 'others' beyond those boundaries; how they resist, violently if necessary, those movements which seek to rearrange the boundaries; and so on. In fact, the nationalism of 'civic nationalism' seems to slide away.

Indeed, civic nationalism as a whole slides away textually. When Ignatieff refers to 'nationalism' without qualification, he means the ethnic variety: 'Nationalism legitimizes an appeal to blood loyalty' (ibid.: 6). Thus, ethnic nationalism appears as if it were the epitome of all nationalism. The 'nationalism', which was repressed, but which now has returned, is, of course, the dangerous variety. Ignatieff's publishers catch the mood on the book jacket: 'Modern nationalism is the language of blood: a call to arms which can end in the horrors of ethnic cleansing.' Surplus nationalism has become the genus; its benign form is expelled from the category.

So long as the 'problems of nationalism' are defined in this way, the ideology, by which established Western nations are reproduced as nations, can be taken for granted. The Gulf War disappears from theoretical attention, as does the nationalism of established, democratic nations. This way of presenting nationalism is widespread. In describing political events in Northern Ireland, the British media typically use the term 'nationalist' to describe those who seek to abolish the border between the United Kingdom and Éire, especially if they advocate violence in the pursuit of these aims. The government of the British nation-state, by contrast, is not called 'nationalist', although it, too, can use force to maintain present national boundaries. Often, the term 'nationalist' seems to exert a magnetic pull upon the critical adjective 'extreme' in the force-field of commonplace semantics. The linkage implies that those who desire to change the political map of nations possess an unwarranted surplus of fervour, which is to be identified as nationalist.

Examples can be given from British newspapers. Here, as elsewhere, it is important not to select illustrations from the popular press, whose chauvinistic excesses have been well documented (Taylor 1991). Nationalism is too general a phenomenon to be projected on to the working-class readers of popular newspapers, as if 'we', the liberal, educated classes, are removed from that sort of thing. 'Our' newspapers, on 'our' daily breakfast tables, present routine flags for 'our' benefit, as do 'our' sociological and psychological theories.

The *Guardian*, Britain's most liberal, left-of-centre quality newspaper, is important in this respect. A detailed analysis would be necessary to sustain the general point about the term 'nationalism', but a couple of illustrative examples can be briefly given. An article on Serbia carried the headline 'Nationalists challenge Milosevic'. The opening sentence asserted: 'President Slobodan Milosevic of Serbia's problems [sic] will mount today when extreme nationalists table a no-confidence motion against his Serbian Socialist party government' (7 October 1993). In the article, the writer does not once use the word 'nationalist' to describe the Serbian government or its President. Milosevic, himself the architect of a Greater Serbia, and hence of a lesser Bosnia and Croatia, is described as consolidating his power, having 'essentially won the wars in Croatia and Bosnia'. The term 'extreme nationalists' refers to the same people as the unqualified 'nationalists' of the headline. Thus, the President and his state are being unmade as 'nationalist'. The territory, gained from the war of expansion, is on its way to international recognition. This flagging of what is nationalism (and by implication what is not nationalism) occurs beyond the level of outward argument. It is ingrained into the very rhetoric of common sense, which provides the linguistic resources for making outward arguments.

A second example also concerns Balkan politics. An article reports the opening of a museum of Serbiana on the Greek island of Corfu. The opening paragraph set the tone:

> As fiery displays of fervent nationalism go, it was a fine one. There was the archbishop with his golden cross giving a blessing that had grown men in tears. Amid flowers and flags, a dinner-jacketed all-male choir sang patriotic melodies. (*Guardian*, 6 September 1993)

The event was not an official state occasion. It was organized by a group which wishes to alter, rather than protect, existing state boundaries. In this context, the adjective 'fiery' takes its textual place as a companion to the word 'nationalism'. The author assumes that readers will be familiar with the notion of 'fiery displays of nationalism', and will appreciate that this was a 'fine' example of a generally understood genus. Official occasions in 'our' established nations, such as dinners for heads of state or the opening of new national monuments, often involve similar elements of display: flags, flowers, divines in funny costumes and suitably patriotic melodies. However, these occasions are rarely described as displays of nationalism, let alone 'fiery nationalism'.

The rhetoric distances 'us' from 'them', 'our' world from 'theirs'. And 'we', writer and readers, are assumed to belong to a reasonable world, a point-zero of nationalism. In these newspaper reports and in Ignatieff's book, nationalism is routinely and implicitly the property of others. Freud claimed that projection depends upon forgetting. He was referring to the individual repressing personal experiences of the past from conscious awareness. There is also, by analogy, a form of collective forgetting and collective projection. Common sense, through gaps in vocabulary and through the pointed rhetoric of cliché, can accomplish what amounts to a collective amnesia. This projection is a social habit of thought. 'Our' nationalism is routinely forgotten, being unnamed as nationalism. Nationalism as a whole is projected on to others. But, again and again, not only 'their' nationalism seems to return; 'ours' does too.

14

GOOD AND BAD NATIONALISMS

Philip Spencer and Howard Wollman

THE JANUS FACE OF NATIONALISM

In a famous and influential article, Tom Nairn suggested that 'all nationalism is both healthy and morbid. Both progress and regress are inscribed in its genetic code from the start' (1997b: 347–8). Nairn was perhaps unusual at the time in trying to deal with the complexity and at times baffling variety of nationalist movements by seeing nationalism as at one and the same time both positive and negative, a legacy perhaps of his background in Marxism. Many other writers have adopted a more dualistic approach, distinguishing more sharply between different kinds of nationalism, marking out more clearly positive and negative poles of reference.[1]

This tendency, to split nationalism into two fundamentally different types, has a long history in the literature, going back at least to the seminal work of Hans Kohn (1965). It can take, as we shall see, a number of different forms, not all of them necessarily consistent or compatible with each other. Whilst this may not in itself be an insuperable problem, there are a number of major difficulties, both theoretical and empirical, with the dualistic approach which cannot be easily resolved.

The theoretical difficulties are partly methodological and partly conceptual. To begin with, distinctions are often formulated in terms of dichotomous Weberian-style ideal types, not existing in a pure form in practice, but useful for comparing against the complexity of political and historical reality. Too often this seems to lead to the complexity being lost sight of in the heat of analysis and to the ideal type or model coming to stand itself for the reality. An analytical distinction (itself problematic) thus comes to be treated as real. At the

Philip Spencer and Howard Wollman (2002), *Nationalism: a Critical Introduction*, London: Sage.

same time, it can allow for, if not actively encourage, a certain slipperiness in argument, as writers attacked for overdoing a distinction between, say, civic and ethnic nationalism can retreat into a defence that they are only making analytical distinctions and that of course most nationalisms are a combination of both. Thus Anthony Smith writes that 'modern nations are simultaneously and necessarily civic and ethnic' (1995: 99). Meanwhile the dichotomy establishes itself thoroughly in the literature.[2]

At the same time, the categories used by different theorists often overlap in ways that confuse and blur the distinctions between good and bad. What are held to be virtues in some accounts are vices in another. More seriously perhaps, the virtues themselves, what is held to make a particular form of nationalism good rather than bad, may have nothing essentially to do with nationalism itself. These supposed virtues may, in other words, be conceptually independent, stand or fall on their own account. Mixing them up with nationalism in one form or another may be both unnecessary and even counterproductive.

Empirically, certain sharp distinctions do not stand up to close scrutiny. Some of the often cited classic historical examples of one type or the other appear to fall rather less than clearly into one side or other of a dichotomy than is often claimed. In the contemporary world too, and perhaps especially, a number of the distinctions are difficult to apply with any conviction. In relation to Western liberal democracies in particular there is a tendency to downplay certain features of nationalism and the nation state whilst maintaining a full critical stance towards other manifestations of nationalism.[3] This is partly due to an ethnocentric bias which privileges the West, and partly due to a blindness to some of the contradictions in liberal nationalism itself. As a result, there seems to be a utopian character to the work of a number of writers as they fail to take account of (to borrow Bogdan Denitch's telling phrase) 'really existing nationalism' (Denitch 1996).

Ultimately this dualistic approach, we argue, raises more problems than it solves. Whilst it would clearly be mistaken to assert that nationalisms are all exactly the same, or to deny that nationalism can take different forms across time and space, it may be more serious to underestimate what apparently different forms of nationalism have in common and the problems they may all pose. For at the heart of nationalism as a political project, whatever form it takes, is a logic that tends towards exclusion. There must after all always be people who are not part of the nation; the nation is always framed with the presumption of the existence of the outsider, the other, against which the nation is itself defined and constructed. The problem of the other is common to all forms of nationalism, constantly creating and recreating the conditions in which supposedly 'good' forms of nationalism turn 'bad'. The problem of dualism is that it obscures and cannot explain this continual slippage, and creates the illusion that somehow or other it can be avoided, when so much of the evidence points the other way.

ONE, TWO, MANY DUALISMS

It is possible to identify a large number of dualistic distinctions in the literature which have these characteristics. A cursory list would include all or some of the following:

Western	Eastern
Political	Cultural
Staatsnation	*Kulturnation*
Civic	Ethnic
Liberal	Illiberal
Individualistic	Collectivist
Voluntarist	Organic
Rational	Mystical/emotional
Universalistic	Particularistic
Patriotism	(Chauvinist) Nationalism
Constitutional	Authoritarian
Historic nations	Non-historic nations
Nationalism of the oppressed	Nationalism of the oppressor
Women-Emancipation nationalism	Patriarchal nationalism

Some of these distinctions in the literature are more influential than others; some are overlapping; some refer to specific writers; others refer to more general tendencies. Whilst there is clearly not space here to provide an exhaustive treatment of all of these, we can highlight and analyse a central set which are closely related in terms of their foci of concern, and which may be understood in a sense as part of the same basic matrix. The contrast specifically between West and East, between the political and the cultural, between the civic and ethnic, are all, we may argue, hewn from the same rock. They emerge to some degree sequentially and to some degree as successive reformulations. Separately and collectively they are arguably at the core of the dualistic enterprise, seeing to arrive at the same point, at a clear and unambiguous point of distinction and contrast. If this point cannot in fact be reached even by these routes, it may be argued, perhaps it cannot be reached at all.

WEST AND EAST

One of the earliest distinctions may be thought of on the face of it as more geographical than conceptual. This is the distinction between nationalism in its Western and its Eastern forms. Although less obviously in vogue today, it has played a prominent role in the work of some major writers on nationalism, from Kohn to John Plamenatz and the late Ernest Gellner, writers whose work has spanned some sixty years and still remains influential today. Of course, this distinction could never be, and was never intended to be, merely geographical. Rather the words 'West' and 'East' functioned as containers, to be filled with a particular (and value-laden) content. According to Kohn (1965), nationalism developed in the West first and along singular lines. It was the product of the Enlightenment, of the age of reason, an essential expression of the confidence of rational, (and especially) bourgeois individuals wishing to pursue their legitimate interests. Eastern nationalism by contrast developed in a profoundly different environment, along quite different lines and, importantly, in reaction to the success and confidence of the West. Plamenatz in turn identifies in the West a

> nationalism of peoples who for some reason feel themselves at a disadvantage but who are nevertheless culturally equipped in ways that favour success and excellence measured by standards which are widely accepted and fast spreading, and which first arose among them and other peoples culturally akin to them. (1976: 33)

In contrast to this, the Eastern model represents

> the nationalism of peoples recently drawn into a civilisation hitherto alien to them and whose ancestral cultures are not adapted to success and excellence by these cosmopolitan and increasingly dominant standards. This is the 'nationalism' of peoples who feel the need to transform themselves, and in so doing to raise themselves; of peoples who come to be called 'backward', and who would not be nationalists of this kind unless they both recognised this backwardness and wanted to overcome it. (ibid.: 33–4)

Both writers seem to suggest that the Eastern model is characterised by an inferiority complex which produces an impatience and intolerance that is a far cry from the rationalistic, constitutional Western model. A similar sense that the West is the model to which others aspire (or ought to) and to which they will sooner or later gravitate underpins Gellner's notion of the different nationalisms of different time zones steadily moving westward as they go (Gellner 1994a).

There are a number of perhaps obvious objections to this whole approach. The West/East dichotomy may be only a metaphor, but it is, even on its own terms, a somewhat crude and inaccurate one, and liable to cause disagreements even among its proponents. Is Germany located in the East? It may be, if one starts in Britain or France. For Kohn it is Eastern, while for Plamenatz it is Western! But what then of Ireland, which Kohn puts in the Eastern camp?

More serious than any difficulties in acknowledging that the world is after all round, not flat, or, more accurately, a globe, is the problem of the set of heavily value-laden assumptions that underpin the use of the concepts of backwardness (Plamenatz), inferiority (Kohn) and incompleteness (Gellner). These may be rooted in what Stuart Hall has called the discourse of the 'West and the Rest', developed over hundreds of years of unequal contact, imperialism and colonialism, founded on elements of power and coercion (Hall 1992b).[4] This discourse has deep historical origins in the form of the opposition between East and West, going back to Roman and Greek hostility to the barbarian Others from the East, to the schism in Christianity between Eastern Orthodoxy and Western Catholicism, to Christianity's struggle with Islam, and to the contempt of some Enlightenment thinkers for the East (Davies 1997). This perception of cultural backwardness has been a major factor in the importance many nations give to being 'European', and in being as near to western or at least central Europe as possible. (It is noticeable for instance how the term 'east-central Europe' has become popular since the fall of communism as one way of carving out more differentiation among the countries of eastern Europe.)[5]

The profoundly ethnocentric sense of Western superiority which informs this particular dualism can then all too easily blind writers to the deficiencies of Western nationalism as they rush to denounce that of the East. For it is not too difficult to point to a number of the characteristics of supposedly 'Eastern' nationalism which appear to feature in Western nationalism, enough to make the distinction murky. Waves of resentment against others (for stealing 'our' jobs, or swamping 'our' culture) have been a staple feature of right-wing (both extreme and mainstream) nationalist discourse in France, Britain and the USA for many years; the fruits of intolerance have produced the widespread occurrence of acts of racial violence in many parts of the 'West' now for decades or more (Björgo & Witte 1996). Even the emotionality attributed to Eastern nationalism has been clearly visible in the West whether in situations such as the Falklands War in Britain, or the more routine celebrations of the nation in sporting triumphs and national commemorations (Billig 1995).

POLITICAL VERSUS CULTURAL NATIONALISM

One of the primary distinctions that filled the East-West containers was the contrast between (Western) political and (Eastern) cultural forms of nationalism. In locating the origins of Western nationalism in the Enlightenment project, Kohn saw it as a part of a more general movement 'to limit governmental power and to secure civic rights. Its purpose was to create a liberal and rational civil society' (1965: 29). Thus for example 'English and American nationalism was, in its origin, connected with the concepts of individual liberty and represented nations firmly constituted in their political life' (ibid.: 30). Intimately connected then with the liberal revolt against absolutism, with the opening up of society, and (it is claimed) with democracy, Western political nationalism was progressive, modern, the creation of the present if not oriented to the future. The cultural form of nationalism, which according to Kohn emerged in the East, was a reaction to this, opposed to its core values and driven by a quite different dynamic. It emerged

> in lands which were in political ideas and social structure less advanced
> than the modern West. There was only a weak middle class: the nation

was split between a feudal aristocracy and a rural proletariat. Thus nationalism became . . . a cultural movement . . . [led] to oppose the 'alien' example and its liberal and rational outlook. (ibid.)

Cultural nationalism looked elsewhere for its justification, finding it not in reason but in emotion, not in the present but in the past, turning inwards, to the imagination, to tradition, to history and to nature.

The sharpness of the contrast between the political and the cultural roots of different forms of nationalism is, however, hard to sustain when we seek to apply it to particular cases. Nations which are purportedly models of the political form of nationalism appear both (positively) to exhibit a signal pride in the achievements of 'their' own culture, and (negatively) to experience recurring anxieties about their health, security, even viability. Such pride may be seen for example to underpin the assimilationist assumptions of, for instance, the French model of republican citizenship. Mark Mitchell and Dave Russell have further argued that 'a logic of assimilation clearly underpins [this] ideal type. Cultural assimilation is the price that must be paid . . . for integration into the political community' (1996: 67).[6] However, one can also note an obsession with culture in France as the basis for national identity, which has little to do with republicanism. Martin Thom has shown how sustained attempts were already being made in the early nineteenth century to use culture to identify a distinctively French national identity as opposed to a supposedly Germanic or Celtic one, concluding that this 'suggests that historians have been in error in ascribing the invention of cultural nationalism to the Germans alone' (1995: 257). On the other hand, from another angle, pride may be replaced by something more negative, by fears that this culture is vulnerable, under attack, threatened by the diluting and sapping presence of particular minorities. Movements have thus arisen (such as the Front National) which (however disingenuously) explicitly eschew the overt racism of predecessors such as the Action Française in asserting the need to defend French culture (Safran 1993).

Whether this amounts to a new form of racism is not the issue here.[7] Rather it is necessary to point to the importance of cultural underpinnings for apparently political nationalisms, underpinnings which have to be fortified and sustained against both external and internal threats. Thus for some the existence of supposedly distinct and different national cultures underpinning the identity of western European states poses a serious barrier to moves in the direction of further European integration (Zetterholm 1994). For others, it is necessary to mount a sustained argument for the existence and defence of a distinct (if not static) national culture against the disintegrating appeals of radical multiculturalists (Miller 1995). This may also involve the imposition of significant restrictions on immigration in order not to stretch the education system and other mechanisms of cultural integration beyond their capacity (Miller 1995: 128). At this point the line between 'open' political and 'closed' cultural nationalism may seem blurred indeed. In a recent work, Smith has gone so far as to suggest that nationalisms of the western European variety can be 'every bit as severe and uncompromising as ethnic nationalisms', arguing that

> the pedagogical narrative of Western democracies turns out to be every bit as demanding and rigorous – and in practice ethnically one-sided – as are those of non-Western authoritarian state-nations, since it assumes the assimilation of ethnic minorities within the borders of the nation state through acculturation to a hegemonic majority ethnic culture. (Smith 1995: 101)

Such dynamics of pride and fear may derive from a profound sense that political nations cannot themselves exist without a vivid and strong sense of their own cultural identity. They may lead to forms of nationalist politics which bear little resemblance to Kohn's optimistic picture, but in which nation states seek both to impose 'their' culture on (selected) others internally (through assimilation) or to defend their cultural identities by excluding or raising barriers against others.

CIVIC VERSUS ETHNIC NATIONALISM

If the distinction between a good political and a bad cultural form of nationalism is then problematic, one alternative may be to distinguish between a civic and an ethnic form. In some ways, this can be seen as an extension or reformulation of the political/cultural distinction, drawing out more fully the implications of the civic element in Kohn's original formulation and, following him, locating this firmly in the West. Thus for Smith, 'historic territory, legal-political community, legal-political equality of members, and common civic culture and ideology; these are the components of the standard Western model of the nation' (1991: 11). Or in Ignatieff's more popular work,

> civic nationalism maintains that the nation should be composed of all those – regardless of race, colour, creed, gender, language or ethnicity – who subscribe to the nation's political creed. This nationalism is called civic because it envisages the nation as a community of equal, rights bearing citizens, united in patriotic attachment to a shared set of political practices and values. (1994: 3–4)

The civic nation is 'an association of citizens' (Schwarzmantel 1991: 207), with rights and obligations. Within the borders of the civic nation, on its soil, all may be citizens, according to the principle of *ius soli*. Membership is thus in some sense open, or at least not closed off in any a priori way.

In the ethnic model, by contrast, the nation is, as Smith defines it, 'first and foremost a community of common descent' (1991: 11). Nations are the product of history and in a sense, to the extent that people are born into them, of nature too. 'Rather than free associations based on residence, they {are} historically determined entities based on ancestry' (Jenkins and Sofos 1996: 15). The nation is thus a given, a fate, from which none may escape. As Smith puts it, 'whether you stayed in your community or emigrated to another, you remained ineluctably, organically a member of the community of your birth, and were for ever stamped by it' (1991: 11). One cannot at the most basic level choose to join this or that nation. The nation is overtly exclusive, closed rather than open. 'No one can become Kurd, Latvian or Tamil through adopting Kurdish etc. ways' (Kellas 1991: 51). Citizenship is acquired by birth, through blood, determined by *ius sanguinis*, not by *ius soli*.

The classic European examples of civic and ethnic nations, again placed along West-East lines, are generally held to be France and Germany. There is a long tradition in the literature, going back to Kohn and forward to the recent work of Rogers Brubaker, for whom even today 'the opposition between French and German understandings of nationhood and forms of nationalism remains indispensable' (1992: 3).[8]

The intellectual origins of this distinction may be traced back to German intellectuals such as Friedrich Meinecke on the one side and French writers such as Jules Michelet and Ernest Renan on the other. Michelet was the great historian and advocate of the egalitarian and humanitarian principles laid down and broadcast to the world by the French revolutionary nation. Renan's seminal lecture, 'What is a Nation?' (1996), is often taken as a basic text for the civic model, 'a vindication,' according to Stuart Woolf for instance, 'of the voluntaristic definition that originated with the French revolution . . . against the insistence on blood and soil that was being affirmed ever more widely in Germany' (1996: 48).

There are a number of problems, however, with this conventional contrast. To begin with, neither Michelet nor Renan, nor their followers, were exactly clear cut or consistent in their approach to the French nation. Michelet's arguments are at best contradictory, undermined by a rather crass chauvinism and at times overt racism. As Tsvetan Todorov shows, 'the image that Michelet seeks to give France belongs to the purest ethnocentric tradition, which consists in attributing superlative qualifications to one's own group, without attempting to justify them' (1993: 217). Renan's arguments are flawed by similar racist assumptions. He did claim famously that 'a nation is the actual consent, the desire to live together . . . The existence of a nation is an everyday plebiscite' (Renan 1994: 17). This formulation, however, was developed in a particular and highly charged political context. At the time Renan was writing, French nationalists were seething with resentment at the recent annexation by Germany of Alsace-Lorraine. The citizenship status of the residents of that area could then, as Patrick Weil has suggested, be argued to turn sharply on competing conceptions of the nation, conceptions which could be articulated as respectively either 'French' or 'German'. One way of understanding Renan's lecture then may be as a political intervention, its dramatic invocation of plebiscites intended to counter other, German, claims to this territory (Weil 1996).

It is not wholly clear, however, how seriously we are intended to take the notion of a daily plebiscite. This seems more of a romantic gesture, part of a rhetoric which has closer affinities than might at first appear with the object of its own critique, rendering any division between (French, Western) rationalism and (German, Eastern) romanticism problematic. As Maxim Silverman has argued,

> an analysis of Renan's lecture shows that his concept of the nation is informed by ideas of the spirit and tradition. Much of the imagery he uses is in keeping with the so-called Germanist tradition . . . his reference to the nation as a 'spiritual principle' invokes the counter-revolutionary discourse informed by the romanticism of Herder. (1992: 20–21)[9]

Renan's arguments are, however, more than merely romantic. The nation, according to Renan, is not only willed in the present but also a matter of culture (suggesting again that the distinction between political and cultural nationalism is flawed), and from this angle rooted in the past. But culture is, as we have seen, a problematic basis for the nation, and often a cover for a more vulgar biological racism. Indeed, as Todorov points out, Renan was a 'willing practitioner of popular racialism' and something of an anti-semite (1993: 228). In reality, Renan's apparently political nationalism was based, as Zeev Sternhell (1991) has argued, on rather different premises, those of a 'cultural determinism strongly influenced by racial determinism'.

This, as Sternhell has indeed suggested, may help to explain a major puzzle about the kind of civic nationalism developed in France. It is often argued that there was a fundamental, irreconcilable conflict between the ethnic nationalism of the right and the civic republican patriotism of the left. This culminated in the Dreyfus Affair, which was in part a dispute about who could and could not be French. The driving obsession on the French right was to reverse the democratic and egalitarian implications of the Revolution. The right was not only Catholic, where the revolution had been anti-clerical, it was also anti-semitic, where the revolution had granted civic rights to Jews. Nationalist ideologues such as Charles Maurras and Maurice Barrès hated the Jews in particular, whom they saw as inherently alien, rootless, incapable of becoming French. National identity for them was rooted in blood and soil. Nationalist movements, from Boulanger to the Action Française, aimed to take over or bring down the hated parliamentary regime in the name of historic French values, in the interests of a French nation, with a sharply differentiated, discrete identity.

How then was it, if the civic nationalism of the left was so different from that of the ethnic and racist right, that in 1914, barely a decade after the end of the affair, left and right could come together so readily in a united defence of the sacred territory of the French nation?

One answer, indicative of a key element in civic nationalism, is that the French left, as much as the right, had at its own core a concern with national unity, and was committed not only to the notion but to the forced construction of a homogenous nation. The state in the Third Republic in fact took great care and devoted considerable resources to ensure that French became the common, dominant language, that a particular understanding of French history was taught to all, that French territory (including Alsace and Lorraine) was seen as eternal, that a common culture was imposed on all living under its sovereignty. Without these efforts, after all, how could peasants and others have been turned into Frenchmen, as Weber (1977) put it, ready not only to take revenge on the hated Germans but also of course to extend the (imperialist) power of the French state over so many others through colonial conquest (plebiscites of course not being for everyone)?

For a key element in the civic nationalism argument is the idea that all are or may be citizens of the nation. This seems rather questionable in the case of France at the time of the Revolution, often taken as the beginning of civic nationalism, when there were after all rather severe restrictions on who was or could be a full member of the nation, not least in terms of gender. The promise of universal citizenship, as it turned out, was not supposed to apply to women (Hufton 1992). On the contrary, a good argument can be made that citizenship was constructed on an essential difference between masculine citizens and female others (Sluga 1998). This was no temporary omission; women gained the right to vote in France only in 1945.

The English example, favoured by other writers, may be no more persuasive. Liah Greenfeld for instance, who has developed a version of the civic-ethnic contrast, connected to the opposition between individualism and collectivism, uses England. For her, the transformation in the meaning of the word 'nation', linked to profound structural transformations in fifteenth- and sixteenth-century English society, produced a form of nationalism which 'elevated every member of the community which it made sovereign' (Greenfield 1992: 487). Within this civic individualist version of the nation, in principle all could be members of a homogeneously noble nation. In reality, as even Greenfeld recognises, this principle was rather heavily compromised, historically, by the systematic exclusion of the vast majority of the population (such as women, servants, Catholics, the poor) from the full exercise of civic rights.

Much the same was true for a very long time after the American Revolution, which founded another favoured civic nation. Civic recognition was withheld, it transpired here, not only from women (Hoff 1994), but from both native Americans and black slaves. Native Americans were explicitly identified as aliens in a court judgment as late as 1831 (Daniels 1998: 42), whilst it took a civil war still decades later for slavery (revealingly not actually mentioned in the Constitution) to be formally ended, athough that did not put an end to major inequalities and to the continuing denial of many of the rights of citizenship. As Etienne Balibar puts it pithily, 'the American "revolutionary nation" built its original ideals on a double repression: that of the Amerindian "natives", and that of the difference between free "White" men and "Black" slaves' (Balibar and Wallerstein 1991: 104).

The ideal of the civic conception of the nation was then, at its inception in these cases, perhaps honoured more in the breach than in the performance. The point here is not to apply anachronistic standards to the past, nor merely to point out the flaws, imitations, and exclusions that were present at the birth of the civic nation. The problem is that these flaws are not simply of historical interest; problems of exclusion from rights of citizenship continue to haunt these very different civic nations, and the problem of the alien other is still a feature of civic nationalism.

IUS SOLI AND IUS SANGUINIS

It is often argued that civic nationhood is more open, more inclusive, more expansive than ethnic nationhood. Since ethnic nationhood is defined in terms of birth, it is only open to those born into the ethnos and closed to those who are not. Different legal principles are supposed to underpin these different conceptions of nationhood. Under *ius soli*, citizenship may be ascribed to all persons residing within a given set of borders. Under *ius sanguinis*, citizenship can only be ascribed to children of citizens. It is, however, difficult to find clear, unambiguous and consistent applications of the principle of *ius soli* in many Western civic nations. Neither France, nor Britain, nor the USA have held consistently and confidently to the principle of *ius soli* for complex reasons that in many ways go to the heart of the problem of the dualistic approach.

It needs to be pointed out, to begin with, that *ius sanguinis* is used even by civic nations. As Michael Mertes has pointed out, 'ius sanguinis is a rule in most places in the world; children of American parents, for instance, are citizens of the United States even if born abroad. Ius soli and, of course, naturalisation, are *additional* ways of conferring citizenship' (1996: 27, our emphasis). Thus, as Brubaker notes, although based to some degree on the principle of *ius sanguinis*, citizenship law in France has supplemented this with significant elements of *ius soli*. He concludes nevertheless that France and Germany represent polar cases: 'French citizenship law includes a substantial territorial component; German citizenship law none at all. Most other Western European *ius sanguinis* countries include some complementary elements of *ius soli*, without going as far as France' (Brubaker 1992: 81). However, whilst this has been the case for much of this century, it was not always so, nor always for the same reasons.

NATIONAL IDENTITY, IMMIGRATION AND CITIZENSHIP – THE FRENCH CASE

Historically *ius soli* in France, far from being the product of democratisation, was the dominant principle before the Revolution, under the ancien régime. It was then pushed back under Napoleon. As Weil notes, 'it was decided that birth within the borders of the country was *not enough to guarantee the loyalty* of the children of those foreigners born in France' (1996: 77, our emphasis). Simple *ius soli* was then rejected and replaced by citizenship based on blood ties. It was not until much later, in the Third Republic, that *ius soli* was *readopted;* again concerns about loyalty were uppermost in the minds of policy makers. Now, in a context of sustained enmity between France and Germany, the presence on French soil of residents who did not possess French citizenship and were therefore not obliged to do military service was seen to be both unfair to French citizens who were burdened by this duty, and potentially dangerous (Wihtol de Wenden, 1994). The *readoption* of *ius soli* in these circumstances may be better understood as a state project to ensure citizenship for the potentially recalcitrant. It was accompanied by a rigorous programme of socialisation, involving what Brubaker himself calls 'moral and civic indoctrination' in a national educational system (1992: 109). This was arguably designed to make loyal citizens of them all, to instil republican loyalties where they did not spontaneously exist.

Whilst sections of the French right have continued to pursue exclusionary objectives, targeting first Jews,[10] and more recently immigrants from Africa, the nationalism of the republican left has not been without its difficulties. As the *foulard* affair (see note 6) demonstrated, its predominantly assimilationist tradition is contradictory, appearing to be universalist and egalitarian but on its own particularist and intolerant terms. If they are to become members of the French nation, immigrants must assimilate to a given, dominant, national culture.

This has a number of consequences. Amongst other things, it leads to a tendency in that culture to render immigrants in some degree invisible in the depiction of the nation's identity whilst at the same time, there is evidence of racist criteria at work in the ways the French state has in reality sought to regulate immigration in the supposed national interest (Noiriel, 1988). Racist views are not of course confined to the elite, republican or not, but powerfully influence dominant conceptions of national identity. Alec Hargreaves has identified a 'broad hierarchical ordering of ethnic categories by the French public [which] has remained fairly stable during the postwar period', although these 'ethnicised categories against which French images of national identity are constructed are seriously at odds with both the *de facto* participation of immigrants and their descendants within French society and with their own sense of belonging' (1995: 155, 159). It has not been easy for the French left to meet the challenge of such sustained racist nationalism, effectively mobilised by movements of the far right, by asserting the principles of the republic when these are themselves so contradictory. Rather what has been required is a move beyond the sacrosanct categories of the national itself, a reinterrogation of republican principles. In fact, as Catherine Lloyd (1998) has shown, the anti-racist movement in France has been impelled to develop along precisely these lines, articulating a demand for a 'new citizenship' which is not rooted in terms of nationality so much as in participation on an equal footing in the polity, in the economy and in society. This movement, Lloyd argues, has been at heart internationalist, challenging and critiquing the inherently ambivalent notion of a French national identity, and seeking to decouple citizenship from nationality altogether.

NATIONAL IDENTITY, IMMIGRATION AND CITIZENSHIP – THE BRITISH CASE

Similar issues arise when we consider the British case, although here the pull of an exclusionary nationalism has been rather more effective. *Ius soli* in Britain was a product not of a political decision but typically (given the absence of a written constitutional tradition) of common law and precedent. In this case, as Cesarani (1996) has pointed out, citizenship laws have developed in a confused and uncertain manner, tied up with shifting definitions of national identity. These have varied over time, depending in good measure on who at any particular point in time has been perceived to have been the feared other. For, as Caryl Phillips has put it, 'Britain has always sought to define her people and by extension the nation itself by identifying those who don't belong' (1997: x). This has taken various forms, from attempts to construct models of the 'true-born Englishman' to the forging of 'Britons', analysed by Linda Colley (1992), in the course of prolonged conflict with France. Whether English or British, this identity has been premised on the existence of a dangerous other, to be suppressed, fought or excluded.[11] Robin Cohen (1997) has also argued that this national identity may have been shaped to a significant extent by exclusionary measures taken to reject or eject those deemed not to fit the prevailing definition. Over time, those so proscribed have included former French allies, Jews (more than once), Lombards, Hansards, Flemings, Calvinists, Catholics, Spanish agents, continental revolutionaries, Germans, Gypsies, Bolsheviks, and especially since the war, black commonwealth citizens. Here, as he notes,

> the Other is a shifting category . . . But all are victims of a nasty version of the old game of 'pass the parcel' [which] gets dumped into the lap of that group the Self, or more exactly the defining agents and agencies of the British identity, most need at that time to distance themselves from and repulse (Cohen 1997: 372–3).

The formulation of the appropriate categories to define who is and is not British has not been easy. At times, it has involved more or less overt racism, as both Miles (1987) and Cesarani (1996) have argued. The attempt to racialise national identity is certainly discernible in a number of legislative initiatives from the 1905 Aliens Act, deliberately constructed to keep out Jews fleeing persecution in Eastern Europe, to the legislation of 1962, 1968, 1971 and 1981, the last of which, Cesarani argues, 'exceeded all previous legislation . . . by abrogating the principle of *ius soli* . . . Such legislation exposed the racialised character of British nationality, reflecting the bitterly polarised and at one extreme, racist understanding of British nationality in the mid-1980s' (1996: 67). This understanding was often obscured if not hidden, as policy makers struggled with the difficulties of formulating a coherent policy on migration in the aftermath of Empire. It had after all been the riches of Empire and the ideology of 'mother country' which drew or encouraged many to come to Britain in the first place. As Kathleen Paul (1997) has argued, this produced a fundamental contradiction between what was initially a formally inclusive legal nationality policy and an informal, exclusive construction of national identity. The resolution of this conflict over time and in sometimes halting stages involved, as she has shown, the construction and pursuit of quite distinct strategies in relation to at least four designated groups. In the immediate post-war period, despite a domestic economic crisis and a labour shortage, white UK residents were encouraged to migrate to designated parts of the Empire. At the same time (and in sharp contrast with the treatment of Jews fleeing persecution from Germany in the 1930s), quite major efforts were made, at considerable cost, to recruit and integrate Europeans from refugee camps. Alongside this, in a more ambivalent way reflecting the tensions of a desire in the wake of independence to both define them as still British but also alien, Irish migrant workers were both recruited and accorded citizenship, whilst being at the same time subjected to sustained discrimination. Finally, in the wake of an immigration encouraged for economic reasons (cheap labour being the uppermost consideration), black migrants from the colonies (particularly from the Caribbean and the Indian sub-continent) were identified as a major problem, requiring a complex but ultimately drastic revision and retraction of citizenship. A succession of Acts as passed (in 1957, 1962, 1968, 1971 and 1981) which 'transformed British citizens into immigrants and immigrants into coloureds' (Paul 1998: 169). This racialisation of national identity, which, as Rich argues, 'drew on deep traditions of nativist reactions' (1990: 106), had the effect of effectively 'controlling the migration of subjects of colour, while allowing white subjects to migrate at will' (Paul 1997: 180).

In recent years, many of the arguments, debates, and exclusions previously visited on 'immigrants' have been reprised in relation to refugees. The 1990s saw a growth in the number of those seeking asylum and a raft of policies designed to exclude as many as possible of those fleeing from political persecution, ethnic conflicts, or those marginalised through discrimination and poverty in the name of supposedly integrating those who remain. The means employed have ranged from attempts to prevent refugees from reaching Britain through action against road hauliers, airlines and ferry companies, through the use of a discourse which has continually sought to separate undeserving 'bogus' or 'abusive' asylum seekers or 'economic migrants' from the deserving refugees, to measures that might deter potential refugees from seeking asylum in the UK in the first place, ensuring that Britain is not seen as a 'soft touch' for asylum seekers.[12] Thus many asylum seekers are held in various forms of detention to prevent them from simply staying in the UK illegally despite the conditions from which they might have fled. In March 2001 the number of those detained was 1,436 with a further 307 in a 'reception centre'. As the Home Office Research Development and Statistics Directorate puts it, 'a total of 1,743 persons not at liberty'. Finally, the Labour Government introduced a system of support that involved the issuing of potentially stigmatising vouchers rather than cash at levels well below the normal welfare benefit levels plus a system of coerced dispersal of asylum seekers round the UK, often to areas of deprivation where they faced isolation, lack of support and racist hostility from the existing residents.[13]

It is difficult to interpret this complex and tortuous history as the expression of a coherent civic nationalism, given the discrimination and systematic inequities which appear to have marked successive revisions of citizenship, or to have a great deal of confidence in the civic character of a nation that has felt impelled to define itself by keeping out so many others on such apparently uncivil grounds.

NATIONAL IDENTITY, IMMIGRATION AND CITIZENSHIP – THE AMERICAN CASE

Many writers have seen the United States as the model civic nation in its openness to others and in the construction of its national identity on the basis of subscription to a liberal political creed. (As we noted earlier, however, this openness applied only rarely if at all to native Americans and the African American descendants of former slaves. After the fifteenth amendment to the US Constitution gave blacks the right to vote, in the South in particular a range of restrictions as introduced in the form of literacy and property tests, poll taxes, and criminal disenfranchisement provisions which had the effect – and the intention – of excluding as many black people as possible from local or national political participation.)[14] Notwithstanding this, in many accounts, the US was not only a nation of immigrants from the beginning but in some ways has always idealised the immigrant. The immigrant is the one who chooses to move, to make something of himself/herself, to make a new life in America (Goodwin-White 1998). This ideal, it is claimed, lay at the heart of the American revolution, which was based on a fusion of democratic, liberal and cosmopolitan principles. For Reed Ueda, the USA was

> historically a country in which heterogeneity formed the basis of the state . . . the state arose from a democratic and cosmopolitan nation shaped largely by immigration. . . . The Revolution popularised a new conception of national identity in the struggle to separate from the English, a new people bred from the frontier and the mingling of several nationalities. (1997: 39, 50)

It is true that the scale and variety of immigration has been greater in the United States than anywhere else in the modern world. Between 1790 and 1970 it has been estimated that something like 50% of population growth was due to immigration whilst even today it is estimated that one third of population growth stems from the same source (Keeley 1993; Hatton and Williamson

1998). However, this has not been a uniform or unproblematic development for a variety of reasons that are particularly pertinent here.

There has from very early on in America been something of what Perea calls a 'love-hate relationship' with immigration (1997: 66). Immigrants from northern and western Europe were not always welcoming to others who wished to follow in their footsteps. A whole battery of legislation has been framed in relation to immigration, from the Alien and Seditions Act of 1798 onwards. (Indeed it has been suggested it was American legislation that some people in Britain took as their model at the end of the 19th century (Cohen 1992).) There have been great surges of national panic over immigration, focusing on a variety of targets from the 'savage' Irish in the 1850s to the Chinese in the 1880s, the Jews and the Catholics in the 1890s, and the Japanese in the 1900s (Reimers 1998). By 1917 the racialised focus of concern was all too clear, culminating in the legislation of 1924 hailed at the time in one newspaper as a 'victory for the Nordic race' (cited by Feagin 1997: 25). This established ethnic quotas designed to encourage immigration from northern and western Europe and exclude others. It was only in 1965 that this racialised system was overturned. In the meantime, there were growing concerns, not new in themselves but particularly acute at the height of the Cold War, about the dangers of ideologically 'unsound' or dangerous immigration (Jacobson 1998). In any event, by the 1980s the consequences of a relatively non-discriminatory policy were beginning to be felt, with a significant influx from Asia and fears of a mass influx from the South, at which point another major campaign began to develop to restrict immigration. Its success in again restricting immigration may be seen as a part of the conservative backlash against the supposedly radical 1960s (Capaldi 1997; Duignan and Gann 1998).

There is much in this that puts into question the romanticised self-image of the identity of a nation that prides itself on being open to the other.[15] It may make more sense to think of this identity not merely as paradoxical but inherently contradictory (Jacobson 1996). On the one hand there is the articulation of democratic, cosmopolitan and egalitarian principles which are at least implicitly universalist. On the other hand, there is, from the very act indeed of separating from Britain, from the Old World, a move towards the particular, to the assertion of uniqueness, of the importance of selection if not even (in its Puritan formulation) of election.[16] Horowitz (1998) claims as its great virtue, that unlike even other republican nations such as France, the US has no core identity because it is continually reshaped by immigration. As we have suggested here, this overstates the continuity of immigration, obscures the selective criteria deployed to control it and understates the effort put in to define who can and cannot be 'American'.

EXCLUSION IN A 'NEW' CIVIC NATION – SOUTH AFRICA

This is not to suggest that immigration poses a special problem for national identity in America, whereas in other countries national identity is more secure.

All national identities, and the nation states that shape and depend upon them, face the same problem to a greater or lesser extent, as even the new civic nation of South Africa is discovering, as Sheila Croucher (1998) has recently and persuasively argued. There is something painfully ironic here, in as much as the struggle against apartheid was conducted on a wider basis than the national, both on a pan-African basis and across continents. Since the collapse of the apartheid system, South Africa has apparently attracted significant immigration, although estimates vary wildly, in the case of illegal immigration for instance between two and eight million (Migration News, 1998). There is here the typical combination of push and pull factors that one might expect in a regional context of extreme differences in wealth. According to one estimate South Africans may be thirty-six times richer on average than Mozambicans (when Americans are 'only' seven times richer than their neighbours to the south (*The Economist*, 4 March 95, cited in Croucher 1998: 645). Croucher argues that immigration here poses a challenge to nation-building on much the same lines as we have suggested it poses to the civic nature of the nation states of France, Britain and the US. The forms of rhetoric and discourse she has identified certainly seem remarkably similar. There is a similar politics of resentment and hostility to immigrants, a similarly invoked sense of a 'nation' under siege, at risk of disappearing under a tide of crime and insatiable demand, a similar sense of overwhelming panic. What is perhaps more tragic than ironic in this case is that, not so deeply buried in such projections onto the negatively defined other, are elements of the very racism from which the people of the region have struggled so hard to escape. A recent report concluded from its survey data that 'South Africans are more hostile to immigration than citizens of any country for which comparable data is available' (Mattes et al. 1999, p. 8), whilst a recent survey found that both blacks and whites prefer white to black immigrants (Migration News, 1998). A report by the Southern African Bishops' Conference in May 1995 attacked the prevailing level of xenophobia in South Africa and concluded that 'one of the main problems is that a variety of people have been lumped together under the title of illegal immigrants, and the whole situation of demonising immigrants is feeding the xenophobia phenomenon' (cited in Human Rights Watch 1998: 2). As a result support was found for forced repatriation of immigrants among 65% of respondents in a recent survey (cited in Human Rights Watch 1998). In 1997 nearly 200,000 immigrants were deported with the number having risen every year since 1994. According to Human Rights Watch,

> Suspected undocumented migrants are identified by the authorities through unreliable means such as complexion, accent, or inoculation marks. We documented cases of persons who claimed they were arrested for being 'too black', having a foreign name, or in one case 'walking like a Mozambican'. (1998: 3)

Immigration has perhaps not so much replaced race as the issue around which the new South Africa defines itself, as Croucher suggests, as subsumed it. Either way, it is clear that we have here yet another case in which a nation, even a supposedly civic one, may be seeking to define itself by those whom it excludes since 'it is by defining who they are not that South Africans are defining who they are' (Croucher 1998: 656).[17]

IMMIGRATION, NATIONAL IDENTITY AND THE NATION STATE

What immigration in all these apparently civic cases has done is to pose a very sharp set of questions about national identity. Questions about who may be included and who must be kept out, about who has rights and who does not, are about the composition and character of the nation, and about the nature of the polity itself. Immigration may periodically have been welcomed, indeed organised, if it has been perceived to be in the national interest but care has always had to be exercised that immigrants were of the right type so that their entry would not subvert the existing, dominant and reified vision of national identity. In all of this the civic nation state has played a central role. For, as Vernon Briggs has pointed out, 'in a world of nation states, immigration control is a discretionary act of government. Regulation is thus directly linked to sovereignty over a particular land area' (1996: 3). In so far as civic nations are defined in terms of their control over territory,[18] it can be argued that they are driven to control immigration. For Paul Boyle et al.,

> the civic conception of the nation has clear implications for migration. If membership of the nation is determined by place of abode . . . Unregulated immigration poses a major threat to such a nation, since it implies a loss of control over who can and cannot become citizens. (1998: 155)[19]

However, in order to justify such regulation, apparently civic nation states have had to engage in a set of mystifications, making arbitrary distinctions, and erecting a host of barriers and gates.

Distinctions for instance between legal and illegal, economic and political, voluntary and forced migration are not only conceptually problematic (Lucassen and Lucassen 1997) but, when used to discriminate, liable to lead to civic nation states breaking their own norms.[20] At the same time, such discriminatory policies have led to a contradictory state of affairs with regard to citizenship within civic nation states, involving distinctions between fully fledged national citizens, denizens (or migrants who have stayed despite assumptions to the contrary) and aliens (Castles and Miller 1998; Hammar 1990; Barbieri 1998). It has been argued that such distinctions (particularly between citizens and denizens) cannot for a variety of reasons be sustained in the long run and are eroding fast (Jacobson 1998; Soysal 1994), but this seems somewhat overstated, if not from our perspective somewhat overoptimistic. There remains still today a significant set of distinctions within the optic of the nation, between the nation's own citizens with (at least formally) full rights; denizens who have some rights but few if any of a political nature; and aliens who have very few.

CITIZENSHIP AND THE NATION – INCLUSION OR EXCLUSION?

Citizenship in the 'civic' nations of France and the United States, as well as in the new South Africa, is thus rather more problematic than the civic model suggests. It is no longer (if it ever was) so open. This, we may suggest, has to do with the way in which the category of the national has taken precedence over that of the citizen. For despite appearances, citizenship and nationality are grounded differently. T. K. Oommen has suggested that citizenship is about equality, a category whose internality to a given society is not questioned, whereas nationality (and he adds, ethnicity) are about kinds of collective identity which precisely raise the possibility of externality. Thus, 'while nationality and ethnicity as identities are exclusionary and could be inequality generating, citizenship can essentially be inclusionary and equality oriented' (Oommen 1997: 35). Now of course it can be argued that, in its own various ways, citizenship too is exclusionary. Minors may be excluded on grounds of age; felons on grounds of their failure to observe the laws; tourists on the grounds that they are not staying long enough to take on the burdens that go with the rights of citizenship. Some would argue that any conception of politics implies some sense of bounded space within which political activity can take place, within which people may be citizens. There is no necessary reason, however, why this space has to be articulated in national terms, why the grounds of exclusion have to be based on the idea of nation, on associated conceptions of national identity. The principles of exclusion from the nation state, even from supposedly civic nation states, are framed characteristically in terms of who is deemed to belong to the nation and who is not, who may or may not threaten the nation's identity, a closure which necessarily has effects not just externally (on those excluded) but also internally (on those included) as well as those caught between nation states, the stateless. Repeatedly within civic nations there has emerged a recurring anxiety about the other, however defined and wherever located, responses to which expose fundamental difficulties with the construction of civic rather than ethnic foundations for the nation. This anxiety may focus on the presence of 'foreigners' of dubious loyalty who may have to have citizenship forced upon them, or from whom it may have to be forcibly wrested. It may generate denial, whether that 'others' have always been 'here', or of 'their' rights once here. It may lead to the erection of barriers to keep 'them' out or to gates to regulate their controlled admission. However, as long as the other is perceived in inherently hostile terms that are also in a fundamental sense constitutive and defining of the identity of the nation itself, the distinction between civic and ethnic is hard to sustain or apply. To see recent policies in particular as merely contingent, the result of specific historically atypical political pressures in the present forcing hitherto impeccably civic nations to abandon or retreat from long-held beliefs or deeply cherished traditions, seems unconvincing. Rather they may be better understood in terms of a shifting repertoire of responses to a problem for which there is, within the nationalist frame of reference, no easy or 'good' answer. The drift back to ethnic criteria, if not all the way to *ius sanguinis*, may be understood as (at best?) a search for firmer ground, a more certain answer to a question that will not go away.

NOTES

1. There are of course some prominent exceptions to this. Carleton Hayes moved from a simpler division into good and bad forms to a six-fold classification of forms of nationalism (Snyder 1990). Giddens (1993) and Kellas (1991) provide threefold classifications.
2. See, for example, Michael Ignatieff's popular book and television series *Blood and Belonging*, or Raymond Breton's analysis of nationalism among French and English speaking inhabitants of Canada (Breton 1988; Ignatieff 1994).
3. For a good discussion of this see again Billig (1995).
4. See too Edward Said's analysis of 'orientalism' (Said 1985).
5. Thus, for example, Holy (1996), in an interesting recent account of Czech national identity from an anthropological perspective, has shown that the Czech view of the Slovaks associates them with the East rather than the West, and that this is associated with a whole set of binary opposites which sees the Czechs as associated with modernity, history, progress, culture, and rationality, while Slovaks are associated with traditionalism, lack of history, underdevelopment, nature and the emotions.
6. This has been seen most clearly in recent years in the so-called *foulard* or head-scarves affair. This cause célèbre, which arose out of the desire of three female Muslim school students to wear headscarves in school, was treated by sections of the left as well as the right as an affront to French culture. Left intellectuals such as Regis Debray wrote a letter to the French education minister warning of 'the Munich of Republican education' (cited by Moruzzi 1994: 659), an extraordinary analogy! In this dispute, as Moruzzi suggests, 'any insistence on serious cultural difference' was seen 'as a perverse refusal of French values, French identity, and the French republican tradition' (p. 660). Thus the assertion of political, secular, and Republican values was at the same time an assertion of a homogeneous French culture (Moruzzi 1994).
7. But see Martin Barker's analysis of the 'new racism' that affirms the inevitable (and 'natural') divisions arising from cultural differences, whilst avoiding the crudity of more overt assertions of inferiority and superiority (Barker 1981). Paul Gilroy too has argued that 'race is now being defined almost exclusively through the ideas of culture and identity' (Gilroy 1993: 57). See also Malik (1996).
8. But note that in a later essay Brubaker has criticised the distinction between civic and ethnic nationalism 'especially in the rather simplistic form in which it is usually applied' as 'both analytically and normatively problematic' (1998, p. 299).
9. Renan insisted in his memoirs on his great admiration for Herder, calling him 'my king of thinkers' (cited in Birnbaum 1992: 379).
10. On the repeated assaults on Jewish citizenship throughout the life of the Third Republic see Birnbaum (1992).
11. The war with revolutionary France, central to Colley's (1992) account, was fought, it may be noted, with another civic nation and involved not only the conflict with a hostile other, but also the repression of radical groups. Colley suggests that the recruitment of volunteers into the militias, from all classes, to face a possible French invasion was a key moment in the creation of a popular British patriotism. To the extent then that the 'British nation' was forged in an explicitly counterrevolutionary project aimed at a hostile other, one might argue that its civic character is at best

     contradictory, rooted in conflict not just with another civic nation but with large sections of its own population.

12. For a full account of some of the worst aspects of the treatment of refugees in the UK see Hayter (2000), especially Chapter 3.

13. These measures were heavily criticised by human rights organisations and voluntary bodies working with refugees. However, even the National Audit Office, which did not question the overall thrust of the policy of dispersal, admitted that its implementation was flawed, that community tensions had 'been raised by emotive and sensational media reporting', and that there were many barriers to asylum seekers getting the support that they needed.

14. This is not of course only of historical significance. Although many of these forms of exclusion were outlawed by the federal government in the 1965 Voting Rights Act, the 2000 presidential election was marred by claims about the exclusion of African American voters in the deciding state of Florida. Among many factors one key issue was the exclusion of ex-felons from the right to vote in Florida along with more than ten other states. In Florida, as a result of this, and of the exclusion of those on probation or parole as well, 31.2% of black males were ineligible to vote! (Human Rights Watch 1998.) When taking into account a host of other irregularities particularly affecting minority voters, noted by the chairwoman of the US Commission on Civil Rights, it is clear that the exclusion of African Americans crucially determined the outcome of the election (CNN 2001).

15. Teitelbaum and Winter suggest that it is best to think about American attitudes to immigration in terms of an ambivalent romanticism (1998, p. 145).

16. As Joel Kovel noted many years ago, there is in such Puritanism 'a powerful tradition of hating strangers, foreigners and subversives' (cited in Feagin 1997: 16).

17. Croucher concludes by making much the same general point about civic nationalism that we have here. 'Civic nationalism, laudable though the goal may seem, overlooks the reality that nationhood, civic or not, is an inherently exclusive concept' (1998: 657).

18. As Anthony Smith puts it, 'it is in the first place, a predominantly spatial or territorial conception . . . [such] nations must possess compact, well-defined territories' (1991: 9).

19. The line between civic and ethnic concepts again becomes blurred at this point. Like Smith, whose definition here they follow, Boyle et al. end up blurring the very distinction with which they began. Since civic nations seem to require a common culture, they are led to conclude that 'modern civic nations have little choice other than to become committed to selectivity in international migration. Such a policy serves to bolster national self-identity and homogeneity, through the admission of certain ethnic, racial and religious groups and the exclusion of others' (Boyle et al. 1998: 156).

20. Noiriel (1993) points out that it is democratic states which have led the way in developing rules for the control of immigration, pointing to the example of France in the 1880s and Britain in 1905.

FURTHER READING

The classic analysis of Eastern and Western nationalism is that by Hans Kohn. A succinct account of his views is contained in his 1965 book *Nationalism: Its Meaning and History* (New York: Anvil). The same distinction, albeit from a different angle and using slightly different terminology, can be found in John Schwarzmantel (1991) *Socialism and the Idea of the Nation* (Brighton: Harvester Wheatsheaf). Rogers Brubaker's (1992) *Citizenship and Nationhood in France and Germany* (Cambridge, MA: Harvard University Press) provides the most important contemporary statement of a fundamental divide. There is an illuminating study of the problematic evolution of different approaches in France and Germany by Patrick Weil in the very interesting set of essays edited by David Cesarani and Mary Fulbrooke (1996), *Citizenship, Nationality, and Identity in Europe* (London: Routledge). These and related issues are also discussed by David Brown (2000), in his *Contemporary Nationalism: Civic, Ethnocultural and Multicultural Politics* (London: Routledge).

PART FIVE
NATIONAL SELF-DETERMINATION AND NATIONALIST MOBILISATION

15

ON NATIONAL SELF-DETERMINATION

Margaret Moore[1]

This paper argues in favour of a conception of self-determination which involves the equal recognition of different national identities. It proceeds by, first, criticizing the dominant territorial (in contrast to national) conception of self-determination. It then addresses three main criticisms of a principle of national self-determination. These are (1) the argument from indeterminacy; (2) the argument from instability; (3) the problem of overlapping nationalities.

This paper argues in favour of a conception of self-determination which involves the *equal* recognition of different national identities. It argues that the claim of a nation to political self-expression should amount to a defensible right, equally possessed by all nations, and that this claim derives from the mere existence of a nation (and does not rest on past injustice or present discrimination).[2]

The paper is divided into two sections. Part one suggests various difficulties – in international law, political practice and philosophical coherence – with the dominant territorial (in contrast to national) conception of self-determination. It argues that international law is riddled with inconsistencies and is ethically unconvincing; that political practice based on this territorial conception of self-determination has failed to generate rules and mechanisms adequate for resolving national conflict; and that the philosophical underpinnings of the territorial conception are also problematic.

In part two, some of the main objections to a principle of national self-determination are considered. One of the reasons why the principle of

Margaret Moore (1997), 'On National Self-determination', *Political Studies*, 45.

self-determination has been conceptualized in territorial terms has been because of (perceived) problems surrounding a principle of *national* self-determination. The paper addresses three criticisms most commonly made of the principle of national self-determination. These are (1) the argument from indeterminacy; (2) the argument from instability; and (3) the problem of overlapping nationalities. I suggest a solution to the problem of indeterminacy, *viz*, the *claim that the idea of* self-determination is indeterminate in the sense that it does not tell us who the peoples are that are entitled to self-determination or the jurisdictional unit to which they are entitled.

In some cases, nations should be able to exercise their right to self-determination by seceding. However, for a variety of reasons, this might not be practical or appropriate. In addressing the third criticism of the idea of national self-determination, the paper explores imaginative ways in which the equal recognition of different national identities might be achieved in situations where secession is not a desirable or practical option.

SELF-DETERMINATION OF PEOPLES IN INTERNATIONAL LAW, PHILOSOPHY AND POLITICAL PRACTICE?

The terminology surrounding issues of nations, nationalism and states is both confused and confusing. Walker Connor has pointed out that writers in both international politics and in the popular media often use the terms 'nation' and 'state' interchangeably, as if they are synonyms.[3] This practice is encouraged by the widespread use of the term 'nation state' which misleadingly suggests that the population of each state is comprised of a single nation. The term 'United Nations' is also misleading and for the same reason. It would be more accurate to call it 'The Assembly of Sovereign States'. In fact, most states are not nationally homogeneous – Japan, Iceland, Korea and a few others are exceptions – but are either comprised of co-existing national communities, i.e., historical communities on what they perceive to be their 'ancestral territory', or people from a variety of ethnic backgrounds who have immigrated to countries like Australia, Canada and the United States.[4]

In multi-nation states, the principle of self-determination of peoples can be politically charged. This principle was understood in the nineteenth century and in the period following World War I as national in form, and so the new states of Eastern Europe were created in 1918 from the ruins of the Austro-Hungarian, Turkish, German and Russian empires in accordance with the idea of *national* self-determination. But because this principle endangered the unity of many multi-national states, the 'people' in question have been conceived, since 1945, not as 'national' peoples, but as the inhabitants of pre-existing political states or colonies; and it was also interpreted as not entailing a right to secession.[5]

The incoherence and ethical contradictions surrounding the right (or principle) of self-determination in international law since 1945 has been extensively documented.[6] The right to 'self-determination of peoples', endorsed in Article 1, par. 2 and Article 55 of the United Nations Charter, is qualified by numerous other articles in the UN Charter affirming the sanctity of the principle of the territorial integrity of states and denying the right of the UN or its member states to intervene in the internal affairs of recognized states.[7] For example, the 1970 UN Declaration regarding the right of secession makes it clear that the UN condemns 'any action aimed at the partial or total disruption of the national unity and territorial integrity of any other state or country'.[8] In 1970, UN Secretary General U Thant argued that the recognition of a state by the international community and its acceptance into the UN implied acceptance of its territorial integrity and sovereignty. He added, 'the United Nations' attitude is unequivocable. As an international organization, the United Nations has never accepted and does not accept and I do not believe it will ever accept the principle of secession of a part of its Member State.'[9]

Elaboration of the right to self-determination by a whole series of resolutions passed by sovereign states, concerned about the potentially destructive effect (for them) of this principle, makes it clear that the 'peoples' in question are not national groups, but, rather, peoples within territorial states; and it could only be invoked by people under colonial rule or people living under alien and racist regimes (Palestinians under Israeli occupation, blacks under apartheid in South Africa, respectively).[10]

However, this very narrow conception of the right to self-determination is inconsistent and ethically problematic. It is difficult to justify why the right to self-determination of peoples living under colonial rule can only be exercised *once* (to restore sovereignty to the people, who had been illegitimately deprived of it by the colonial power) but can never be used again.[11] This makes sense in terms of the political interests of sovereign states who are concerned about their territorial integrity, but certainly not to unhappy national groups inside these states who question the legitimacy of the states. Indeed, the moral idea justifying both democracy and decolonization is that political power should be in the hands of the people over whom it is exercised; and this provides some basis for condemning, for example, states dominated by a particular national group which exercises power and control over another national group. It might be politically correct to describe only Western powers controlling overseas territories as imperialists, but it is not factually correct: the term 'imperialism' can be coherently and persuasively applied to any attempt by one people to dominate politically another people, especially if the latter perceive the rule to be hostile to their national identity.[12]

Other inconsistencies flow from this very narrow interpretation of the principle of self-determination of peoples.[13] Why, for example, should a *majority* suffering racist discrimination (blacks in South Africa under apartheid) be entitled to self-determination but not *minorities* in a state who are suffering under racist or discriminatory policies (a much more common phenomenon)? And why are Palestinians the only people living under 'alien' rule when there are many national groups which perceive the state as alien to them and hostile to their national identity?

The tendency in international law since 1945 to treat national and cultural identity as irrelevant is mirrored in political philosophy, which also abstracts from issues of national and cultural identity. John Rawls's influential *A Theory of Justice* is typical: he stipulates at the beginning that he is concerned with justice *within* a single society, or state, and leaves out of consideration the important question of justifying state boundaries, and hence all issues relating to membership.[14] The *political* significance of cultural and especially national identity is ignored, because the argument appeals to a conception of fundamental *human* interests and then erects liberal rights and rules on that basis.

The dissolution of the former Soviet Union and former Yugoslavia, in particular, has given new urgency to the need to consider the appropriate relation of national identity to the state and international state system. The inconsistencies and ethical shortcomings of international law are not merely a theoretical or conceptual problem, but a pressing practical issue. In the former Soviet Union, the West supported Gorbachev, who had no democratic legitimacy and very little popular support, against popular democratically-elected national leaders, until it was apparent, on the ground, that the Soviet Union had collapsed. Similarly, the response of the international community to the dissolution of the former Yugoslavia was first to try to hold Yugoslavia together, thereby wasting valuable time in which they could have searched for a just settlement of these rival claims to national self-determination.

Faced with the collapse of these federations, the (belated) response of the international community – the UN and the EU, in particular – was to recognize the self-determination of peoples, defined in territorial terms, as members of specific republics, but not as national groups. Federations could disintegrate along the lines of their constituent units, but there was to be no re-consideration of borders, 'no secessions from secessions'.[15] This was so, even though it was evident that many people living within the republican borders of the former Yugoslavia did not share this view.

The Badinter Arbitration Committee on the former Yugoslavia, set up by the EU, concluded that 'whatever the circumstances, the right to self-determination must not involve changes to existing frontiers at the time of independence'.[16] Once secession was inevitable, or had occurred *de facto*, the international community reluctantly accepted it, but attempted to limit its 'damage' by applying a territorial understanding of 'peoples'. Indeed, the Badinter Arbitration Committee specifically mentioned concern about the 'stability of frontiers', even in a case (the former Yugoslavia) where the *external* frontier (of the former Yugoslavia) was not being disputed; and it justified its decision in terms of the principle of 'territorial integrity', which it described as 'this great principle of peace, indispensable to international stability'.[17]

Whatever one might think of the merits of this (and related) legal decision(s), it is now widely accepted that the international community's response in the Balkans was profoundly inadequate, at least in the sense that they did not have rules or procedural mechanisms adequate to achieve peace. The idea of national self-determination has profound resonance across the globe – from Northern Ireland to Kashmir – and it is necessary to elaborate ways of dealing with the national dimension of these conflicts, so that a peaceful solution can be achieved.

The inadequacy of the *territorial* conception of peoples, which promises to extend civic equality and fair treatment to all members of the state, is apparent not only to the people who consider the formal extension of equality to them as insufficient, holding out instead for the political recognition of their identity,[18] it is also becoming something of a commonplace in liberal political philosophy.[19] There has been a flurry of recent work in this field arguing that the conceptions of state neutrality and formal equality of citizens, embedded in a territorial understanding of citizenship, are inadequate in dealing with issues of national and cultural identity. Tamir, in her book *Liberal Nationalism*, argues for the importance of a defensible nationalism, which, she claims, can be reconciled with the principles of liberalism. In his book *Multicultural Citizenship*, Kymlicka argues that the liberal commitment to equality and autonomy can be used to support a theory of special rights for national minorities. And Miller's *On Nationality* defends what he calls the 'nationality principle' on the grounds that ties between people are necessary to support a redistributive practice.

One common argument running throughout these otherwise very different works is that it is no longer tenable to reject the claims of nationalists out of hand on the grounds that nationalism is inherently divisive, parochial and unjustifiable. It is hypocritical for large states, with a secure national identity and political institutions expressive of that identity, to demonize the nationalism of smaller peoples, who aspire to make political claims on behalf of their own nations. In practice, most liberal polities are expressive of a particular cultural identity. France creates Frenchmen: it teaches French history and traditions, the French language; the United Kingdom teaches British history, the English language and so on. Indeed, almost all liberal states have a dominant culture and value system, from which some national minorities feel marginalized. The problem is not that these societies are insufficiently liberal and that a more fully liberal society would be neutral on issues of culture and nationality. As Kymlicka argues persuasively, it is not *possible* to be neutral on issues of relevance to national identity: the state must make some decisions on which language(s) should be used in government, the bureaucracy, the courts, and schools.[20]

The increasing recognition, then, of the difficulties, both philosophical and practical, facing the territorial understanding of peoples, on which the prevailing idea of self-determination in international law is based, points to the need to reconsider whether the principle of *national* self-determination might not be an appropriate starting-point for the resolution of national conflicts. Specifically, a consistent and ethically principled approach to conflicting claims of national self-determination, based on the recognition of national identity, is necessary. In the next section, I will consider three objections to the idea of national self-determination, for these objections inform the view that the idea of self-determination can only be understood in territorial terms, and not applied to national 'peoples'.

OBJECTIONS TO NATIONAL SELF-DETERMINATION

The indeterminacy problem

One of the most serious objections raised to the principle of national self-determination is that the concept, in itself, does not tell us who the peoples are that are entitled to self-determination or the jurisdictional unit that they are entitled to. Appealing to democratic criteria is not helpful, critics claim, because the idea that we should let the people decide is 'ridiculous because the people cannot decide until somebody decides who are the people'.[21]

The problem of indeterminacy is a serious criticism, which must be addressed if the principle of self-determination is going to be helpful in resolving national conflicts. Some of the difficulty arises, however, because of a misguided attempt to specify objective criteria for delimiting national identity. This quest is misguided, because there are good reasons to understand a 'nation' as *subjectively* defined. On this view, the term 'nation' refers to a group of people who identify themselves as belonging to a particular nation group, who are usually ensconced on a particular historical territory, and who have a sense of affinity to people sharing that identity. It is not necessary to specify which traits define a group seeking self-determination. As Philpott argues, 'Why need we try [to establish historical, linguistic or racial tests to delimit a seceding group]? If Lithuanians, Croatians, East Pakistanis or Tibetans express a desire for self-determination, we do not ask what characteristics make them Lithuanians, Croatians, East Pakistanis, or Tibetans. This is a matter for scholars of Slavic, Middle Eastern, and Asian cultures.'[22] In practice, it is not difficult to discern which groups seek greater independence or autonomy. The main difficulty arises not from the subjective criterion but from cases where communities are intermingled and it seems that the self-determination of one group must be compromised to take into account the equally good claims of another group.

The subjective definition of national identity not only circumvents the problem of specifying objective criteria for identifying nations, but it also helps to point the way toward resolving the problem of specifying a jurisdictional unit. The jurisdictional unit in which a plebiscite is held is also essentially contested: as Barry has argued, in a case where the majority of people in an area want the boundaries of that area to be the boundaries of the state and a minority do not, the 'issue is in effect decided by the choice of the area of the plebiscite'.[23] In the case of Quebec, for example, a referendum on secession may yield different results if the jurisdictional unit is taken to be the whole of Canada, or the province of Quebec, or only part of the province of Quebec.[24]

Just as it is unacceptable for one nation to determine whether another group is indeed a nation, so it is unacceptable for one nation to define as essential to its territory land on which resides people who do not conceive of themselves as members of the nation in question. Thus, if a group did attempt to define its area of jurisdiction too broadly – *viz.*, it attempted to include territory and a people who do not conceive of themselves as belonging to that group – it would leave itself open to the possibility that the minority nation would hold its own referendum in its own self-defined area of jurisdiction. This follows from the view, advanced here, that national identity is subjectively-defined. Thus, this conception leaves open the possibility of recursive secession, as does Beran's theory, but with the important difference that Beran's theory is individualist, whereas this theory grants the right of self-determination to national groups,[25] and requires us to distinguish between a dissenter (a member of the seceding national group who, say, disagrees with the decision to secede) and a national minority (a member of a different national group).[26]

The view sketched here, in which nationality is subjectively defined, and self-determination confined to areas which encapsulate territory where the national group resides, is justified in terms of liberal-democratic norms. It is consistent with the liberal emphasis on autonomy, for it places importance on people's own conceptions and identities.[27] Indeed, the requirement that the identification of a national group can only be by the people themselves can be conceptualized in terms of the idea of external preferences, a concept which was first expounded in liberal political philosophy by Ronald Dworkin. Dworkin argued that internal preferences – preferences over how one lives one's own life – are legitimate from a liberal standpoint, but that external preferences – preferences over how *others* live their lives – are unacceptable or illegitimate in liberal political philosophy.[28]

It is consistent with democratic principles because it means that, as far as possible, the territory which the group claims encapsulates that group and does not illegitimately also encapsulate another group which does not conceive of itself as a member of the nation. This would mean, for example, that the native peoples in northern Quebec, who have a distinct history and culture, and who conceive of themselves as distinct nations, should *not* be included as Quebecois and that the appropriate jurisdictional unit for a plebiscite on this issue would recognize this fact, and not include native lands of northern Quebec.

One advantage of conceiving of national identities in subjective terms, and jurisdictional units in terms of the area on which the national group resides, is that it avoids the problem of contested definitions of what 'really' constitutes a nation. Identification of a national group by others (by people outside the group) is often used to *deny* particular national identities. Thus, Turkey has frequently referred to the Kurdish population in the south-east corner of Turkey, not as Kurds, but as 'mountain Turks'. In this way, Turkey denies their distinctive national identity, and so can ignore the political claims to self-determination which flow from this. Greek nationalists deny that Macedonians are a distinctive national group: they claim that the Macedonians in northern Greece are really Greeks; and Bulgarian nationalists claim that Macedonians in the former Yugoslavia are really Bulgarians.

It is implicit on this conception that *historic* ties to a place are insufficient to generate rights to control a territory. Appealing to historic links can legitimize claims to vast areas, and legitimize many different irredentist claims. In an absurd, but revealing, example, James A. Graff points out that 'one could press claims to all of the Levant, including the Holy Land and most of North Africa, in the name of the Greek Orthodox people, insisting on a "return" to territory that was the homeland for people of that faith community during centuries of Byzantine rule'.[29] Thus, the Greek nationalist claim to the mainly Slavic-speaking Macedonia in the former Yugoslavia would be deemed unacceptable on the principles I am outlining. Similarly, the Serb occupation of the Kosovo region, which has a 90% Albanian population, on historic grounds, is also unjust. Historic monuments and national sites can legitimate a *prima facie* case in favour of rights of *access* but not to control over the territory in which these national sites are located.

The argument from instability

Another concern that has been expressed about the principle of national self-determination is that its acceptance would be destabilizing for the international state system. Some of the concern focuses on the nature of nationalism itself; some on the destabilizing effects of a principle which, it is alleged, would licence a secessionist free-for-all and lead to the break-up of most of the world's states. The first kind of criticism focuses on the potentially aggrandizing and threatening nature of the nationalist mentality. Nationalists prefer their own nation over others (this would seem to be definitionally true); therefore, nationalists seek to advance the interests of their own nation at the expense of other nations. However, we should not assume (as many liberal cosmopolitans do)[30] that nationalism is irrational and therefore incapable of recognizing any limits on its demands or the similar feelings of other people.

The basic normative idea of national self-determination involves the (institutional) recognition of people's collective (national) identity through self-government, and this recognition *as* a nation is given by other nations. In other words, nationalism in itself is no more aggrandizing than individualism. It can, of course, take an aggrandizing form, just as the individual liberty principle can take an aggrandizing form. I might think that the exercise of *my* individual freedom is more important than anyone else's freedom, and I might seek whatever I want, without regard for the interests of others. But liberals recognize that the unrestrained pursuit of individual liberty would be destabilizing, and could only be secured at the expense of other people's liberty. The solution to this problem has been the equal liberty principle: each person can pursue his/her liberty *as long* as she respects the rights or legitimate interests of others. This is the essence of Mill's harm principle.

Similarly, nationalism does not need to take an aggrandizing form: indeed, the only stable, coherent legitimate nationalism is one which recognizes, not only the rights of one's own nation to self-determination (whatever form that takes) but also the equal rights of other nations.[31] This is a logical point, as well as a practical one: if feelings of communal identity, and aspirations to have political institutions which express that identity, are important to *me*, and justify my claims to self-determination, they might also be important to others who belong to a different nation, and also seek rights to self-determination. Indeed, this idea is central to most forms of nationalism: the basic idea is that of humanity belonging to a family of nations, and each nation having its own right to self-determination, and being recognized (institutionally) as a nation *by* other nations and operating *among* other nations.[32] The requirement that nations are subjectively defined, and that the jurisdictional unit for a democratic plebiscite is confined to territory in which the national group resides, addresses the concern about the potentially aggrandizing nature of nationalism.

Moreover, it would seem that the equal political recognition of distinct nations might *facilitate* international cooperation and obedience to international norms. When insecure peoples face other insecure peoples, their identity uncertain, they may be led to adopt an aggressive and expansionist policy in order to secure their place in the community of nations. The hope is to make themselves economically and militarily viable, and this might be possible only with increased territory and population. To avoid this, it would seem prudent to include peoples in international organizations, not through denying their national identity but through *recognizing* it. Although the EU could be viewed primarily as an economic association of sovereign states, it does suggest that sometimes societies are prepared to give up some sovereignty, prepared to abide by international norms, if their own identity is secure and is recognized. In an international context of open markets and a common defence policy, it is possible for small nations, such as Luxembourg, to be 'viable'. In this way, international organizations can reduce the incentive of particular nations to be aggrandizing – reduce the incentive for nations to secure more territory and thereby enhance their economic and military viability. Not only can multilateral organizations reduce the need for increased territory but also acceptance into these international communities and recognition of national identity within these organizations is itself an incentive to behave according to accepted international norms.

A more serious charge against the principle of national self-determination is that the implementation of this principle would be potentially disastrous, leading to the break-up of many of the world's states. In his book *Nations and Nationalism*, Ernest Gellner argues that the principle of national self-determination is impractical because there are many potential nations but only room for a small number of political units.[33]

Gellner's criterion for determining a 'potential nation' is language: he does not argue that each one of these linguistic groups now, or even at some future time, is likely to have nationalist aspirations. This hypothetical form of argument does not address the issue of the circumstances in which ethnic or linguistic groups become transformed into nations, or the possibility of the opposite trend occurring, as when a linguistic group becomes assimilated or when a particular national identification encompasses more than one ethnic or linguistic group (as, for example, in Switzerland).

It is difficult to be certain what is meant by the idea that there is only 'room' for a small number of political units. If this refers to the fact that many national groups are not geographically concentrated, and so any claim to self-determination must take into account the equally good claims of another group, then this is an important consideration (which I deal with below). But part of the force of the objection may stem from a bias against small states. It is difficult to know *a priori* how small is too small. Many self-determining states that are small – Andorra, Liechtenstein and Singapore, to name a few – are doing quite well.[34] Obviously, size is a potentially relevant consideration: there are functions that a state must perform, such as maintain domestic order and provide basic goods and services, and self-determination which took the form of independent statehood would be inappropriate for a unit which could not perform the basic functions of a state.

Moreover, this consequentialist form of argument against the principle of national self-determination appeals mainly to the need for stability, and while this is an important practical and moral consideration, it is not an absolute value. It needs to be weighed against the problem of states ruling without the consent of the people, and denying legitimate feelings of communal identity. There is an important moral distinction between insisting on the inviolability of territorial boundaries against *external* aggression and insisting on them against the people themselves. Instead of treating the two together, it would surely make more sense to elaborate criteria according to which national self-determination might be justifiable, rather than treat internal national dissent as inherently bad because destabilizing. After all, freedom of speech and political dissent can be viewed as destablizing; but that is not normally viewed as a good (legitimate) reason for suppressing them.

The model that I propose as a way of dealing with claims to national self-determination does have two safeguards which are designed to address concerns about the dynamic effects of recognizing the legitimacy of self-determination along national lines. First, on my conception, any claim to self-determination must be subject to a free and fair democratic referendum or plebiscite on this issue in order to establish consent. The basic idea which justifies democratic decision making within a political unit – that people are capable of making decisions about their political future – also justifies decisions on self-determination. determination. If the unit is so small and resource-poor that the people it encompasses will be impoverished, then this is obviously a factor which must be considered by the people themselves in a vote. Second, the requirement that the jurisdictional unit cannot encapsulate geographically concentrated national minorities which do not wish to secede would be a considerable practical deterrent for many secessionist movements, which may be reluctant to recognize similar rights (to self-determination) for their own national minorities.

The problem of overlapping nationalities

Thus far I have been suggesting that the model regarding secession that the international community should be aiming to duplicate is similar in kind to the peaceful 1905 secession of Norway from Sweden. This was not justified on the grounds of past injustice or genocidal threat.[35] Growing Norwegian nationalism simply meant that Norwegians identified with each other and not with Swedes, they therefore sought their own political community.[36] Although Norwegians and Swedes now share many of the same liberal-democratic values and the two states have peaceful relations with each other, it is hard to think of a compelling argument why there should be one state in the region rather than two.

This brings me to the most serious problem with any claim to national self-determination. In cases where the national group is geographically concentrated, claims to self-determination (including a right to secession) may be quite straightforward. But this is not typical, because, frequently, two national communities are intermingled and the self-determination of one national group may threaten to compromise the self-determination of another national group.

Redrawing boundaries often does not solve the fundamental problem of majorities and minorities, because there is frequently no way of drawing boundaries which would result in a homogeneous political community. In some cases, although the majority-minority problem cannot always be completely overcome, the *extent* of minority dissatisfaction and the numbers of people who are dissatisfied can be reduced. Suppose, for example, that a present border arrangement leaves 60% of the population happy and 40% unhappy. It is not possible to make everyone happy, but redrawing the boundaries would make 85% happy and 15% unhappy. This is morally and practically relevant. While politicans dislike appealing to such utilitarian calculations, because they raise the spectre of 'sacrificing' some for the benefit of others, there is sometimes no alternative to counting numbers and trying to do the best one can (within the limits of legitimate action): sometimes no arrangement can satisfy everyone.

This is not a mere theoretical issue of morality: it is also an issue with important practical consequences for long-term stability. The aim behind the partition of Ireland in 1921 was not simply the separation of two rival groups into two homogeneous units. Such an aim would have been consistent with a principle of national self-determination. The 1921 settlement created the territory of Northern Ireland in such a way that (i) it guaranteed an in-built Protestant majority (assuming that Catholics did not out-reproduce Protestants); and (ii) it secured the maximum sustainable amount of territory for the province.[37] This partition arrangement resulted in a large Catholic minority – over a third of the entire population – in the province as a whole; and Catholic *majorities* in two of the six counties – Fermanagh and Tyrone – and almost all of the local government areas contiguous with the border.[38] This has meant, first, that the partitionist settlement was unjust, because the British state was aggrandizing, *viz.*, claiming two counties with majority Catholic (Irish nationalist) populations; and it has also meant – though this was not of course foreseen – that the entity, which contained a large, dissatisfied national minority, was unworkable. Indeed, it has been suggested that, had the province not contained the two nationalist counties, Fermanagh and Tyrone, the 'Troubles' would either have been easily contained or would not have occurred.[39] It seems obvious from this that the *size* of unhappy minorities is relevant to the practical issue of political stability. (This does not mean that a repartition of Northern Ireland is an attractive option, for reasons that I will outline below.)

The principle that I have advanced – that of giving *equal* recognition to different national identities – cannot be achieved by the partition of different national communities in cases where national groups are thoroughly mixed. But the subjective definition of a nation, and the definition of jurisdictional unit which I have outlined, enable us to identify these cases and attempt to achieve the equal recognition of different national identities through other means.

In the former Yugoslavia, for example, the secession of Slovenia was fairly straightforward: Slovenia was relatively homogeneous (about 90% Slovenian), and its 10% Serb minority was not geographically concentrated. It made sense, therefore, to accommodate this minority through a system of minority rights within an independent Slovenia.

In Bosnia-Hercegovina, by contrast, the situation was quite different. According to the 1991 census, Bosnia-Hercegovina comprised 44% Slav Muslim, 31% Serb, 17% Croat, and 5% Yugoslav (in practice, people in, or children of, mixed marriages). It had no dominant national group and no neat dividing line along which to fragment, because, with the exception of Croat-populated western Hercegovina, the different national groups were thoroughly mixed.[40] In Bosnia, then, there was no way of drawing boundaries which would have 'solved' the nationalities problem by separating antagonistic groups. Nevertheless, acceptance of the principle of (non-aggrandizing) national self-determination has important practical and moral policy implications for such a situation. Recognition of (1) the importance and legitimacy of national ties, combined with (2) the view that internal borders are not inviolable, but must have demonstrated democratic legitimacy, would have led the international community to develop a different policy with regard to Bosnia. The West would not have been eager to extend international recognition to a *civic* Bosnian state, in which all people have rights *as individuals*. The obvious route, following from acceptance of these two principles, would have been negotiations with all national groups to arrive at a solution which recognizes the *equal* right of all nationalities.

Moreover, the definition of national group and jurisdictional unit which I have outlined would have enabled us to identify whether or not a secessionist solution was appropriate. Any application of the principle of recursive secession (secession from a secession) in Bosnia-Hercegovina would not have resulted in a satisfactory settlement, but would have involved a patchwork of enclaves or pockets of sovereign units throughout the republic. Where the communities are intermingled in this way, and the domino threat is genuine, different mechanisms for realizing the fundamental principle of giving equal recognition to national identities are necessary. One possible arrangement, among others, would have been a confederal state, in which the constituent elements are subject to a unifying treaty for certain purposes, but retain their individual sovereignty and international identity for other purposes.[41] This would have enabled the Serb and Croat national groups to develop links with their co-nationals in Serbia and Croatia, without violating the equal right of the Bosnian Muslims to determine their own group's future.

Similarly, in Northern Ireland, a partitionist settlement is not optimal, because the existence of both communities in enclaves throughout the province, but particularly in Belfast, means that there is no way to solve the fundamental problem of majority and minority. Giving importance to national self-determination without domination requires imaginative solutions, which go beyond a purely 'internal' settlement. Specifically, the Anglo-Irish Agreement of 1985 points the way toward an internal power-sharing government combined with a joint role for the British and Irish governments in governing Northern Ireland which involves the dual recognition of national identities. In other words, it is through the *equal* recognition of the distinct national identities that nationally divided communities have the best hope of achieving lasting peace.[42]

CONCLUSION

In this paper, I have argued in favour of a conception of national self-determination which involves the equal recognition of different national identities. I have offered reasons why a territorial conception of self-determination is inadequate, and have attempted to counter three arguments which are commonly made against the principle of national self-determination.

First, I have argued that the concept of national self-determination is not indeterminate: a subjective understanding of nationality combined with a conception of jurisdictional unit based on consent specify both who the people are and the territory to which they are entitled.

Second, I have considered the argument that the principle of national self-determination is inherently divisive and destabilizing to the international state system. I have not dismissed the latter concern, but I have suggested that political instability is sometimes caused by the *failure* to accommodate national identities, and that the international community can play an important role in encouraging the development of non-aggrandizing forms of nationalism.

Finally, I have argued that national self-determination cannot always take the form of independent statehood in situations where one national group's right to self-determination would hinder or adversely affect another group's equally good right to self-determination. I have suggested that the subjective understanding of nation and jurisdictional unit help to specify precisely those situations in which more imaginative constitutional arrangements, based on the *equal* recognition of different national identities, are necessary.

NOTES

1. The author would like to thank R. Beiner, J. McGarry, W. Norman, the participants of the Toronto chapter for the Study of Political Thought and the anonymous referees for *Political Studies* for helpful comments on earlier drafts of this essay. She is grateful to the Social Science and Humanities Research Council of Canada for financial support and H. Ristau for research assistance.
2. This is in contrast to A. Buchanan's argument in *Secession: the Morality of Political Divorce from Fort Sumter to Lithuania and Quebec.* (Boulder CO, Westview, 1991). Buchanan dismisses the idea of national self-determination, arguing instead that the strongest justificatory argument for secession is when liberal precepts of justice have been violated.
3. W. Connor, *Ethnonationalism: the Quest for Understanding* (Princeton NJ, Princeton University Press, 1994), ch. 4.
4. This distinction is explored in W. Kymlicka, *Multicultural Citizenship* (Oxford, Clarendon, 1995).
5. A. Heraclides, *The Self-determination of Minorities in International Politics* (London, Frank Cass, 1991), pp. 21–2.
6. See R. Emerson, 'Self-determination', *American Journal of International Law*, 65 (1971), 464–6; R. Higgins, *Problems and Progress: International Law and How We Use It* (Oxford, Clarendon, 1994); A. Heraclides, 'Secession, self-determination and nonintervention: in quest of a normative symbiosis', *Journal of International Affairs*, 45 (1992), 399–420; B. O'Leary, 'Determining our selves; on the norm of national self-determination', Paper Presented to the International Political Science Association, Berlin, Germany (August, 1994).
7. See Emerson, 'Self-determination', p. 463.
8. Quoted in Heraclides, *The Self-determination of Minorities in International Politics*, p. 21.
9. This was in the context of the attempted secession by Biafra of Nigeria. Quoted in Emerson. 'Self-determination', p. 464.
10. A. Michalska, 'Rights of Peoples to Self-determination in International Law' in W. Twining (ed.), *Issues of Self-determination* (Aberdeen, Aberdeen University Press, 1991), p. 80; D. Horowitz 'Self-determination; philosophy, politics and law' (unpublished paper), pp. 27–8.
11. This point is made by O'Leary, 'Determining our selves', p. 3.
12. Most theories of imperialism are Marxist and are linked by Marxists to capitalism. However many people have called the Soviet rule over non-Russian nationalities 'Russian imperialism' and emphasized the continuity between Tsarist and Communist nationalities policies. See H. Seton Watson, *Nations and States: an Enquiry into the Origins of Nations and the Politics of Nationalism* (London, Methuen, 1977), pp. 77–87, 188–91.
13. These arguments are also found in O'Leary, 'Determining our selves', pp. 1–3; Horowitz, 'Self-determination', pp. 27–34.
14. J. Rawls, *A Theory of Justice* (Oxford, Oxford University Press, 1971), p. 4.
15. Horowitz, 'Self-determination', p. 15.
16. A. Pellet, 'The opinions of the Badinter Arbitration Committee: a second breath for the self-determination of peoples', *European Journal of International Law*, 3 (1992), 184.
17. Pellet, 'The opinions of the Badinter Arbitration Committee', p. 180.
18. Some examples are: Quebecois in Canada, native peoples in Quebec, Catholics in Northern Ireland, Croats and Serbs in Bosnia-Hercegovina.
19. Y. Tamir, *Liberal Nationalism* (Princeton NJ, Princeton University Press, 1993); Kymlicka. *Multicultural Citizenship*; D. Miller, *On Nationality* (Oxford, Clarendon, 1995); C. Taylor, *Multiculturalism and the Politics of Recognition* (Princeton NJ, Princeton University Press, 1992).

20. For a more elaborate discussion of this, see Kymlicka's *Multicultural Citizenship*, pp. 4–6.
21. I. Jennings, *The Approach to Self-Government* (Cambridge, Cambridge University Press, 1956), p. 56.
22. D. Philpott, 'In defense of self-determination', *Ethics*, 105 (1995), p. 365.
23. B. Barry, 'Self-Government Revisited' in *Democracy and Power* (Oxford, Clarendon, 1991), p. 162.
24. Natives in Quebec (Cree, Inuit, Montagnais and Mohawks) claim that they too are nations and so entitled to self-determination; that they never gave up rights to their territories; and that the future of their lands should be decided by their own referendum on the issue.
25. H. Beran, 'A liberal theory of secession', *Political Studies*, 32 (1984), 21–31.
26. The requirement that decisions be binding even on those who disagree is not itself controversial, as all democratic decisions do this. The differential treatment of dissidents and minorities follows from the recognition of the importance (to many people) of national identity.
27. The connection between a choice or consent theory of national self-determination and liberalism has been well-documented. See Beran, 'A liberal theory of secession'; C. Wellman, 'A defense of secession and political self-determination', *Philosophy & Public Affairs*, 24 (1995), 142–71; Philpott, 'In defence of self-determination'; D. Gauthier, 'Breaking up: an essay on secession', *Canadian Journal of Philosophy*, 24 (1994), 357–72; K. Neilsen, 'Secession: the case of Quebec', *Journal of Applied Philosophy*, 10 (1993), 29–43.
28. R. Dworkin first elaborated these concepts in order to rule out racist preferences. See R. Dworkin, *Taking Rights Seriously* (Cambridge MA, Harvard University Press, 1977), pp. 233–4.
29. J. Graff, 'Human Rights, Peoples, and Self-determination' in J. Baker (ed.), *Group Rights* (Toronto, University of Toronto Press, 1994), p. 211.
30. This view is sometimes expressed by liberal philosophers and theorists. J. Dunn describes national attachments and national identities as 'the starkest political shame of the twentieth century, the deepest, most intractable and yet most unanticipated blot on the political history of the world since the year 1900'. See J. Dunn, *Western Political Theory in the Face of the Future* (Cambridge, Cambridge University Press, 1979), p. 59. Michael Ignatieff's popular exploration of national conflict from a liberal perspective is organized according to a fundamental dichotomy between liberal cosmopolitanism, with which Ignatieff identifies, and nationalism, which he variously represents as tending toward violence, authoritarianism and a primitive Hobbesian state of nature. M. Ignatieff, *Blood and Belonging: Journeys into the New Nationalism* (Harmondsworth, Penguin, 1993), pp. 5, 6, 16.
31. See B. Barry, 'Nationalism' in D. Miller, J. Coleman, W. Connolly and A. Ryan (eds), *The Blackwell Encyclopaedia of Political Thought* (Oxford, Basil Blackwell, 1987), pp. 352–5.
32. The importance of recognition is persuasively discussed by Taylor, *Multiculturalism and the Politics of Recognition*, pp. 40–4, 58–61.
33. E. Gellner, *Nations and Nationalism* (Ithaca NY, Cornell University Press, 1983), p. 2.
34. This point is made by Philpott, 'In defense of self-determination', p. 366.
35. A Buchanan adopts stringent liberal (justice-related) criteria for permitting secession.
36. See R. Lindgren, *Norway-Sweden: Union, Disunion and Scandinavian Integration* (Princeton NJ, Princeton University Press, 1959), especially pp. 49–51.
37. J. McGarry and B. O'Leary, 'Northern Ireland's Options: a Framework and Analysis' in McGarry and B. O'Leary (eds), *The Future of Northern Ireland* (Oxford, Clarendon, 1990), pp. 270–3.
38. McGarry and O'Leary, 'Northern Ireland's Options'.

39. Liam Kennedy, 'Repartition' in McGarry and O'Leary, *The Future of Northern Ireland*, pp. 143–6.
40. C. Bennett, *Yugoslavia's Bloody Collapse; Causes, Course and Consequences* (New York, New York University Press, 1995), p. 53.
41. For a discussion of these options, see D. Elazar, *Federalism and the Way to Peace* (Queen's University (Kingston, Ontario), Institute of Intergovernmental Affairs, 1994).
42. See the excellent book by J. McGarry and B. O'Leary, *Explaining Northern Ireland* (Oxford, Blackwell, 1995).

16

WHOSE IMAGINED COMMUNITY?

Partha Chatterjee

Nationalism has once more appeared on the agenda of world affairs. Almost every day, state leaders and political analysts in Western countries declare that with 'the collapse of communism' (that is the term they use; what they mean is presumably the collapse of Soviet socialism), the principal danger to world peace is now posed by the resurgence of nationalism in different parts of the world. Since in this day and age a phenomenon has first to be recognized as a 'problem' before it can claim the attention of people whose business it is to decide what should concern the public, nationalism seems to have regained sufficient notoriety for it to be liberated from the arcane practices of 'area specialists' and made once more a subject of general debate.

However, this very mode of its return to the agenda of world politics has, it seems to me, hopelessly prejudiced the discussion on the subject. In the 1950s and 1960s, nationalism was still regarded as a feature of the victorious anti-colonial struggles in Asia and Africa. But simultaneously, as the new institutional practices of economy and polity in the postcolonial states were disciplined and normalized under the conceptual rubrics of 'development' and 'modernization', nationalism was already being relegated to the domain of the particular histories of this or that colonial empire. And in those specialized histories defined by the unprepossessing contents of colonial archives, the emancipatory aspects of nationalism were undermined by countless revelations of secret deals, manipulations, and the cynical pursuit of private interests. By the 1970s, nationalism had become a matter of ethnic politics, the reason why people in the Third World killed each other – sometimes in wars between regular

Partha Chatterjee (1993), *The Nation and Its Fragments*, Princeton, NJ: Princeton University Press.

armies, sometimes, more distressingly, in cruel and often protracted civil wars, and increasingly, it seemed, by technologically sophisticated and virtually unstoppable acts of terrorism. The leaders of the African struggles against colonialism and racism had spoiled their records by becoming heads of corrupt, fractious, and often brutal regimes; Gandhi had been appropriated by such marginal cults as pacifism and vegetarianism; and even Ho Chi Minh in his moment of glory was caught in the unyielding polarities of the Cold War. Nothing, it would seem, was left in the legacy of nationalism to make people in the Western world feel good about it.

This recent genealogy of the idea explains why nationalism is now viewed as a dark, elemental, unpredictable force of primordial nature threatening the orderly calm of civilized life. What had once been successfully relegated to the outer peripheries of the earth is now seen picking its way back toward Europe, through the long-forgotten provinces of the Habsburg, the tsarist, and the Ottoman empires. Like drugs, terrorism, and illegal immigration, it is one more product of the Third World that the West dislikes but is powerless to prohibit.

In light of the current discussions on the subject in the media, it is surprising to recall that not many years ago nationalism was generally considered one of Europe's most magnificent gifts to the rest of the world. It is also not often remembered today that the two greatest wars of the twentieth century, engulfing as they did virtually every part of the globe, were brought about by Europe's failure to manage its own ethnic nationalisms. Whether of the 'good' variety or the 'bad', nationalism was entirely a product of the political history of Europe. Notwithstanding the celebration of the various unifying tendencies in Europe today and of the political consensus in the West as a whole, there may be in the recent amnesia on the origins of nationalism more than a hint of anxiety about whether it has quite been tamed in the land of its birth.

In all this time, the 'area specialists', the historians of the colonial world, working their way cheerlessly through musty files of administrative reports and official correspondence in colonial archives in London or Paris or Amsterdam, had of course never forgotten how nationalism arrived in the colonies. Everyone agreed that it was a European import; the debates in the 1960s and 1970s in the historiographies of Africa or India or Indonesia were about what had become of the idea and who was responsible for it. These debates between a new generation of nationalist historians and those whom they dubbed 'colonialists' were vigorous and often acrimonious, but they were largely confined to the specialized territories of 'area studies'; no one else took much notice of them.

Ten years ago, it was one such area specialist who managed to raise once more the question of the origin and spread of nationalism in the framework of a universal history. Benedict Anderson demonstrated with much subtlety and originality that nations were not the determinate products of given sociological conditions such as language or race or religion; they had been, in Europe and everywhere else in the world, imagined into existence.[1] He also described some of the major institutional forms through which this imagined community came to acquire concrete shape, especially the institutions of what he so ingeniously called 'print-capitalism'. He then argued that the historical experience of nationalism in Western Europe, in the Americas, and in Russia had supplied for all subsequent nationalisms a set of modular forms from which nationalist elites in Asia and Africa had chosen the ones they liked.

Anderson's book has been, I think, the most influential in the last few years in generating new theoretical ideas on nationalism, an influence that of course, it is needless to add, is confined almost exclusively to academic writings. Contrary to the largely uninformed exoticization of nationalism in the popular media in the West, the theoretical tendency represented by Anderson certainly attempts to treat the phenomenon as part of the universal history of the modern world.

I have one central objection to Anderson's argument. If nationalisms in the rest of the world have to choose their imagined community from certain 'modular' forms already made available to them by Europe and the Americas, what do they have left to imagine? History, it would seem, has decreed that we in the postcolonial world shall only be perpetual consumers of modernity. Europe and the Americas, the only true subjects of history, have thought out on our behalf not only the script of colonial enlightenment and exploitation, but also that of our anti-colonial resistance and postcolonial misery. Even our imaginations must remain forever colonized.

I object to this argument not for any sentimental reason. I object because I cannot reconcile it with the evidence on anti-colonial nationalism. The most powerful as well as the most creative results of the nationalist imagination in Asia and Africa are posited not on an identity but rather on a *difference* with the 'modular' forms of the national society propagated by the modern West. How can we ignore this without reducing the experience of anti-colonial nationalism to a caricature of itself?

To be fair to Anderson, it must be said that he is not alone to blame. The difficulty, I am now convinced, arises because we have all taken the claims of nationalism to be a *political* movement much too literally and much too seriously.

In India, for instance, any standard nationalist history will tell us that nationalism proper began in 1885 with the formation of the Indian National Congress. It might also tell us that the decade preceding this was a period of preparation, when several provincial political associations were formed. Prior to that, from the 1820s to the 1870s, was the period of 'social reform', when colonial enlightenment was beginning to 'modernize' the customs and institutions of a traditional society and the political spirit was still very much that of collaboration with the colonial regime: nationalism had still not emerged.

This history, when submitted to a sophisticated sociological analysis, cannot but converge with Anderson's formulations. In fact, since it seeks to replicate in its own history the history of the modern state in Europe, nationalism's self-representation will inevitably corroborate Anderson's decoding of the nationalist myth. I think, however, that, as history, nationalism's autobiography is fundamentally flawed.

By my reading, anti-colonial nationalism creates its own domain of sovereignty within colonial society well before it begins its political battle with the imperial power. It does this by dividing the world of social institutions and practices into two domains – the material and the spiritual. The material is the domain of the 'outside', of the economy and of state-craft, of science and technology, a domain where the West had proved its superiority and the East had succumbed. In this domain, then, Western superiority had to be acknowledged and its accomplishments carefully studied and replicated. The spiritual, on the other hand, is an 'inner' domain bearing the 'essential' marks of cultural identity. The greater one's success in imitating Western skills in the material domain, therefore, the greater the need to preserve the distinctness of one's spiritual culture. This formula is, I think, a fundamental feature of anti-colonial nationalisms in Asia and Africa.[2]

There are several implications. First, nationalism declares the domain of the spiritual its sovereign territory and refuses to allow the colonial power to intervene in that domain. If I may return to the Indian example, the period of 'social reform' was actually made up of two distinct phases. In the earlier phase, Indian reformers looked to the colonial authorities to bring about by state action the reform of traditional institutions and customs. In the latter phase, although the need for change was not disputed, there was a strong resistance to allowing the colonial state to intervene in matters affecting 'national culture'. The second phase, in my argument, was already the period of nationalism.

The colonial state, in other words, is kept out of the 'inner' domain of national culture; but it is not as though this so-called spiritual domain is left unchanged. In fact, here nationalism launches its most powerful, creative, and historically significant project: to fashion a 'modern' national culture that is nevertheless not Western. If the nation is an imagined community, then this is where it is brought into being. In this, its true and essential domain, the nation is already sovereign, even when the state is in the hands of the colonial power. The dynamics of this historical project is completely missed in conventional histories in which the story of nationalism begins with the contest for political power.

I wish to highlight here several areas within the so-called spiritual domain that nationalism transforms in the course of its journey. I will confine my illustrations to Bengal, with whose history I am most familiar.

The first such area is that of language. Anderson is entirely correct in his suggestion that it is 'print-capitalism' which provides the new institutional space for the development of the modern 'national' language.[3] However, the specificities of the colonial situation do not allow a simple transposition of European patterns of development. In Bengal, for instance, it is at the initiative of the East

India Company and the European missionaries that the first printed books are produced in Bengali at the end of the eighteenth century and the first narrative prose compositions commissioned at the beginning of the nineteenth. At the same time, the first half of the nineteenth century is when English completely displaces Persian as the language of bureaucracy and emerges as the most powerful vehicle of intellectual influence on a new Bengali elite. The crucial moment in the development of the modern Bengali language comes, however, in midcentury, when this bilingual elite makes it a cultural project to provide its mother tongue with the necessary linguistic equipment to enable it to become an adequate language for 'modern' culture. An entire institutional network of printing presses, publishing houses, newspapers, magazines, and literary societies is created around this time, *outside* the purview of the state and the European missionaries, through which the new language, modern and standardized, is given shape. The bilingual intelligentsia came to think of its own language as belonging to that inner domain of cultural identity, from which the colonial intruder had to be kept out; language therefore became a zone over which the nation first had to declare its sovereignty and then had to transform in order to make it adequate for the modern world.

Here the modular influences of modern European languages and literatures did not necessarily produce similar consequences. In the case of the new literary genres and aesthetic conventions, for instance, whereas European influences undoubtedly shaped explicit critical discourse, it was also widely believed that European conventions were inappropriate and misleading in judging literary productions in modern Bengali. To this day there is a clear hiatus in this area between the terms of academic criticism and those of literary practice. To give an example, let me briefly discuss Bengali drama.

Drama is the modern literary genre that is the least commended on aesthetic grounds by critics of Bengali literature. Yet it is the form in which the bilingual elite has found its largest audience. When it appeared in its modern form in the middle of the nineteenth century, the new Bengali drama had two models available to it: one, the modern European drama as it had developed since Shakespeare and Molière, and two, the virtually forgotten corpus of Sanskrit drama, now restored to a reputation of classical excellence because of the praises showered on it by Orientalist scholars from Europe. The literary criteria that would presumably direct the new drama into the privileged domain of a modern national culture were therefore clearly set by modular forms provided by Europe. But the performative practices of the new institution of the public theatre made it impossible for those criteria to be applied to plays written for the theatre. The conventions that would enable a play to succeed on the Calcutta stage were very different from the conventions approved by critics schooled in the traditions of European drama. The tensions have not been resolved to this day. What thrives as mainstream public theatre in West Bengal or Bangladesh today is modern urban theatre, national and clearly distinguishable from 'folk theatre'. It is produced and largely patronized by the literate urban middle classes. Yet their aesthetic conventions fail to meet the standards set by the modular literary forms adopted from Europe.

Even in the case of the novel, that celebrated artifice of the nationalist imagination in which the community is made to live and love in 'homogeneous time',[4] the modular forms do not necessarily have an easy passage. The novel was a principal form through which the bilingual elite in Bengal fashioned a new narrative prose. In the devising of this prose, the influence of the two available models – modern English and classical Sanskrit – was obvious. And yet, as the practice of the form gained greater popularity, it was remarkable how frequently in the course of their narrative Bengali novelists shifted from the disciplined forms of authorial prose to the direct recording of living speech. Looking at the pages of some of the most popular novels in Bengali, it is often difficult to tell whether one is reading a novel or a play. Having created a modern prose language in the fashion of the approved modular forms, the literati, in their search for artistic truthfulness, apparently found it necessary to escape as often as possible the rigidities of that prose.

The desire to construct an aesthetic form that was modern and national, and yet recognizably different from the Western, was shown in perhaps its most exaggerated shape in the efforts in the early twentieth century of the so-called Bengal school of art. It was through these efforts that, on the one hand, an institutional space was created for the modern professional artist in India, as distinct from the traditional craftsman, for the dissemination through exhibition and print of the products of art and for the creation of a public schooled in the new aesthetic norms. Yet this agenda for the construction of a modernized artistic space was accompanied, on the other hand, by a fervent ideological programme for an art that was distinctly 'Indian', that is, different from the 'Western'.[5] Although the specific style developed by the Bengal school for a new Indian art failed to hold its ground for very long, the fundamental agenda posed by its efforts continues to be pursued to this day, namely, to develop an art that would be modern and at the same time recognizably Indian.

Alongside the institutions of print-capitalism was created a new network of secondary schools. Once again, nationalism sought to bring this area under its jurisdiction long before the domain of the state had become a matter of contention. In Bengal, from the second half of the nineteenth century, it was the new elite that took the lead in mobilizing a 'national' effort to start schools in every part of the province and then to produce a suitable educational literature. Coupled with print-capitalism, the institutions of secondary education provided the space where the new language and literature were both generalized and normalized – outside the domain of the state. It was only when this space was opened up, outside the influence of both the colonial state and the European missionaries, that it became legitimate for women, for instance, to be sent to school. It was also in this period, from around the turn of the century, that the University of Calcutta was turned from an institution of colonial education to a distinctly national institution, in its curriculum, its faculty, and its sources of funding.[6]

Another area in that inner domain of national culture was the family. The assertion here of autonomy and difference was perhaps the most dramatic. The European criticism of Indian 'tradition' as barbaric had focused to a large extent on religious beliefs and practices, especially those relating to the treatment of women. The early phase of 'social reform' through the agency of the colonial power had also concentrated on the same issues. In that early phase, therefore, this area had been identified as essential to 'Indian tradition'. The nationalist move began by disputing the choice of agency. Unlike the early reformers, nationalists were not prepared to allow the colonial state to legislate the reform of 'traditional' society. They asserted that only the nation itself could have the right to intervene in such an essential aspect of its cultural identity.

As it happened, the domain of the family and the position of women underwent considerable change in the world of the nationalist middle class. It was undoubtedly a new patriarchy that was brought into existence, different from the 'traditional' order but also explicitly claiming to be different from the 'Western' family. The 'new woman' was to be modern, but she would also have to display the signs of national tradition and therefore would be essentially different from the 'Western' woman.

The history of nationalism as a political movement tends to focus primarily on its contest with the colonial power in the domain of the outside, that is, the material domain of the state. This is a different history from the one I have outlined. It is also a history in which nationalism has no option but to choose its forms from the gallery of 'models' offered by European and American nation-states: 'difference' is not a viable criterion in the domain of the material.

In this outer domain, nationalism begins its journey (after, let us remember, it has already proclaimed its sovereignty in the inner domain) by inserting itself into a new public sphere constituted by the processes and forms of the modern (in this case, colonial) state. In the beginning, nationalism's task is to overcome the subordination of the colonized middle class, that is, to challenge the 'rule of colonial difference' in the domain of the state. The colonial state, we must remember, was not just the agency that brought the modular forms of the modern state to the colonies; it was also an agency that was destined never to fulfil the normalizing mission of the modern state because the premiss of its power was a rule of colonial difference, namely, the preservation of the alienness of the ruling group.

As the institutions of the modern state were elaborated in the colony, especially in the second half of the nineteenth century, the ruling European groups found it necessary to lay down – in law-making, in the bureaucracy, in the administration of justice, and in the recognition by the state of a legitimate domain of public opinion – the precise difference between the rulers and the ruled. If Indians had to be admitted into the judiciary, could they be allowed to try Europeans? Was it right that Indians should enter the civil service by taking the same examinations as British graduates? If European newspapers in India were given the right of free speech, could the same apply to native newspapers? Ironically, it became the historical task of nationalism, which insisted on its own marks of cultural difference with the West, to demand that there be no rule of difference in the domain of the state.

In time, with the growing strength of nationalist politics, this domain became more extensive and internally differentiated and finally took on the form of the national, that is, postcolonial, state. The dominant elements of its self-definition, at least in postcolonial India, were drawn from the ideology of the modern liberal-democratic state.

In accordance with liberal ideology, the public was now distinguished from the domain of the private. The state was required to protect the inviolability of the private self in relation to other private selves. The legitimacy of the state in carrying out this function was to be guaranteed by its indifference to concrete differences between private selves – differences, that is, of race, language, religion, class, caste, and so forth.

The trouble was that the moral-intellectual leadership of the nationalist elite operated in a field constituted by a very different set of distinctions – those between the spiritual and the material, the inner and the outer, the essential and the inessential. That contested field over which nationalism had proclaimed its sovereignty and where it had imagined its true community was neither coextensive with nor coincidental to the field constituted by the public/private distinction. In the former field, the hegemonic project of nationalism could hardly make the distinctions of language, religion, caste, or class a matter of indifference to itself. The project was that of cultural 'normalization', like, as Anderson suggests, bourgeois hegemonic projects everywhere, but with the all-important difference that it had to choose its site of autonomy from a position of subordination to a colonial regime that had on its side the most universalist justificatory resources produced by post-Enlightenment social thought.

The result is that autonomous forms of imagination of the community were, and continue to be, overwhelmed and swamped by the history of the post-colonial state. Here lies the root of our postcolonial misery: not in our inability to think out new forms of the modern community but in our surrender to the old forms of the modern state. If the nation is an imagined community and if nations must also take the form of states, then our theoretical language must allow us to talk about community and state at the same time. I do not think our present theoretical language allows us to do this.

Writing just before his death, Bipinchandra Pal (1858–1932), the fiery leader of the Swadeshi movement in Bengal and a principal figure in the pre-Gandhian Congress, described the boarding-houses in which students lived in the Calcutta of his youth:

Students' messes in Calcutta, in my college days, fifty-six years ago, were like small republics and were managed on strictly democratic lines. Everything was decided by the voice of the majority of the members of the mess. At the end of every month a manager was elected by the whole 'House', so to say, and he was charged with the collection of the dues of the members, and the general supervision of the food and establishment of the mess. . . . A successful manager was frequently begged to accept re-election; while the more careless and lazy members, who had often to pay out of their own pockets for their mismanagement, tried to avoid this honour.

. . . Disputes between one member and another were settled by a 'Court' of the whole 'House'; and we sat night after night, I remember, in examining these cases; and never was the decision of this 'Court' questioned or disobeyed by any member. Nor were the members of the mess at all helpless in the matter of duly enforcing their verdict upon an offending colleague. For they could always threaten the recalcitrant member either with expulsion from the mess, or if he refused to go, with the entire responsibility of the rent being thrown on him. . . . And such was the force of public opinion in these small republics that I have known of cases of this punishment on offending members, which so worked upon them that after a week of their expulsion from a mess, they looked as if they had just come out of some prolonged or serious spell of sickness. . . .

The composition of our mess called for some sort of a compromise between the so-called orthodox and the Brahmo and other heterodox members of our republic. So a rule was passed by the unanimous vote of the whole 'House', that no member should bring any food to the house . . . which outraged the feelings of Hindu orthodoxy. It was however clearly understood that the members of the mess, as a body and even individually, would not interfere with what any one took outside the house. So we were free to go and have all sorts of forbidden food either at the Great Eastern Hotel, which some of us commenced to occasionally patronise later on, or anywhere else.[7]

The interesting point in this description is not so much the exaggerated and obviously romanticized portrayal in miniature of the imagined political form of the self-governing nation, but rather the repeated use of the institutional terms of modern European civic and political life (republic, democracy, majority, unanimity, election, House, Court, and so on) to describe a set of activities that had to be performed on material utterly incongruous with that civil society. The question of a 'compromise' on the food habits of members is really settled not on a principle of demarcating the 'private' from the 'public' but of separating the domains of the 'inside' and the 'outside', the inside being a space where 'unanimity' had to prevail, while the outside was a realm of individual freedom. Notwithstanding the 'unanimous vote of the whole House', the force that determined the unanimity in the inner domain was not the voting procedure decided upon by individual members coming together in a body but rather the consensus of a community – institutionally novel (because, after all, the Calcutta boarding-house was unprecedented in 'tradition'), internally differentiated, but nevertheless a community whose claims preceded those of its individual members.

But Bipinchandra's use of the terms of parliamentary procedure to describe the 'communitarian' activities of a boarding-house standing in place of the nation must not be dismissed as a mere anomaly. His language is indicative of the very real imbrication of two discourses, and correspondingly of two domains, of politics. The attempt has been made in recent Indian historiography to talk of these as the domains of 'elite' and 'subaltern' politics.[8] But one of the important results of this historiographical approach has been precisely the demonstration that each domain has not only acted in opposition to and as a limit upon the other but, through this process of struggle, has also shaped the emergent form of the other. Thus, the presence of populist or communitarian elements in the liberal constitutional order of the postcolonial state ought not to be read as a sign of the inauthenticity or disingenuousness of elite politics; it is rather a recognition in the elite domain of the very real presence of an arena of subaltern politics over which it must dominate and yet which also had to be negotiated on its own terms for the purposes of producing consent. On the other hand, the domain of subaltern politics has increasingly become familiar with, and even adapted itself to, the institutional forms characteristic of the elite domain. The point, therefore, is no longer one of simply demarcating and identifying the two domains in their separateness, which is what was required in order first to break down the totalizing claims of a nationalist historiography. Now the task is to trace in their mutually conditioned historicities the specific forms that have appeared, on the one hand, in the domain defined by the hegemonic project of nationalist modernity, and on the other, in the numerous fragmented resistances to that normalizing project.

This is the exercise I wish to carry out. Since the problem will be directly posed of the limits to the supposed universality of the modern regime of power and with it of the post-Enlightenment disciplines of knowledge, it might appear as though the exercise is meant to emphasize once more an 'Indian' (or an 'Oriental') exceptionalism. In fact, however, the objective of my exercise is rather more complicated, and considerably more ambitious. It includes not only an identification of the discursive conditions that make such theories of Indian exceptionalism possible, but also a demonstration that the alleged exceptions actually inhere as forcibly suppressed elements even in the supposedly universal forms of the modern regime of power.

The latter demonstration enables us to make the argument that the universalist claims of modern Western social philosophy are themselves limited by the contingencies of global power. In other words, 'Western universalism' no less than 'Oriental exceptionalism' can be shown to be only a particular form of a richer, more diverse, and differentiated conceptualization of a new universal idea. This might allow us the possibility not only to think of new forms of the modern community, which, as I argue, the nationalist experience in Asia and Africa has done from its birth, but, much more decisively, to think of new forms of the modern state.

The project then is to claim for us, the once-colonized, our freedom of imagination. Claims, we know only too well, can be made only as contestations in a field of power. Studies will necessarily bear, for each specific disciplinary field, the imprint of an unresolved contest. To make a claim on behalf of the fragment is also, not surprisingly, to produce a discourse that is itself fragmentary. It is redundant to make apologies for this.

NOTES

1. Benedict Anderson, *Imagined Communities: Reflections on the Origin and Spread of Nationalism*, London 1983.
2. This is a central argument of my book *Nationalist Thought and the Colonial World: A Derivative Discourse?*, London 1986.
3. Anderson, *Imagined Communities*, pp. 17–49.
4. Ibid., pp. 28–40.
5. The history of this artistic movement has been recently studied in detail by Tapati Guha-Thalkurta, *The Making of a New 'Indian' Art: Artists, Aesthetics and Nationalism in Bengal 1850–1920*, Cambridge 1992.
6. See Anilchandra Banerjee, 'Years of Consolidation: 1883–1904'; Tripurari Chakravarti, 'The University and the Government: 1904–24'; and Pramathanath Banerjee, 'Reform and Reorganization: 1904–24', in Niharranjan Ray and Pratulchandra Gupta, eds, *Hundred Years of the University of Calcutta*, Calcutta 1957, pp. 129–78, 179–210 and 211–318.
7. Bipinchandra Pal, *Memories of My Life and Times*, Calcutta 1932, reprinted 1973, pp. 157–60.
8. Represented by the various essays in Ranajit Guha, ed., *Subaltern Studies*, vols 1–6, Delhi 1982–90. The programmatic statement of this approach is in Ranajit Guha, 'On Some Aspects of the Historiography of Colonial India', in Guha, ed., *Subaltern Studies* vol. 1, Delhi 1982, pp. 1–8.

17

CONSTRUCTING NATIONAL AND CULTURAL IDENTITIES IN SUB-SAHARAN FRANCOPHONE AFRICA

Dominic Thomas

> To tell the truth, I must say the country concerned is *not on any map*. If you want to find it, it's in time that you must go searching.
>
> Henri Lopes, *The Laughing-Cry*[1]

As the twentieth century comes to an end, we have become increasingly accustomed to images of world leaders gathering for economic summits. Little more than one hundred years ago, in 1884, the members of some fourteen international delegations representing the superpowers of the age assembled in Berlin to divide the African continent among themselves. We know today that this meeting triggered the 'scramble for Africa', and that it was nothing but a pretext for economic exploitation, veiled in arguments for Christianity and civilization. However, when the participants at the Berlin Conference divided Africa, they failed to consider the cultural, linguistic and ethnic boundaries which distinguished African peoples. The African leaders of postcolonial nation states have had to confront these complex realities in their attempt to construct national identity within the boundaries established by Western powers. As the various superpowers gather today, one cannot help but wonder why they have not been joined at the conference table by the leaders of politically independent *African nations*.

Defining African nationalisms

The problems associated with the concept of 'nationalism' in the African

Dominic Thomas (1997), 'Constructing national and cultural identities in sub-Saharan Francophone Africa', in Stuart Murray (ed.), *Not on Any Map: Essays on Postcoloniality and Cultural Nationalism*, Exeter: Exeter University Press.

context are inextricably linked to, and complicated by, the historical determination of the territorial borders following the Berlin Conference and its neglect for heterogeneous realities. In the African context, nationalism has come to signify the attempt to bring together peoples who were not linguistically, ethnically or culturally homogeneous within given territorial boundaries and to build the nation state. As James Coleman has argued, 'a colonial nationalist movement directs its efforts toward the attainment of two main objectives: (1) the achievement of self-government and (2) the creation of a cultural or political sense of nationality and unity within the boundaries of the area of the nation to be.'[2] It is the relationship between the cultural and the political that are of particular interest to me here, and I propose to explore it within the context of francophone sub-Saharan Africa. Many of the issues and arguments I raise will of course be pertinent to other areas of Africa.

The concept of nationhood describes various stages of communality and collectivity. Coleman's comprehensive description of the various manifestations of these 'nationalisms' is most useful:

> **Pan-Africanism**: race, continent, or subcontinent.
> **Nationalism**: colonial territory to a new state or nation.
> **Ethnic nationalisms/ethnicity**: *historic*-ethnolinguistic collectivities with previous political unity; *situational*- large-scale collectivities acquiring identity and self-consciousness through supertribalization.
> **Tribalism/micronationalism**: small-scale ethnolinguistic, kinship-defined collectivities.
> **Regionalism or localism**: any collectivity which asserted itself against alien rule prior to the emergence of an organized territorial nationalist movement as the presumptive successor regime.[3]

While these various collectivities represent attempts to forge community, I would argue that it is essentially with the struggle for independence that the nation becomes an object of public consciousness, since it is at this historical juncture that nation-building becomes the responsibility of the State. Somewhat paradoxically, an important moment in the process of national consciousness in francophone postcolonial cultures came from the exposure of African soldiers, (collectively designated as the '*tirailleurs sénégalais*') fighting for France in Europe during the Second World War, to French denunciations of the invading German forces; the French invocation of nationalism as a response to this territorial invasion led many Africans to reflect on the analogies with the colonial situation in Africa.

ACQUIRING POWER

As V. Y. Mudimbe has argued, 'Up to the 1920s, the entire framework of African social studies was consistent with the rationale of an epistemological field in its sociopolitical expressions of conquest . . . Socially, they were tools strengthening a new organization of power and its political methods of reduction, namely assimilation or indirect rule.'[4] Assimilation describes the French colonial policy which sought to impose French language and culture on its colonial subjects, while indirect rule refers to the British model which was fundamentally concerned with economic and political exploitation. These colonial models of dominance and authority (of power that is), were challenged by the *négritude* movement and the discourse it generated, and announced, as Mudimbe has argued, the first 'signs of an African will for power'.[5] The essential tenets of the *négritude* movement were to rehabilitate the idea of Blackness through the glorification of the African past, to dignify tradition and culture, and in the process to dispel the Western reductionist vision Africans had been subjected to for generations. This would also transform the superior-inferior relationship that had come to characterize Western and African relations, and simultaneously empower Africans. The *négritude* movement was soon politicized and came to play a significant role in the politics of nationalism both in the movement towards independence but also in the post-independence structuring of newly-independent *countries*.

MAINTAINING POWER

In order to avoid potential conflict, the Organization for African Unity (OAU) encouraged African leaders at independence to accept the existing colonial territorial borders, and to undertake the task of promoting national unity. Newly-independent governments identified the importance of recognition in the international community, and the juridical legitimacy it conferred upon the State. United Nations documents during the early 1960s are particularly revealing, in their concern with portraying their leaders fully engaged in government.

African governments simultaneously attempted to promote a national culture, common heritage, and collective memory in order to justify the construction of the nation state. As Coleman has explained, 'it is a posttribal, postfeudal terminal community which has emerged from the shattering forces of disintegration that characterize modernity . . . there must be a much greater awareness of a closeness of contact with "national" compatriots as well as with the "national" government.'[6] The task of constructing identities required a renunciation and denunciation of the French assimilationalist paradigm, and this dimension was implicit to much *négritude*. This was also one of the reasons why Marxism-Leninism proved attractive to a number of African countries (for example Mali and Congo), since the rejection of colonialism and imperialism that was so central to the writings of Lenin and Stalin, coincided with the opposition shared by Africans to the colonizing powers. Since independence, African countries have experimented with political systems as diverse as multi-party democracies, monarchies, single-party structures, military dictatorships and Marxist-Leninist parties. However, the frequency of *coups d'état* and the ease with which governments have been overthrown, underlines the fact that these structures were unstable and characterized by fragile alignments. Furthermore, the military in Africa soon relinquished its initial apolitical status, and entered the realm of politics.

One of the most influential and interesting leaders in post-colonial Africa was the *négritude* poet Léopold Sédar Senghor. Senghor served as President of Senegal for some twenty years (1960–1980). The Senghorian-*négritude* view of Africa played a determining role in the postcolonial nation-building process and division of power, to the extent that it offered a model of African unity and co-existence. Irving Markovitz has described Senghor's influence in the following terms: 'observers have called Senghor one of Africa's architects of a revigorated, dynamic socialism; they have held him responsible for a dramatic cultural and moral break with the values of Western civilization and the creation of a new, uniquely African civilization and systems of values.'[7] As Ali Mazrui has shown, Zaire's President Mobutu Sese Seko transformed this 'paradigm of authenticity' and has 'argued eloquently that, while *négritude* as a literary movement was a rebellion against the contempt which others (e.g., Europeans) felt towards Africa, *authenticity* as a political stance was a rebellion against the contempt many Africans felt towards *themselves*'.[8] Allegiance to an African past and unity have provided key tenets to the policies of African leaders, as they implemented them with their own variations. Senghor's writings during that period reflect the transformations in his thinking as it evolved, as Mudimbe has described it, from *négritude* to Marxism and finally to universal civilization.[9]

As I have argued, national consciousness emerged during the colonial era as a unified attempt to rid the African continent of colonial oppressors. Africans from all over the continent joined forces in the colonized territories and formed a united front against the common oppressor. However, these alignments were not conceived as permanent associations and unity soon came to signify sameness, that is to say assimilation to the views and philosophies of the new postcolonial élites who controlled and manipulated power.

Manipulating power

It is essential for us to explore the emergence of various power mechanisms in the African context, since, as Achille Mbembe has argued, 'to account for postcolonial relations is thus to pay attention to the workings of power in its minute details, and to the principles of assemblage which give rise to its efficacy'.[10] The term 'power' signifies a number of phenomena, but it is used here, as Henry Bretton defined it in his book *Power and Politics in Africa*, 'to connote any extension of will or physical ability beyond an individual or group to effect certain goals in relation to other individuals or groups'.[11] The manner in which power has been acquired, maintained and manipulated by the various agents is essential to our understanding of nationalism in the African context.

Patrick Chabal has addressed the question of power and violence in post-colonial Africa, and distinguished between two types of violence, namely 'active violence' and 'passive violence'. Whereas the former includes torture, execution, detention, et cetera, the latter designates incompetence, economic considerations, hunger, famine, embezzlement, and so forth. Indeed, as Max Weber has demonstrated, 'the use of force is regarded as legitimate only in so far as it is either permitted by the State or prescribed by it . . . the claim of the modern state to monopolize the use of force is as essential to it as its character of compulsory jurisdiction and of continuous operation.'[12] These types of violence feature prominently in a number of literary works, in their portrayal of what Chabal has described as:

> A political order that is exclusively governed by a moral economy founded on violence . . . This regression of the political toward raw violence in turn lowers human psychology to its most basic expression: it is a return to the survival of the fittest and to a political economy made up of rape, theft, barter and robbery.[13]

The suitability, or at least the effectiveness of the models I have discussed to the African context, can in part be gauged by considering the predicament of the postcolonies. Africans were only allowed limited participation in the leadership hierarchy under French direct rule, and therefore gained only little experience with power. This factor does not in itself explain the situation in the postcolony today, since the problems faced by countries that were subjected to British indirect rule, which did allow greater participation, are analogous.[14] However, if one examines these colonial mechanisms of rule, one can see how, after independence, they came to be duplicated in spaces that were not ethnically homogeneous, and thus generated the situation which characterizes postcolonial Africa. As Kwame Anthony Appiah has argued in his book, *In My Father's House*:

> In most places, however, the new states brought together peoples who spoke different languages, had different religious traditions and notions of property, and were politically (and in particular, hierarchically) integrated to different – often radically different – degrees . . . even the states with the smallest populations were by and large not ethnically homogeneous.[15]

The structures and alignments that were in place on the pre-contact African continent were all dismantled by the colonial powers. This process of erasure and domination ensured that any subsequent autonomous rule would have to be undertaken according to colonial alignments. The colonial authorities employed such terms as 'tribalism' and 'ethnicity' to further their *divide ut imperes* policy. However, it was not just the colonial measures undertaken to restrict nomadic existence and the process of 'fluid' exchanges which Jean-Loup Amselle has described in *Au coeur de l'ethnie (The Heart of the Ethnic Group)* but rather the colonial practices themselves (economic, regional, social) which generated a 'tribalist ideology' (encompassing factionalism, tribalism and micro-nationalism).[16]

The 'tribalist ideology' described by Amselle has come to represent the principal obstacle to the nation-building process to the extent that it has been politicized and employed by postcolonial rulers, in the same way that the colonial powers did, to fuel ethnic animosity and generate instability. As Crawford Young has argued, ' "Nation" as an imagined community of anti-colonial combat . . . was relatively unproblematic . . . But "nation", once independence was won, required the postcolonial state as vehicle: thus its imperative of "national integration".'[17] The initial model for nation-building consisted in bringing together heterogeneous peoples, and foregrounded the willingness to incorporate and validate this sociological plurality. However, in the name of 'national integration' and unity, governments have failed to recognize this diversity and accordingly to authenticate individual aspirations; the instability of postcolonial environments can thus be seen as an affirmation of peoples' refusal to assimilate their respective identities to a monolithic national paradigm.

In his book, *Technology, Tradition and the State in Africa*, Jack Goody attested to the conflict characteristic of pre-colonial Africa. While it is vital to recognize the often violent character of pre-colonial relations, it is the aliena-tion, assimilation and violence associated with colonial rule which comes closest to the sophisticated and technologically advanced mechanisms of repression and exploitation (such as torture, propaganda, communication technology et cetera) that are at work in the postcolony today. Assimilationist policy was the order of the day under French rule, but similar philosophies have prevailed in the postcolony at the service of nationalistic, unifying policies, that are just as oppressive and exclusive. The territorial borders may have been artificial and arbitrary in their original conception, but they nevertheless became political, legal and administrative realities at independence. Indeed, as Denis Austin has stated, 'cartographically, Africa certainly exists.'[18] The colonial period mod-ernized Africa, and created cities and infrastructures, shipping and trading lanes, et cetera, which favoured a number of regions over others (coastal over inland, for example). This situation was further complicated by the fact that the artificial boundaries demarcated by the colonial powers provided the frame-work for the emergence of national consciousness as the driving force behind the struggle for independence, but once this end had been achieved, the very precondition for its continuity depended on its sustained and unified opposition to the colonial powers. This has generated a very complex situation, in that the State (government authorities) has been able to justify the promotion of nationalism as a measure to exclude colonial domination.

The fight against the common oppressor (Western colonists) was indeed sanctified by international law: 'All peoples have the right of self-determination. By virtue of that right they freely determine their political status and freely pursue their economic, social and cultural development.'[19] Somewhat para-doxically, self-determination generated a situation of dependency on the auton-omous national State. Initially, however, there was much debate concerning the definition of a 'people and of what 'self-determination' itself signified. The history of decolonization has underlined this, since countries achieved independence at different historical periods, as their associations with the former Western colonizing powers were redefined. The 1950s and 1960s witnessed self-determination by most African countries; for most of francophone sub-Saharan Africa, 1960 proved to be the determining year (Cameroon, Central African Republic, Gabon, Congo, Zaire, and so forth). However, some African countries only achieved independence much later (Zimbabwe in 1980, Mozambique in 1975, Angola in 1975). There is little ambiguity today concerning the significance of 'self-determination' and 'peoples'; they correspond respectively to the autonomous government of a sovereign territory, and to the 'nationals' who reside there. Attention has instead shifted towards the problem of validating and recognizing diversity in these nation states, and to the complex task of constructing identity.

THE RIGHT TO VIOLENCE AND THE RIGHT TO SILENCE: HUMAN RIGHTS IN AFRICA

Once power has been acquired and concentrated in the hands of a power élite, the concern turns towards maintaining it. African postcolonial governments have promoted a unifying discourse, and opposition and dissent have often become treasonable offences. The government is always greater than the individual, since when violence is perpetrated by them, it is legal and legitimized in its own name.[20] Debate is stifled and alternative discourse is deemed unacceptable. While governments have been eager to promote an official culture, the complex political realities have in turn forced writers and other dissidents to situate themselves in relation to this national paradigm. As Timothy Brennan has demonstrated, 'it is not that people, or the artists who speak for them, can imagine no other applications, but that the solutions to dependency are only collective, and the territorial legacies of the last 200 years provide the collectivity no other basis upon which to fight dependency.'[21]

Political constitutions accord legitimacy to sovereign nations and to their governments. An interesting parallel can be drawn between the foundations of constitutional legislation in the West and in Africa, particularly since African constitutions are usually duplicated according to Western models. As Susan Waltz has explained:

> In the West, the two principal human rights documents – the French Déclaration des droits de l'homme et du citoyen and the U.S. Bill of Rights – were drafted explicitly to limit the arbitrary powers of government. Both documents seek to protect individual liberties against the oppression of those who govern, and both assure due process of law for those accused of wrongdoing.[22]

However, as Waltz goes on to point out, 'so long as authority has control in nondemocratic regimes, it is difficult to imagine that such groups [human rights organizations] will be appreciated.'[23] Recent events in the Republic of the Congo illustrate some of these considerations.

The Congo has a particularly complicated history of ethnic instability. In 1991, the Congolese Government stated that it had 'reaffirmed its faith in the principles of pluralist democracy, to the rights outlined by the International Charter on Human and Peoples' Rights adopted in 1981 by the Organization for African Unity and the African Charter on Human and Peoples' Rights adopted in 1991 by the sovereign National Conference'.[24] Within the framework of this discussion, the following 'articles' in the Congolese Constitution are the most pertinent:

> Article 7: The human person is sacred. The state has a duty to respect and protect human life. Every citizen has the right to freely develop her/his personality as long as they respect the rights of others and civil order.
> Article 8: The freedom of the human person is inviolable. Any act of torture, any inhumane or degrading treatment are prohibited. No one can be arrested or detained arbitrarily.
> Article 13: No citizen may be interned on the national territory, except in those instances provided for by the law. No citizen can be forced for political reasons to reside away from her/his dwelling place or in exile.[25]

The new Constitution thus recognizes that dissent and opposition are lawful, but also the illegality of torture. Since the National Conference was held in 1991 and the Congo became a pluralist democracy, the sociological reality has remained problematic. Political alignment has taken place according to ethnic criteria, and this has in turn exacerbated ethnic animosity, and precluded the possibility of genuine social reform. Furthermore, the previous pattern of military engagement in government has been duplicated. It would seem that the future lies in the irony of the new Constitution and the apparent contradiction that is contained in its wording. The very use of the word 'reaffirm' confirms the previous Constitution's faith in the fundamental principles of human rights, but history has shown that it chose to ignore them. The problem lies once again in the policy of national integration, and the uses that are made of State security to achieve that goal. 'Security' is a broad term, and governments have been able to exercise their constitutional, and therefore legitimate, 'right to violence'. An Amnesty International report entitled 'Torture as Policy' has described this process: 'Torture is usually part of the state-controlled machinery to suppress dissent. Concentrated in the torturer's electrode or syringe is the power and responsibility of the state . . . Torture is most often used as an integral part of a government's security strategy.'[26] The ways in which the abuses of this State 'violence' are exposed are essential to our understanding of the construction of nationalism and national culture.

FROM BERLIN TO THE END OF THE MILLENNIUM

Official discourse in postcolonial Africa has called for the elimination of ethnicity, tribalism and regionalism, but yet the State has simultaneously relied on these phenomena to manipulate power. Recent events in African politics have pointed to possible alternative structures as frameworks for transition. One of the most significant efforts has been the staging of National Conferences (Benin 1990, Congo 1991, Togo 1991), prompted by the imperative of seeking new and innovative frameworks for the postcolony, given the failure of existing ones. Governments need to demonstrate a willingness to distance themselves from the political paradigm according to which unity is synonymous with unanimity; they must accept the complexity of the social reality, and validate plurality as a prerequisite to the construction of the national space. The situation is further complicated by the continued exploitation of the African continent by neo-colonial powers, the International Monetary Fund, and other such organizations.[27] Unless this relationship is redefined and Western powers recognize that their activities preclude the possibility of progress, it does not seem likely that the foreseeable future will offer us the spectacle of African leaders joining these superpowers at conference tables or 'summits'. The twentieth century will have ended with such instability and overt violations of the most fundamental basic human rights, that it is impossible to feel that there has been any progress since the 1884–1885 Berlin Conference. Recent events in countries such as Angola, Burundi, the Congo, Nigeria, Rwanda, Somalia, and Zaire confirm this. One can only hope that increased discourse and exposure of these realities will allow us to articulate different observations by the end of the twenty-first century.

NOTES

1. Henri Lopes, *Le Pleurer-Rire* (Paris: Présence Africaine, 1982) p. 58; *The Laughing Cry*, trans. Gerald Moore (London: Readers international Inc., 1987) p. 40. Quotations from Lopes' work are cited in the text with the abbreviation 'PR' and 'LC', and followed by the page reference.
2. James Smoot Coleman, *Nationalism and Development in Africa: Selected Essays*, ed. Richard L. Skar (Berkeley and Los Angeles: University of California Press, 1994) p. 34.
3. Coleman, p. 122.
4. V. Y. Mudimbe, *The Invention of Africa: Gnosis, Philosophy and the Order of Knowledge* (Bloomington and Indianapolis: Indiana University Press, 1988) p. 83.
5. Mudimbe, p. 83.
6. Coleman, p. 21.
7. Irving Markovitz, *Léopold Sédar Senghor and the Politics of Negritude* (New York: Atheneum, 1969) p. 3.
8. Ali A. Mazrui, 'On Poets-Presidents and Philosopher Kings', *Research in African Literature* 21, no. 2 (Summer 1990) p. 14.
9. Mudimbe, p. 93.
10. Achille Mbembe, 'The Banality of Power and the Aesthetics of Vulgarity in the Postcolony', *Public Culture: Society for Transnational Cultural Studies* 4, no. 2 (Spring 1992) p. 4.

11. Henry Bretton, *Power and Politics in Africa* (Chicago: Aldine Publishing Company, 1973) p. 8.
12. Max Weber, in Guenther Roth and Claus Wittich (eds), *Economy and Society: An Outline of an Interpretative Sociology* (Berkeley and Los Angeles: University of California Press, 1978) p. 56.
13. Patrick Chabal, 'Pouvoir et violence en Afrique postcoloniale', *Politique Africaine* 42 (June 1991) pp. 58–9. My translation.
14. In anglophone African literature, the novels of Ngugi wa Thiong'o, Chinua Achebe and Nuruddin Farah, among others, attest to this.
15. Kwame Anthony Appiah, *My Father's House: Africa in the Philosophy of Culture* (New York: Oxford University Press, 1992) pp. 161–2.
16. Jean-Loup Amselle, 'Ethnies et espaces: Pour une anthropologie topologique' in Jean-Loup Amselle and Elikia M'Bokolo (eds), *Au coeur de l'ethnie: Ethnies, tribalisme et état en Afrique*, (Paris: La Découverte, 1985).
17. Crawford Young, 'Evolving modes of consciousness and ideology: nationality and ethnicity' in David E. Apter and Carl G. Rosberg (eds), *Political Development and the New Realism in Sub-Saharan Africa* (Charlottesville: University of Virginia Press, 1994) p. 72.
18. Denis Austin, 'Pax Africa' in Simon Baynham (ed), *Military Power in Black Africa* (London: Croom Helm, 1986) p. 166.
19. This is from the United Nations Charter, cited in Richard Pierre and Claude and Burns H. Weston (eds), *Human Rights in the World Community: Issues and Action* (Philadelphia: University of Pennsylvania Press, 1992) p. 424.
20. For an analysis of the processes through which power is accumulated and its use legitimated, see Achille Mbembe, 'Pouvoir, violence et accumulation' in Jean-François Bayart, Comi Toulabor et Achille Mbembe (eds), *La Politique par la basse en Afrique Noire: Contributions à une problématique de la démocracie* (Paris: Karthala, 1992).
21. Timothy Brennan, 'The national longing for form' in Homi K. Bhabha (ed), *Nation and Narration*, (London and New York: Routledge, 1990) p. 58.
22. Susan E. Waltz, *Human Rights and Reform: Changing the Face of North African Politics* (Berkeley and Los Angeles: University of California Press, 1995) p. 14.
23. Waltz, p. 14.
24. F. Eboussi Boulaga, *Les Conférences nationales en Afrique noire: Une affaire à suivre* (Paris: Karthala, 1993) p. 196. My translation.
25. Eboussi Boulaga, pp. 197–8.
26. Cited in Claude and Weston, p. 79.
27. Mongo Beti has addressed this question in his recent *La France contre Afrique: Retour au Cameroon* (Paris: La Découverte, 1993).

18

HOW NATIONALISMS SPREAD – EASTERN EUROPE ADRIFT THE TIDES AND CYCLES OF NATIONALIST CONTENTION[1]

Mark Beissinger

'One word dominated our conversation – struggle. . . . Struggle, struggle, struggle.' Two Soviet journalists attempting to interview activists of the Latvian Popular Front, as reported in *Pravda*, March 1, 1989.

'We are living in an extremely condensed historical period. Social processes which earlier required decades now develop in a matter of months.'
Literaturnaia gazeta, September 13, 1989.

NATIONALISM, John Breuilly tells us, 'is, above and beyond all else, about politics, and that politics is about power' (1982: 1–2). Yet, in explaining how and why nationalisms spread, many scholars write about nationalism as if it were more a matter of communication or contagion than contention.

Early theorists of nationalism, such as Hans Kohn, Carleton Hayes, and Elie Kedourie, treated nationalism as an ideology and approached the subject as a branch of the history of ideas. Whereas Kohn attributed the spread of nationalism as a 'state of mind' to the 'the power of an idea' (specifically, the overwhelming attractiveness of notions of self-determination provoked by the French Revolution (1967: 16)), Kedourie (1993) viewed its spread as an almost accidental infection, a false and dangerous ideological obsession kindled by political philosophers in the human mind.[2] Hayes failed altogether to produce an explanation for why nationalism spread.[3] For other early theorists,

Mark R. Beissinger (1996), 'How nationalisms spread: Eastern Europe adrift the tides and cycles of nationalist contention', *Social Research*, 63:1.

Le Bon's notion of the 'maddening crowd' and understandings of nationalism as ideological or emotional dementia were appealing explanations for addressing what appeared to them as the essential irrationality of ethnic separatism and national self-assertion.[4] For primordialists, residues of 'primordial sentiments' were seen as spreading in emotional contagions in societies experiencing the stresses of modernization, leading to intergroup conflicts that threatened to overwhelm the rational, modernized sector of society (Shils 1957; Geertz 1963). Such images remain common today in the study of nationalism. They have little to do with the reality of nationalist mobilization, as a careful analysis of the most recent waves of nationalism in the former Soviet Union and East Europe indicates.

To some degree, the continued power of these images has been due to an excessive focus on the activities of nationalist intellectuals as opposed to what are arguably the two most important *dramatis personae* in any nationalist politics: state and society. Liah Greenfeld, for instance, in her magisterial study of the rise of nationalist discourse, argues that the spread of nationalism from a small intellectual elite to society at large, 'an important and interesting topic in itself, doubtless increased the efficacy of national identity as a force of social mobilization, but it had no significant impact on the character of specific nationalisms' (Greenfeld 1992: 22–3).[5] Miroslav Hroch similarly focuses his attention on what he terms Phase B in the development of nationalism (the period of patriotic agitation), which he calls 'the most important phase,' largely ignoring how and why the emergence of nationalist counter-elites leads to the rise of mass national movements (Phase C), although he notes that 'Phase B was not necessarily destined to pass over into Phase C' (Hroch 1985: 22–4). In an article entitled 'When Is a Nation?' Walker Connor bemoaned the fact that scholars of nationalism have focused excessively on the 'musings of elites whose generalizations concerning the existence of national consciousness are highly suspect.' By contrast, nationalism should be understood as 'a mass, not an elite phenomenon,' although the moment when 'a sufficient portion of a people has internalized the national identity in order to cause nationalism to become an effective force for mobilizing the masses' does not lend itself to easy identification (Connor 1990).[6]

Understanding the origins of nationalist ideas is a different exercise than understanding how and why nationalism attains its political potency as a mass phenomenon and how it manifests itself in a specific location, in a specific manner, at a specific moment in time. 'Nationalism as such is fated to prevail,' wrote the late Ernest Gellner, 'but not any one particular nationalism' (1983: 47).[7] As Kedourie came to recognize on the eve of his death:

> To narrate the spread, influence and operation of nationalism in various politics is to write a history of events, rather than of ideas. It is a matter of understanding a polity in its particular time, place and circumstances, and of following the activity of specific political agents acting in context of their own specific and peculiar conditions. The coherence of contingent events is not the same as the coherence of contingent ideas, and

the historian has to order his strategies accordingly . . . (Kedourie 1993: 139).

Nations exist, we are told, because people 'think the nation' (Anderson 1991). But in spite of the importance of culture and ideas in nationalist politics, in reality the only way that we know that nationalisms exist is through behaviors: through the collective behaviors and state actions that they engender. In this respect, nationalist discourse should be understood less as the history of ideas than as a form of collective behavior – one greatly influenced by the context in which the speaker is located. Nationalism achieves political potency only in the form of collective discourse, mass mobilization, or state practice. But it manifests itself in other areas of social behavior as well. There is a 'quiet' politics of nationalism, a politics in which state institutions remain dominant and nationalist contestation turns around efforts to institutionalize behaviors and identities to prevent challenges to official conceptions of nationhood or to prepare for moments when direct contestation becomes possible, the latter often revolving around what Scott calls 'hidden transcripts of resistance' (Scott 1991). And there is a 'noisy' politics of nationalism, precipitated by an opening of political opportunities in which the political order and its institutions come under direct challenge and contest. As Gellner noted, '[n]ationalism is like gravity, an important and pervasive force, but not, at *most* times, strong enough to be violently disruptive' (1994: xi).

When state and society are restored to their rightful places in the study of nationalism, it becomes clear that nationalism is essentially a contentious political activity, one which contests a particular crystallization of the state's physical, human, or cultural boundaries.[8] The modern state as it emerged since the seventeenth century has inherently involved a bounded community, both in terms of physical territory, the populations afforded membership, and the dominant rules of cultural interaction.[9] These boundaries represent, in Ian Lustick's terms, 'institutional constraints . . . which advantage certain groups and rival elites within the state at the expense of others' (Lustick 1993: 41). Nationalism is not about ancient enmities or even always about ethnicity, but rather about authority over a set of objects in politics, about the drawing of the physical, human, and cultural boundaries of the state and the life chances that people believe are associated with these definitions of boundaries. In this sense, nationalism differs from ethnic political action in much the same way that an object differs grammatically from a subject. Nationalism overlaps and intersects with ethnic political action but is defined not by the subject engaged in it, but primarily by its orientation toward a particular type of goal: the definition or redefinition of the physical, human, or cultural boundaries of the polity.

States need to be understood in part as repositories of cultural interest; while the degree to which cultural interests are embedded in states varies, no state is entirely culturally neutral. Nationalism is a contentious political activity in at least three senses. As a form of political practice, it generates controversy, for interests are closely bound with any given crystallization of a state's physical, human, and cultural boundaries. As a mode of political discourse, nationalism inherently involves a contestable claim, an inherently ambiguous claim subject to contestation: there is no 'objective' answer to the question of what the proper human, physical, and cultural bounds of the state should be. Finally, as a form of action, nationalism involves groups that contest a given crystallization of a state's physical, human, or cultural boundaries through various forms of mobilization and state practice. Nationalist contention is an iterative process; the boundaries of states are continually subjected to challenge and normalization, and previous attempts to contest boundaries are connected with subsequent attempts, viewed by challengers as part of a broader drama of national struggle, and consciously embedded into collective memory (itself an act of nationalist contestation) (Halbwachs 1980).

'Every nation has several moments which may be called great,' Merab Kostava, the Georgian nationalist leader, told hundreds of thousands of Georgians massed outside of the House of Government in the late hours of April 8, 1989, the night of the infamous Tbilisi massacre, when army troops stormed the square, killing twenty and injuring hundreds in an attempt to seize back control over the city. 'For Georgia that time has come now' (*Ekspress khronika*, no. 15, April 10, 1990). Like other modes of political contestation, nationalist contention has tended to emerge in the political arena in defined historical periods – in the context of cycles of contention and in regional or world-historical tides of contention that encompass particular areas of the world or families of polities. I use the terms 'tide of contention' or 'tide of mobilization' to describe a series of related mobilizational waves and cycles that are transnational in character, encompassing multiple polities.[10] Historically, these tides of contention have been accompanied by numerous bursts of nationalist discourse, waves of nationalist mobilization, and eruptions of interstate violence which, when reaching fruition, have brought about tectonic change in the character of the state system. Rarely has the remaking of the physical, human, or cultural boundaries of states been an isolated action without connection to other states. The noisy politics of nationalism is almost always a transnational phenomenon that is itself bounded by time and space. The French Revolution unleashed the first tide of nationalist contention, in which multiple polities within Europe became engulfed in a struggle to redefine the boundaries of their political communities (Dann and Dinwiddy 1988). The year 1848 was known for many years in Europe as 'the springtime of nations,' when, as Kedourie noted, 'a great upsurge of nationalist claims and ambitions' burst forth (1993: xii). Another tide of nationalist mobilization swept the Russian, Ottoman, and Austro-Hungarian empires from the second half of the nineteenth century through the First World War, when new states arose, in Peter Alter's words, 'like a wave sweeping across the land between Finland and Yugoslavia' (1989: 109). The rise of fascism in interwar Europe and the wave of decolonization that followed the Second World War represented the first truly global tides of nationalist contention. Historically, tides of nationalist contention emerged concomitantly with the emergence of both the national state and the social movement, the latter, as Charles Tilly noted, pitting challengers 'against the people who run national states' (1984: 304). The notions of boundedness and the revolution in communications which gave rise to both the modern state and the modern nation also gave rise to the modern social movement and inserted it into a transnational dialectic with similar phenomena in other locales.[11]

The latest tide of nationalist contention – emerging in 1987 in what was then the Soviet Union and subsequently spreading to the west and south – provides a unique opportunity to study how nationalism spreads to envelop numerous groups within a single polity and ultimately to encompass multiple states. It has been both a regional and a global tide of contentious behavior, spilling over into adjacent regions of Eastern Europe but echoing to farther corners of the globe as well. In what follows, I use examples from the former Soviet Union and Eastern Europe to illustrate how attention needs to be refocused on nationalism as a form of contentious politics. A contentious theory of nationalism helps us to understand the interrelationships between nationalisms, the connection between their 'quiet' and 'noisy' politics, the various forms which they assume, and the contingent nature of the substantiation of nations.

NATIONALISM AND INSTITUTIONAL CHANGE: AN ARMENIAN EXAMPLE

Scholars who study mobilizational politics have come to realize that contention is punctuated by broader cycles of mobilization – parabolas of protest which rise and fall largely as this collective action relates to what is happening inside political institutions (Tarrow 1989a, 1989b; McAdam 1982; Eisinger 1973). The same is true of nationalist contention as well. Not all contentious mass actions or even waves of mobilization ultimately build into cycles; some indeed are cut short through state repression or cooptation,[12] while in other cases mobilizational politics never materializes. Moreover, nationalist contention does occur outside of mobilizational cycles. But in times of 'normalized' politics, a given crystallization of state boundaries is backed by the effective authority of the state and is not subject to open challenge from within. In such conditions, there is a strong tendency for individuals to adjust their beliefs to the boundaries of the possible, accepting a given institutional arrangement as unalterable and even natural. In 1913, for instance, on the eve of the war which gave birth to the Czechoslovak state that he founded, Tomás Masaryk stated that '[j]ust because I cannot indulge in dreams of its collapse and know that, whether good or bad, it will continue, I am most deeply concerned that we should make something of this Austria' (quoted in Skilling 1992: 228). State institutions seek to promote this kind of hardening of boundaries within mass consciousness and among potential challengers by establishing a frame of discourse aimed at molding attitudes to the 'reality' which these institutions project, turning boundaries into 'unquestioned features of . . . public life' and 'part of the natural order of things for the overwhelming majority of the population' (Lustick 1993: 44). Essentially, when we talk about the spread of nationalism, we are talking not about processes of communication or contagion, but about the politics by which the hitherto impossible, implicit, and inconceivable come to be viewed by large numbers of people as thinkable, desirable, and even conventional.

There is considerable empirical evidence showing not only that 'people change their minds radically' during a cycle of contention, but also that 'these changes are remarkably stable' once a cycle of contention winds down (Klandermans 1992: 81–2) – that is, that cycles of contention are associated with the rise and institutionalization of new collective beliefs and identities. As we have come to realize, identities are situational, embedded, and overlapping – sometimes submerged, sometimes suppressed, and sometimes affirmed. But identities also need to be distinguished from the meanings attached to identities; usually identities contain a range of action-oriented collective beliefs which provide them with a sense of purpose and meaning. In phases of quiescence, the salience of specific identities and the collective meanings attached to them are formed through routine acts of discourse and behavior in formal or informal institutional settings. In phases of contention, social movements seek to disrupt these routines to bring about discursive transformations in society. Identities and/or certain ranges of collective beliefs associated with identities that previously remained submerged or suppressed are given substance through new forms of behavior which link individual beliefs into new patterns of social interaction. Mobilization provides the occasion for individuals to 'switch worlds,' in Berger and Luckmann's phrase, not only by expanding the boundaries of the possible, thereby making the unthinkable thinkable, but also by guiding individuals to a new social reality through a combination of personal networks and cathartic experiences emerging from specific events (Berger and Luckman 1966: pp. 144–5).

The USSR elevated the politics of controlling imaginations to an art, declaring that the nationalities question had been 'solved' forever and marginalizing nationalist dissent in support of this 'reality.' As Gorbachev has admitted, the regime itself came to believe its own rhetoric, blinding it to the latent potency of nationalist appeals and to the potentiality of the breakup of the country.[13] While many of the accusations against Sovietologists for their defects of vision in predicting the collapse of the USSR are deserved (they also established a discursive frame that largely excluded the possibility of state collapse), these charges must be understood in context; even the vast majority of Soviet dissidents in 1987 (including most non-Russian dissidents) did not imagine the collapse of the USSR,[14] and the discursive frame concocted by the Soviet state strongly colored the ways in which nationalists and populations formulated their aims. As one Western scholar has noted, to utter the words 'secession' or 'independence' in public in Lithuania in August 1988 seemed 'a daring act,' with most Sajudis activists believing that 'it was unrealistic . . . to think seriously about Lithuanian independence within the next ten to fifteen years'

(Senn 1990: 151–2). Rein Taagepera has similarly noted in Estonia that 'for the majority independence seemed either a pipe dream in 1987, or something one could think about only after meaningful autonomy was attained,' and it was only in fall 1989 that a majority of Estonians came to believe in the real possibility of attaining independence (1993: 127).

Waves of mass mobilization are usually triggered by change within institutions: by significant divisions within political elites and shifts in the political opportunities facing activists and populations. They are characteristic of transitional polities, not stable or stagnant polities. This is precisely why nationalism remains very much a 'disease of transition,' as has often been noted by observers. In most circumstances, institutional change and the emergence of political opportunities are necessary to bring nationalist challenges into being, for otherwise groups seeking to challenge the boundaries of the polity, as well as the populations they seek to mobilize, are unlikely to believe even in the possibility, let alone the desirability, of such actions. But whether a wave of mobilization builds into a cycle of mobilization within a particular population depends very much on the degree to which mobilization can be sustained over time, presenting a consistent challenge to a regime or eventually becoming institutionalized within the state itself. It is here – at the intersection of opportunity and identity – that nationalism and national identities ultimately acquire substance or grow tenuous. Anyone can declare a nation into existence; there is no shortage of failed experiments in 'nation-building,' including several addressed in this article. A nation whose tangibility is never affirmed through unimpeded and inclusive public discourse, voluntary support for state action, or autonomous mass mobilization can hardly be said to exist other than in name only. Elites may believe such a nation exists, and may even act in its name. But unless the nation extends into the beliefs and behaviors of society, such a farce runs a great risk of eventually being punctured.

As we know, the French Revolution began neither as a national nor a class struggle but eventually became both (Mann 1993b: p. 167). Similarly, the mobilizational waves unleashed by *glasnost'* did not begin as national struggles but gradually grew into them. *Glasnost'* altered the boundaries of the possible, giving rise to iterative attempts by nationalist groupings to test the political waters through acts of mobilization. By altering public expectations of the possible, liberalization significantly changed the boundaries of the thinkable and created interstices into which nationalist mobilization flowed.

A short sketch of the onset of Armenian mobilization over the Karabakh issue – the first major wave of nationalist mobilization in the *glasnost'* era – provides a glimpse into the ways in which political opportunity and the interaction of events structured nationalist politics in the early part of the cycle. While there is considerable evidence that Armenians never reconciled themselves to Azerbaidzhani control over Karabakh and the issue was raised regularly from the 1920s on through petitions, letter-writing campaigns, official appeals by party officials, and occasional demonstrations, these efforts were ignored by Moscow and their initiators subjected to persecution by local Azerbaidzhani authorities (Chorbajian et al. 1994: 144–7; Birch 1987; Suny 1983: 80–1). Indeed, the Soviet press portrayed the issue as if it 'had been settled once and for all' (Suny 1993: 188–9). But the situation changed with the inauguration of *glasnost'*. In July 1987, Karen Demirchian, longtime first secretary of the Armenian Communist Party, was harshly criticized at a republican party Central Committee plenum for tolerating corruption and favoritism. This was understood as signalling an effort to undermine Demirchian and to replace him with a reformist leader. Soon, articles appeared in the central press attacking Demirchian; one such piece, on the harmful pollutants emitted by chemical plants in Yerevan, described the local communist leadership as a mafia unconcerned with the health of the population. It was widely interpreted as 'a maneuver by the central authorities to provoke a popular uprising against the local authorities, which would be the pretext for their removal' (Verluise 1995: 84).[15] On September 1st, several hundred Armenians demonstrated in front of a polluting synthetic rubber plant, with no attempt by the authorities to repress them. In mid-October another unsanctioned ecological demonstration attracting up to 5,000 participants took place in Yerevan, again with little reaction by the authorities (*Vesti iz SSSR*, no. 19/20–5, 1987, p. 6; *Glasnost'*, no. 8, November 1987, pp. 46–7; *Glasnost'*, no. 10, 1987, p. 8).[16] The following day, a 1,000-strong demonstration displaying portraits of Gorbachev and calling for transfer of the territory to Armenia occurred in Yerevan in solidarity with the Armenians of Karabakh. This 'slippage' of demands – from ecology to nationalism – was a pattern that repeated itself throughout much of the former Soviet Union, as nationalist counter-elites probed the limits of the permissible. In this case the demonstration was brutally broken up by the police when demonstrators refused to heed calls to disperse (*Vesti iz SSSR*, 19/20–5, 1987, p. 6; *Radio Liberty Research Report*, no. 44/187, October 20, 1987, p. 2). However, already by this time the rudiments of nationalist social movement organization began to emerge.

Demirchian hung to his post despite persistent attacks on him. But by January 1988, encouraged by the broadening limits of public debate, the attacks upon Stalinism at the October 1987 Central Committee Plenum, sympathetic statements by several Gorbachev advisors (some of them Armenian) over the Karabakh issue, the retirement of former Azerbaidzhani party boss Heydar Aliev from the Politburo, the emergence of open conflict within the Politburo as a result of Yeltsin's resignation, and widespread rumors that Moscow intended to look into the problem,[17] the Karabakh Armenians pressed their claims. As Georgii Shakhnazarov, a Gorbachev advisor and himself an Armenian from Karabakh, later noted about those who organized the campaign for unification, 'the freedom that loomed on the horizon was embodied in their consciousness primarily by the possibility of uniting with their homeland' (Shakhnazarov 1993: 206). In August 1987, the Karabakh Armenians had sent a petition to the Central Committee in Moscow signed by 75 thousand people in favor of transferring Karabakh to Armenia. The petition was ignored until an official delegation from Karabakh arrived in Moscow in January to press the issue; they were promised that their appeal would be reviewed. But in early February a negative answer was crudely relayed from the Central Committee apparatus (Ryzhkov 1992: 203; *Vesti iz SSSR*, no. 4, 1988, p. 1).[18] This in turn unleashed a coordinated campaign of civil disobedience by Armenians throughout Nagorno-Karabakh, with calls for the regional Soviet to convene to recognize the territory as part of Armenia. The campaign appears to have been organized in part by forces within the local party organization itself.[19] In the meantime, in Yerevan a series of ecological demonstrations were taking place over construction of a new chemical plant on the outskirts of the city. When news that the regional Soviet in Stepanakert had approved an appeal for unification with Armenia reached Yerevan, as well as a second rejection from Moscow, the ecological demonstrations quickly grew into manifestations of support for the Karabakh Armenians, attracting up to thirty thousand people (*Vesti iz SSSR*, no. 4, 1988, p. 2; Verluise 1995: 86). On the night of February 21st anti-Armenian pogroms broke out in the town of Gadrut in Nagorno-Karabakh, injuring 16 and killing 2. This in turn led to enormous demonstrations in Yerevan of up to a million people calling for transfer of the territory to Armenia and physical protection of Armenians living in Karabakh. Demonstrators carried portraits of Gorbachev with the inscription 'We believe in you' (*Vesti iz SSSR*, no. 4–1, 1988). Even Demirchian came to support the Karabakh cause, pressing the issue before the Politburo (Gorbachev 1995: 502); indeed, there is some suspicion that Demirchian, facing pressure for his resignation from Moscow, tolerated the demonstrations in Yerevan as a way of building popular support (*Ekspress khronika*, no. 52, Dec. 17–24, 1991, p. 6). On February 24th, the Organizational Committee for the Issue of the Reunification of Karabakh with Armenia sprang into existence. The following day Gorbachev met with two of its representatives, agreeing on February 26th to a program of measures proposed by them to strengthen the cultural and economic autonomy of the Karabakh Armenians in exchange for taking the territorial issue off the agenda and calling a halt to demonstrations (Shakhnazarov 1993: 205–10). By February 27th participation in nationalist demonstrations in Yerevan dropped sharply, ceasing entirely on February 28th. Ironically, it was precisely as the Armenian mobilization in Yerevan wound down that rallies organized by Azerbaidzhani refugees from Armenia began to gather on the central square of the industrial town of Sumgait in Azerbaidzhan, leading ultimately to an orgy of anti-Armenian violence. As one study notes, 1988 became known among Armenians as 'the year when everything was possible' (Chorbajian et al. 1994: 149).

The rest, as they say, is history. But there are several features of the origins of the Armenian wave of mobilization that deserve careful attention, for they repeat themselves in most cases of successful mobilization throughout the cycle. Most striking, of course, is how shifts in authority within the state led to an explosion of public expectations, a slippage of protest activity from within-system demands to those directly challenging the parameters of the official boundary regime, and ultimately to a shift in the frame of public discourse over boundary issues. Shifting a discursive frame was neither a matter of communication nor of contagion, but rather an iterative process of groping and probing on the part of nationalist counter-elites in response to the openings that specific acts of government provided. The most effective force for mobilizing populations, however, remained violence – through the sense of victimization and activization of ethnic boundaries which it produced. Here, we should note as well the contingency of nationalist mobilization and its dialectical relationship with other nationalisms and with state actions. Had Gorbachev, for instance, acceded to the petition of Karabakh Armenians for the transfer of the territory to Armenia, one might well imagine how this would have transformed the entire politics of the issue. But as we now know from the memoir literature, the Soviet leadership took seriously the problem of analogy; it viewed the entire affair through the prism of a 'domino theory,' fearing the encouragement which one boundary change might give to other groups seeking to challenge boundaries. Actually, there had been regular border adjustments among republics in the Stalin and Khrushchev periods; simply between 1930 and 1970 thirty border changes were effected among the federal units of the USSR, including the transfer of Crimea from the Russian Federation to Ukraine. But during the Brezhnev period a discursive frame that essentially froze internal boundaries became ensconced. The Gorbachev leadership unanimously defended this policy, even after it was evident, in the words of former Prime Minister Nikolai Ryzhkov, that 'the fire of the conflict would not die down' (1992: 203–4) and that the old frame had already been transcended by developments on the ground. As Gorbachev told the Politburo at its July 4th, 1988 meeting, 'Reviewing boundaries is unrealistic; that would mean going down a disastrous path, and not only in these regions' (*Soiuz mozhno . . .* 1995: 30). But the gap between the Soviet leadership's discourse over boundaries and its inability to enforce it ultimately turned the Karabakh events into, as former Politburo member Vadim Medvedev put it, 'a detonator for sharpening other national problems and conflicts' (1994:63).

FROM STATE TO EMPIRE: THE FORMATION
AND SPREAD OF A NATIONALIST MASTER FRAME

A single wave hardly makes a cycle of contention. Had nationalist mobilization in the former Soviet Union stopped over the issue of Karabakh and other internal boundary changes, the Soviet flag would probably still be hoisted over the Kremlin. But nationalisms have a profound effect on one another. They are in this sense transnational and interrelated phenomena, not merely a collection of individual and isolated stories.

In his study of the Italian cycle of contention, Sidney Tarrow noted that contention diffuses largely as a response to the successes achieved by others in their efforts to contest the state. As he observed, protest cycles emerge 'through imitation, comparison, the transfer of forms and themes of protest from one sector to another, and direct reaction on the part of those whose interests had been affected by earlier protests' (Tarrow 1989a: 223). Serbian success in confronting the Turks in the early nineteenth century encouraged Greek efforts to do the same. The success of Mussolini's march on Rome in 1922 brought about a rash of right-wing nationalist challenges throughout Europe.

In the former Soviet Union, the events surrounding Nagorno-Karabakh and the activities of other 'early risers' within the *glasnost'* mobilizational cycle not only made clear the growing political space that had been made available to contest the state, but also indicated the regime's vulnerability to a particular form of mobilization – the mass demonstration. The reimagining of nations throughout the former Soviet Union coincided with the rise of the demonstration as a form of political action and contestation, both constituting parts of the resonant 'master frame' (Snow and Benford 1992) that characterized the mobilizational cycle. The association of the demonstration with the rise of nationalism is hardly accidental. In his memoirs Gavriil Popov notes the liberating sensations that he felt from the first major demonstrations in Moscow in May 1989: 'For the first time in my life I saw tens of thousands of free people' (Popov 1994: 65). In addition to its disruptive effects upon the government, the demonstration became the occasion for reconstituting the boundaries of the nation, flaunting the lack of support for the regime through the power of numbers and puncturing longstanding legitimating myths propagated by the regime that it had 'solved' the nationalities problem or represented the interests of 'the people.' Through the demonstration, the Soviet population was guided to a new consciousness. 'Every day here in the square,' a Tadzhik newspaper editor wrote about the wave of mass protest which overtook that republic at the end of 1991, 'was like ten days in school for the people' (quoted in *The New York Times*, June 9, 1992, p. A1).

Nationalism in this sense is a modular form of political behavior; a specific module of contentious action or discursive frame can easily be transferred from one context to another, although whether these modules resonate within specific populations is as much a factor of context as it is a product of the features of the modules themselves.[20] The specific master frame that became the subject of imitation throughout the former Soviet Union by groups seeking to contend the state during this period, however, was not developed in Armenia but rather in the Baltic. Baltic nationalisms operated parallel and in interaction with one another, due largely to the similar relationship these three peoples had with the Soviet state and their geographic proximity. The association, symmetry, and coordination among Baltic nationalisms is further evidence of how analogy constitutes a critical process in the spread of nationalism. Here the pattern at first developed much as in Armenia: a series of environmental demonstrations over industrial pollution and development in Latvia and Estonia became the occasions for the expression of anti-Muscovite sentiments over the central government's 'colonial' style of management, while dissident groups previously marginalized and seeking to raise broader boundary issues utilized the opportunity afforded by the political opening to mobilize and put forth their own national agendas. The difference in the Baltic was that the boundary issue was one of secession from the USSR rather than the redefinition of interrepublican boundaries. From April 1987 through May 1988, well before the rise of mass secessionist movements, more than 21 demonstrations occurred throughout the Baltic that raised secessionist demands, most of them attracting anywhere from a few hundred participants to ten thousand. But these minor disturbances were little more than a nuisance to the authorities. Even as late as February 1988, on the occasion of the 70th anniversary of Lithuanian independence, Western journalists noted that the dominant mood in Lithuania was one of 'public nonchalance, . . . not a feeling of hostility' (quoted in Senn 1990: 34). By spring 1988 the issue of Stalin's victims, now openly debated in Moscow in the aftermath of Gorbachev's denunciation of Stalinism at the October 1987 plenum, gave rise to a ferment across the Baltic, raising the thorny issues of Stalinist deportations and repressions, the Molotov-Ribbentrop Pact, and by implication Baltic membership in the Soviet Union. From the beginning Baltic nationalism had a strong anti-central, anti-bureaucratic temper which paralleled closely Gorbachev's attacks upon the Soviet central bureaucracy in 1987 and 1988. The popular fronts which sprang into existence in spring 1988 all defined themselves initially as movements for *perestroika*, not for independence, and Gorbachev and other reformers largely interpreted them through the lens of their struggle against bureaucratic domination throughout Soviet life (Cherniaev 1993: 143–4). But bureaucratic and imperial domination were difficult to separate within the Soviet context,[21] and ultimately the opportunity to express anti-center sentiment allowed the possibility of slippage into an antiimperial discourse.

The Soviet Union always straddled the divide between empire and state, and it was the inability of Soviet reformers to make clear this distinction which prevented them from averting Soviet collapse.[22] Ian Lustick has pointed to the powerful effects which images of state and empire have upon those to whom they are addressed; as he notes, 'in the modern world, empires are expected to break apart,' and secession and decolonization have been turned into categories used by politicians 'to label what they do to prevent or achieve changes in the shape of a state' (Lustick 1993: 22–3). In the late twentieth century, empires have come to represent the antithesis of the norms of the modern state system. They have become one of the several alter-egos for polities claiming the status of states, embodying an essential rejection of the norms and practices of dominant groups within these states and constituting a term of opprobrium and reproof by those claiming the status of nation and seeking a major alteration in state boundaries. The master frame of nationalism which spread throughout much of the Soviet Union was essentially an anti-colonial frame. What once was routinely referred to as a state suddenly came to be universally condemned as an empire. The dominant view of the collapse of the Soviet Union today is that the Soviet Union was an empire and therefore its dissolution was inevitable. However, it is now routinely referred to as an empire precisely because it did break up. The real question raised by the disintegration of the Soviet Union is not whether the break-up of the Soviet empire was inevitable, but rather how the Soviet Union, once universally regarded as a state, came to be seen by large numbers of people as an empire, and therefore its collapse as inevitable.[23]

And it is here that we can appreciate the significance of what Aristide Zolberg and Sidney Tarrow have called 'moments of madness' (Zolberg 1972; Tarrow 1989a: 79–80) for the study of nationalism. It is these moments, when the social world seemingly is turned upside-down and the authority of the existing order grows bare, that a revolution in collective imagination, or 'cognitive liberation,' as McAdam calls it (1982: 36–59), occurs, as official frames of discourse come loose and are transcended. Three patterns of consciousness change as they related to patterns of mobilization marked the Soviet experience – exemplified by the rise of secessionist sentiment in Lithuania, Armenia, and Ukraine respectively.

The Lithuanians illustrate a pattern of consciousness change typical of early risers, in which the task of counter-elites was one of emboldening publics to express openly that which they traditionally feared to express – a situation Timur Kuran refers to as 'preference falsification' (Kuran 1989). In Lithuania secessionist demands lay implicit in most early demonstrations but were usually not forthrightly voiced. As nationalist protest gathered speed, the Politburo sent a mission led by Aleksandr Yakovlev to Vilnius in early August 1988 to investigate the situation. Yakovlev shocked his Lithuanian hosts by publicly supporting the Sajudis movement against the local party bureaucracy. Kazimera Prunskiene later noted that '[i]n 1988 Sajudis divided time into "pre-Yakovlev" and "post-Yakovlev"' (quoted in Senn 1995: 25). As one eyewitness described the changes in consciousness which subsequently ripened at a mass meeting on August 23rd, the anniversary of the Molotov-Ribbentrop Pact: 'the public behavior of Lithuanians changed radically . . . The public now spoke more freely of its concerns; it raised new demands' (Senn 1990: 132, 136). When local party officials tried to make a stand against growing secessionist sentiment at the end of September by suppressing unsanctioned nationalist rallies, the move backfired, leading Sajudis to call for the resignation of party boss Ringaudas Songaila. His resignation in October and replacement by Algirdas Brazauskas demonstrated the power of the movement, but an ambiguity still remained in Sajudis' public stances over whether it stood for sovereignty within a reformed Soviet Union or for independence. It was not really until February 1989, when Brazauskas sanctioned Lithuanian Independence Day as a public holiday, that Sajudis leaders, at a rally numbering in the hundreds of thousands, unabashedly proclaimed independence as a goal (*Vesti iz SSSR*, no. 4–7, 1989, p. 7). Still, Brazauskas continued his delicate balancing act with the Kremlin for at least a half-year more, all the while gradually positioning his own party for separation from Moscow.

By contrast, the Armenian and Ukrainian cases represent less instances of preference falsification than cases of preference change – that is, the emergence and spread of new ranges of collective beliefs about nationhood that were largely absent in mass consciousness on the eve of mobilization. Secessionist demands among Armenians were first voiced largely as a bargaining chip with central and local authorities in the Armenian struggle over Karabakh. They subsequently took on larger meaning as social movements grew frustrated with Moscow's policies – and specifically its refusal to change internal boundaries. Only in the fall of 1989, in response to a new wave of violence over Karabakh and continued disappointment with Moscow's policies, did sustained secessionist mobilization emerge for the first time in Armenia. As Lev Ter-Petrossian indicated the rationale behind his republic's drive for independence on the eve of the break-up of the USSR, Armenia had been forced to take steps in the direction of secession, since the Soviet government had been 'backing away from Armenia, leaving it one on one with its problems' (*Moscow News*, no. 23, 1991, p. 8).

The Ukrainians represented yet a third pattern typical of late risers within the mobilizational cycle. Over the course of 1990 and 1991, Ukraine witnessed a major transformation in public attitudes toward secession. Through January 1990 nearly all secessionist mobilization in Ukraine was concentrated in the West, and the handful of secessionist demonstrations that took place elsewhere never succeeded in gaining more than 10 thousand participants at most at any single event. But the East European revolutions of late 1989, the republican elections of early 1990, and the parade of sovereignties that broke out throughout the former Soviet Union in the summer of 1990 led to an explosion of efforts to spread secessionist sentiment throughout Ukraine. This campaign culminated in the clear 'moment of madness' in Ukrainian politics – October 1990, when massive student strikes and a wave of protest forced the communist-dominated parliament to seek the resignation of the prime minister, to vote that military service outside of Ukraine for inhabitants of Ukraine would be on a voluntary basis only, and to declare that Ukraine's participation in a new union treaty would have to wait until a new Ukrainian constitution had been drawn up. This transformative set of events partially institutionalized secessionist sentiment by bringing to power a new government that spoke ambiguously about Ukraine's relationship with the center and about ensuring Ukrainian sovereignty and independence.

One of the hallmarks of politics in the Soviet Union in its final years was the mercurial character of identities, a massive reimagining of political communities, not simply an assertion of old identities. Popular fronts along the Baltic model sprang up throughout most of the former Soviet Union by the summer and fall of 1988. They borrowed their tactics of contestation directly from the Balts, relying primarily on the demonstration as a means for mobilizing opinion and disrupting normalized politics. They also drew heavily on the programmatic documents of the Baltic fronts, incorporating the anti-imperial paradigm along with specific demands and goals.[24] Indicative of its power, even the Russians came in large numbers to embrace this master frame. 'Communists are internal occupiers!' a slogan at a Leningrad election rally in March 1990 put it (*Yezhednevnaia glasnost* March 3, 1990). Boris Yeltsin, in his speech in May 1990 calling for the passage of a Russian declaration of sovereignty vis-à-vis the Soviet government, referred to 'the longstanding imperial policy of the center' toward Russia (*Izvestiia*, May 25, 1990). Eventually, empire-consciousness among Russians reached the point where even the director of the Institute of Ethnography of the USSR Academy of Sciences, on the eve of the break-up of the Soviet Union, was referring instinctively to the very government he was advising as an 'empire' (Tishkov 1991). Indeed, if he is to be believed, already by summer 1989 at least one of Gorbachev's chief advisors had come to the conclusion that 'the collapse of the empire was inevitable' (Cherniaev 1993: 296).[25]

The spread of the anti-imperial master frame was not merely a matter of shifting authority, analogy, alienation from state policy, and bandwagoning. Nationalist movements also consciously attempted to reproduce themselves throughout the former Soviet Union, both out of philosophical and strategic considerations. The leaders of the Baltic fronts 'insisted that their own interpretation of self-determination had applicability throughout the Soviet Union' and 'called not only for their own self-determination but also for that of all the titular nationalities of Soviet republics' (Muiznieks 1995: 4). 'There cannot be a sovereign Estonia,' Edgar Savisaar noted in October 1988, 'if Lithuania, Latvia, and other republics are not sovereign' (Radio Vilnius, in *Foreign Broadcast Information Service, Daily Report: Soviet Union*, October 31, 1988, p. 50). In the Italian mobilizational cycle, diffusion of contention was in part a purposive process that had 'a powerful organizational component from the start' (Tarrow 1989a: 225). Similarly, Baltic fronts vigorously organized to extend their influence throughout the former Soviet Union by aiding the spread of the master frame which they themselves had pioneered. This they did through numerous means: the production of Russian-language newspapers intended for consumption outside the Baltic; dispatching emissaries to engage in agitation or to provide advice about the organization of social movements; hosting 'foreign delegations' from other republics and providing nascent social movements with a safe haven from which to operate; and printing newspapers and other materials for social movements from other republics that lacked printing facilities (Muiznieks 1995: pp. 5–11). The mechanics of organizing contentious acts were overtly taught and propagated between groups, including the spread of manuals on how to organize demonstrations. In short, the spread of nationalism in the former Soviet Union was both a process of push and pull, as nationalist movements struggled to institutionalize themselves through their own reproduction.

NOTES

1. Research on protest mobilization in the former Soviet Union was carried out under the auspices of grants from the National Council for Soviet and East European Research, the National Science Foundation, the International Research and Exchanges Board, and the Graduate School of the University of Wisconsin-Madison, as well as a fellowship from the Woodrow Wilson International Center for Scholars. The author gratefully acknowledges their support.

2. As Ernest Gellner caricatured this position, nationalism is an ideological invention which 'might not have happened, if only those damned busy-body interfering European thinkers, not content to leave well enough alone, had not concocted it and fatefully injected it into the bloodstream of otherwise viable political communities' (1983: 56).

3. 'What has given great vogue to nationalism in modern times? We really do not know. As it is, we have to content ourselves with hypotheses and suggestions. Of these the most plausible would appear to be the underlying tendency in modern times to regard the national state as the medium through which civilization is best assured and advanced' (Hayes 1931: 302).

4. On the connection between early theories of nationalism and Le Bon's social psychology, see Smith 1986: 7, 227. For a recent view that treats nationalism as an 'intrinsically absurd' phenomenon, see Pfaff 1993.

5. Greenfeld goes on to argue that 'the character of every national identity was defined in the early phase' of the formation of national identity, when *ressentiment* took hold within elite segments of society. 'Its effect, in the political, social, and cultural constitution of the respective nations, as well as their historical record, are attributable to this original definition which set the goals for mobilization, not to the nationalization of the masses.'

6. For a critique of the excess focus in the study of mobilizational politics on social movements rather than the way in which they interact with and resonate in society, see Oliver 1989.

7. As Gellner noted in a subsequent publication, his theory sought to explain 'why nationalism, relatively inconspicuous in the past, is so very salient in our age.' But '[i]t does not explain why, for instance, German nationalism should have become quite so virulent during the Nazi period. Or again, it fails to explain the firm commitment of anglophone Canadians to the existing Canadian political unit, notwithstanding the fact that anglophone Canadians at any rate have not the slightest difficulty operating within the polity of the USA' (Gellner 1994: 44–5).

8. On the notion of the crystallization of state institutions, see Mann 1993b: 75–81.

9. See, for instance, Brubaker 1992: 21–34; Mann 1993b: 57, 83; Gellner 1983.

10. Nationalism is often thought of in terms of tides but is rarely analyzed in the context of tides. For one use of the term in reference to the transitional spread of contention over issues of cultural pluralism, see Young 1993. On the notion of contentious collective action, see the work of Charles Tilly, in particular Tilly 1978, 1986, 1995. The difference between a tide of contention and a cycle of contention largely inheres in the transnationality of the former. In recent years, specialists on protest cycles have increasingly pointed to the transnationality of these phenomena. See, in particular, Tarrow 1994.

11. See, for instance, Tarrow 1994: 48–78.

12. See, for instance, Brockett 1991: 267.

13. Gorbachev notes the significant loss of time that transpired in dealing with nationality issues while his own thinking traversed the path from a 'traditional position' to one aimed at transforming the union to a looser 'federation of sovereign states' (Gorbachev 1995: 496). See also Medvedev 1994: 237.

14. Writing in 1969, Andrei Amalrik was one of the few who clearly foresaw the break-up of the USSR along national lines, although he believed it would be precipitated by a war with China, not by internal reform. See Amalrik 1970: 62–5.
15. Indeed, in 1987 Gorbachev viewed *glasnost'* and the demonstrations that it provoked as means for fostering change within republican and provincial elites who were resisting his efforts at reform and defended those initiating demonstrations against his colleagues in the Politburo. See Gorbachev 1995: 318; Cherniaev 1993: 149–50.
16. Organizers were merely called into the KGB for 'a conversation.'
17. See the report at the emergency meeting of the Politburo on February 21st, as recounted in Vorotnikov 1995: 193–4; Suny 1993: 197.
18. The Central Committee apparatus had received 500 letters over the previous three years complaining about the situation in Karabakh. The letters were largely ignored. See *Soiuz mozhno* [. . .] 1995: 22.
19. While the leadership of the local party apparatus in Karabakh generally opposed the campaign, one of the main organizers was an *instruktor* of the Nagorno-Karabakh *obkom*. The local party apparatus apparently did not attempt to block the demonstrations, and efforts by Baku to bully the local party *aktiv* into opposing the campaign failed. Gorbachev 1995: 502; Vorotnikov 1995: 194–5.
20. A similar point is made by Anderson in his discussion of 'official nationalism' in the nineteenth century. See Anderson 1991: 86–7. For the notion of collective action as modular, see Tarrow 1994: 31–47.
21. Givi Gumbaridze, first secretary of the Georgian Communist Party, reflected the inability to dissociate the two when he warned his fellow Georgians in spring 1989 against the then widespread tendency 'to confuse anger against bureaucratic fiat with anti-Russian sentiment' (*Zaria vostoka*, June 9, 1989, p. 1).
22. Some, such as Gavriil Popov, argued that it was possible to exorcise the imperial persona of the USSR and arrive at a legitimate state. But once the imperial persona of the Soviet state came to be widely recognized as such, even by Russians, how one might go about doing this became a nearly impossible task to conceive. See Popov 1994: 364–5.
23. For an elaboration of this issue and its key role in the 'master frame' of nationalism that spread through much of the former Soviet Union, see Beissinger 1993, 1995.
24. This was particularly true of Ukranian, Moldavian, Georgian, and Belorussian movements, but the Baltic example had a strong influence elsewhere as well. See Muiznieks 1995.
25. While Cherniaev had responsibility for foreign relations, the particular passage cited here deals with the Soviet 'empire' in its internal configuration.

FURTHER READING

For a useful historical survey and discussion of the development of the idea of self-determination in theory and practice, it is still worth reading Alfred Cobban's (1969) *The Nation-State and National Self-Determination* (London: Fontana). A sharp and critical discussion of the concept is provided by Benjamin Neuberger (1997) in his 'National self-determination – dilemmas of a concept', (*Nations and Nationalism*, 1, 3). For a Marxist approach to this question, see Nigel Harris (1992), *National Liberation* (Harmondsworth: Penguin). A key figure in the literature on anti-colonialism is Frantz Fanon, whose work has been particularly influential on post-colonial writing, see especially his *The Wretched of the Earth* (Harmondsworth: Penguin, 2001). A wide-ranging set of essays from a post-colonial perspective can be found in the collection edited by Anne McClintock, Aamir Mufti and Ella Shohat (1997), *Dangerous Liaisons – Gender, Nation and Postcolonial Perspectives* (Minneapolis: University of Minnesota Press). Mark Beissinger (2002) provides an impressive and detailed elaboration of his arguments and data in *Nationalist Mobilization and the Collapse of the Soviet State: A Tidal Approach to the Study of Nationalism* (Cambridge: Cambridge University Press). The revival of nationalism in Eastern Europe gets thoughtful treatment in Rogers Brubaker (1996), *Nationalism Reframed: Nationalism and the National Question in the New Europe* (Cambridge: Cambridge University Press). Michael Keating (2001) has written a useful comparative survey of three major examples of new forms of constitutional nationalism in the West in his *Nations Against the State: The New Politics of Nationalism in Quebec, Catalonia, and Scotland* (2nd ed.) (Basingstoke: Macmillan). A further perspective on stateless nations with a broader range of examples is provided by Montserrat Guibernau's (1999) *Nations without States* (Cambridge: Polity).

PART SIX
GLOBALISATION, CITIZENSHIP
AND NATIONALISM

19

HAS GLOBALISATION ENDED THE RISE
AND RISE OF THE NATION-STATE?

Michael Mann

INTRODUCTION

The human sciences seem full of enthusiasts claiming that a new form of human society is emerging. The most enthusiastic compare today with the eighteenth century, whose Industrial Revolution, whose 'modernism' and whose 'Enlightenment' supposedly revolutionized human society. They say we are in the throes of a comparable transition to a 'post-industrial' or 'postmodern' society. Other terminologies imply rather less revolutionary change. Terms such as 'late capitalism', 'late modernity' or 'radical modernity' are used to suggest varying degrees of continuous versus disruptive change. 'Globalist' words also invoke varying degrees of enthusiasm: 'global capitalism' may refer only to a major extension of an old economy, while 'global society' usually implies a radically novel phenomenon in the history of human society.

The enthusiasts comprise a very varied group of *littérateurs*, *philosophes*, historians, sociologists, political and business economists, geographers and environmentalists. They agree about very little – especially about whether the changes are to be welcomed. But on one point they do agree: contemporary changes are weakening the nation-state. From postmodernists like Baudrillard or Lyotard or Jameson to geographers like Harvey or Taylor to sociologists like Giddens or Lash and Urry, to the business economists well represented by *The Economist*, come similar statements about the 'undermining', 'under-cutting',

Michael Mann (1997), 'Has globalization ended the rise and rise of the nation-state?', *Review of International Political Economy*, 4:3.

'outflanking' or 'marginalization' of the nation-state (for recent exemplars, see Taylor 1996; Lash and Urry 1994; Featherstone 1990; Harvey 1989; *The Economist* 1995). Some qualify this in one respect. Since 'ethnicity' looms large in scenarios of 'postmodern fragmentation', these often see national*ism* as resurgent in the world today. But for the old nation-state, we find largely epitaphs.

Many enthusiasts are west Europeans – not surprisingly, since this particular region of the globe offers most political support to their epitaph for the state. Many (both marxian and neoclassical) are materialists who point to the great changes under way in capitalism and believe these will necessarily transform the rest of the social structure. The core of most arguments rests on the techno-logical-informational innovations of our times. Transport and information systems providing rapid (often instantaneous) access to the world provide the infrastructures of a global society. I accept that this potential infrastructure of globalism exists: the logistics of communication and so of power have indeed been revolutionized. Persons, goods and especially messages circulate the globe so that the enthusiastic vision of a single global society is a technologically possible one. But is it actuality? To suggest that it is, various groups of enthusiasts advance four main theses.

1. Capitalism, now become global, transnational, post-industrial, 'infor-mational', consumerist, neoliberal and 'restructured', is undermining the nation-state – its macroeconomic planning, its collectivist welfare state, its citizens' sense of collective identity, its general caging of social life.
2. New 'global limits', especially environmental and population threats, producing perhaps a new 'risk society', have become too broad and too menacing to be handled by the nation-state alone.
3. 'Identity politics' and 'new social movements', using new technology, increase the salience of diverse local and transnational identities at the expense of both national identities and those broad class identities which were traditionally handled by the nation-state. For this and for the previous reason we are witnessing the stirrings of a new transnational 'civil society', social movements for peace, human rights and environ-mental and social reform which are becoming truly global.
4. Post-nuclearism undermines state sovereignty and 'hard geo-politics', since mass mobilization warfare underpinned much of modern state expansion yet is now irrational. Martin Shaw's perception of the emergence of a 'world state' is perhaps the most measured version of this thesis (see Shaw 1997). It is very much a minority view in the discipline of International Relations, most of which remains attached to the study of the sovereign state.

So the empirical part of this article will investigate whether these four nation-state-weakening theses are correct. Since they downplay political power rela-tions, it also considers two political counter-theses.

A. State institutions, both domestic and geopolitical, still have causal efficacy because they too (like economic, ideological and military institutions) provide necessary conditions for social existence:[1] the regulation of aspects of social life which are distinctively 'territorially centred' (see Mann 1986, ch. 1). Thus they cannot be the mere consequence of other sources of social power.

B. Since states vary greatly, if (A) is true, these variations will cause variations in other spheres of social life. Even within Europe states differ in size, power, geography and degree of centralization. Across the globe, variations dramatically increase: in degree of democracy, level of development, infrastructural power, geopolitical power, national indebtedness, etc. They also inhabit very different regional settings. Can contemporary capitalism, even if reinforced by environmental limits, 'cultural postmodernity' and demilitarization, render all this variation irrelevant, and have the *same* effects on all countries? Or will these variations cause variation among these forces, and so limit globalization?

Only the most breathless of enthusiasts would deny all validity to these counter-theses – or to the survival of the nation-state as wielder of some economic, ideological, military and political resources. The task is to establish *degrees* of relative causality: to what extent is the nation-state being transformed, to what extent is it declining – or even perhaps still growing?

But to establish this we must also make some conceptual distinctions. We can roughly distinguish five socio-spatial networks of social interaction in the world today:

1. *local* networks – which for present purposes just means subnational networks of interaction;
2. *national* networks, structured or (more neutrally) bounded by the nation-state;
3. *inter-national* networks, that is relations between nationally constituted networks. Most obviously, these include the 'hard geopolitics' of inter-state relations which centre on war, peace and alliances. But they also include 'soft geopolitics' between states – negotiations about more peaceable and particular matters like air transport communications, tax treaties, air pollution, etc. And they include relations between networks that are more nationally than state-constituted: for example, the emergence of 'national champions' playing on a broader playing-field – whether these are football teams or giant corporations;
4. *transnational* networks, passing right through national boundaries, being unaffected by them. These might not be very extensive – perhaps a religious sect organized across two neighbouring countries – or they might be continent-wide or even worldwide. Many transnational

arguments about contemporary society rest on a 'macro-regional' base. Examples are the frequent distinctions between 'Liberal/Anglo-Saxon', 'Nordic / Social Democratic' or 'Christian Democratic/corporatist' forms of contemporary social organization;

5. *global* networks cover the world as a whole – or, perhaps more realistically, they cover most of it. But we should distinguish between networks which radiate universalistically or particularistically across the globe. The feminist movement may spread through almost all countries, but usually only among rather particular, smallish groups. The Catholic Church has some presence in all continents but only has quite a narrow base across Asia, while being near-universal across Latin America. The capitalism evoked by many of the enthusiasts is a universal global network, evenly diffusing through economic and social life just about everywhere. Thus global networks might be formed by either a single universal network or by a more segmented series of networks between which existed rather particularistic relations.

Over the last centuries local interaction networks have clearly diminished in relative weight; while longer-distance networks – national, inter-national and transnational – have become denser, structuring more of people's lives. Genuinely global networks have emerged relatively recently. Note that global networks need not be the same as transnational networks, though many enthusiasts equate them. Nor are they necessarily economic in nature. Global networks may be constituted by geopolitics (as Shaw argues) or by ideological movements like a religion or socialism or feminism or neoliberalism – the combination amounting perhaps to a new transnational civil society.

Since national and inter-national networks are constituted or fundamentally constrained by the nation-state, the future of the nation-state thus turns critically upon the answer to two questions: *Is the social significance of national and inter-national networks declining relative to some combination of local and transnational networks? And to the extent that global networks are emerging, what is the relative contribution to them of national/inter-national versus local/ transnational networks?*

THE 'MODEST NATION-STATE' OF THE NORTH

I start with the most familiar and dominant form of state in the world today. In the 'west', or more precisely the 'northwest' of western Europe and its white colonies, arose a state claiming formal political sovereignty over 'its' territories and a legitimacy based on the 'people' or 'nation' inhabiting them. This is what we mean by the nation-state.

The regulatory powers of such states expanded through several centuries. First, from the end of the Middle Ages they increasingly plausibly claimed a monopoly of judicial regulation and military force. Then, in the eighteenth and especially the nineteenth centuries they sponsored integrating communications infrastructures and basic control of the poor. The twentieth century saw welfare states, macroeconomic planning and the mobilization of mass citizen nationalism. All the while more states legitimated themselves in terms of 'the people', either 'representing' the people (liberal democracies) or 'organically embodying' it (authoritarian regimes), with varying degrees of civil, political and social citizenship. To a degree, therefore, northwesterners became 'caged' into national interaction networks, and these became supplemented by the inter-national relations between nation-states which we know by the term 'geopolitics'.

This is the now familiar story of 'the rise and rise' of the nation-state and the nation-state system – to which I have contributed myself (Mann, 1986, 1993b). Yet we should note that the expansion of these national and inter-national networks always proceeded *alongside* the expansion of certain 'transnational' power relations, especially those of industrial capitalism and its attendant ideologies (liberalism, socialism), plus the broader cultural networks provided in the northwest by European / Christian /'white' senses of collective identity. National and inter-national interaction networks thus grew much more at the expense of local than of transnational networks. For example, in the very period in the late nineteenth century when European states were deepening their national education and public health infrastructures, raising tariffs and beginning to drift nearer to war against each other (examples of national and international caging), transnational trade was rocketing to form the same proportion of world production as it now forms, and the north-western powers were acting together, with a smug sense of cultural superiority, to Christianize, exploit and drug the Chinese. Indeed nation-state growth *presupposed* a broader global expansion, most obviously to finance it, but also perhaps because a sense of nationhood may have presupposed the sense of European / Christian / white superiority which endowed *all* the classes and both sexes of the northwest with a sense of their own moral worth and equality. Indeed, the last great expansionist surge of the nation-state, from 1945 to the 1960s, may have also involved both. States were flush with funds from massive economic expansion and they possessed the war- and reconstruction-generated institutions to spend them; and northwestern nations, having taught their colonials the values of 'civilization', now 'granted' them independence in their own European form, as nation-states. Thus the past saw the rise of transnational capitalism and cultural identities alongside the rise of the nation-state and its inter-national system. They have always possessed a complex combination of relative autonomy and symbiotic interdependence.

Most northwestern states also *lost* certain functions during the period of their expansion. As they became more 'secular', they relinquished powers over moral regulation, which they had in principle possessed in association with Churches (though Church rather than state infra-structures had usually enforced such moral regulation in earlier centuries). Remember also that most of economic life had never come into the realm of the state: we call it 'private' property. Thus much of social life remained or became *more* private, outside the sphere of competence of the nation-state, even during its great period of expansion. Property remained private, gays remained in the closet. Capitalism and morality were substantially autonomous of the state. I suggest later that moral autonomy is now declining.

Thus only a 'modest nation-state' became dominant in the northwest. In the course of the twentieth century it defeated three rivals. One was the 'multinational empire': the dynastic empires of the Habsburgs, Romanovs and Ottomans, with weaker states and little national identity – a less 'nation-statist' alternative. But the other two defeated states were actually far more nation-statist. Fascism sought a much stronger, authoritarian state which would supposedly embody the essence of a more rigidly and more ethnically defined nation. By 1945 fascism was discredited – at least for the two generations which have followed. State socialism also sought a stronger state (supposedly only in the short run). Though not strictly nationalist, its increasing tendency to equate the proletariat with a broader 'people' or 'masses' gave it a similar principle of legitimation. And its economic autarchy and rigid surveillance greatly intensified its 'national' caging. Its discrediting lasted longer and seemed finished (for the present) by 1991. Both of these defeated regimes also claimed a monopoly of morality, which the 'modest nation-state' never did. It was the responsibility of the state to cultivate 'Soviet Man' or what was 'consciously German'. Had these more ambitious 'nation-states' both triumphed and the world had then globalized, its global society would have been constituted by a segmental series of global networks between which the most particularistic, and probably warlike, relations would have existed. Since they did not, any subsequent globalism might be expected to be rather more universal in character.

Since 1945 the modest victor further diffused across almost all the rest of 'the north', i.e. the whole European continent and increasing regions of East and South Asia. Its formal trappings have also dominated 'the south', while all states meet in a forum called 'The United Nations'. The modest nation-state might seem to dominate the entire globe. In some limited senses it actually does. Only a few states do not base their legitimacy on the nation, or lack a monopoly of domestic coercion or real territorial boundedness. Almost all manage to implement policies oriented towards basic population control, health and education. Plunging mortality and rising literacy have multiple causes but some lie in the realm of effective public policy. For these reasons I will go ahead and describe contemporary states as nation-states. Yet most of them actually possess rather limited control over their territories and boundaries, while their claims to represent the nation are often specious. For much of the world a *true* nation-state remains more aspiration for the future than present reality. The nation-state's rise has been global, but modest and very uneven. The modest nation-state came to dominate the 'north', has been part of its expansion and represents a desired future for the bulk of the world's people. Is all this now threatened?

The Capitalist threat

The enthusiasts have correctly identified many important transformations of capitalism. It is not necessary here to document capitalism's use of new 'informational' and 'post-industrial' technology to expand through much of the world and penetrate more of social life. But how great is its threat to the nation-state? And just how 'global' and/or 'transnational' is it?

In a formal geographic sense capitalism *is* now more or less global. Two great geopolitical events permitted massive extension. First, decolonization largely ended the segmentation of the world economy into separate imperial zones. Second, the collapse of Soviet autarchy opened up most of Eurasia to capitalist penetration. Only Iran, China and a handful of smaller communist countries now maintain partial blockages, and these are declining or may be expected to start declining soon. China retains distinct property forms (mixing private with varieties of public ownership and control), and there still also remain (declining) areas of subsistence economy scattered through the world. Yet capitalist commodity exchange clearly dominates. With no confident adversary in sight, capitalism is becoming – at least minimally – global. That was not so in 1940, or even in 1980. It is obviously a major transformation.

But are its global networks 'pure' in the sense of being singularly universal, or do other more particularistic principles of social organization also help constitute them? An economy may be global, but this may be conferred by help from national and inter-national networks of interaction. After all, more than 80 per cent of world production is still for the domestic national market. Since economic statistics are gathered at the level of the nation-state, it is unknown what is the relative contribution to this of truly national exchanges compared to the contributions made by multiple local interaction networks. The national economy is presumably considerably less integrated than the statistic suggests – especially in backward countries and bigger advanced countries like the USA or Australia. Yet the nation-state clearly does systematically structure many economic networks. The ownership, assets and R&D of 'multinational' corporations (including banks, mutuals and insurance firms) remain disproportionately in their 'home' state, and they still lean on it for human capital (education), communications infrastructures and economic protectionism (Carnoy 1993; Castells 1993). Nonetheless, even among the more fixed multinationals, their sales reach, organization of production and investment flows are also substantially transnational. Strategic alliances with corporations of other 'nationality' are now proliferating, weakening the national identity of property – though many of these arrangements occur to evade protectionism and might decline if it did.

Finance is far more transnational, as evidenced by the growing complexity of financial markets and of the models supposed to be capable of explaining them – from random walk to chaos theories. Yet its institutions continue to exhibit bureaucratic regularity, much of it with a pronounced national character. The employees of Nikko Europe start their London workday before the Tokyo stock market closes. They relay the latest information first to their European-based customers, who are actually mostly Japanese corporations. Then, as Wall Street awakes, the information is transmitted westward and London shuts down for the night. Financial markets also reveal a national/transnational duality. On the one hand, trading in government bonds, in currencies, in futures and in wholesale dealing between banks, is largely transnational, often distinctively 'offshore', slushing through the boundaries of states subject to very few controls. On the other hand, company shares tend to be fixed to particular national stock markets and to national corporate laws and accountancy practices (Wade 1996).

Of course, western Europe has gone more transnational, sponsoring a unique degree of continental economic integration. Here lies a genuine single market, a movement which will probably end in a single currency within twenty years (at least in its core), and predominantly 'Euro-' rather than national attempts at protectionism. Here 'national champion' corporations are becoming 'Euro-champions', assisted as much by EU government as by the nation-state.

Obviously, such economic complexities should be explored at a much greater length than I can attempt here. But two points emerge: Europe is extreme (this will be further explored later), and real capitalist interaction networks remain profoundly mixed. Symbiosis between the national and the transnational remains.

A third point also emerges: most 'transnational' economic relations cannot be necessarily equated with a global universalism. The bulk of capitalist activity is more 'trilateral' than global, being concentrated in the three regions of the advanced 'north': Europe, North America and East Asia. These contain over 85 per cent of world trade, over 90 per cent of production in advanced sectors like electronics, plus the headquarters of all but a handful of the top 100 multi-nationals (including banks). This does not necessarily mean capitalism is not global. It may only indicate that the north is rich, the south is poor – and that both are locked together in a global network of interaction. But it does suggest that capitalism retains a geo-economic order, dominated by the economies of the advanced nation-states. Clusters of nation-states provide the stratification order of globalism. Among other consequences, this protects the citizens of the north: the poorly educated child of an unskilled worker in Britain or the United States will enjoy far better material conditions of existence (including twenty more years of life) than will his/her counterpart in Brazil or India. True, inequalities within all these nation-states are widening, yet it is almost inconceivable that the bulk of the privileges of national citizens in northern countries could be removed. That would cause such social disorder as to be incommensurate with a stable and profitable capitalism. The nation-state provides some of the structure, and some of the stratification structure, of the global networks of capitalism. If the commodity rules, it only does so entwined with the rule of – especially northern – citizenship.

The global economy is also subject to loose and predominantly 'soft' inter-national regulation in the shape of organizations like G7, GATT, the World Bank or the IMF. These are also northern-dominated. Some of these are involved in seemingly endless negotiations of trade liberalization – and these are likely to drag on a lot longer since national governments have been recently raising non-tariff barriers. We are nowhere near global free trade, but we may be moving a little closer and this is at present ideologically dominant. But is this just another liberalization phase in the normal historical oscillation around the middle zone between the free trade and protectionist poles? That depends on the resolution of other tendencies discussed in this article.

So, at the moment and probably also for the near future, a rapidly globalizing economy does not only acquire its character from transnational networks of interaction. What adds up to the global is a very complex mix of the local, the national, the inter-national (represented in my discussion mostly by northern trilateralism) – and the truly transnational. The *transnational* commodity does not rule the globe.

Over time some of these national and inter-national structurings may decline. Northern domination of the world economy may diminish because of the pressures of comparative advantage. Apart from very high-tech activities, much productive enterprise may migrate to the lower costs of the south, producing more globalization (though not necessarily much reducing inequality). But so far migration has operated not by some 'transnational' logic (of random walk?) but by some combination of four other principles: the possession of useful natural resources, geographical propinquity (neighbouring countries), geopolitical alliances (friendly countries), and state and civil society stability (predictable countries). Whereas the first factor is found fairly randomly through the world – and so oil alone can develop rather backward, distant countries – the last three factors are generally interconnected. The historical development of the major northern economies emerged amid broader regional settings, from which neighbouring states and societies also benefited. Thus expansion has mostly been to the Koreas and the Mexicos, friendly neighbours with relatively developed nations and states, rather than, say, to most African countries. Nor does most growth take a regional, 'enclave' pattern within states (except where raw materials matter, or where extension is over a border and the neighbouring government sponsors 'enterprise zones'). Development then tends to diffuse across the core territories of these states, aiding the development of their overall civil societies and their drift towards becoming nation-states. Thus extension of the north – and so globalization – has depended upon, and in turn reinforced, the nation-states benefiting from it. This form of globalization reinforces national networks of interaction.

Since finance capital seems more transnational than industrial capital, its constraints upon the nation-state are usually those most emphasized by the enthusiasts. Its mobility and velocity produce financial movements which dwarf the fiscal resources of states and which constrain two of the three props of post-war state fiscal policy – interest rates and currency valuation (taxation being less affected). Yet it is difficult to assess the overall significance of this, for two reasons. First, the numbers do not offer real precision about power relations. Since currencies, shares, futures, etc. can be traded many times over in a single day, the paper value of 'financial flows' vastly exceeds that of world trade, and continues to grow. But power cannot be simply read off such sums. What are being traded are property rights to raw materials, manufactured goods and (increasingly) services, almost all of which have much greater fixity of location and therefore presumably a degree of national identity.

Second, it is not clear how effective macroeconomic planning ever was in the northwest. It *seemed* effective while massive growth was occurring and governments had access to surpluses. Many were able to be mildly interventionist (though selective incentives were generally more effective than physical controls). But since then we have seen the collapse not only of Keynesian economics but also of economic theory in general. Economists now more or less admit they have no explanation of any of the great booms or slumps of the twentieth century (or at least one that does not depend on singular events like great world wars). Macroeconomic planning was a general ideology surrounding some highly abstract concepts, from which were precariously derived some technical tools (including, most fundamentally, national accounting) and policies (which in fact also depended on contingencies). Macroeconomic planning still contains such a mixture, though its emphasis has changed. The ideological pretensions and the ability to expand spending have certainly declined. Thus we may expect looser and fiscally more cautious national/inter-national (i.e. trilateral) macro-economic policies: a proliferation of G7 and GATT guidelines and piecemeal liberalizing agreements; MITI-style[2] collaboration and incentive programmes more than nationalization or direct state investment; central banks more than politicians; less the pretence of controlling markets than of signalling intentions to them; and, above all, no increases in taxation masquerading as grandiose economic theory.

Nor are the reasons for these less than dramatic power reductions easy to interpret. As the economy has internationalized, real living standards have stagnated and inequalities widened (apart from East Asia). If national governments are increasingly constrained in their economic planning and welfarist pretensions, this might be due to either transnational tendencies or recession – transformations such as 'restructuring' may be a response to both. For example, Latin American 'import-substitution' policies throve on the regional economic expansion made possible by the Second World War; this expansion collapsed under the mountain of indebtedness accumulated by easy credit during the 1970s followed by the stagnation and inflation of the 1980s. 'Restructuring' is now extreme across much of the region, virtually eliminating national macroeconomic planning and trimming welfare states. But this may result less from transnationalism than from the power conferred on finance capital and its major institutions by the burden of debt: the creditors can enforce repayment terms. The creditors comprise the usual mixed bag: banks with national identities but transnational activities, inter-national and predominantly northern agencies like the World Bank and the IMF, and the US government with the dual motive of protecting American investors and making the region more geopolitically and geoeconomically friendly/subordinate to itself. In contrast, however, current Korean 'restructuring' can be a mere reorientation of rather stronger macroeconomic policy because, though it had considerable debt, its economic growth meant the debt could be paid off and further foreign investment attracted.

Similarly, the fiscal crisis afflicting most states of the north and south alike may be more the product of recession than of transnational capitalism. My previous work (Mann 1986, 1993a, 1993b) gives me the confidence to say that, at least since the thirteenth century, citizens have only consistently agreed to pay a higher proportion of their incomes in taxes during wartime. Their reluctance to stump up during the peaceful 1970s and later, in a period of recession (when their real incomes were stagnant or falling), is hardly surprising. It is the historical norm, not the unique product of 'postmodernity' or 'globalism'. Political movements resting traditionally on the nation-state, like Social Democracy, Christian Democracy and the US Democratic Party, have indeed entered something of a crisis. They have stalled and entered modest decline (more in terms of their ability to devise radical policies than to attract votes). Again, it is not entirely clear why. Did it result from the new powers of transnational capital (plus perhaps Euro-institutions in Europe) or from citizens refusing to support 'tax and spend' policies amid stagnant or declining real incomes? Probably both, but I have not yet seen the research which could clearly differentiate these rival hypotheses. Of course, if growth does not resume, or if its unevenness continues to widen inequality and deepen unemployment, some of its political effects in weakening the Centre-Left might be similar to those identified by the enthusiasts. Social citizenship seems to have peaked in the north and it may now be in moderate secular decline. Yet this could be reversed by a variety of future trends: economic recovery, changing demographics (i.e. an ageing or a better-educated population should reduce unemployment and so inequality) or political backlashes.

Yet national economies also vary considerably – in their prosperity, their cohesion and their power. Consider first the three main regions of the north. North America is dominated by its superpower, the USA. This has an unusual state, dominated by its unique war machine and (rather meagre) social security system. Most other governmental activities which in most other northern countries are mainly the province of the central state (criminal justice, education and most welfare programmes) are the concern of fifty separate 'states' or local governments in the USA. Three major industries are closely entwined with the federal government, agriculture, the military-industrial complex and health care, and may be said to be somewhat (if particularistically) planned. They are likely to remain so – though the current plan is to downsize the military by just under a quarter over two decades. Many other industries have closer relations with 'state' and local governments, for example property development and construction. Federal legislation has been traditionally tight in the area of labour relations and monopolies, especially restraining the growth of US unions and banks. But there has been little macroeconomic planning by any level of government. The principal 'planning' agency (over interest rates) is the Federal Reserve Bank, which is largely autonomous of government. There is no serious American industrial policy; this is left to the post-war power-houses of the US economy, the large corporations. Much of this is due to the radical separation of powers enshrined by the US constitution. A coordinated political economy cannot easily be run by a President and his cabinet, two Houses of Congress, a Supreme Court and fifty 'states' (which are also fragmented by the same separation of powers) – especially when they belong to different political parties. Thus it is difficult to see much of a weakening of US government powers, since these were never exercised very actively. Of course, recession alone means they cannot be exercised now. Amid stagnant family living standards, no government agency can raise the taxes to throw money after any policy. On the other hand, in certain other respects, it might be said that the American nation-state is actually tightening. Organizations as diverse as banks, TV stations and newspapers are becoming more nationally integrated and the recent absorption of staggering numbers of immigrants (immigration is back to the pre-1914 level) by the school system and the labour market indicates formidable national solidarity.

Of course, the USA has been influenced by capitalist transformations. Competitive pressures from the two other northern geo-economies have been most visible in the creation of NAFTA, a free trade area embracing the USA, Canada and Mexico, with some prospects for its eventual extension to other stable economies in Central and South America. Though the Canadian and US economies were similarly advanced and already partially integrated, the combination of 'southern' Mexico and the 'northern' USA has led some to view NAFTA as a microcosm of the new global economy. Yet Mexico exemplifies those 'principles of orderly extension' I noted earlier. It is a neighbour, a friend and a very stable state: ruled for seventy years by a single party, mildly coercive but so far capable of responding institutionally to pressure. It provides quite good infrastructures and a fairly literate and healthy labour force, and a nation beset by no general civil conflict.[3]

US hegemony in the continent also makes NAFTA unique – and very different to the European Union. Canada is an advanced but small client economy with a weak state – perhaps shortly to disintegrate. Mexico is much poorer, and has recently become more debt-ridden and a little less politically stable. But the USA is itself wavering, beset by doubts about free trade and Latino immigration, and its political fragmentation makes coordinated decision making difficult. Thus NAFTA embodies three distinct power processes: it is a kind of 'mini global economy'; yet it is also geopolitically dominated by one nation-state; and this nation-state has a peculiarly fragmented polity and political economy. The combination of the three is unique in the world, but – as we are seeing – the entwining of transnational capitalist transformation with political and geopolitical institutions is quite normal.

East Asia is at present also dominated by a single nation-state, though Japan is not a military superpower. Japanese political economy differs from both North American and European, with far more coordination between the state and capitalist corporations (and, in a more dependent role, the labour unions): 'Governing the market', Wade (1990) calls it; 'Governed interdependence', say Weiss and Hobson (1995). Such national coordination has been adapted in varying forms across the smaller economies of East Asia. These include active industrial policies centring on selective tax rates or conditional subsidies for key or export sectors, public absorbing of risk for innovation and government coordination of inter-firm collaboration for technology upgrading (Weiss, 1995). These countries also have political stability and an advanced civil, i.e. 'national', society which is stable, literate and broadly honest. They have also experienced phenomenal growth. Though growth is stuttering in Japan, this is not true of the rest of East Asia.

Thus these East Asian governments have a buoyant tax base and the growth to support debt, and their countries are attractive to foreign investors. They can raise taxes to expand welfare and they can bargain with foreign business from a position of strength. They have fairly equal income distribution and they provide extensive public services like education and housing. They protect their domestic industries, if in different ways. Korea and Malaysia have their own automobile industries behind protectionist markets. Thailand takes a different East Asian tack. Japanese automobile plants are already there, the American majors are now negotiating to move in plants. The Thai government seems to deal from strength. It offers no tax breaks and requires substantial local component ratios. The Philippines offers a much bigger domestic market, big tax concessions and no strings. Yet the auto manufacturers prefer Thailand. Why? They say it is because the Thai government is both more honest and more stable. American and Japanese accountants can calculate future profit and loss much more precisely there (*USA Today*, 5 March 1966). Presumably not all the desirable difference comes from the characteristics of government. Thai society probably also embodies more literacy, more discipline, more honesty. But these are *all* characteristics of a national network of interaction, of the nation-state. East Asia offers different combinations of capitalist transformation and nation-states.

Europe is the only one of the three regions to have experienced significant political transformation.[4] This has reduced what we might call the 'particularistic' autonomy of its member states. They can no longer do their own peculiar things across many policy areas – from the labels on products to the torturing of suspected terrorists. In the long run this may impact on major constitutional variations. The increasing lobbying pressure on both Euro- and national government (which must now represent more interests more effectively than it did in the past), combined with the EU's regional policy (offering many financial resources), seems likely to produce more uniform distribution of power between central and local government. Constitutional rights of citizens and minorities are also converging. The states are both converging and losing powers to Brussels.

The original impetus for all this was mainly geopolitical and military: to prevent a third devastating war in the continent, more specifically to bind Germany into a peaceful concert of nation-states. The United States had its own, primarily geopolitical, reasons for encouraging it. Thus the 'Six' and the 'Nine' were being bound together before much of the capitalist transformation had occurred. But since the chosen mechanisms of binding were primarily economic, they were then intensified by this transformation. The economy of Europe has thus been substantially transnationalized.

Yet the European Union also remains an association between nation-states, an inter-national network of interaction. Specific geopolitical agreements between Germany and France, with the support of their client Benelux states, have always been its motor of growth. Germany and France, like the other states, have lost many particularistic autonomies. But, when allied, they remain the masters on most big issues. Ask Germans what economic sovereignty, ask the French what political sovereignty they have lost, and they are hard pressed to answer. The minor and economically weaker states may seem to have lost more, but their sovereignty on the big issues was more limited in the past. Britain has stood to lose most, because of its historic geopolitical independence from the rest of Europe. And they vote and acquire ministries based on a combination of their population size and economic muscle. 'They' are states and national economies, represented by statesmen (and women) and national technocrats and business leaders. This is not traditional 'hard' geopolitics, since the agenda is primarily economic and the participants believe war between them is unthinkable. It is 'soft' geopolitics structured by much denser inter-national (plus the remaining national) networks of interaction.

Thus Europe has been politically and economically transformed, with a substantial decline in the particularistic autonomy and sovereignty of its nation-states. Though the mechanisms for negotiating these transfers of powers have been largely geopolitical (supplemented by the enthusiasm of Euro-wide federalists), they are institutionalized through rules, institutions and practices that have become fairly transnational, transforming social expectations right across Europe. Yet all this coexists with a far denser, if 'softer', set of inter-national networks. Since the density of both is historically unprecedented – no Delian or Hanseatic League or confederacy ever penetrated so transnationally or inter-nationally into social life – we have no political term to describe it. The political legacy of the Greek language is finally superseded. Maybe the best term is just 'Euro'. If so, it may not be the future of the world.

It would be unwise to generalize about 'the south', given its variety. Some of it may well follow East Asia into the north. A genuine transnational penetration would integrate bits of territory here, there and everywhere, by 'random walk', almost regardless of state boundaries. But this seems rather unlikely, since stable government, social order, and education and health systems still seem the minimum of what substantial foreign investment and economic development require, and geopolitical alliances retain some, though less, relevance (unless some new world tension replaces the old Cold War). These all require social organization coordinated at the national or state level. What other agency can provide them? If Chile is making it into the north, then it will be because its already fairly stable state and civil society were reinforced by a firm anti-Leftism, a state-imposed order and a state-imposed economic neoliberalism which were attractive to foreign investors, especially the USA. If the richer Arab countries make it, it will be because of their oil – but this has also been accompanied by formidable states. China and India – one-third of the world's population – offer different combinations of massive economic resources, strong civil (i.e. 'national') societies and ambitious state regulation. Will the sense of national citizenship in such countries be diminished or strengthened by economic success? Surely it will be strengthened.

At the other extreme deeply troubled states in Africa seem to be fragmenting for premodern rather than postmodern reasons. Their claim to modernity, including the constitution of a nation-state, proved paperthin. International capitalism would like to prop them up, not to fragment them. But it has insufficient local power or attention-span to do so. There are more attractive areas, with stronger states and civil societies.

Thus the vital issue for the nation-state across most of the world is the level of development – of the economy narrowly considered, but also of two of the preconditions of this: the 'civility' of the country and the infrastructural capacity of the state. The entwined expansion of all three produced the nation-state in the northwest and its extension to a broader north. If world development stalls, then so will the extension of the nation-state; indeed, some 'paper' nation-states may collapse. But if development is possible, it will occur in those countries which most resemble nation-states and it will in turn enhance them.

But suppose that the drift of the economy is towards more and more transnational globalism, that free trade is largely achieved as the EU, NAFTA, the Asian and Pacific Conference countries and other trade groups merge under the loose umbrella of GATT, that multinationals become more cosmopolitan, that development of the south becomes more diffuse, less nation-state-centric. Would this amount to a single transnational/global economy in which the commodity and the single market ruled universally?

The answer is both yes and no. All goods and services would then have a price on a single market and capitalist enterprises would organize their financing, production and exchange. 'Consumerism' already dominates, some of the enthusiasts say; business accountancy practices spread through previously insulated institutions like civil services or universities; and athletes sell their skills to the highest bidder on free and relatively new markets. Such commodity penetration would broaden.

But even so, the rules of those markets might still have their particularities, some being the effects of national and inter-national networks of interaction. Though a far broader range of goods are now bought and sold, many of the most important ones are not actually sold as commodities on free markets. None of the three biggest industries in the US economy, defence, health care and (probably) illicit drugs, are simply dominated by commodity production, though all involve considerable transnational networks. In defence the government is a monopolistic customer for hi-tech weapons systems and it decides what other states (friendly ones) will be allowed as customers; supply is not very competitive (sometimes only one manufacturer will 'tender' and sometimes profit is calculated on a cost-plus basis). The weapons embody more 'use' than 'exchange' value – the USA *must* have them, almost regardless of cost, and the corporation can produce them without much thought of market risk. The health care industry offers its wares more competitively, though the industry has a peculiar multi-tiered structure, involving considerable bureaucracies (of insurance companies, Health Maintenance Organizations, etc.), organizationally differentiated according to the customer's ability to pay. And again, for customers who can afford to pay, the product is more of a use than an exchange value. Health preservation (defined by current medical practices and power) is desired at almost any price. Of course, both these industries involve massive multinational corporations and the global finance networks involved in their investment. But these are funnelled into organizations with distinctive national and (in the case of defence) inter-national organization. In the third industry, illicit drugs, the delivery to the consumer seems largely commodity exchange. But the industry is also structured by the intersection of law and state policing of its boundaries with distinctively criminal organization of secrecy and violence. Addiction also produces consumers for whom the product is a use value, to be obtained at almost any price (including crime). Thus the commodity need not rule, even through an eminently capitalist-seeming economy. The economy involves diverse social practices and values, which provide their own 'blockages' to the rule of commodity exchange.

Though the capitalist economy is now significantly global, its globalism is 'impure', a combination of both the transnational and the inter-national. The potential universalism of the former is undercut by the particularisms of nation-states – and indeed also by the particularisms of human social practices at large.

ENVIRONMENTAL LIMITS, NEW SOCIAL MOVEMENTS AND A NEW TRANSNATIONAL CIVIL SOCIETY

Through population growth, soil and plant erosion, water shortages, atmospheric pollution and climate change, we encounter a second form of globalism – reinforced by the dangers of biological, chemical and nuclear warfare alluded to later. We are indeed living in Beck's 'risk society' (though this is not the only society we are living in) and have only done so in the second half of the twentieth century. On some of these issues the traditional 'solution' of letting the south or the poor starve can endure. But on others, humanity together faces severe risks. These are not identical to the risks of capitalism, though the two are deeply entwined (since capitalism is now the dominant form of economic production). The 'mastery' and 'exploitation' of nature, and the enormous increase in human potentiality to do so throughout the globe, are also attributable to industrialism and to the other modes of production developed in the modern period. State socialism (and fascism too) was even more destructive of the environment, while the petty commodity production of small peasants has also been forced into many destructive practices. Nation-states, scientific establishments and (until the last few years) virtually all modern institutions contributed their piece of destruction. And rampant population growth also has sources other than capitalism, for example military, religious and patriarchal practices. To deal with these risks responses must go beyond the nation-state and capitalism alike.

Present responses on environmental issues seem mainly two-fold. First, organizations are already in action embodying variant forms of the famous environmental maxim 'Think globally, act locally'. These are mainly mixed local-transnational pressure groups and NGOs, some of them formal pressure groups (like Greenpeace), others carried by professional and scientific networks (of soil scientists, ornithologists, demographers, etc.). They are more 'modern' than 'postmodern', since they reject scientific-material exploitation of nature on primarily scientific and social-scientific grounds. Though their elites originated in the north, they have increasingly spread globally, among both highly educated southern elites and among diverse, and rather particular, groups threatened by real material problems. Such networks use the most modern and global means of communication. In exploiting these, they sometimes outflank national government and international capital alike – as consumers mobilized through western Europe to boycott Shell, humiliate the British government, and force the towing back of the Brent Spar oil platform in 1995. We may expect more of this.

Is this a 'global civil society'? Its structure is not entirely new: in the early twentieth century socialists (and, to a lesser extent, anarchists, pacifists and fascists) also generated extensive transnational networks covering much of the globe, using similarly advanced technology (printing presses, immediate trans-lation, dictaphones, etc. – see Trotsky's remarkable study in Mexico City). The socialists launched a wave of revolutions, some successful, most unsuccessful. Many of the more idealistic proponents of the notion of a new civil society expect its scale eventually to dwarf such historical analogies.

Second, however, there is also increasing deployment of intergovernmental agencies: macroregional and continental agencies, UN conferences, etc. Their key participants, those who could implement coordinated policy decisions, are representatives of nation-states. 'Soft geopolitics' is becoming denser in this arena too. The other main delegates are the 'experts' mentioned two paragraphs above, who lead a double life. Though nurtured in transnational professional associations, they must adopt the perspective of the nation-state, persuading governments that global concerns are actually in the national interest. Some hit on excellent wheezes. Some American ornithologist managed to persuade the State Department to insert into its aid programme to Belize a requirement to protect a rare bird of which the Belize planners had not previously heard. More significantly, feminists involved in development agencies are pressuring reactionary dictators in the south to put more resources into the education of women since this will reduce the birth rate (one of the primary goals of almost all southern governments).

Thus environmental issues mainly encourage dual networks of interaction, one a potentially local/transnational civil society, the other inter-national, in the form of 'soft' geopolitics. The former may transcend the nation-state, the latter coordinate states more tightly together, though perhaps in partly consensual terms which are not incompatible with a gradual spread of a civil society. Again it is a mixed story.

And this is also the case with others among the 'new social movements'. It is usually argued that those concerned with the 'new politics' of identity – of gender, sexuality, lifestyle, age cohort, religion and ethnicity – weaken national (and nationally regulated class) identities, replacing or supplementing them with local-cum-transnational sources of identity. Ethnic politics are too variable to be dealt with in a few paragraphs [. . .] So one sentence will do here: ethnic politics may fragment existing states, but – given the defeat of alternative multinational and socialist states – they fragment them into more, supposedly more authentic, nation-states. But for other social movements based on identity politics, I wish to argue that on balance they strengthen existing nation-states.

I argued earlier that the 'moderate nation-state' began by staying out of areas of social life considered 'private'. The household was especially sacred, and states stayed outside the family life of all but the very poor. Secular states generally lacked their own moral concerns, taking over moral conceptions from religion. Their legislation might firmly prohibit certain forms of personal behaviour yet government relied more on citizens' internalizing morality than on enforcement. Where citizens did not wish to comply, they privately evaded – and states usually lacked effective infrastructures of enforcement. Apparent exceptions – child and female labour prohibitions were the main nineteenth-century instance of new legislation being enforced – resulted because they were believed to violate the patriarchal household and Christian sexual conduct.

The twentieth century changed this, through new political movements and the penetration of the welfare state into the private realm. States are now asked to legislate and enforce moral conduct in what had been hitherto private arenas. I can no longer pollute the public environment by smoking. My dog's defecations are also more restricted. I can no longer beat my wife or children. If I leave them, I must make due provision for their wellbeing. Much of the new legislation is paradoxically framed in the spirit not of restrictiveness, but of extending personal freedoms. Gays may practise their lifestyle openly; women may abort unwanted foetuses. But this results not in a neoliberal absence of state regulation; it would only if there could be some consensual final resting-post for definitions of what is public and what is private. Instead it produces a continuous, highly contentious political debate and legislative stream. May gays get married, rear children, join the military, run scout troops? For how long, for what reasons, in what ways and in what type of clinic can women abort foetuses? Does the presumptive father have any say? We need laws on all these issues and for the complicated welfare entitlements they imply. Thus passionate pressure groups organize and 'culture wars' appear. The USA is extreme, both its main political parties partially hijacked by these 'new social movements'. But most countries across the world are now politicized by such moral issues.

These culture wars do involve some transnational and some global interaction networks. Feminists, gays, religious fundamentalists, etc. use emerging global networks of communication and NGOs, and they focus energies on the UN as well as their own state. However, most contending actors demand *more* regulation by their own nation-state through its legal or welfare agencies: to restrict or liberalize abortion, pre-marital conception and single parenting; to clarify harassment, child abuse and rape and the evidence needed to prosecute them; to guarantee or restrict the rights of those with unorthodox sexual preferences or lifestyles. Since authoritative social regulation remains overwhelmingly the province of the nation-state, the emergence of new identities may ultimately reinvigorate its politics and broaden its scope. New social movements claim to be turned off by class politics. Perhaps class politics will decline – but not national politics in general.

POST-MILITARISM AND A NEW WORLD ORDER

As Martin Shaw argues, it is in the realm of hard geopolitics that the northern nation-states have experienced the most radical transformation – because this is where they learned the bitterest lessons. In the two great northern wars (more commonly called the world wars) they suffered perhaps 70–80 million dead – as a direct consequence of the nation-state system.[5] Through those wars they also pioneered weapons so devastating that they could no longer be actually used for any rational 'hard geopolitical' purpose. Northern states are now less willing to engage themselves in wholesale war than almost any states in history. The original backbone of the nation-state is turning to jelly.

But again our three regions vary. None are more reluctant militarists than the Europeans, the guilty perpetrators of both wars, reliant for their defence for the last fifty years on the USA and presently faced by no serious threat to their security. Though the EU contains two nuclear powers, has its Franco-German brigade and its curious Western European [Defence] Union, all this is less significant than the unprecedented virtual absence of serious 'hard geopolitics' within Europe. Germans remain the most constrained of all by anti-militarism. The determination to break with the terrible character of European history is probably the most causally determining modern transformation of all, and the one which is most encroaching upon traditional national sovereignties. But to make European history the general pattern of the world would be ethnocentric in the extreme. And if it was, then the analogy would require more than just a restructuring of capitalism reinforced by a 'cultural turn'. The analogy would require future wars killing many millions of people in other regions of the world, before they too cried 'enough'.

Yet most Japanese may also have cried 'enough'. They are at present reluctant militarists. Some Japanese politicians are bolder than their German counterparts in expressing nationalism, but they still get slapped down. Yet East Asia is potentially an insecure region. The United States differs again. It suffered little during the two great northern wars – indeed its economy greatly benefited. It is a military superpower, still projects a standing armed force of 1,200,000 into the next century, and still modernizes its hardware. It remains the global policeman, a role which European and Japanese governments are keen to see continue and may even help finance. But even in the USA defence cuts have been sizeable and it is doubtful that the American electorate has the stomach for warfare in which many American lives would be lost. In any case these northern regions dominate the world without war.

The world nonetheless remains conflict-ridden, with a substantial place for 'hard' geopolitics. Consider this list: rising ethnic separatism, conflict between potentially nuclear states like India and Pakistan or the two Chinas, China's geopolitical role incommensurate with its real strength, the instability of Russia and some smaller well-armed powers, the prevalence of military regimes in the world, the likely proliferation of nuclear weapons and the largely uncontrolled current spread of chemical and biological weapons through the world. Who knows what eco-tensions, resulting from water shortages, foreign-dominated exploitation of a country's habitat, etc. might lurk around the corner? It is unlikely militarism or war will just go away. All these threats constitute serious obstacles to the diffusion of transnational and universal global networks.

The threats could conceivably be contained by a global geopolitical order, though this would be partially segmented. It must centre for the foreseeable future on the USA, flanked perhaps by greater coordination with the bigger northern states and with the United Nations. Shaw sees their combination as providing an emerging global order, though acknowledging that it is not a true 'state' and that it remains dual, torn between what he calls its 'western' and 'world' components. Actually, it seems a triad, since its core is not western but American – adding a further level of unreliability. The American electorate may not wish to provide the 'mercenaries' to police the world. It may agree to police its neighbours, a few strategic places and vital resources like oil, but not most of the world – or the more powerful rivals. It seems a long way to either a transnational or a geopolitical order for the world as a whole.

And even the more warlike scenarios mentioned above would not actually be on a par with the nation-state's horrendous past. 'Hard' geopolitics – that is, terrible wars – caused its initial growth and remained one-half of it until recently. Hard geopolitics are now in relative decline in the north, though not everywhere. Though the dangers presented by weapons of war have increased, these actually reduce the mobilizing power of states. If states have lost some of their traditional core, are they therefore in general decline? The argument seems most plausible in Europe, least across large swathes of the south. Moreover, we have seen that 'soft' geopolitics may be rising to complement the hard variety, buttressed by the new national mobilizations described above.

CONCLUSION

This article has analysed four supposed 'threats' to contemporary nation-states: capitalist transformation, environmental limits, identity politics and post-militarism. We must beware the more enthusiastic of the globalists and transnationalists. With little sense of history, they exaggerate the former strength of nation-states; with little sense of global variety, they exaggerate their current decline; with little sense of their plurality, they downplay inter-national relations. In all four spheres of 'threat' we must distinguish: (a) differential impacts on different types of state in different regions; (b) trends weakening *and* some trends strengthening nation-states; (c) trends displacing national regulation to inter-national as well as to transnational networks; (d) trends simultaneously strengthening nation-states *and* transnationalism.

I have hazarded some generalizations. Capitalist transformation seems to be somewhat weakening the most advanced nation-states of the north yet successful economic development would strengthen nation-states elsewhere. The decline of militarism and 'hard geopolitics' in the north weakens its traditional nation-state core there. Yet the first three supposed 'threats' should actually intensify and make more dense the inter-national networks of 'soft geopolitics'. And identity politics may (contrary to most views) actually strengthen nation-states. These patterns are too varied and contradictory, and the future too murky, to permit us to argue simply that the nation-state and the nation-state system are *either* strengthening *or* weakening. It seems rather that (despite some postmodernists), as the world becomes more integrated, it is *local* interaction networks that continue to decline – though the fragmentation of some presently existing states into smaller ethnically defined states would be something of a counter-trend, i.e. the reduction of the nation-state to a more local level.

Global interaction networks are indeed strengthening. But they entwine three main elements. First, part of their force derives from the more global scale of transnational relations originating principally from the technology and social relations of capitalism. But these do not have the power to impose a singular universalism on global networks. Thus, second, global networks are also modestly segmented by the particularities of nation-states, especially the more powerful ones of the north. Third, that segmentation is mediated by inter-national relations. These include some 'hard' politics, and if these turned again to major wars or international tensions, then segmentation would actually increase. Yet at present the expansion of 'soft' geopolitics is more striking, and this is rather more congenial to transnationalism. Is this a single 'global society'? Not in the strongest sense often implied by the more enthusiastic theorists. These global networks contain no singular, relatively systemic principle of interaction or integration. My own view of 'society' is less demanding, since I conceive of human societies as always formed of multiple, overlapping and intersecting networks of interaction. Globalism is unlikely to change this. Human interaction networks are now penetrating the globe, but in multiple, variable and uneven fashion.

NOTES

1. Clearly, stateless societies existed (indeed they dominated much of human existence on earth) and they still exist in the world today. But states seem necessary to advanced social life – though anarchists disagree.
2. MITI – the highly interventionist Japanese Ministry of Trade and Industry.
3. Chiapas is the only province where ethnic conflict can plausibly arise, since *mestizos* dominate everywhere else. This is because Chiapas was acquired from Guatemala in the 1920s.
4. I have discussed this in more detail, and with some comparisons with other regions, in an earlier article (Mann, 1993b). As the present article indicates, however, my views have since modified in certain respects.
5. Obviously, these wars had complex causes. However, as I have tried to show in the case of the First World War (see Mann, 1993a: Ch. 21), they centre on the institutions of the nation-state more than they do on any other power organization (such as capitalism).

20

CITIZENSHIP AND THE OTHER IN THE AGE OF MIGRATION

Stephen Castles

In the past half-century, the democratic nation-state has become the global norm as the principal unit of political organization. Within it, people are defined as citizens with rights and obligations laid down by constitutions and laws. There is, of course, a gap between the principle and the reality: the majority of the 185 states within the United Nations cannot claim to be stable democracies in which all citizens are truly equal before the law. Where democracy does not yet exist those in power claim that this is due to economic deprivation or histories of colonialism, foreign domination and internal conflict. Democratic citizenship is the goal.

The paradox is that, just as the nation-state has achieved almost universal acceptance, it appears increasingly precarious: globalization is eroding national boundaries and breaking the nexus between territory and power. This challenge has multiple dimensions:

- The emergence of global markets and transnational corporations with economic power greater than many states.
- The increasing role of supranational bodies in regulating inter-state relations and individual rights.
- The emergence of global cultural industries based on new communication techniques.
- The growth in international migration since 1945 and especially since about 1980.

Stephen Castles (2000), *Ethnicity and Globalization*, London: Sage.

This last dimension of globalization is my main theme. In the age of migration (Castles and Miller 1998) a major problem arises: if the citizen is a person who belongs both culturally and politically to one specific nation-state, what of migrants who settle in one country without abandoning their cultural belonging in another? The migrant has always been the 'Other' of the nation. National identity is often asserted through a process of exclusion – feelings of belonging depend on being able to say who does not belong. But if the Other is part of society (as a worker, parent or tax-payer, for example), how can national distinctiveness be maintained? Moreover, the increase in the number of people with transnational identities – as shown by multiple citizenship, and by family, social and economic connections in more than one country – questions the principle of nation-state exclusivity (Basch et al. 1994).

Globalization makes it necessary to work out new modes of inclusion for 'the citizen who does not belong'. The problem is all the more acute in that cultural difference within nation-states is increasing at a time when new forms of economic and social polarization are also emerging. Ethnic exclusion and social exclusion are linked in complex ways.[1]

[. . .]

CITIZENSHIP AND NATIONALITY

It is necessary first to discuss some of the inherent contradictions of the nation-state and of citizenship. It is significant that today's global association of *states* is actually called the United *Nations*, indicating that we find it hard today to conceive of a state that is not also a nation. A *state* refers to a legal and political organization which controls a certain territory. A *nation* is a cultural community of people who believe that they have a common heritage and a common destiny (see Seton-Watson 1977; Smith 1991). Both are of great antiquity, but their linking as a *nation-state* is relatively new, dating from the eighteenth and nineteenth centuries. The juxtaposition of nation and state has many problems which I cannot go into here (see Castles 1998). I will focus on just two key issues: the contradiction between citizenship and nationality, and the contradiction between the active and the passive citizen.

An essential feature of a democratic nation-state is the integration of all its inhabitants into the political community and their equality as citizens. As a political community, the nation-state claims to be inclusive of all people in its territory, while those outside are excluded. In the 'universal state', all citizens are meant to be free and equal persons, who, as citizens, are homogeneous individuals (Rawls 1985: 232–4). This requires a separation between a people's political rights and obligations and their membership of specific groups, based on ethnicity, religion, social class or regional location.

The notion of the free citizen goes back to medieval towns, which developed as places of refuge from feudal servitude and as the location of the new classes of merchants and artisans. But in the era of modernity, citizenship no longer referred to the city, but to the nation-state. Becoming a citizen depended on membership of a specific national community (for example, being French, German, Italian). A *citizen* was always also a member of a nation, a *national*. So citizenship is meant to be universalistic and above cultural difference, yet it exists only in the context of a nation-state, which is based on cultural specificity – on the belief in being different from other nations.

Since very few nation-states actually start off with a single national group, the question is how the varying ethnic groups in a territory are to be moulded into one nation. This *obliteration of difference* may take place by means of the forcible imposition of the culture of the dominant group; for instance, through the prohibition of minority languages, schools and festivals. The process may be a more gradual and consensual one, in which groups grow together through economic and social interaction and the development of a common language and shared institutions, such as schools, church and military service. Most nation-states have elements of both repression and evolution.

States vary in the degree to which ethnic nationalism is subordinated to universalism. The ultra-nationalism of the nineteenth-century German *Kultur-nation* was in strong contrast to the French *Staatsnation* created by the democratic revolution of 1789. This civic nation was regarded as a political project capable of transcending the tension between universalism and particu-larism and of assimilating ethnic or religious minorities (Schnapper 1994: 83–114). Yet the claim of transcending culture was dubious: even in France, nation-state formation involved linguistic homogenization, political centralization and compulsory assimilation. The key to success was the long duration of the process of conquering and homogenizing surrounding peoples, starting in the fifteenth century, and only completed towards the end of the nineteenth century. This, in the famous formulation of Renan (1992), gave people 'time to forget' the history of their own oppression, which had made them into one nation. But, even over centuries, some people did not forget, which is why there have been separatist movements in Corsica and Languedoc.

This fundamental contradiction between citizen and national is at the root of many of the conflicts that tore Europe apart in the nineteenth and twentieth centuries, such as anti-semitism, racism and nationalism. It was never fully overcome within the nation-state model: the wars triggered by rival nationalisms were only ended through *supranational* approaches after 1945 – and even then not completely, as the example of former Yugoslavia has shown.

THE PASSIVE AND THE ACTIVE CITIZEN

The contradiction between citizen and national cuts across another crucial dichotomy: that between the passive and the active citizen. According to seventeenth-century social-contract theory, a sovereign could only rule with the consent of the people, but once this consent was given the people had a duty to obey the constitutionally enacted laws. In the pre-1914 German *Rechtsstaat*, the passive citizen had obligations towards the state and rights to protection from unlawful state action, but had no right to question state authority.

By contrast, the French Revolution of 1789 led to a notion of citizenship as an assertion of political will, which has to be constantly renewed through participation in the process of law-making (summed up in Renan's designation of the nation as 'the daily plebiscite'). The essence of citizenship was a set of procedures designed to guarantee equal participation in the expression of political will. This popular sovereignty was the basis for the legal rights laid down in the Declaration of the Rights of Man and the Citizen. Citizenship meant participation as an equal in the public sphere, while protecting the right to be different in the private sphere. In principle there was no link between being a citizen and belonging to the French cultural community: the 1793 Constitution virtually gave citizenship at will to resident foreigners (Davidson 1997: 45).

The principle of equal citizenship was always incomplete – above all, women were excluded. Moreover, it was linked to the exclusion of the external Other: the democratic citizen was always also the 'warrior-citizen'. The right to vote was explicitly linked to conscription. Nevertheless, the conflict between active and passive notions of the citizen was – and remains – one of the great political divides within modern nation-states. Democratic movements have struggled for the enfranchisement of previously excluded groups, such as workers and women. Conservatives have always opposed popular sovereignty because it restricts the rights of those with wealth and power. Today, the growing complexity of society and state make it difficult for the popular will to control the decisions of experts and technocrats.

What is important in our context is that the notion of the active citizen inevitably leads to demands for broadening the rights of citizenship. A person cannot participate in political processes without a certain minimum standard of education and of economic and social well-being. Political rights are meaningless in the long run unless they are linked to social rights. This principle was asserted by European labour movements from the late nineteenth century, and given real substance in the post-war European welfare states.

The roll-back of social citizenship since the 1970s is the expression of an ideological offensive against the idea of the active citizen with social rights. New right ideologies are reasserting the notion of the citizen as a person who fits into the community by working and obeying the law. The task of the state is to guarantee the private realm by maintaining law and order and minimizing intervention in economic and social affairs (Mead 1986). Underlying this ideology is the economic and social crisis brought about by global economic restructuring. The question is how high wages and the welfare state can be maintained in a world where the old industrial countries are no longer dominant.

THE IMMIGRATION OF THE IRREDUCIBLE OTHER

Globalization and international migration exacerbate the contradictions of citizenship. Today, there are at least 100 million people resident outside their country of birth. This is only a small proportion of the world's population, yet the consequences are much broader, affecting migrants' families, their communities of origin, and the places where they settle. Moreover, the effects of migration are felt most in areas already undergoing rapid change. Economic and social transformation in poor areas lead to emigration, while the destinations may be global cities with burgeoning service economies, or new industrial countries undergoing rapid urbanization.

The significance of migration for citizenship is felt at the intersection between the two basic contradictions discussed above. The principle of citizenship for all members of society demands the inclusion of new ethnic minorities into the political community; the principle of national belonging demands their exclusion. Similarly, the principle of active citizenship demands giving minorities the economic and social rights needed for full participation. But the current rollback in the welfare state makes it difficult to admit new groups and to provide the conditions they need to achieve full societal membership.

Immigration and growing cultural diversity poses a dual challenge to nation-states. First, admitting the Other into the national community through citizenship and equal rights appears as a threat to national cohesion and identity. The process of immigration has become so rapid that there is no time to obliterate difference, let alone to forget it. This problem is all the more acute when the Other comes from former colonies, where their otherness (expressed both through phenotypical and cultural difference) has been constructed both as inferiority and as a danger to 'Judeo-Christian civilization'.

Secondly, at a time of economic decline, sharing a shrinking social cake with new groups appears as a threat to the conditions of the local working class. The social polarization brought about by economic restructuring and policies of privatization and deregulation leaves little room for minority rights. It is much easier to turn these groups into the scapegoats for the social crisis, by blaming them not only for their own marginality, but also for the decline in general standards. Migration is therefore seen as a central aspect of the North-South conflict, and migrants may be perceived as infiltrators who will drag the rich countries down to Third-World poverty. The 'enemy within' is the racialized 'underclass' in the new urban 'ghettos'.

The immigration of the irreducible Other creates a dilemma for Western countries because it exacerbates the existing contradictions of the nation-state model at the very moment when this model is in any case being undermined by globalization. To what extent does this also apply to the new immigration countries of Asia? There are clearly some important differences. The long historical process which led to the emergence of the democratic citizenry in Europe has no parallel in Asia. The idea of popular sovereignty is relatively new and untried, while the practice of achieving political objectives through negotiation within complex authoritarian structures has a long tradition. The Western model of the nation-state and citizenship came to Asia mediated through the distorting mirror of colonialism. France offered citizenship to some of the colonized people of Indo-China; Britain and The Netherlands made colonized people into subjects of their monarchs; the USA preached democratic values in the Philippines. But such ideals were always tarnished by the realities of dispossession, exploitation and racism.

Yet at the same time colonialism was so effective in destroying previous state-forms that liberation movements usually set out to take over the Western model – often with the ideal of giving reality to democratic principles that had been mere hypocrisy in their colonial guise. The new post-colonial states were largely based on the Western form, but without the historical process that had led to its emergence. Above all, the democratic citizen was absent. Anti-colonial trade unions, parties and movements tried to create a democratic-nationalist con-sciousness. They often failed: military rule or other forms of authoritarianism quickly became the norm, although there has been a shift towards greater democracy in some countries in the past twenty years (see Rodan 1996).

Post-colonial nation-states developed so quickly that there was no 'time to forget'. Ruling elites were incapable of homogenizing the various ethnic and national groups brought together by colonialism into one people. In some cases, colonialism had cut across traditional ethnic boundaries; in others long-stand-ing ethnic divisions were exacerbated by colonialism (such as the situation of the Chinese in South-east Asia); in yet others, colonial labour recruitment had created new minorities (for example, the Indians in Malaysia). Where there were cleavages of religion, ethnicity, culture or economic interests, the rule of a dominant group was often imposed by force.

This is not to argue that there have not been successful examples of nation-building: Singapore, Indonesia and Malaysia all provide models for building unity on diversity. Rather, the point is that the development of national consciousness is a difficult and as yet incomplete process. The national and the citizen are not generally emerging in parallel, as was the experience in at least some European countries. The strains arising from attempts to develop a single national commu-nity out of diverse cultures may make it all the harder to include immigrants into the nation. 'Late nations' are generally the most nationalistic ones.

BECOMING A CITIZEN

How have immigration countries dealt with the dilemmas outlined above? Becoming a citizen is clearly of crucial importance to an immigrant. But gaining formal *access to citizenship* – symbolized by getting the passport of the country of residence – is only one aspect of this. Equally important is the extent to which people belonging to distinct groups of the population actually achieve *sub-stantial citizenship*: that is equal chances of participation in various areas of society, such as politics, work and social security. This section deals with access to citizenship while the following one will examine substantial citizenship. The discussion concentrates on older immigration countries (Western Europe, North America and Australia) due to lack of information on newer immi-grant-receiving countries.

Rules for formal access to citizenship are highly complicated and are in a state of flux. Laws on citizenship or nationality derive from two competing principles: *ius sanguinis* (literally, law of the blood), which is based on descent from a national of the country concerned, and *ius soli* (literally, law of the soil), which is based on birth in the territory of the country. *Ius sanguinis* is often linked to an ethnic or folk model of the nation-state (the German *Kulturnation*), while *ius soli* generally relates to a nation-state built through incorporation of diverse groups on a single territory (as in the case of the United Kingdom). *Ius sanguinis* has been seen historically as appropriate for an emigration country (like Germany, Spain or Greece) which wished to retain the allegiance of people who had settled elsewhere. A 'law of return' to reintegrate former emigrants may be based on this principle, as in the case of contemporary Germany and its *Aussiedler* (ethnic Germans from Eastern Europe). *Ius soli*, on the other hand, is particularly useful for integrating immigrants of diverse national origins into a new nation, which is why it has been adopted in the former British colonies (USA, Australia and so on) and former Spanish colonies in Latin America. In practice, all modern states have citizenship rules based on a combination of *ius sanguinis* and *ius soli*, although one or the other may be clearly predominant. For instance, *ius soli*, countries use the *ius sanguinis* principle to confer citizenship on children of their citizens born overseas. A further principle is growing in significance at present: *ius domicili* (law of residence) according to which people may gain an entitlement to citizenship through residence in the territory of a country.

However, some general trends can be made out (Çinar 1994; Guimezanes 1995). Half a century of large-scale immigration to Western nations is leading to a grudging realization that people of diverse ethno-cultural backgrounds are there for good, and that there is no real alternative to incorporating them as citizens. This recognition has been easier for some countries than others. Classical immigration countries like the USA, Canada and Australia have been able to continue their traditions of incorporating newcomers as citizens, although they have had to drop practices of racial selectivity and find new ways of dealing with cultural difference. Immigrants are encouraged to become citizens with automatic citizenship for their children. These countries seem highly inclusive. However, it may be argued that the real decision on citizenship is made when immigration applications are rejected or accepted, rather then later on when settlers apply for naturalization. Selectivity of immigrants according to economic, social and humanitarian criteria may be based on (possibly unconscious) political and cultural biases.

European countries, with their strong historical links between imagined cultural community and political belonging, have found it more difficult to change their access criteria. None the less, naturalization rules have been gradually relaxed to grant citizenship to long-standing foreign residents. Many observers speak of a cross-national convergence of rules, but a comparison of actual practices and outcomes shows that major differences still exist. Table

23.1 presents a comparison of naturalization figures. Naturalization rates are still very low in the *ius sanguinis* countries which used to recruit guest-workers: Germany, Austria and Switzerland. Countries with models combining elements of *ius soli* and *ius sanguinis* – France, Belgium, the UK – have intermediate rates. Sweden and The Netherlands have done most to change rules to include immigrants and now have naturalization rates close to those of Australia or Canada.

Measures are also being introduced to facilitate access to citizenship for the second and subsequent generations through the extension of *ius soli* or through various combinations of *ius soli*, *ius sanguinis* and *ius domicili*. Immigrants' children are automatically citizens in the USA, Australia, Canada and the UK. The overwhelming majority become citizens on reaching adulthood in France, Sweden, The Netherlands, Belgium and Italy. Despite recent changes, rules are still restrictive in Germany, Austria and Switzerland, so that many young people remain foreigners in their country of birth and upbringing.

Table 20.1 *Naturalizations in selected countries 1988 and 1995*

Country	1988		1995	
	No. of naturalizations	Naturalization rate[1]	No. of naturalizations	Naturalization rate[1]
Australia	81,218	57	114,757	74
Belgium	8,366	10	26,109	29
Canada	58,810	n.a.	227,720	n.a.
France	46,351	13	59,988	17
Germany (FR)	16,660	4	31,888	5
Japan	5,767	6	14,104	10
Netherlands	9,110	14	71,440	98
Sweden	17,966	43	31,993	60
Switzerland	11,356	11	16,795	12
UK	64,600	35	40,500	19
USA	242,063	n.a.	445,853	n.a.

n.a. = not available.

1. The naturalization rate is defined as the number of naturalizations per thousand foreign residents. The calculated naturalization rate for Australia is based on an estimate for foreign resident population, assuming that 60 per cent of overseas-born persons are Australian citizens. The naturalization rate for France is calculated using the foreign resident population figure for 1990. The German naturalization figure excludes naturalization based on legal entitlement, which applies mainly to 'ethnic Germans' from Eastern Europe. The comparison has only indicative value, as definitions and procedures vary from country to country.

Sources: Australian census 1996, preliminary figures; OECD (1997: Table III. 1, Tables A.1, B3, and C5)

Another general trend is that towards dual or multiple citizenship. Although many governments reject this due to fears of 'divided loyalties', there are now millions of people with two or more passports. The rapid increase reflects both the reality of migrants' dual national affiliations and the growth in bi-national marriages. This contributes to the erosion of notions of exclusive national belonging.

Several states have created systems of quasi-citizenship, through which long-term residents are granted some but not all of the rights of citizenship (for instance, local but not national voting rights) (Hammar 1990). Such measures do improve the legal and psychological security of settlers but seem fundamentally unstable because they create a two-class system of citizenship which is inconsistent with democratic principles. However, once immigrants have civil and social rights, they are in a better position to demand political rights. Citizenship of the European Union (EU) is a special form of quasi-citizenship. It is linked to citizenship of a member-state and confers only limited political rights, though quite considerable social rights. EU citizenship does nothing for the millions of 'extra-communitarians' and is seen by some as one aspect of the construction of an exclusionary European identity. But, like other types of quasi-citizenship, EU citizenship could be an important stepping-stone towards full membership. The question is whether this will be membership of an exclusionary nation-state or of a new type of transnational democratic entity (Martiniello 1994).

Issues of formal access to citizenship for immigrants are thus far from resolved. Large numbers of people still have ambiguous and disadvantaged legal positions. In some countries, a generation of young people is reaching maturity without equal rights in their country of birth. Populations can be divided up into *full citizens*, *denizens*, (people with limited citizenship rights) and *margizens* (undocumented immigrants or other people with insecure legal status) (Martiniello 1994). Such legal differentiation reinforces social divisions and racism against minorities.

MINORITIES AND RIGHTS

The rise of the welfare state after 1945 led to debates on the contradiction between formal political membership and persistence of severe economic and social disadvantage. Welfare state theorists in Britain, Scandinavia and other European countries (Townsend 1979; Turner 1992) argued that a bundle of social rights, including the rights to work, education and certain basic social standards, were essential for members of the working class to be full citizens. On this basis, T. H. Marshall (1950, 1964) developed his famous notion of three types of citizenship rights, which had developed in historical progression: *civil rights*, *political rights* and *social rights*.

Such debates have become all the more significant today. In all the old industrial countries, certain social groups are becoming spatially segregated and cut off from mainstream economic and social frameworks. Some US urban sociologists (for example, Wilson 1987, 1994) refer to such groups as the 'underclass', while most European observers prefer the concept of 'social exclusion' (Cross and Keith 1993; Mingione 1996). A high proportion of the socially excluded in Western countries belong to ethnic minorities, defined on the basis of race, culture or origins. There is a clear trend towards the *racialization* or *ethnicization of poverty* (Schierup 1997).

It would be useful to review the rights of ethnic minorities according to Marshall's triad of civil, political and social rights. This task cannot be carried out adequately here, but a few key issues can be mentioned. In principle, *civil rights*[2] are guaranteed by law for everyone (including non-citizens) in a democratic state. Moreover, as Soysal (1994) has pointed out, the rights of non-citizens have in many cases been expanded through supranational legal norms laid down by such bodies as the United Nations, the International Labour Organization and the Council of Europe. However, civil rights guaranteed by law to ethnic minorities are frequently violated in practice, often by powerful institutions such as the police, prisons and courts. For instance, indigenous peoples such as Australian Aborigines suffer extremely high rates of incarceration and of death in custody (HREOC 1991). Police brutality against African-Americans is also well documented.

The prevalence of racist violence can in itself be seen as a constraint on civil rights, for it severely reduces minority members' chances of equal participation in society. In the USA, 'hate organizations', such as the Ku Klux Klan, neo-Nazi groups and 'militia' organizations, carry out campaigns of violence and intimidation against African-Americans and other minorities. European countries have also experienced growing racist violence since the 1970s. The situation deteriorated further as the end of the Cold War coincided with a serious recession. 'By the early 1990s, many groups of people have had to face racist violence and harassment as a threatening part of everyday life' (Björgo and Witte 1993: 1). These groups included immigrants and asylum-seekers, but also long-standing minorities such as Jews and gypsies.

The situation with regard to *political rights*[3] is highly complex: many resident non-citizens are denied political rights, while others have been granted limited rights, such as the vote in local elections. On the other hand, minorities which do have formal citizenship may have little real chance of political participation. In Australia, indigenous people make up less than 2 per cent of the population, and there are few constituencies where they have a chance of securing representation. Their only way of making their voice heard is through special representative bodies, such as the Aboriginal and Torres Strait Islander Commission (ATSIC). However, its prerogatives are limited and insecure, as was shown in 1996 when the Liberal–National government took steps to curtail its autonomy in financial matters.

Different categories of rights are interdependent. Criteria of exclusion based on socio-economic position and on minority status may be mutually reinforcing: in the USA, large numbers of the poor and of ethnic minorities are not even registered as voters. Even in presidential elections, only about half the population votes, while the proportion is far lower in congressional and state elections.

Current trends are leading to a weakening of *social rights*[4] for many ethnic minority members. Two main situations may be distinguished. First, the majority of immigrants and their descendants do not live in enclaves nor find employment in workplaces separate from those of the majority populations. Yet their position is frequently precarious: the combination of only partial incorporation into mainstream economic and social systems with continuing processes of racialization makes them highly vulnerable. This situation may be referred to as *social segmentation* (Cross 1995).

Secondly, some minority groups are highly vulnerable due to their weak legal position, racial stigmatization, lack of human capital and specific historical conditions of conflict. These groups include indigenous peoples in North America and Australia, African-Americans in the USA, Afro-Caribbeans and South Asians in Britain and asylum-seekers everywhere. Groups on the verge of such situations include Muslim immigrants in most countries, some (but not all) Hispanics in the USA, and certain Asian groups (especially those of refugee origin). These groups are likely to suffer *social exclusion*. As Mingione (1996: 12) argues, their disadvantage is so severe as to weaken the social bond and to question the strength of citizenship as an integrating force in contemporary society.

However, Marshall's triad of civil, political and social rights is inadequate to understand fully the situation of ethnic minorities today. It is necessary to add the additional categories of gender rights and cultural rights. In Western countries, women were excluded from formal citizenship and legal equality until quite recently (Pateman 1988): women got the vote in 1902 in Australia, 1918 in Britain,[5] 1920 in the USA, and in 1944 in France. Although explicit legal discrimination had disappeared in most places by the 1970s, the legacy of historical subordination remains: women have worse jobs, lower incomes, low rates of participation in political decision-making processes, and are still seen as primarily responsible for the domestic sphere (Gregory 1987; Meehan 1993: 101–20; Vogel 1994: 85).

Ethnic minority women are in a double bind: they are marginalized both through subordinating constructions of gender and through ethnic and racial stigmatization. These are not simply additive processes, where two forms of discrimination reinforce each other. Rather, racialization of minority women takes specific forms within the reproduction of gendered social relations (Anthias and Yuval-Davis 1989; Brah 1993; Lutz et al. 1995). These interlocking processes can be observed in many social arenas, including:

- ideological discourses on nation and community;
- notions of sexuality;
- legal rules on immigration and nationality;
- mechanisms of labour market segmentation;
- the spatial ordering of social relations;
- the construction of socio-cultural norms.

Minority women cannot become full citizens simply by achieving formal equality because this will not overcome sexist and racist discourses. Rather they need specific rights, which recognize the historical forms in which their oppression and exclusion have been constructed. Iris Young (1989) argues that this can only be achieved, first, through 'mechanisms for group representation' of previously excluded groups, and, secondly, through 'the articulation of special rights that attend to group differences in order to undermine oppression and disadvantage'.

A similar point can be made with regard to cultural rights. Since the nation-state is based on the obliteration of minority cultures, the maintenance of immigrant cultures and languages can become a stigma used to justify the inferiority of minorities. On the other hand, giving up the original culture and accepting assimilation can lead to even greater marginalization for minorities because it means losing the self-esteem and the community solidarity needed to survive in an often hostile environment. Therefore, minorities demand the rights both to the maintenance of their original culture and to social equality within the country of settlement. This duality of social and cultural rights is accepted in countries with policies of multiculturalism, like Australia, Canada and Sweden. It seems an essential aspect of citizenship in a culturally diverse society (Castles 1994).

RACIALIZATION AND COMMUNITY FORMATION

Until quite recently, the prevailing view in most immigration countries was that the problem of cultural diversity would solve itself over time through the assimilation of minorities. This is still the dominant ideology in some countries, most notably France. But the belief in assimilation is becoming harder to sustain. The capability of the nation-state to 're-socialize' immigrants is being undermined both by globalizing tendencies and by a decline in social solidarity (Schnapper 1994). At the same time, immigrants find it easier to maintain their cultural and other links with their areas of origin through better communication and frequent visits.

This situation gives rise to two closely linked phenomena: racialization (or ethnicization) of minorities and community formation. Racialization arises from the combined effects of all the exclusionary effects already discussed in this chapter. Racial discrimination and violence, spatial segregation, economic disadvantage and social exclusion all work together to create ethnic or racial minorities which are clearly identifiable. Racialization as a discursive process goes a step further by blaming the minorities for their social isolation, and by portraying them as a threat to society. For example, Susan Smith has shown how residential segregation in Britain was presented as the choice of immigrants, who wanted to live together in a 'black inner city'. The development of minority neighbourhoods then appeared as the result of 'natural processes' of racial differentiation, rather than as the consequence of economic and social exclusion. Minority areas were portrayed as a threat to morality and public order. Welfare dependency, crime, vice and dangerous religious and political ideologies were seen as cancers which developed in such areas, and might spread to threaten the whole society. This laid the ground for a racialization of politics in the 1960s: extreme-right groups and sections of the Conservative Party mobilized public opinion around demands to stop immigration and curtail the rights of existing immigrants (Smith 1993b).

The response by minorities to racialization is to maintain their cultures and languages, and to develop community solidarity. In the early stages of a migratory process, immigrant groups normally cluster together and develop their own infrastructure – businesses, religious institutions, associations – as a way of coping with the new social situation. In time, successful immigrants make links with mainstream economic and social frameworks, and move out into other areas. When such shifts are blocked by racial discrimination and violence, and by lack of economic opportunities, members of minorities have to focus their activities within the ethnic community, and this stimulates the development of religious, political and economic institutions. This in turn increases the suspicions of the majority population that 'alien enclaves' are developing. Ethnic segregation is thus a self-fulfilling prophecy, originating in exclusionary discourses. However, extreme separatism – such as Islamic fundamentalist groups in France, Germany and Britain – is very much the exception. In most cases, ethnic mobilization, especially by members of the second generation, is concerned with combating discrimination and achieving equal treatment within mainstream society.

In France, Catherine Wihtol de Wenden (1988, 1995) has shown how forms of ethnic mobilization changed at different stages of migration and settlement:

1. Immigrants as foreigners and workers (1950s and 1960s). Migrant workers originally became politicized with reference to home-country issues, as well as with regard to industrial and trade-union action.
2. Immigrants as purveyors of traditional culture (from the 1970s). Both European and African workers of the first generation formed religious and cultural associations concerned with maintaining the traditions of the area of origin. These associations contributed to the internal cohesion of immigrant families and groups without necessarily integrating them into French society.
3. The second generation of immigrants as political actors (1980s and 1990s). Associations were formed to fight against racism, to lobby for civic rights and for new citizenship laws, to promote socio-cultural integration in the suburbs, to organize help with home work, and to offer help with work-seeking and new business ventures.

The movement of the *beurs* (youth of North African origin) has become an important cultural and political force in France (Bouamama 1994). New forms of citizenship appeared in urban struggles when *beurs* asserted that they were 'citizens by participation' without necessarily being nationals. The notion of a 'new citizenship' was viewed as the answer to a crisis in democracy caused both by the rise of individualism and the growth of collective identities. Members of the second generation demanded participatory citizenship in a multicultural society, based on residence rather than nationality or descent (Wihtol de Wenden 1995). Cultural symbols and ethnic community solidarity play an important part in the development of movements for equal participation in the wider society without loss of identity. This presents a major challenge to traditional forms of national belonging (Bouamama et al. 1992).

Towards post-national belonging

My central conclusion is that the nation-state model, which asserts (or seeks to create) congruity between nationality and citizenship, cannot offer an adequate basis for societal belonging in the age of globalization and migration. The continuing attempt to base citizenship on membership of an imagined cultural community leads to political and social exclusion and the racialization of difference. Such trends do not just disadvantage minorities – they also lead to social divisions and political conflicts for the societies concerned. Three sets of principles arise from this conclusion.

1. The need for citizenship rules which guarantee formal inclusion of all permanent residents of a given country. A notion of *porous borders* is required, with admission rules and rights based on people's real societal membership (cf. Bauböck 1994). Where people belong to more than one society there may need to be differential or segmented forms of citizenship, which recognize the different modes of participation.

2. The need for economic and social policies which make social citizenship possible for all, and which overcome trends to racialization of social exclusion and poverty. Since there can be no political equality without certain basic social standards, there is a need for a social safety-net for all, as well as affirmative action policies to facilitate the inclusion of previously excluded groups. Here the principle of interdependence of civil, political, social, gender and cultural rights must be stressed.

3. The need for institutional change. Existing constitutions, laws, political parties and economic organizations all embody the dominant cultural values of the era in which they were constructed. These cultural values are based on the idea of a distinctive national community, with fixed boundaries to the outside world. If belonging is uncoupled from nationality, new members of society are likely to question and change existing structures (Habermas 1994).

It is very easy to put forward such principles, but much harder to achieve them in practice. It is important to examine actual political tendencies, which are in fact quite contradictory: on the one hand, attempts are being made to shore up the old nation-state model, while, on the other, certain changes point to the possibility of devising new modes of belonging. I will conclude by giving a few examples.

With regard to formal inclusion, it may be argued that significant changes are gradually eroding the link between citizenship and nationality. Every major immigration country has altered its naturalization rules in recent times. There is a trend towards easier naturalization for immigrants and stronger entitlement to citizenship for their children. Dual citizenship is also burgeoning. This has often meant relaxing the requirement for prior cultural assimilation: the new citizens are not yet nationals, and may never become so. Moreover, many immigrants unable to secure full citizenship are obtaining some crucial rights through national and supranational legal norms. Regional political integration (above all the European Union) is creating new forms of political belonging decoupled from nationality. But there are also countervailing tendencies: the tightening of immigration and refugee rules is leading to an increase in the number of illegal residents. Moreover, minority members are often unable to obtain their formal rights in practice.

The picture is far less positive with regard to social citizenship. Current trends towards the economic polarization of Western societies and the dismantling of welfare systems make it much more difficult for minorities to achieve the minimum standards necessary for genuine participation. The racialization of social exclusion creates both the material and the ideological conditions for deep societal divisions. Anti-discrimination laws and affirmative action policies have not been very effective in preventing such developments. Here the key to change may lie in social movements, in which ethnic solidarity is used as an instrument to achieve societal inclusion and equality.

Finally, the question of institutional change is the one which rouses most resistance from dominant groups. The idea of changing time-honoured institutions is a threat both to identity and vested interests. Here the need of minorities for the removal of cultural biases has to be linked to the need of the wider population for greater participation. Under existing political arrangements, popular sovereignty has been steadily eroded by the power of experts and the decline of the public sphere. In response, citizens' groups and social movements have demanded 'more democracy in more places' – that is, the decentralization of decision-making to the lowest possible level. New technological developments – such as 'electronic democracy' – could be used to allow much wider participation by citizens. Within such a general movement for democratization, minority demands for a new citizenship may play an important part.

NOTES

1. Many of the ideas in this chapter arise from joint work with Alastair Davidson.
2. Civil rights include freedom and inviolability of the person; freedom of expression; freedom of religion; protection from unlawful acts by the state, such as imprisonment or forced labour; equality before the law; prohibition of discrimination on grounds of gender, origins, race, language or beliefs.

3. Political rights include the right to vote and to stand for office at the various levels of government; freedom of assembly and of association; freedom of information (including access to the information needed to understand complex issues in contemporary societies).
4. Social rights include the right to work; equality of opportunity (in education, the labour market, etc.); entitlement to welfare benefits and social services in the event of unemployment or inability to work; entitlement to health services; entitlement to a certain standard of education.
5. But British women got the vote only from the age of 30 in 1918; enfranchisement on the same terms as men came ten years later.

21

CULTURE AND POLITICAL COMMUNITY – NATIONAL, GLOBAL AND COSMOPOLITAN

David Held

This 'window' explores the impact on national culture of the globalization of communications and cultural life. It is in four parts. In the first part, the historical background to the debate about the nature and prospects of national culture is explored. The second and third sections examine the debate in an era of increasing transborder cultural interchange. Two positions are set out: the traditionalist or modern, territorial, state-based conception of the enduring significance of national identity and the cultural globalist position – the view that global popular culture, consumption orientations and hybrid identities are transforming cultural life. These positions are related to the development of political community and, in particular, to accounts about the proper nature and locus of the political good. The fourth and final part draws on aspects of both accounts, and points toward an alternative formulation, which appears a better fit with, and more appropriate to, cultural and political life in the contemporary age.

HISTORICAL BACKDROP

The globalization of culture has a long history. The formation and expansion of the great world religions are profound examples of the capacity of ideas and beliefs to cross great distances with decisive social impacts. No less important are the great pre-modern empires such as the Roman Empire, which, in the absence of a direct military and political control, held its domains together through a shared and extensive ruling class culture (Millar *et al.* 1967; Mann

David Held (2002), 'Culture and political community: national, global, and cosmopolitan', in Steven Vertovec and Robin Cohen, *Conceiving Cosmopolitanism: Theory, Context, and Practice*, Oxford: Oxford University Press.

1986). For most of human history, these extensive ruling cultures passed through a fragmented mosaic of local cultures and particularisms; little stood between the political centre and the village. It was only with the emergence of nation-states and national cultures that a form of cultural identity coalesced between these two poles.

With the rise of nation-states and nationalist projects, the spatial organization of culture was transformed. Nation-states took control of educational practices, linguistic policies, postal systems, and so on. However, from the eighteenth century, as European empires expanded and as a series of technological innovations began to have far-reaching practical effects (regularized mechanical transport and the telegraph most notably), new forms of cultural globalization crystallized. The most important ideas and arguments to emerge from the West during this era were science, liberalism and socialism (Held *et al.* 1999, ch. 7). Each of these modes of thought – and the practices that went with them – transformed the ruling cultures of almost every society on the planet. They have certainly had a more considerable impact on national and local cultures than Nike, Coca-Cola, McDonald's and a host of pop groups.

However, in the period since the Second World War, the extensity, intensity, speed and sheer volume of cultural communication are unsurpassed at a global level (UNESCO 1950, 1986, 1989; OECD 1997). The global diffusion of radio, television, the Internet, satellite and digital technologies has made instantaneous communication possible, rendered many border checks and controls over information ineffective, and exposed an enormous constituency to diverse cultural outputs and values. A telling example is the viewing figures for *Baywatch*; over two billion people are estimated to have watched each episode. While linguistic differences continue to be a barrier to these processes, the global dominance of English provides a linguistic infrastructure that parallels the technological infrastructures of the era. In contrast to earlier periods in which states and theocracies were central to cultural globalization, the current era is one in which corporations are the central producers and distributors of cultural products. Corporations have replaced states and theocracies as the key producers and distributors of cultural products. Private international institutions are not new but their mass impact is. News agencies and publishing houses in previous eras had a much more limited reach than the consumer goods and cultural output of the global corporations today.

Though the vast majority of these cultural products come from the USA, this does not amount to a simple case of 'cultural imperialism', One of the surprising features of our global age is how robust national and local cultures have proved to be. National institutions remain central to public life; while national audiences constantly re-interpret foreign products in novel ways (see Thompson 1995). The central question is the future impact of communication and cultural flows on local and national cultures, and on our sense of personal identity, national identity and politics. The next section turns to the debate on this.

National culture and its presuppositions

The rise of the modern nation-state and nationalist movements altered the landscape of political identity. The conditions involved in the creation of the modern state often helped generate a sense of nationhood. In particular, the military and administrative requirements of the modern state 'politicized' social relations and day-to-day activities (Giddens 1985; Mann 1986). Gradually, people became aware of their membership in a shared political community, with a common fate. Although the nature of this emergent identity was often initially vague, it grew more definite and precise over time (Therborn 1977; Turner 1986; Mann 1987).

The consolidation of the ideas and narratives of the nation and nationhood has been linked to many factors including the attempt by ruling elites and governments to create a new identity that would legitimize the enhancement of state power and the coordination of policy (Breuilly 1992); the creation, via a mass education system, of a common framework of understanding – ideas, meanings, practices – to enhance the process of state coordinated modernization (Gellner 1983); the emergence of new communication systems – particularly new media (such as printing and the telegraph), independent publishers and a free market for printed material – which facilitated interclass communication and the diffusion of national histories, myths and rituals, that is a new imagined community (Anderson 1983); and building on an historic sense of homeland and deeply-rooted memories, the consolidation of ethnic communities via a common public culture, shared legal rights and duties and an economy creating mobility for its members within a bounded territory (Smith 1986, 1995).

Even where the establishment of a national identity was an explicit political project pursued by elites, it was rarely their complete invention. That nationalist elites actively sought to generate a sense of nationality and a commitment to the nation – a 'national community of fate' – is well documented. But 'it does not follow', as one observer aptly noted, that such elites 'invented nations where none existed' (Smith 1990: 180–1). The 'nation-to-be' was not any large, social or cultural entity; rather, it was a 'community of history and culture', occupying a particular territory, and often laying claim to a distinctive tradition of common rights and duties for its members. Accordingly, many nations were 'built up on the basis of pre-modern "ethnic cores" whose myths and memories, values and symbols shaped the culture and boundaries of the nation that modern elites managed to forge' (see Smith 1986; 1990: 180). The identity that nationalists strove to uphold depended, in significant part, on uncovering and exploiting a community's 'ethno-history' and on highlighting its distinctiveness in the world of competing political and cultural values (cf. Hall 1992a).

Of course, the construction of nations, national identities and nation-states has always been harshly contested and the conditions for the successful development of each never fully overlapped with that of the others (see Held *et al.* 1999: 48–9, 336–40). The fixed borders of the modern state have generally embraced a diversity of ethnic, cultural and linguistic groups with mixed leanings and allegiances. The relationships between these groups, and between these groups and states, has been chequered and often a source of bitter conflict. In the late nineteenth and twentieth centuries, nationalism became a force that supported and buttressed state formation in certain places (e.g., in France) and challenged or refashioned it elsewhere – for instance, in multiethnic states such as Spain or the United Kingdom (Held *et al.* 1999: 337–8).

However, despite the diversity of nationalisms and their political aims, and the fact that most national cultures are less than two hundred years old, these 'new' political forces created fundamentally novel terms of political reference in the modern world – terms of reference that appear so well rooted today that many, if not the overwhelming majority, peoples take them as given and practically natural (see Barry 1998). In fact, advocates of the primacy of national identity juxtapose its enduring qualities and the deep appeal of national cultures with the ephemeral and ersatz qualities of the products of the transnational media corporations (Smith 1990; Brown 1995). Since national cultures have been centrally concerned with consolidating the relationships between political identity, self-determination and the powers of the state, they are, and will remain, so the argument runs, formidably important sources of ethical and political direction.

The political significance of nationalism, along with the development and consolidation of the state, has been at the heart of modern political theory. Political theory, by and large, has taken the nation-state as a fixed point of reference and has sought to place the state at the centre of interpretations of the nature and proper form of the political good (Dunn 1990: 142–60). The theory and practice of liberal democracy has added important nuances to this position. For within the framework of liberal democracy, while territorial boundaries and the nation-state demarcate the proper spatial limits of the political good, the articulation of the political good is directly linked to the national citizenry. The political good is inherent in, and is to be specified by, a process of political participation in which the collective will is determined through the medium of elected representatives (Bobbio 1989: 144).

The theory of the political good in the modern territorial polity rests on a number of assumptions that repay an effort of clarification (see Held 1995, chapter 10; Miller 1995, 1999). These are that a political community is properly constituted and bounded when:

1. its members have a common socio-cultural identity; that is, they share an understanding, explicit or implicit, of a distinctive culture, tradition, language and homeland, which binds them together as a group and forms a (if not the) basis (acknowledged or unacknowledged) of their activities;
2. there is a common framework of 'prejudices', purposes and objectives that generates a common political ethos, namely an imagined 'com-

munity of fate' that connects its envoys directly to a common political project – the notion that they form a people who should govern themselves;

3. an institutional structure exists – or is in the process of development – that protects and represents the community, acts on its behalf and promotes the collective interest;

4. 'congruence' and 'symmetry' prevail between a community's 'governors' and 'governed', between political decision-makers and decision-takers. That is to say, national communities 'programme' the actions, decisions and policies of their governments, and governments determine what is right or appropriate for their citizens; and

5. members enjoy, because of the presence of the above conditions, a common structure of rights and duties, namely they can lay claim to and can reasonably expect certain kinds of equal treatment, that is certain types of egalitarian principles of justice and political participation.

According to this account, appropriate conceptions of what is right for the political community and its citizens follow from its cultural, political and institutional roots, traditions and boundaries. These generate the resources – conceptual and organizational – for the determination of its fate and fortunes. And the underlying principle of justification involves a significant communitarian thought: ethical discourse cannot be detached from the 'form of life' of a community; the categories of political discourse are integral to a particular tradition; and the values of such a community take precedence over or trump global requirements (MacIntyre 1981, 1988; Walzer 1983; Miller 1988).

THE GLOBALIZATION OF COMMUNICATIONS AND CULTURE

Globalists take issue with each of these propositions, and they mount a sustained critique of them. First, shared identity in political communities historically has been the result of intensive efforts of political construction; it has never been a given (cf. Anderson 1983; Gellner 1983; Smith 1986, 1995). Even within the boundaries of old-established communities, cultural and political identity is often disputed by and across social classes, gender divisions, local allegiances, ethnic groupings and the generations. The existence of a shared political identity cannot simply be read off vociferously proclaimed symbols of national identity. The meaning of such symbols is contested and the 'ethos' of a community frequently debated. The common values of a community may be subject to intense dispute. Justice, accountability and the rule of law are just a few terms around which there may appear to be a shared language and, yet, fiercely different conceptions of these may be present. In fact, if by a political consensus is meant normative integration within a community, then it is all too rare (Held 1996, part 2; and see below).

Political identity is only by exception, for instance during wars, a singular, unitary phenomenon. Moreover, contemporary 'reflexive' political agents, subject to an extraordinary diversity of information and communication, can be influenced by images, concepts, lifestyles and ideas from well beyond their immediate communities and can come to identify with groups beyond their borders – ethnic, religious, social and political (Keck and Sikkink 1998; Thompson 1998; Held *et al.* 1999, chapter 8). Further, while there is no reason to suppose that they will uncritically identify with any one of these, self-chosen ideas, commitments or relations may well be more important for some people's identity than 'membership in a community of birth' (Thompson, 1998: 190; cf. Giddens 1991; Tamir 1993). Cultural and political identity today is constantly under review and reconstruction.

Second, the argument that locates cultural value and the political good firmly within the terrain of the nation-state fails to consider or properly appreciate the diversity of political communities that individuals can appreciate, and the fact that individuals can involve themselves coherently in different associations or collectivities at different levels and for different purposes (Thompson 1998). It is perfectly possible, for example, to enjoy membership and voting rights in Scotland, the United Kingdom and Europe without necessarily threatening one's identification or allegiances to any one of these three political entities (see Archibugi *et al.* 1998). It is perfectly possible, in addition, to identify closely with the aims and ambitions of a transnational social movement – whether concerned with environmental, gender or human rights issues – without compromising other more local political commitments. Such a pluralization of political orientations and allegiances can be linked to the erosion of the state's capacity to sustain a singular political identity in the face of migration, the movement of labour and the globalization of communications. Increasingly, successful political communities have to work with, not against, a multiplicity of identities, cultures and ethnic groupings. Multiculturalism, not national culture, is increasingly the norm.

Third, globalization has 'hollowed-out' states, eroding their sovereignty and autonomy. State institutions and political agents are, globalists contend, increasingly like 'zombies' (Beck 1992; Giddens 1999*b*). Contemporary political strategies involve easing adaptation to world markets and transnational economic flows. Adjustment to the international economy – above all to global financial markets – becomes a fixed point of orientation in economic and social policy. The 'decision signals' of these markets, and of their leading agents and forces, become a, if not the, standard of rational decision-making. States no longer have the capacity and policy instruments they require to contest the imperatives of global economic change; instead, they must help individual citizens to go where they want to go via the provision of social, cultural and educational resources (Giddens 1999*a*). Accordingly, the roles of the state as a protector and representative of the territorial community, as a collector and (re)allocator of resources among its members, as a promoter of an independent, deliberatively tested shared good are all in decline.

Fourth, the fate of a national community is no longer in its own hands. Regional and global economic, environmental and political processes profoundly redefine the content of national decision-making. In addition, decisions made by quasi-regional or quasi-supranational organizations such as the EU, the World Trade Organization (WTO), the International Monetary Fund (IMF) or NATO diminish the range of political options open to given national 'majorities'. In a similar vein, decisions by particular states – not just the most economically or militarily powerful nations – can ramify across borders, circumscribing and reshaping the political terrain. Political communities are, thus, embedded in a substantial range of processes that connect them in complex configurations, making them all too often decision-takers, not decision-makers.

Fifth, national communities are locked into webs of regional and global governance that alter and compromise their capacity to provide a common structure of rights, duties and welfare to their citizens. From human rights to trade regimes, political power is being re-articulated and reconfigured. Increasingly, contemporary patterns of globalization are associated with a multilayered system of governance. Locked into an array of geographically diverse forces, national governments are having to reconsider their roles and functions. Although the intensification of regional and global political relations has diminished the powers of national governments, it is recognized ever more that the nurturing and enhancement of the political good requires coordinated multilateral action, for instance to prevent global recession and enhance sustainable growth, to protect human rights and intercede where they are grossly violated and to act to avoid environmental catastrophes such as ozone depletion or global warming. A shift is taking place from government to multilevel global governance. Accordingly, the institutional nexus of the political good is being reconfigured.

Each of the five propositions set forth by the theorists of national culture and of the modern national state can be contrasted with positions held by the globalists. Thus, the political community and the political good need, on the globalists' account, to be understood as follows:

1. Individuals increasingly have complex loyalties and multi-layered identities, corresponding to the globalization of economic and cultural forces and the reconfiguration of political power.
2. The continuing development of regional, international and global flows of resources and networks of interaction, along with the recognition by growing numbers of people of the increasing interconnectedness of political communities – in domains as diverse as the social, cultural, economic and environmental – generates an awareness of overlapping 'collective fortunes' that require collective solutions. Political community begins to be re-imagined in regional and global terms.

3. An institutional structure exists comprising elements of local, national, regional and global governance. At different levels, individual communities (albeit often imperfectly) are protected and represented; their collective interests require both multilateral advancement and domestic (local and national) adjustment if they are to be sustained and promoted.

4. Complex economic, social and environmental processes, shifting networks of regional and international agencies and the decision outcomes of many states cut across spatially delimited, national locales with determinate consequences for their agendas and policy options. Globalization alters decisively what it is that a national community can ask of its government, what politicians can promise and deliver, and the range of people(s) affected by government outputs. Political communities are 'reprogrammed'.

5. The rights, duties and welfare of individuals can only be adequately entrenched if they are underwritten by regional and global regimes, laws and institutions. The promotion of the political good and of egalitarian principles of justice and political participation are rightly pursued at regional and global levels. Their conditions of possibility are inextricably linked to the establishment of transnational organizations and institutions of governance. In a global age, transnational organizations and institutions are the basis of cooperative relations and just conduct.

Accordingly, what is right for the individual political community and its citizens, in the globalists' account, must follow from reflection on the processes that generate an intermingling of national fortunes. The contemporary world 'is not a world of closed communities with mutually impenetrable ways of thought, self-sufficient economies and ideally sovereign states' (O'Neill 1991: 282). Not only is ethical discourse separable from forms of life in a national community, it is also developing today at the intersection and interstices of overlapping communities, traditions and languages. Its categories are increasingly the result of the mediation of different cultures, communication processes and modes of understanding. There are not enough good reasons for allowing, in principle, the values of individual political communities to trump or take precedence over global principles of justice and political participation. While for the traditionalists ethical discourse is, and remains, firmly rooted in the bounded political community, for the globalists it belongs squarely to the world of 'breached boundaries' – the 'world community' or global order.

COSMOPOLITAN ALTERNATIVES

There is insufficient space here to appraise all the claims of these two positions. But by way of a conclusion, I would like to make a number of additional points, and indicate the plausibility of a third position – neither traditionalist, nor globalist, but cosmopolitan.

The leading claims of the globalists are at their strongest when focused on institutional and process change in the domains of economics, politics and the environment, but they are at their most vulnerable when considering the movements of people, their attachments and their cultural and moral identities. For the available evidence suggests that national (and local) cultures remain robust; national institutions continue in many states to have a central impact on public life; national television and radio broadcasting continue to enjoy substantial audiences; the organization of the press and news coverage retain strong national roots and imported foreign products are constantly read and reinterpreted in novel ways by national audiences (Miller 1992; Liebes and Katz 1993; Thompson 1995). Moreover, the evidence indicates that there is no simple common global pool of memories, no common global way of thinking, and no 'universal history' in and through which people can unite. There is only a manifold set of political meanings and systems through which any new global awareness, or multicultural politics, or human rights discourse must struggle for survival (see Bozeman 1984). Given the deep roots of national cultures and ethno-histories, and the many ways they are often refashioned, this can hardly be a surprise. Despite the vast flows of information, imagery and people around the world, there are only a few signs, at best, of a universal or global history in the making, and few signs of a decline in the importance of nationalism.

There has been a shift from government to multi-level governance, from the modern state to a multi-layered system of power and authority, from relatively discrete national communication and economic systems to their more complex and diverse enmeshment at regional and global levels. Yet, there are few grounds for thinking that a concomitant widespread pluralization of political identities has taken place. One exception to this is to be found among the elites of the global order – the networks of experts and specialists, senior administrative personnel and transnational business groups – and those who track and contest their activities, the loose constellation of social movements, trade unionists and (a few) politicians and intellectuals. The globalists' emphasis on the pluralization of political identities is overstated. What one commentator has written about the EU applies, in many respects, to the rest of the world: 'The central paradox . . . is that governance is becoming increasingly a multi-level, intricately institutionalized activity, while representation, loyalty and identity remain stubbornly rooted in the traditional institutions of the nation-state' (Wallace 1999: 521).

Hence, the shift from government to governance is an unstable shift, capable of reversal in some respects, and certainly capable of engendering a fierce reaction – a reaction drawing on nostalgia, romanticized conceptions of political community, hostility to outsiders (refugees, immigrants), and a search for a pure national state (e.g., in the politics of Haider in Austria). But this reaction itself is likely to be highly unstable, and a relatively short-term phenomenon. To understand why this is so, nationalism has to be desegregated. As 'cultural nationalism' it is, and in all likelihood will remain, central to people's identity; however, as political nationalism – the assertion of the exclusive political priority of national identity and the national interest – it cannot deliver many sought-after public goods and values without seeking accommodation with others, in and through regional and global collaboration. In this respect, only a cosmopolitan outlook can, ultimately, accommodate itself to the political challenges of a more global era, marked by overlapping communities of fate and multi-layered politics. Unlike political nationalism, cosmopolitanism registers and reflects the multiplicity of issues, questions, processes and problems that affect and bind people together, irrespective of where they were born or reside.

Cosmopolitanism is concerned to disclose the cultural, ethical and legal basis of political order in a world where political communities and states matter, but not only and exclusively. It dates at least to the Stoics' description of themselves as cosmopolitans – 'human beings living in a world of human beings and only incidentally members of polities' (Barry 1999: 35). The Stoic emphasis on the morally contingent nature of membership of a political community seems anachronistic after 200 years of nationalism. But what is neither anachronistic nor misplaced is the recognition of the necessary partiality, one-sidedness and limitedness of 'reasons of political community' or 'reasons of state' when judged from the perspective of a world of 'overlapping communities of fate' – where the trajectories of each and every country are tightly entwined. Cosmopolitanism today must take this as a starting point, and build a robust conception of the proper basis of political community and the relations among communities. The Kantian understanding of this, based on a model of human interaction anchored in co-presence, cannot be an adequate basis of this (Held 1995, ch. 10). Cosmopolitanism needs to be reworked for another age.

What would such a cosmopolitanism amount to? In the little space available here, I cannot unpack what I take to be the multi-dimensional nature of cosmopolitanism. But I would like to end with a few words about cultural cosmopolitanism. Cultural cosmopolitanism is not at loggerheads with national culture; it does not deny cultural difference or the enduring significance of national tradition. It is not against cultural diversity. Few, if any, contemporary cosmopolitans hold such views (see, e.g., Waldron 1999; Barry 2000). Rather, cultural cosmopolitanism should be understood as the capacity to mediate between national cultures, communities of fate and alternative styles of life. It encompasses the possibility of dialogue with the traditions and discourses of others with the aim of expanding the horizons of one's own framework of meaning and prejudice (Gadamer 1975). Political agents who can 'reason from the point of view of others' are better equipped to resolve, and resolve fairly, the challenging transboundary issues that create overlapping communities of fate. The development of this kind of cultural cosmopolitanism depends on the recognition by growing numbers of peoples of the increasing interconnectedness of political communities in diverse domains, and the development of an understanding of overlapping 'collective fortunes' that require collective solutions – locally, nationally, regionally and globally.

Cultural cosmopolitanism emphasizes the possible fluidity of individual identity – 'people's remarkable capacity to forge new identities using materials from diverse cultural sources, and to flourish while so doing' (Scheffler 1999: 257). It celebrates, as Rushdie put it, 'hybridity, impurity, intermingling, the transformation that comes of new and unexpected combinations of human beings, cultures, ideas, politics, movies, songs' (quoted in Waldron, 1992: 751). But it is *the ability to stand outside a singular location (the location of one's birth, land, upbringing, conversion) and to mediate traditions* that lies at its core. However, there are no guarantees about the extent to which such an outlook will prevail. For it has to survive and jostle for recognition alongside deeply held national, ethnic and religious traditions (Held and McGrew 2000: 13–18 and part 3). It is a cultural and cognitive orientation, not an inevitability of history.

The core requirements of cultural cosmopolitanism include:

1. recognition of the increasing interconnectedness of political communities in diverse domains including the social, economic and environmental;
2. development of an understanding of overlapping 'collective fortunes' that require collective solutions – locally, nationally, regionally and globally; and
3. the celebration of difference, diversity and hybridity while learning how to 'reason from the point of view of others' and mediate traditions.

Like national culture, cultural cosmopolitanism is a cultural project, but with one difference: it is better adapted and suited to our regional and global age.

FURTHER READING

The Global Transformations Reader: An Introduction to the Globalization Debate (2003) edited by David Held and Anthony McGrew (Cambridge: Polity) provides a useful introduction to the relevant debates about the extent and impacts of globalization. Yasmin Soysal (1994), *Limits of Citizenship: Migrants and Postnational Membership in Europe* (Chicago: Chicago University Press) provides a clear argument for the emergence of a new postnational model of citizenship. The possibilities and limitations of cosmopolitan politics are debated in Daniele Archibugi's (2003) edited collection *Debating Cosmopolitics* (London: Verso). For further analysis of the issues of migration and citizenship in the light of the rise of universal human rights principles see David Jacobson (1997), *Rights across Borders – Immigration and the Decline of Citizenship* (Baltimore: Johns Hopkins University Press). Nigel Dower (2003) examines the arguments from ethical, social and political theory for and against the view that we are global citizens in *An Introduction to Global Citizenship* (Edinburgh: Edinburgh University Press).

REFERENCES

Acton, E. (1996), 'Nationality', in G. Balakrishnan (ed.), *Mapping the Nation*, London: Blackwell.

Adams, M. (1990), *The Great Adventure: Male Desire and the Coming of World War I*, Bloomington: Indiana University Press.

Almond, G. and Pye, L. (eds) (1965), *Comparative Political Culture*, Princeton, NJ: Princeton University Press.

Alter, P. (1989), *Nationalism*, London: Edward Arnold.

Alvarez, S. (1990), *Engendering Democracy in Brazil: Women's Movements in Transition Politics*, Princeton, NJ: Princeton University Press.

Amalrik, A. (1970), *Will the Soviet Union Survive until 1984?*, New York: Harper and Row.

Anderson, B. (1983), *Imagined Communities: Reflections on the Origins and Spread of Nationalism*, London: Verso.

Anderson, B. (1991), *Imagined Communities: Reflections on the Origins and Spread of Nationalism*, 2nd ed., London: Verso.

Anderson, P. (1974), *Lineages of the Absolutist State*, London: New Left Books.

Anthias, F. and Yuval-Davis, N. (1989), 'Introduction', in F. Anthias and N. Yuval-Davis (eds), *Woman–Nation–State*, Basingstoke and London: Macmillan, pp. 1–15.

Anthias, F. and Yuval-Davis, N. (1992), *Racialized Boundaries: Race, Nation, Gender, Colour and Class and the Anti-Racist Struggle*, London: Routledge.

Archetti, E. (1999), *Masculinities: Football, Polo and the Tango in Argentina*, Oxford: Berg.

Archibugi, D. (1998), 'Principles of cosmopolitan democracy', in D. Archibugi, D. Held and M. Köhler (eds), *Re-Imagining Political Community*, Cambridge: Polity Press, pp. 198–228.

Armstrong, J. (1982), *Nations before Nationalism*, Chapel Hill: University of North Carolina Press.

Augustin, E. (ed.) (1993), *Palestinian Women: Identity and Experience*, London: Zed.

Balibar, E. and Wallerstein, I. (1991), *Race, Nation, Class: Ambiguous Identities*, London: Verso.

Banks, M. (1996), *Ethnicity: Anthropological Constructions*, London: Routledge.

Banton, M. (1967), *Race Relations*, London: Tavistock.

Banton, M. (1983), *Racial and Ethnic Competition*, Cambridge: Cambridge University Press.

Barbieri, W. (1998), *Ethics of Citizenship: Immigration and Group Rights in Germany*, Durham, NC: Duke University Press.

Barker, M. (1981), *The New Racism: Conservatives and the Ideology of the Tribe*, London: Junction.

Barkow, J., Cosmides, L. and Tooby, J. (eds) (1992), *The Adapted Mind: Evolutionary Psychology and the Generation of Culture*, Oxford: Oxford University Press.

Barry, B. (1998), 'The limits of cultural politics', *Review of International Studies*, 24:3, 307–19.

Barry, B. (1999), 'Statism and nationalism: a cosmopolitan critique', in I. Shapiro and L. Brilmayer (eds), *Global Justice*, New York: New York University Press.

Barry, B. (2000), *Culture and Equality*, Cambridge: Polity Press.

Barthes, R. (1977), *Roland Barthes*, Basingstoke: Macmillan.

Barthes, R. (1983), 'Myth today', in R. Barthes, *Selected Writings*, ed. and intr. S. Sontag, London: Fontana.

Basch, L., Glick-Schiller, N. and Blanc, C. (1994), *Nations Unbound: Transnational Projects, Post-Colonial Predicaments, and Deterritorialized Nation-States*, New York: Gordon and Breach.

Bauböck, R. (1994), 'Changing the boundaries of citizenship: the inclusion of immigrants in democratic policies', in R. Bauböck (ed.), *From Aliens to Citizens*, Aldershot: Avebury, pp. 199–232.

Baumann, G. (1996), *Contesting Culture: Discourses of Identity in Multi-Ethnic London*, Cambridge: Cambridge University Press.

Beattie, G. (1993), *We Are the People*, London: Mandarin.

Beck, U. (1992), *Risk Society: Towards a New Modernity*, London: Sage.

Bederman, G. (1995), *Manliness and Civilization: A Cultural History of Gender and Race in the United States 1880–1917*, Chicago: University of Chicago Press.

Beissinger, M. (1993), 'Demise of an empire-state: identity, legitimacy, and the deconstruction of Soviet politics', in M. Young (ed.) *The Rising Tide of Cultural Pluralism: The Nation-State at Bay?*, Madison: University of Wisconsin Press, pp. 93–115.

Beissinger, M. (1995), 'The persisting ambiguity of empire', *Post-Soviet Affairs*, 11:2, 149–84.

Benda, H. and Larkin, J. (eds) (1967), *The World of Southeast Asia: Selected Historical Readings*, New York: Harper and Row.

Benda-Beckmann, K. von and Verkuyten, M. (eds) (1995), *Nationalism, Ethnicity and Cultural Identity in Europe*, Utrecht: European Research Centre on Migration and Ethnic Relations, Utrecht University.

Benedict, B. (1965), *Mauritius: Problems of a Plural Society*, London: Pall Mall.

Benner, E. (1995), *Really Existing Nationalisms: A Post-Communist View from Marx and Engels*, Oxford: Oxford University Press.

Berberi, Y. (1993), 'Active in politics and women's affairs in Gaza', in E. Augustin (ed.), *Palestinian Women: Identity and Experience*, London: Zed, pp. 43–54.

Berger, P. and Luckmann, T. (1966), *The Social Construction of Reality: A Treatise in the Sociology of Knowledge*, Garden City, NJ: Doubleday.

Bhabha, H. (ed.) (1990), *Nation and Narration*, London and New York: Routledge.

Billig, M. (1990), 'Collective memory, ideology and the British Royal Family', in D. Middleton and D. Edwards (eds), *Collective Remembering*, London: Sage.

Billig, M. (1991), *Ideology and Opinions*, London: Sage.

Billig, M. (1992), *Talking of the Royal Family*, London: Routledge.

Billig, M. (1995), *Banal Nationalism*, London: Sage.

Billig, M. and Edwards, D. (1994), 'La construction sociale de la mémoire', *La Recherche*, 25, 742–5.

Birch, J. (1987), 'Border disputes and disputed borders in the Soviet federal system', *Nationalities Papers*, 15:1, 43–69.

Birnbaum, P. (1992), *Anti-Semitism in France: A Political History from Léon Blum to the Present*, Oxford: Blackwell.

Björgo, T. and Witte, R. (1993), 'Introduction', in T. Björgo and R. Witte (eds), *Racist Violence in Europe*, London: Macmillan, pp. 1–16.

Björgo, T. and Witte, R. (1996), *Racist Violence and the State: A Comparative Analysis of Britain, France and the Netherlands*, Harlow: Addison-Wesley Longman.

Blackbourne, D. and Eley, G. (1991), *The Peculiarities of German History*, Oxford: Oxford University Press.

Blanning, T. (1986), *The Origins of the French Revolutionary Wars*, London: Longman.

Bloch, M. (1961), *Feudal Society*, tr. I. Manyon, 2 vols, Chicago: University of Chicago Press.

Bobbio, N. (1989), *Democracy and Dictatorship*, Cambridge: Polity Press.

Bocock, R. (1974), *Ritual in Industrial Society*, London: George Allen and Unwin.

Bologh, R. (1990), *Love or Greatness: Max Weber and Masculine Thinking – A Feminist Inquiry*, London: Unwin Hyman.

Bouamama, S. (1994), *Dix ans de marche des beurs*, Paris: Desclée de Brouwer.

Bouamama, S., Cordeiro, A. and Roux, M. (1992), *La Citoyenneté dans tous ses états*, Paris: CIEMI l'Harmattan.

Boulding, E. (1977), *Women in the Twentieth Century World*, Beverly Hills, CA: Sage.

Bourdieu, P. (1990), *The Logic of Practice*, Cambridge: Polity Press.

Boyle, P., Halfacre, K. and Robinson, V. (1998), *Exploring Contemporary Migration*, London: Longman.

Bozeman, A. B. (1984), 'The international order in a multicultural world', in H. Bull and A. Watson (eds), *The Expansion of International Society*, Oxford: Oxford University Press, pp. 387–406.

Brah, A. (1993), 'Difference, diversity, differentiation: processes of racialisation and gender', in J. Wrench and J. Solomos (eds), *Racism and Migration in Western Europe*, Oxford: Berg, pp. 195–214.

Breuilly, J. (1985), 'Reflections on nationalism', *Philosophy of the Social Sciences*, 15, 65–75.

Breuilly, J. (1993), *Nationalism and the State*, Chicago and Manchester: Chicago University Press/Manchester University Press.

Breuilly, J. (1996), 'Approaches to nationalism', in G. Balakrishnan (ed.), *Mapping the Nation*, London and New York: Verso, pp. 146–74.

Briggs, V. (1996), *Mass Immigration and the National Interest*, Armonk, NY: M. E. Sharpe.

Brockett, C. (1991), 'The structure of political opportunities and peasant mobilization in Central America', *Comparative Politics*, 23:3, 253–74.

Brogan, H. (1986), *The Pelican History of the United States of America*, Harmondsworth: Pelican.

Brown, C. (1995), 'International political theory and the idea of world community', in K. Booth and S. Smith (eds), *International Relations Theory Today*, Cambridge: Polity Press, pp. 90–109.

Brown, W. (1988), *Manhood and Politics: A Feminist Reading in Political Theory*, Totowa, NJ: Rowman and Littlefield.

Brown, W. (1992), 'Finding the man in the state', *Feminist Studies*, 18, 7–34.

Brownmiller, S. (1975), *Against Our Will: Men, Women, and Rape*, New York: Bantam.

Brubaker, R. (1992), *Citizenship and Nationhood in France and Germany*, Cambridge: Cambridge University Press.

Brubaker, R. (1996), *Nationalism Reframed: Nationalism and the National Question in the New Europe*, Cambridge: Cambridge University Press.

Brubaker, R. (1998) 'Myths and misconceptions in the study of nationalism', in J. Hall (ed.), *The State of the Nation: Ernest Gellner and the Theory of Nationalism*, Cambridge: Cambridge University Press.

Campbell, J. and Sherrard, P. (1968), *Modern Greece*, London: Ernest Benn.

Carnes, M. (1989), *Secret Ritual and Manhood in Victorian America*, New Haven, CT: Yale University Press.

Carnes, M. (1990), 'Middle-class men and the solace of fraternal ritual', in M. Carnes and C. Griffen (eds), *Meanings for Manhood: Constructions of Masculinity in Victorian America*, Chicago: University of Chicago Press, pp. 37–66.

Carnoy, M. (1993), 'Whither the nation-state?', in M. Carnoy (ed.), *The New Global Economy in the Information Age*, College Park: Pennsylvania State University Press.

Castells, M. (1993), 'The informational economy and the new international division of labor', in M. Carnoy (ed.), *The New Global Economy in the Information Age*, College Park: Pennsylvania State University Press.

Castles, S. (1994), 'Democracy and multicultural citizenship: Australian debates and their relevance for western Europe', in R. Bauböck (ed.), *From Aliens to Citizens*, Aldershot: Avebury, pp. 3–27.

Castles, S. (1998), 'Globalisation and the ambiguities of national citizenship', in R. Bauböck and J. Rundle (eds), *Blurred Boundaries: Migration, Ethnicity, Citizenship*, Aldershot: Avebury.

Castles, S. and Miller, M. (1998), *The Age of Migration: International Population Movements in the Modern World*, 2nd ed., Basingstoke: Macmillan.

Castles, S. and Miller, M. (2003), *The Age of Migration: International Population Movements in the Modern World*, 3rd ed., Basingstoke: Macmillan.

Cavalli-Sforza, L., Menozzi, P. and Piazza, A. (eds) (1994), *The History and Geography of Human Genes*, Princeton, NJ: Princeton University Press.

Cesarani, D. (1996), 'The changing character of citizenship in Britain and Europe', in D. Cesarani and M. Fulbrooke (eds), *Citizenship, Nationality and Migration in Europe*, London: Routledge.

Chaney, D. (1993), *Fictions of Collective Life*, London: Routledge.

Chapman, M., McDonald, M. and Tonkin, E. (1989), 'Introduction: history and social anthropology', in E. Tonkin, M. McDonald and M. Chapman (eds), *History and Ethnicity*, London: Routledge, pp. 1–21.

Cherniaev, A. (1993), *Shest' let s Gorbachevym*, Moscow: Progress.

Chodorow, N. (1978), *The Reproduction of Mothering*, Berkeley: University of California Press.

Chorbajian, L., Donabedian, P. and Mutafian, C. (1994), *The Caucasian Knot: The History and Geo-Politics of Nagorno-Karabakh*, London: Zed.

Çinar, D. (1994), 'From aliens to citizens: a comparative analysis of rules of transition', in R. Bauböck (ed.), *From Aliens to Citizens*, Aldershot: Avebury, pp. 49–72.

CNN (2001), 'Official: Florida disenfranchised minority voters', <http://www.cnn.com/2001/allpolitics/03/09/florida.election/index.htm1>.

Coakley, J. (ed.) (1992), *The Social Origins of Nationalist Movements*, London: Sage.

Cobban, A. (1968), *Rousseau and the Modern State*, London: George Allen and Unwin.

Cobban, A. (1969), *The Nation-State and National Self-Determination*, London: Fontana.

Cocks, J. (2002), *Passion and Paradox: Intellectuals Confront the National Question*, Princeton, NJ: Princeton University Press.

Cohen, A. (1985), *The Symbolic Construction of Community*, New York: Tavistock.

Cohen, A. (1994), *Self Consciousness: An Alternative Anthropology of Identity*, London: Routledge.

Cohen, R. (1978), 'Ethnicity: problem and focus in anthropology', *Annual Review of Anthropology*, 7, 379–404.

Cohen, R. (1997), 'Shaping the nation, excluding the other: the deportation of migrants from Britain', in J. Lucassen and L. Lucassen (eds), *Migration, Migration History, History*, Berne: Peter Lang.

Cohen, S. (1992), *Imagine There's No Countries: 1992 and International Immigration*

Controls against Migrants, Immigrants and Refugees, Manchester: Greater Manchester Immigration Aid Unit.

Cohn, C. (1987), 'Sex and death in the rational world of defense intellectuals', *Signs*, 12, 687–718.

Cohn, C. (1990), ' "Clean bombs" and clean language', in J. B. Elshtain and S. Tobias (eds), *Women, Militarism, and War: Essays in History, Politics, and Social Theory*, Savage, MD: Rowman and Littlefield, pp. 33–55.

Cohn, C. (1993), 'Wars, wimps, and women: talking gender and thinking war', in M.

Colley, L. (1992), *Britons: Forging the Nation 1707–1837*, New Haven, CT and London: Yale University Press.

Condor, S. (1996), 'Unimagined community? Some social psychological issues concerning English national identity', in G. Breakwell and E. Lyons (eds), *Changing European Identities*, Oxford: Butterworth-Heinemann.

Connell, R. (1987), *Gender and Power: Society, the Person and Sexual Politics*, Palo Alto, CA: Stanford University Press.

Connell, R. (1995), *Masculinities*, Berkeley: University of California Press.

Connor, W. (1972), 'Nation-building or nation-destroying?', *World Politics*, 24, 319–55.

Connor, W. (1978), 'A nation is a nation, is a state, is an ethnic group, is a . . .', *Ethnic and Racial Studies*, 1:4, 378–400.

Connor, W. (1990), 'When is a nation?', *Ethnic and Racial Studies*, 13:1, 92–103.

Connor, W. (1994), *Ethno-Nationalism: The Quest for Understanding*, Princeton, NJ: Princeton University Press.

Conversi, D. (1997), *The Basques, the Catalans and Spain: Alternative Routes to Nationalist Mobilisation*, London: C. Hurst.

Cross, M. (1995), 'Race, class formation and political interests: a comparison of Amsterdam and London', in A. Hargreaves and J. Leaman (eds), *Racism, Ethnicity and Politics in Contemporary Europe*, Aldershot: Edward Elgar, pp. 47–78.

Cross, M. and Keith, M. (1993), *Racism, the City and the State*, London: Routledge.

Croucher, S. (1998), 'South Africa's illegal aliens: constructing national boundaries in a post-apartheid state', *Ethnic and Racial Studies*, 21:4, 638–60.

Daniels, R. (1998), 'What is an American? Ethnicity, race, the Constitution and the immigrant in early American history', in D. Jacobson (ed.), *The Immigration Reader: America in a Multi-Disciplinary Perspective*, Oxford: Blackwell.

Dann, O. and Dinwiddy, J. (eds) (1988), *Nationalism in the Age of the French Revolution*, London: Hambledon Press.

Davidson, A. (1997), *From Subject to Citizen: Australian Citizenship in the Twentieth Century*, Cambridge: Cambridge University Press.

Davies, N. (1997), 'West best, East beast?', *Oxford Today*, 9:2.

Davis, H. (ed.) (1976), *Selected Writings by Rosa Luxemburg on the National Question*, New York: Monthly Review Press.

Davis, K., Liejenaar, M. and Oldersma, J. (1991), *The Gender of Power*, Newbury Park, CA: Sage.

Delanty, G. (1995), *Inventing Europe: Idea, Identity, Reality*, Basingstoke: Macmillan.

Denitch, B. (1996), *Ethnic Nationalism: The Tragic Death of Yugoslavia*, Minneapolis: University of Minnesota Press.

Deutsch, K. (1966), *Nationalism and Social Communication*, Cambridge, MA: MIT Press.

Donaldson, M. (1993), 'What is hegemonic masculinity?', *Theory and Society*, 22, 643–57.

Duignan, P. and Gann, L. (1998), *The Debate in the United States over Immigration*, Stanford, CA: Hoover Institution Press.

Dumont, L. (1992), *L'Idéologie allemande*, Paris: Seuil.

Dunn, J. (1990), *Interpreting Political Responsibility*, Cambridge: Polity Press.

Duroche, L. (1991), 'Men fearing men: on the nineteenth-century origins of modern homophobia', *Men's Studies Review*, 8, 3–7.

Eagleton, T. (1991), *Ideology: An Introduction*, London: Verso.

The Economist (1995), 'The world economy: who's in the driving seat?', 7 October.

Edgerton, L. (1987), 'Public protest, domestic acquiescence: women in Northern Ireland', in R. Ridd and H. Callaway (eds), *Women and Political Conflict*, New York: New York University Press, pp. 61–83.

Eisenstadt, S. and Rokkan, S. (1973), *Building States and Nations*, Beverly Hills, CA: Sage.

Eisenstein, E. (1968), 'Some conjectures about the impact of printing on Western society and thought: a preliminary report', *Journal of Modern History*, 40:1, 1–56.

Eisenstein, H. (1985), 'The gender of bureaucracy: reflections on feminism and the state', in J. Goodnow and C. Pateman (eds), *Women: Social Science and Public Policy*, Sydney: Allen and Unwin, pp. 104–15.

Eisinger, P. (1973), 'The conditions of protest behavior in American cities', *American Political Science Review*, 67, 11–28.

El-Solh, C. and Mabro, J. (1994), 'Introduction: Islam and Muslim women', in C. El-Solh and J. Mabro (eds), *Muslim Women's Choices: Religious Belief and Social Reality*, Providence, RI: Berg, pp. 1–32.

Enloe, C. (1990), *Bananas, Beaches, and Bases: Making Feminist Sense of International Politics*, Berkeley: University of California Press.

Enloe, C. (1993), *The Morning After: Sexual Politics at the End of the Cold War*, Berkeley: University of California Press.

Eriksen, T. (1988), *Communicating Cultural Difference and Identity: Ethnicity and Nationalism in Mauritius*, Oslo: Department of Social Anthropology, University of Oslo.

Eriksen, T. (1990), 'Linguistic diversity and the quest for national identity: the case of Mauritius', *Ethnic and Racial Studies*, 13:1, 1–24.

Eriksen, T. (1991), 'Ethnicity versus nationalism', *Journal of Peace Research*, 28:3, 263–78.

Eriksen, T. (1992), *Us and Them in Modern Societies: Ethnicity and Nationalism in Trinidad, Mauritius and Beyond*, Oslo: Scandinavian University Press.

Eriksen, T. (1993a), *Ethnicity and Nationalism*, London and Boulder, CO: Pluto Press.

Eriksen, T. (1993b), 'Formal and informal nationalism', *Ethnic and Racial Studies*, 16:1, 1–25.

Eriksen, T. (1993c), 'A non-ethnic, future-oriented nationalism? Mauritius as an exemplary case', *Ethnos*, 58:3–4, 197–221.

Eriksen, T. (1998), *Common Denominators: Politics, Ideology and Compromise in Mauritius*, Oxford: Berg.

Espiritu, Y. (1996), *Asian American Women and Men: Labor, Laws, and Love*, Thousand Oaks, CA: Sage.

Fairclough, N. (1992), *Discourse and Social Change*, Cambridge: Polity Press.

Feagin, J. (1997), 'Old wine in new bottles', in J. Perea (ed.), *Immigrants Out! The New Nativism and the Anti-Immigrant Impulse in the United States*, New York: New York University Press.

Featherstone, M. (1990), 'Global culture: an introduction', *Theory, Culture and Society*, 7.

Febvre, L. and Martin, H-J. (1976), *The Coming of the Book: The Impact of Printing 1450–1800*, tr. D. Gerard, London: New Left Books.

Fenton, S. (1999), *Ethnicity: Racism, Class and Culture*, London: Macmillan.

Finley, M. (1986), *The Use and Abuse of History*, London: Hogarth Press.

Firth, R. (1973), *Symbols: Public and Private*, London: George Allen and Unwin.

Fishman, J., Ferguson, C. and Dasgupta, J. (1968), *Language Problems of Developing Countries*, New York: John Wiley and Sons.

Fondation Hardt (1962), *Entretiens sur l'antiquité classique VIII: Grecs et barbares*, Geneva: Fondation Hardt.

Forsythe, D. (1989), 'German identity and the problem of history', in E. Tonkin, M. McDonald and M. Chapman (eds), *History and Ethnicity*, London: Routledge, pp. 137–56.

Franzway, S., Court, D. and Connell, R. W. (1989), *Staking a Claim: Feminism, Bureaucracy, and the State*, Cambridge: Polity Press.

Freud, S. (1923), *The Standard Edition of the Complete Psychological Works of Sigmund Freud, vol. 21: The Ego and the Id*, London: Hogarth Press and Institute of Psychoanalysis.

Gadamer, G-H. (1975), *Truth and Method*, London: Sheed and Ward.

Gaitskell, D. and Unterhalter, E. (1989), 'Mothers of the nation: a comparative analysis of nation, race, and motherhood in Afrikaner Nationalism and the African National Congress', in N. Yuval-Davis and F. Anthias (eds), *Woman-Nation-State*, New York: St Martin's Press, pp. 58–78.

Geertz, C. (1963), 'The integrative revolution: primordial sentiments and civil politics in the new states', in C. Geertz (ed.), *Old Societies and New States*, New York: Free Press, pp. 105–57.

Gellner, E. (1964), *Thought and Change*, London: Weidenfeld and Nicolson.

Gellner, E. (1983), *Nations and Nationalism*, Oxford: Blackwell.

Gellner, E. (1988), *Plough, Sword and Book: The Structure of Human History*, London: Collins Harvill.

Gellner, E. (1994a), *Conditions of Liberty: Civil Society and Its Rivals*, London: Hamish Hamilton.

Gellner, E. (1994b), *Encounters with Nationalism*, Cambridge, MA: Blackwell.

Gellner, E. and Ionescu, G. (eds) (1970), *Populism: Its Meanings and National Characteristics*, London: Weidenfeld and Nicolson.

Gerth, H. H. and Mills, C. (1948), *From Max Weber: Essays in Sociology*, London: Routledge and Kegan Paul.

Gerzon, M. (1982), *A Choice of Heroes: The Changing Faces of American Manhood*, Boston: Houghton Mifflin.

Gibson, J. (1994), *Warrior Dreams: Violence and Manhood in Post-Vietnam America*, New York: Hill and Wang.

Giddens, A. (1985), *A Contemporary Critique of Historical Materialism, vol. 2: The Nation-State and Violence*, Cambridge: Polity Press.

Giddens, A. (1987), *Social Theory and Modern Sociology*, Cambridge: Polity Press.

Giddens, A. (1991), *Modernity and Self-Identity*, Cambridge: Polity Press.

Giddens, A. (1993), *Sociology*, Cambridge: Polity Press.

Giddens, A. (1999a), *The Third Way*, Cambridge: Polity Press.

Giddens, A. (1999b), *Runaway World*, London: Profile.

Gildea, R. (1994), *The Past in French History*, New Haven, CT and London: Yale University Press.

Gilmore, D. (1990), *Manhood in the Making: Cultural Concepts of Masculinity*, New Haven, CT: Yale University Press.

Gilroy, P. (1993), 'The peculiarities of the black English', in P. Gilroy, *Small Acts: Thoughts on the Politics of Black Cultures*, London: Serpent's Tail.

Gilroy, P. (2000), *Against Race: Imagining Political Culture beyond the Color Line*, Cambridge, MA Belknap Press.

Glazer, N. and Moynihan, D. (1975), *Beyond the Melting-Pot*, Cambridge, MA: Harvard University Press.

Goodwin-White, J. (1998), 'Where the maps are not yet finished', in D. Jacobson (ed.), *The Immigration Reader: America in a Multi-Disciplinary Perspective*, Oxford: Blackwell.

Gorbachev, M. (1995), *Zhizn' i reformy, vol. 1*, Moscow: Novosti.

Grant, J. and Tancred, P. (1992), 'A feminist perspective on state bureaucracy', in A. J. Mills and P. Tancred (eds), *Gendering Organizational Analysis*, Newbury Park, CA: Sage, pp. 112–28.

Green, M. (1993), *The Adventurous Male: Chapters in the History of the White Male Mind*, University Park, PA: Penn State University Press.

Greenfeld, L. (1992), *Nationalism: Five Roads to Modernity*, Cambridge: Cambridge University Press.

Gregory, J. (1987), *Sex, Race and the Law*, London: Sage.

Guibernau, M. (1996), *Nationalisms: The Nation-State and Nationalism in the Twentieth Century*, Cambridge: Polity Press.

Guibernau, M. (1999), *Nations Without States*, Cambridge: Polity Press.

Guimezanes, N. (1995), 'Acquisition of nationality in OECD countries', in OECD (ed.), *Trends in International Migration: Annual Report*, Paris, OECD, pp. 157–79.

Gurr, T. (1970), *Why Men Rebel*, Princeton, NJ: Princeton University Press.

Habermas, J. (1994), 'Struggles for recognition in the democratic constitutional state', in A. Gutmann (ed.), *Multiculturalism: Examining the Politics of Recognition*, Princeton, NJ: Princeton University Press, pp. 107–48.

Hainsworth, P. (1992), 'The extreme right in post-war France: the emergence and success of the Front National', in P. Hainsworth (ed.), *The Extreme Right in Europe and the USA*, London: Pinter.

Halbwachs, M. (1980), *The Collective Memory*, New York: Harper and Row.

Hall, S. (1992a), 'The question of cultural identity', in S. Hall, D. Held and A. McGrew (eds), *Global Culture: Nationalism, Globalization and Modernity*, London: Sage, pp. 237–51.

Hall, S. (1992b), 'The West and the rest', in S. Hall and B. Gieben (eds), *Formations of Modernity*, Cambridge: Polity Press.

Hammar, T. (1990), *Democracy and the Nation-State: Aliens, Denizens and Citizens in a World of International Migration*, Aldershot: Avebury.

Hart, G. (1991), 'Engendering everyday resistance: gender, patronage, and production in politics in rural Malaysia', *Journal of Peasant Studies*, 19, 93–121.

Hartsock, N. (1983), *Money, Sex, and Power: Toward a Feminist Historical Materialism*, New York: Longman.

Hartsock, N. (1984), 'Prologue to a feminist critique of war and polities', in J. Stiehm (ed.), *Women's Views of the Political World of Men*, Dobbs Ferry, NY: Transnational Publishers, pp. 123–50.

Harvey, D. (1989), *The Condition of Postmodernity*, Oxford: Blackwell.

Hasan, Z. (1994), 'Introduction: contextualising gender and identity in contemporary India', in Z. Hasan (ed.), *Forging Identities: Gender, Communities, and State in India*, Boulder, CO: Westview Press, pp. viii–xxiv.

Hastings, A. (1997), *The Construction of Nationhood: Ethnicity, Religion and Nationalism*, Cambridge: Cambridge University Press.

Hatton, T. and Williamson, J. (1998), *The Age of Mass Migration*, Oxford: Oxford University Press.

Hayes, C. (1931), *The Historical Evolution of Nationalism*, New York: Russell and Russell.

Hayter, T. (2000), *Open Borders: The Case against Immigration Controls*, London: Pluto Press.

Hearn, J. (1987), *The Gender of Oppression*, Brighton: Wheatsheaf.

Hearn, J. (1992), *Men in the Public Eye: The Construction and Deconstruction of Public Men and Public Patriarchies*, London: Routledge.

Heesterman, J. C. (1978), 'Was there an Indian reaction? Western expansion in Indian perspective', in H. L. Wesseling (ed.), *Expansion and Reaction: Essays on European Expansion and Reaction in Asia and Africa*, Leiden: Leiden University Press, pp. 31–58.

Held, D. (1995), *Democracy and the Global Order: From the Modern State to Cosmopolitan Governance*, Cambridge: Polity Press.

Held, D. (1996), *Models of Democracy*, 2nd ed., Cambridge: Polity Press.

Held, D. and McGrew, A. (eds) (2000), *The Global Transformation Reader*, Cambridge: Polity Press.

Held, D., McGrew, A., Goldblatt, D. and Perraton, J. (1999), *Global Transformations: Politics, Economics and Culture*, Cambridge: Polity Press.

Hélie-Lucas, M.-A. (1988), 'The role of women during the Algerian liberation struggle and after: nationalism as a concept and as a practice towards both the power of the army and the militarization of the people', in T. E. Isaksson (ed.), *Women and the Military System*, New York: St Martin's Press, pp. 171–89.

Herder, J. (1969), 'Essay on the origin of language', in J. Herder, *J. G. Herder on Social and Political Culture*, tr. and ed. F. Barnard, Cambridge: Cambridge University Press.

Hernes, H. (1987), *Welfare State and Woman Power: Essays in State Feminism*, New York: Oxford University Press.

Hobsbawm, E. (1990), *Nations and Nationalism since 1780: Programme, Myth, Reality*, Cambridge: Cambridge University Press.

Hobsbawm, E. (1992), 'Nationalism: whose fault-line is it anyway?', *Anthropology Today*, February.

Hobsbawm, E. and Ranger, T. (1983), *The Invention of Tradition*, Cambridge: Cambridge University Press.

Hoff, J. (1994), 'Citizenship and nationalism', *Journal of Women's History*, 6:1, 1–6.

Hoganson, K. (1995), 'The manly ideals of politics and the imperialist impulse: gender, US political culture and the Spanish-American Wars', PhD dissertation, Yale University.

Haganson, K. (1996), 'Fighting over the fathers: the gendered and generational bases of political legitimacy in the Philippine debate 1898–1902', paper presented at the annual meeting of the Men's Studies Association, Washington, DC, March.

Holy, L. (1996), *The Little Czech and the Great Czech Nation*, Cambridge: Cambridge University Press.

Horowitz, D. (1985), *Ethnic Groups in Conflict*, Berkeley and Los Angeles: University of California Press.

Horowitz, D. (1998), 'Immigration and group politics in France and America', in D. Jacobson (ed.), *The Immigration Reader: America in a Multi-Disciplinary Perspective*, Oxford: Blackwell.

Horrocks, R. (1994), *Masculinity in Crisis: Myths, Fantasies, and Realities*, New York: St Martin's Press.

Hosking, G. and Schöpflin, G. (eds) (1997), *Myths and Nationhood*, London: C. Hurst.

HREOC (Human Rights and Equal Opportunity Commission) (1991), *Racist Violence: Report of the National Inquiry into Racist Violence in Australia*, Canberra: AGPS.

Hroch, M. (1985), *Social Preconditions of National Revival in Europe: A Comparative Analysis of the Social Composition of Patriotic Groups among the Smaller European Nations*, Cambridge: Cambridge University Press.

Hufton, O. (1992), *Women and the Limits of Citizenship in the French Revolution*, Toronto: University of Toronto Press.

Human Rights Watch (1998), *'Prohibited Persons': Abuse of Undocumented Migrants, Asylum Seekers, and Refugees in South Africa*, New York: Human Rights Watch, <http://www.hrw.org/reports98/sareport>.

Husbands, C. (1992), 'Belgium: Flemish legions on the march', in P. Hainsworth (ed.), *The Extreme Right in Europe and the USA*, London: Pinter.

Hutchinson, J. (1987), *The Dynamics of Cultural Nationalism: The Gaelic Revival and the Creation of the Irish Nation State*, London: Allen and Unwin.

Hutchinson, J. (1994), *Modern Nationalism*, London: Fontana.

Ignatieff, M. (1993), *Blood and Belonging: Journeys into the New Nationalism*, London: BBC/Chatto and Windus.

Ignatieff, M. (1994), *Blood and Belonging: Journeys into the New Nationalism*, pbk ed., London: Vintage.

Jacobson, D. (1997), *Rights across Borders: Immigration and the Decline of Citizenship*, Baltimore: Johns Hopkins University Press.

Jacobson, D. (1998) 'Introduction: an American journey', in D. Jacobson (ed.), *The Immigration Reader: America in a Multidisciplinary Perspective*, Oxford: Blackwell.

Jayawardena, K. (1986), *Feminism and Nationalism in the Third World*, London: Zed.

Jenkins, B. and Sofos, A. S. (eds) (1996), *Nation and Identity in Contemporary Europe*, London: Routledge.

Jenkins, R. (1986), 'Social anthropological models of inter-ethnic relations', in J. Rex and D. Mason (eds), *Theories of Race and Race Relations*, Cambridge: Cambridge University Press, pp. 170–86.

Jenkins, R. (1997), *Rethinking Ethnicity: Arguments and Explorations*, London: Sage.

Jennings, H. and Madge, C. (1987), *May 12 1937: Mass Observation Day Survey*, London: Faber and Faber.

Jennings, I. (1956) *The Approach to Self-Government*, Cambridge: Cambridge University Press.

Jones, A. (1994), 'Gender and ethnic conflict in ex-Yugoslavia', *Ethnic and Racial Studies*, 17:1, 114–34.

Julius Caesar (1951), *The Conquest of Gaul*, Baltimore: Penguin.

Kandiyoti, D. (1991), *Women, Islam, and the State*, Philadelphia: Temple University Press.

Kapferer, B. (1988), *Legends of People, Myths of State: Violence, Intolerance, and Political Culture in Sri Lanka and Australia*, Washington: Smithsonian Institution Press.

Kaplan, T. (1982), 'Female consciousness and collective action: the case of Barcelona 1910–1918', *Signs*, 7, 545–66.

Karlen, A. (1971), *Sexuality and Homosexuality: A New View*, New York: W. W. Norton.

Kauffman, C. (1982), *Faith and Fraternalism: The History of the Knights of Columbus 1882–1982*, New York: Harper and Row.

Keating, M. (2001), *Nations against the State: The New Politics of Nationalism in Quebec, Catalonia and Scotland*, 2nd ed., Basingstoke: Macmillan.

Keck, M. and Sikkink, K. (1998), *Activists beyond Borders*, Ithaca, NY: Cornell University Press.

Kedourie, E. (1960), *Nationalism*, 3rd ed., London: Hutchinson.

Kedourie, E. (1993), *Nationalism*, 4th ed., Oxford: Blackwell.

Keeley, C. (1993), 'The USA: retaining a fair immigration policy', in D. Kubat (ed.), *The Politics of Migration Policies*, 2nd ed., New York: Centre for Migration Studies.

Kellas, J. (1991), *The Politics of Nationalism and Ethnicity*, London: Macmillan.

Kemiläinen, A. (1964), *Nationalism: Problems Concerning the Word, the Concept and Classification*, Jyväskylä: Kustantajat.

Kennedy, M., Lubelska, C. and Walsh, V. (1992), *Making Connections: Women's Studies, Women's Movements, Women's Lives*, London: Taylor and Francis.

Kimmel, M. (1995), *Manhood in America: A Cultural History*, New York: Basic Books.

Kimmel, M. and Messner, M. (1995), *Men's Lives*, New York: Allyn and Bacon.

Kionka, R. and Vetik, P. (1996), 'Estonia and the Estonians', in G. Smith, *The Nationalities Question in the Post-Soviet States*, Basingstoke: Macmillan.

Klandermans, B. (1992), 'The social construction of protest and multiorganizational fields', in A. Morris and C. McClurg Mueller (eds), *Frontiers in Social Movement Theory*, New Haven, CT: Yale University Press, pp. 77–103.

Kohn, H. (1944), *The Idea of Nationalism: A Study in its Origins and Background*, New York: Collier.

Kohn, H. (1962), *The Age of Nationalism*, New York: Harper.

Kohn, H. (1965), *Nationalism: Its Meaning and History*, New York: Anvil.

Kohn, H. (1967), *The Idea of Nationalism: A Study in Its Origins and Background*, New York: Collier.

Koonz, C. (1987), *Mothers in the Fatherland: Women, the Family, and Nazi Politics*, New York: St Martin's Press.

Koven, S. (1991), 'From rough lads to hooligans: boy life, national culture, and social reform', in A. Parker, M. Russo, D. Sommer and P. Yaeger (eds), *Nationalisms and Sexualities*, New York: Routledge, pp. 365–91.

Kumar, A. (1972), 'Diponegoro (1778?–1855)', *Indonesia*, 13, 69–118.

Kuran, T. (1989), 'Sparks and prairie fires: a theory of unanticipated political revolution', *Public Choice*, 61:1, 41–74.

Kutschera, C. (1996), 'Algeria's fighting women', *Middle East*, April, 40–41.

Langer, E. (1989), *Mindfulness*, Reading, MA: Addison-Wesley.

Lartichaux, J.-Y. (1977), 'Linguistic politics during the French Revolution', *Diogenes*, 97, 65–84.

Lash, S. and Urry, J. (1994), *Economies of Signs and Space*, London: Sage.

Lawrence, T. E. (1926), *Seven Pillars of Wisdom: A Triumph*, New York: Doubleday.

Layoun, M. (1991), 'Telling spaces: Palestinian women and the engendering of national narratives', in A. Parker, M. Russo, D. Sommer and P. Yaeger (eds), *Nationalisms and Sexualities*, New York: Routledge, pp. 407–23.

Levant, R. (1997), 'The masculinity crisis', *Journal of Men's Studies*, 5, 221–31.

Leverenz, D. (1989), *Manhood and the American Renaissance*, Ithaca, NY: Cornell University Press.

Liebes, T. and Katz, E. (1993), *The Export of Meaning: Cross-Cultural Readings of Dallas*, Cambridge: Polity Press.

Lievesley, G. (1996), 'Stages of growth? Women dealing with the state and each other in Peru', in S. M. Rai and G. Lievesley (eds), *Women and the State: International Perspectives*, London: Taylor and Francis, pp. 45–60.

Lipset, S. (1963), *Political Man*, London: Heinemann.

Llobera, J. (1994), *The God of Modernity*, Oxford: Berg.

Lloyd, C. (1998), *Discourses of Anti-Recism in France*, Aldershot: Ashgate.

Lucassen, J. and Lucassen, L. (1997), 'Introduction: old paradigms and new perspectives', in J. Lucassen and L. Lucassen (eds), *Migration, Migration History, History*, Berne: Peter Lang.

Lustick, I. (1993), *Unsettled States, Disputed Lands: Britain and Ireland, France and Algeria, Israel and the West Bank-Gaza*, Ithaca, NY: Cornell University Press.

Luszki, W. (1991), *A Rape of Justice: MacArthur and the New Guinea Hangings*, Lanham, MD: Madison.

Lutz, H., Phoenix, A. and Yuval-Davis, N. (1995), 'Introduction: nationalism, racism and gender', in H. Lutz, A. Phoenix and N. Yuval-Davis (eds), *Crossfires: Nationalism, Racism and Gender in Europe*, London: Pluto Press, pp. 1–25.

MacAloon, J. (1981), *This Great Symbol: Pierre de Coubertin and the Origins of the Modern Olympic Games*, Chicago: University of Chicago Press.

MacAloon, J. (1984), 'Olympic Games and the theory of spectacle in modern societies', in J. MacAloon (ed.), *Rite, Drama, Festival, Spectacle: Rehearsals toward a Theory of Cultural Performances*, Philadelphia: Institute for the Study of Human Issues, pp. 241–80.

MacClancy, J. (ed.) (1996), *Sport, Identity and Ethnicity*, Oxford: Berg.

MacIntyre, A. (1981), *After Virtue*, London: Duckworth.

MacIntyre, A. (1988), *Whose Justice? Which Rationality?*, London: Duckworth.

MacKenzie, J. (1987), 'The imperial pioneer and hunter and the British masculine stereotype in late Victorian and Edwardian times', in J. A. Mangan and J. Walvin (eds), *Manliness and Morality: Middle-Class Masculinity in Britain and America 1800–1940*, Manchester: Manchester University Press, pp. 176–98.

MacKinnon, C. (1989), *Toward a Feminist Theory of the State*, Cambridge, MA: Harvard University Press.

Macleod, A. (1991), *Accommodating Protest: Working Women, the New Veiling, and Change in Cairo*, New York: Columbia University Press.

Makhlouf, C. (1979), *Changing Veils: Women and Modernisation in North Yemen*, Austin: University of Texas Press.

Malik, K. (1996), *The Meaning of Race: Race, History and Culture in Western Society*, Basingstoke: Macmillan.

Manastra, N. (1993), 'Palestinian women: between tradition and revolution', in E. Augustin (ed.), *Palestinian Women: Identity and Experience*, London: Zed, pp. 7–21.

Mann, M. (1986), *The Sources of Social Power, vol. 1: A History of Power from the Beginning to* AD1760, Cambridge: Cambridge University Press.

Mann, M. (1987), 'Ruling strategies and citizenship', *Sociology*, 21:3, 339–54.

Mann, M. (1993a), 'Nation-states in Europe and other continents: diversifying, developing, not dying', *Dædalus*, Summer.

Mann, M. (1993b), *The Sources of Social Power, vol. 2: The Rise of Classes and Nation States 1760–1914*, Cambridge: Cambridge University Press.

Marshall, T. H. (1950), *Citizenship and Social Class*, Cambridge: Cambridge University Press.

Marshall, T. H. (1963), *Class, Citizenship, and Social Development*, Westport, CT: Greenwood.

Marshall, T. H. (1964), 'Citizenship and social class', in T. H. Marshall, *Class, Citizenship, and Social Development: Essays by T. H. Marshall*, New York: Anchor.

Martiniello, M. (1994), 'Citizenship of the European Union: a critical view', in R. Bauböck (ed.), *From Aliens to Citizens*, Aldershot: Avebury, pp. 29–48.

Marvin, C. (1991), 'Theorizing the flagbody: symbolic dimensions of the flag', *Critical Studies in Mass Communication*, 8, 119–38.

Massad, J. (1995), 'Conceiving the masculine: gender and Palestinian nationalism', *Middle East Journal*, 49, 467–83.

Mattes, R., Taylor, D. M., McDonald, D. A., Poore, A. and Richmond, W. (1999), *Still Waiting for the Barbarians: SA Attitudes to Immigrants and Immigration*, Southern Africa Migration Project Migration Policy Series 14, Cape Town and Kingston, Ont.: Idasa/Queen's University.

Mazzini, G. (1891), *Life and Writings, Autobiographical and Political*, London: Smith, Elder.

McAdam, D. (1982), *Political Process and the Development of Black Insurgency 1930–1970*, Chicago: University of Chicago Press.

McClintock, A. (1991), ' "No longer in a future Heaven": woman and nationalism in South Africa', *Transition*, 51, 104–23.

McClintock, A. (1995), *Imperial Leather: Race, Gender and Sexuality in the Colonial Contest*, London: Routledge.

McLellan, D. (1986), *Ideology*, Milton Keynes: Open University Press.

Medvedev, V. (1994), *V kommande Gorbacheva: Vzgliad iznutri*, Moscow: Bylina.

Meehan, E. (1993), *Citizenship and the European Community*, London: Sage.

Mehdid, M. (1996), 'En-gendering the nation-state: woman, patriarchy and politics in Algeria', in S. M. Rai and G. Lievesley (eds), *Women and the State: International Perspectives*, London: Taylor and Francis, pp. 78–102.

Meinecke, F. (1919), *Weltbürgertum und Nationalstaat*, 5th ed., Munich: R. Oldenbourg.

Mernissi, F. (1987), *Beyond the Veil: Male-Female Dynamics in Modern Islamic Societies*, Bloomington: University of Indiana Press.

Mertes, M. (1996), 'Germany's social and political culture: change through consensus?', in M. Mertes, M. Muller and H. Winkler (eds), *In Search of Germany*, New Brunswick, NJ: Transaction.

Messerschmidt, J. (1993), *Masculinities and Crime*, Lanham, MD: Rowman and Little-field.

Messner, M. (1997), *Politics of Masculinities: Men in Movements*, Thousand Oaks, CA: Sage.

Migration News (1998), 'South Africa', *Migration News*, 5:11, <http://migration.ucdavis.edu/mn/more.php?id=1684_0_5_0>.

Miles, R. (1987), 'Recent marxist theories of nationalism and the issue of racism', *British Journal of Sociology*, 38:1, 24–43.

Mill, J. S. (1996), 'On nationality', in S. Woolf, (ed.), *Nationalism in Europe 1815 to the Present*, London: Routledge.

Millar, F., Frye, R., Berciu, D., Talbot Rice, T. and Kossack, G. (1967), *The Roman Empire and Its Neighbours*, London: Weidenfeld and Nicolson.

Miller, D. (1988), 'The ethical significance of nationality', *Ethics*, 98, 647–62.

Miller, D. (1992), '*The Young and the Restless* in Trinidad: a case of the local and the global in mass consumption', in R. Silverstone and E. Hirsch (eds), *Consuming Technology*, London: Routledge, pp. 163–82.

Miller, D. (1995), *On Nationality*, Oxford: Oxford University Press.

Miller, D. (1999), 'Justice and inequality', in A. Hurrell and N. Woods (eds), *Inequality, Globalization, and World Politics*, Oxford: Oxford University Press, pp. 147–210.

Mingione, E. (1996), 'Urban poverty in the advanced industrial world: concepts, analysis and debates', in E. Mingione (ed.), *Urban Poverty and the Underclass*, Oxford: Blackwell, pp. 3–40.

Mitchell, J. (1996), *Strategies for Self-Government: The Campaigns for a Scottish Parliament*, Edinburgh: Polygon.

Mitchison, R. (ed.) (1980), *The Roots of Nationalism: Studies in Northern Europe*, Edinburgh: John Donald.

Moghadam, V. (1991a), 'Neo-patriarchy in the Middle East', in H. Bresheeth and N. Yuval (eds), *The Gulf War and the New World Order*, London: Zed.

Moghadam, V. (1991b), 'Revolution, Islam, and women: sexual politics in Iran and Afghanistan', in A. Parker, M. Russo, D. Sommer and P. Yaeger (eds), *Nationalisms and Sexualities*, New York: Routledge, pp. 424–46.

Moghadam, V. (ed.) (1994), *Gender and National Identity: Women and Politics in Muslim Societies*, London: Zed.

Moore, B. Jr (1966), *The Social Origins of Dictatorship and Democracy: Lord and Peasant in the Making of the Modern World*, Boston: Beacon Press.

Morgan, D. (1992), *Discovering Men*, London: Routledge.

Morris, E. (1979), *The Rise of Theodore Roosevelt*, New York: Ballantine.

Moruzzi, N. (1994), 'A problem with headscarves: contemporary complexities of political and social identity', *Political Theory*, 22:4, 653–72.

Moscovici, S. (1983), 'The phenomenon of social representations', in R. Farr and S.

Moscovici (eds), *Social Representations*, Cambridge: Cambridge University Press.

Mosse, G. (1985), *Nationalism and Sexuality: Middle-Class Morality and Sexual Norms in Modern Europe*, Madison: University of Wisconsin Press.

Mosse, G. (1996), *The Image of Man: The Creation of Modern Masculinity*, New York: Oxford University Press.

Motyl, A. (1990), *Sovietology, Rationality, Nationality: Coming to Grips with Nationalism in the USSR*, New York: Columbia University Press.

Muiznieks, N. (1995), 'The influence of the Baltic popular movements on the process of Soviet disintegration', *Europe-Asia Studies*, 47:1, 3–26.

Mukarker, F. (1993), 'Life between Palestine and Germany: two cultures, two lives', in E. Augustin (ed.), *Palestinian Women: Identity and Experience*, London: Zed, pp. 93–107.

Nagel, J. (1996), *American Indian Ethnic Renewal: Red Power and the Resurgence of Identity and Culture*, New York: Oxford University Press.

Nairn, T. (1977), *The Break-Up of Britain: Crisis and Neo-Nationalism*, London: New Left Books.

Nairn, T. (ed.) (1997a), *Faces of Nationalism: Janus Revisited*, London: Verso.

Nairn, T. (1997b), 'Introduction: on studying nationalism', in T. Nairn (ed.), *Faces of Nationalism: Janus Revisited*, London: Verso.

Nakano Glenn, E. (1995), 'The race and gender construction of citizenship: from categorical exclusion to stratified citizenship', paper presented at the annual meeting of the American Sociological Association, Washington, DC, August.

Nategh, H. (1987), 'Women: damned of the Iranian Revolution', in R. Ridd and H. Callaway, *Women and Political Conflict*, New York: New York University Press, pp. 45–60.

Noiriel, G. (1988), *Le Creuset français: Histoire de l'immigration XIXe–XXe siècles*, Paris: Seuil.

Noiriel, G. (1993), *La Tyrannie du national: Le Droit d'asile en Europe 1793–1993*, Paris: Calmann-Lévy.

Nørgaard, O. et al (1996), *The Baltic States after Independence*, Cheltenham: Edward Elgar.

Nye, R. (1993), *Masculinity and Male Codes of Honour in Modern France*, New York: Oxford University Press.

OECD (1997), *Communications Outlook*, Paris: Organization for Economic Cooperation and Development.

Oliver, P. (1989), 'Bringing the crowd back in: the nonorganizational elements of social movements', in L. Kriesberg (ed.), *Research in Social Movements, Conflicts and Change, vol. 11*, Greenwich, CT: JAI Press, pp. 1–30.

O'Neill, O. (1991), 'Transnational justice', in D. Held (ed.), *Political Theory Today*, Cambridge: Polity Press, pp. 276–304.

Oommen, T. (1997), *Citizenship and National Identity from Colonialism to Globalism*, New Delhi: Sage.

Orr, J. (1994), 'Masculinity in trouble: a comparison of the primitive masculinity movement of the late 19th century and the modern mythopoetic men's movement', paper presented at the annual meeting of the Midwest Sociological Society, March, St Louis.

Pateman, C. (1988), *The Sexual Contract*, Cambridge: Polity Press.

Pateman, C. (1989), *The Disorder of Women: Democracy, Feminism and Political Theory*, Palo Alto, CA: Stanford University Press.

Paul, K. (1997), *Whitewashing Britain: Race and Citizenship in the Postwar Era*, New York: Cornell University Press.

Peel, J. (1989), 'The cultural work of Yoruba ethno-genesis', in E. Tonkin, M. McDonald and M. Chapman (eds) (1989), *History and Ethnicity*, London and New York: Routledge, pp. 198–215.

Perea, J. (1997), 'Introduction', in J. Perea (ed.), *Immigrants Out! The New Nativism and the Anti-Immigrant Impulse in the United States*, New York: New York University Press.

Perrin, W. G. (1922), *British Flags: Their Early History and Their Development at Sea*, Cambridge: Cambridge University Press.

Pfaff, W. (1993), *The Wrath of Nations: Civilization and the Furies of Nationalism*, New York: Touchstone.

Pfeil, F. (1994), 'No Basta Teorizar: in-difference to solidarity in contemporary fiction, theory, and practice', in I. Grewal and C. Kaplan (eds), *Scattered Hegemonies: Postmodemity and Transnational Feminist Practices*, Minneapolis: University of Minnesota Press, pp. 197–230.

Pfeil, F. (1995), *White Guys: Studies in Postmodern Domination and Difference*, London: Verso.

Pinard, M. and Hamilton, R. (1984), 'The class bases of the Quebec independence movement: conjectures and evidence', *Ethnic and Racial Studies*, 7:1, 19–54.

Plamenatz, J. (1976), 'Two types of nationalism', in E. Kamenka (ed.), *Nationalism: The Nature and Evolution of an Idea*, London: Edward Arnold.

Poliakov, L. (1974), *The Aryan Myth*, New York: Basic Books.

Polo, M. (1946), *The Travels of Marco Polo*, tr. and ed. W. Marsden, London and New York: Everyman's Library.

Popov, G. (1994), *Snova v oppozitsii*, Moscow: Galaktika.

Preuss, A. (1924), *A Dictionary of Secret and Other Societies*, St Louis: B. Herder.

Rawls, J. (1971), *A Theory of Justice*, Oxford: Oxford University Press, p. 4.

Rawls, J. (1985), 'Justice as fairness: political not metaphysical', *Philosophy and Public Affairs*, 14:3, 223–51.

Reimers, D. (1998), *Unwelcome Strangers: American Identity and the Turn against Immigration*, New York: Columbia University Press.

Renan, E. (1990), 'What is a nation?', in H. Bhabha (ed.), *Nation and Narration*, London: Routledge.

Renan, E. (1992), *Qu'est-ce qu'une nation? et autres essais politiques*, intr. J. Roman, Paris: Presses Pocket.

Renan, E. (1994), 'What is a nation?', in J. Hutchinson and A. Smith (eds), *Nationalism*, Oxford: Oxford University Press.

Renan, E. (1996), 'What is a nation?', in S. Woolf (ed.), *Nationalism in Europe 1815 to the Present*, London: Routledge.

Reynolds, S. (1983), 'Medieval *origines gentium* and the community of the realm', *History*, 68, 375–90.

Rich, P. (1990), 'Patriotism and the idea of citizenship in postwar British politics', in E. Vogel and M. Moran (eds), *Frontiers of Citizenship*, New York: St. Martin's Press.

Ricoeur, P. (1986), *Lectures on Ideology and Utopia*, New York: Columbia University Press.

Rodan, G. (ed.) (1996), *Political Oppositions in Industralising Asia*, London: Routledge.

Rogowski, R. (1985), 'Causes and varieties of nationalism: a rationalist account', in E. Tiryakian and R. Rogowski (eds), *New Nationalisms of the Developed West*, Boston: Allen and Unwin.

Rosenberg, C. (1980), 'Sexuality, class and role in 19th-century America', in E. Pleck and J. H. Pleck (eds), *The American Man*, Englewood Cliffs, NJ: Prentice-Hall, pp. 219–54.

Rotundo, A. (1987), 'Learning about manhood: gender ideals and the middle-class family in nineteenth-century America', in J. A. Mangan and J. Walvin (eds), *Manliness and Morality: Middle-Class Masculinity in Britain and America 1800–1940*, Manchester: Manchester University Press, pp. 35–51.

Rotundo, A. (1993), *American Manhood: Transformations in Masculinity from the Revolution to the Modern Era*, New York: Basic Books.

Rupp, L. and Taylor, V. (1987), *Survival in the Doldrums: The American Women's Rights Movement 1945 to the 1960s*, New York: Oxford University Press.

Rustow, D. (1967), *A World of Nations*, Washington: Brookings Institution.

Ryzhkov, N. (1992), *Perestroika: Istoriia predatel'stv*, Moscow: Novosti.

Safran, W. (1993) 'The National Front in France – from lunatic fringe to limited respectability', in P. Merkl and L. Weinberg (eds), *Encounters with the Contemporary Radical Right*, Oxford: Westview Press.

Sahlins, P. (1989), *Boundaries: The Making of France and Spain in the Pyrenees*, Berkeley: University of California Press.

Said, E. (1985), *Orientalism*, Harmondsworth: Penguin.

Salas, E. (1994), 'The Soldadera in the Mexican Revolution: war and men's illusions', in H. Fowler-Salamini and M. K. Vaughan (eds), *Women of the Mexican Countryside 1850–1990*, Tucson: University of Arizona Press, pp. 93–105.

Saunders, K. (1995), 'In a cloud of lust: black GIs and sex in World War II', in J. Damousi and M. Lake (eds), *Gender and War: Australians at War in the Twentieth Century*, Cambridge: Cambridge University Press, pp. 178–90.

Sayigh, R. and Peteet, J. (1987), 'Between two fires: Palestinian women in Lebanon', in R. Ridd and H. Callaway, *Women and Political Conflict*, New York: New York University Press, pp. 106–37.

Schama, S. (1987), *The Embarrassment of Riches: An Interpretation of Dutch Culture in the Golden Age*, London: Collins.

Scheffler, S. (1999), 'Conceptions of cosmopolitanism', *Utilitas*, 11:3, 255–76.

Schierup, C.-U. (1997), 'Multipoverty Europe: reflections on migration, citizenship and social exclusion in the European Union and the United States', Umea: unpublished manuscript.

Schlesinger, P. (1991), *Media, State and Nation*, London: Sage.

Schnapper, D. (1994), *La Communauté des citoyens*, Paris: Gallimard.

Schwalbe, M. (1995), *Unlocking the Iron Cage: A Critical Appreciation of Mythopoetic Men's Work*, New York: Oxford University Press.

Schwarzmantel, J. (1991), *Socialism and the Idea of the Nation*, Brighton: Harvester Wheatsheaf.

Scott, J. (1985), *Weapons of the Weak: Everyday Forms of Peasant Resistance*, New Haven, CT: Yale University Press.

Scott, J. (1991), *Domination and the Arts of Resistance: Hidden Transcripts*, New Haven, CT: Yale University Press.

Semmel, B. (1986), *Liberalism and Naval Strategy: Ideology, Interest and Sea Power during the Pax Britannica*, London: Allen and Unwin.

Senn, A. (1990), *Lithuania Awakening*, Berkeley: University of California Press.

Senn, A. (1995), *Gorbachev's Failure in Lithuania*, New York: St Martin's Press.

Seton-Watson, H. (1977), *Nations and States: An Enquiry into the Origins of Nations and the Politics of Nationalism*, Boulder, CO and London: Westview Press/Methuen.

Shakhnazarov, G. (1993), *Tsena svobody: Reformatsiia Gorbacheva glazami ego pomoshchnika*, Moscow: Rossika.

Shaw, M. (1997), 'The state of globalization: towards a theory of state transformation', *Review of International Political Economy*, 4:3, 497–513.

Shelton, A. (1987), 'Rosa Luxemburg and the national question', *East European Quarterly*, 21:3.

Shils, E. (1957), 'Primordial, personal, sacred and civil ties', *British Journal of Sociology*, 7, 113–45.

Silber, N. (1993), *The Romance of Reunion: Northerners and the South 1886–1900*, Chapel Hill: University of North Carolina Press.

Silverman, M. (1992), *Deconstructing the Nation: Immigration, Racism and Citizenship in Modern France*, London: Routledge.

Sinha, M. (1995), *Colonial Masculinity: The 'Manly Englishman' and the 'Effeminate Bengali' in the Late Nineteenth Century*, Manchester: Manchester University Press.

Skilling, H. (1992), 'T. G. Masaryk, arch-critic of Austro-Hungarian foreign policy', in L. Matejka (ed.), *Cross Currents: A Yearbook of Central European Culture*, New Haven, CT: Yale University Press.

Skocpol, T. (1979), *States and Social Revolutions: A Comparative Analysis of France, Russia, and China*, New York: Cambridge University Press.

Skocpol, T. (1992), *Protecting Soldiers and Mothers: The Political Origins of Social Policy in the US*, Cambridge, MA: Harvard University Press.

Skurski, J. (1994), 'The ambiguities of authenticity: *Doña Bárbara* and the construction of national identity', *Poetics Today*, 15, 605–42.

Sluga, G. (1998), 'Identity, gender and the history of European nations and nationalisms', *Nations and Nationalism*, 4:1, 87–111.

Smith, A. (1971), *Theories of Nationalism*, London and New York: Duckworth/Harper and Row.

Smith, A. (1981a), *The Ethnic Revival in the Modern World*, Cambridge: Cambridge University Press.

Smith, A. (1981b), 'States and homelands: the social and geopolitical implications of national territory', *Millennium*, 10:3, 187–202.

Smith, A. (1986), *The Ethnic Origins of Nations*, Oxford: Blackwell.

Smith, A. (1989), 'The origins of nations', *Ethnic and Racial Studies*, 12:3, 340–67.

Smith, A. (1990), 'Towards a global culture?', in M. Featherstone (ed.), *Global Culture: Nationalism, Globalization and Modernity*, London: Sage, pp. 171–92.

Smith, A. (1991), *National Identity*, Harmondsworth: Penguin.

Smith, A. (1995), *Nations and Nationalism in a Global Era*, Cambridge: Polity Press.

Smith, A. (1998), *Nationalism and Modernism: A Critical Survey of Recent Theories of Nations and Nationalism*, London and New York: Routledge.

Smith, M. G. (1965), *The Plural Society of the British West Indies*, London: Sangster's.

Smith, S. (1993b), 'Residential segregation and the politics of racialisation', in M. Cross and M. Keith (eds), *Racism, the City and the State*, London: Routledge, pp. 128–43.

Snow, D. and Benford, R. (1992), 'Master frames and cycles of protest', in A. Morris and C. McClurg Mueller (eds), *Frontiers in Social Movement Theory*, New Haven, CT: Yale University Press, pp. 133–55.

Snyder, L. (1954), *The Meaning of Nationalism*, New Brunswick, NJ: Rutgers University Press.

Snyder, L. (ed.) (1990), *Encyclopedia of Nationalism*, Chicago: St. James Press.

Soysal, Y. (1994), *Limits of Citizenship: Migrants and Postnational Membership in Europe*, Chicago: Chicago University Press.

Springhall, J. (1987), 'Building character in the British boy: the attempt to extend Christian manliness to working-class adolescents 1880–1940', in J. A. Mangan and J. Walvin (eds), *Manliness and Morality: Middle-Class Masculinity in Britain and America 1800–1940*, Manchester: Manchester University Press, pp. 52–74.

Steinberg, S. (1966), *Five Hundred Years of Printing*, rev. ed., Harmondsworth: Penguin.

Steinfels, P. (1995), 'In Algeria, women are caught in the cross-fire of men's religious and ideological wars', *New York Times*, 1 July, pp. 8, 10.

Sternhell, Z. (1991), 'The political culture of nationalism', in R. Tombs (ed.), *Nationhood and Nationalism in France: From Boulangism to the Great War 1889–1918*, London: HarperCollins.

Stone, N. (1983), *Europe Transformed 1878–1919*, London: Fontana.

Sturdevant, S. and Stoltzfus, B. (1992), *Let the Good Times Roll: Prostitution and the US Military in Asia*, New York: New Press.

Suny, R. (1983), *Armenia in the Twentieth Century*, Chico, CA: Scholars Press.

Suny, R. (1993), *Revenge of the Past: Nationalism, Revolution, and the Collapse of the Soviet Union*, Palo Alto, CA: Stanford University Press.

Taagepera, R. (1993), *Estonia: Return to Independence*, Boulder, CO: Westview Press.

Tamir, Y. (1993), *Liberal Nationalism*, Princeton, NJ: Princeton University Press.

Tarrow, S. (1989a), *Democracy and Disorder: Protest and Politics in Italy 1965–1975*, Oxford: Oxford University Press.

Tarrow, S. (1989b), *Struggle, Politics, and Reform: Collective Action, Social Movements, and Cycles of Protest*, Ithaca, NY: Cornell Studies in International Affairs.

Tarrow, S. (1994), *Power in Movement: Social Movements, Collective Action and Politics*, Cambridge: Cambridge University Press.

Taylor, P. (1996), 'Embedded statism and the social sciences: opening up to new spaces', *Environment and Planning A*, 28:11.

Taylor, S. J. (1991), *Shock! Horror! The Tabloids in Action*, London: Corgi.

Tehranian, M. (1993), 'Ethnic discourse and the new world dysorder: a communitarian perspective', in C. Roach (ed.), *Communication and Culture in War and Peace*, Newbury Park, CA: Sage.

Teitelbaum, M. and Winter, J. (1998), *A Question of Numbers: High Migration, Low Fertility, and the Politics of National Identity*, New York: Hill and Wang.

Therborn, G. (1977), 'The rule of capital and the rise of democracy', *New Left Review*, 13.

Theroux, P. (1985), *Sunrise with Seamonsters*, Boston: Houghton-Mifflin.

Theweleit, K. (1987), *Male Fantasies*, tr. Stephen Conway, Minneapolis: University of Minnesota Press, vol. 1.

Thom, M. (1995), *Republics, Nations and Tribes*, London: Verso.

Thomas, D. (1992), *Criminal Injustice: Violence against Women in Brazil – an Americas Watch Report*, New York: Human Rights Watch.

Thompson, J. (1998), 'Community identity and world citizenship', in D. Archibugi, D. Held and M. Köhler (eds), *Re-Imagining Political Community: Studies in Cosmopolitan Democracy*, Cambridge: Polity Press, pp. 179–97.

Thompson, J. B. (1995), *The Media and Modernity*, Cambridge: Polity Press.

Tilly, C. (1978), *From Mobilization to Revolution*, Reading, MA: Addison-Wesley.

Tilly, C. (1984), 'Social movements and national politics', in C. Bright and S. Harding (eds), *Statemaking and Social Movements: Essays in History and Theory*, Ann Arbor: University of Michigan Press.

Tilly, C. (1986), *The Contentious French*, Cambridge, MA: Harvard University Press.

Tilly, C. (1995), 'Contentious repertoires in Great Britain 1758–1834', in M. Traugott (ed.), *Repertoires and Cycles of Collective Action*, Durham, NC: Duke University Press, pp. 15–42.

Tishkov, V. (1991), 'The Soviet empire before and after perestroika', paper presented at the United Nations Workshop on Ethnic Conflict and Development, 3–6 June.

Tivey, L. (ed.) (1980), *The Nation-State*, Oxford: Martin Robertson.

Todorov, T. (1993), *On Human Diversity: Nationalism, Racism, and Exoticism in French Thought*, Cambridge, MA: Harvard University Press.

Tohidi, N. (1991), 'Gender and Islamic fundamentalism: feminist politics in Iran', in C. T. Mohanty, A. Russo and L. Torres (eds), *Third World Women and the Politics of Feminism*, Bloomington: Indiana University Press, pp. 251–65.

Tonkin, E., McDonald, M. and Chapman, M. (eds) (1989), *History and Ethnicity*, London and New York: Routledge.

Townsend, P. (1979), *Poverty in the United Kingdom*, London: Penguin.

Turner, B. (1986), *Citizenship and Capitalism: The Debate over Reformism*, London: Allen and Unwin.

Turner, B. (1992), 'Outline of a theory of citizenship', in C. Mouffe (ed.), *Dimensions of Radical Democracy: Pluralism, Citizenship, Community*, London and New York: Verso, pp. 33–62.

Ueda, R. (1997), 'An immigration country of assimilative pluralism', in K. Bade and M. Wiener (eds), *Migration Past, Migration Future*, Oxford: Berghahn.

UNESCO (1950), *World Communications Report*, Paris: United Nations Educational, Scientific and Cultural Organization.

UNESCO (1986), *International Flows of Selected Cultural Goods*, Paris: United Nations Educational, Scientific and Cultural Organization.

UNESCO (1989), *World Communications Report*, Paris: United Nations Educational, Scientific and Cultural Organization.

Urdang, S. (1989), *And Still They Dance: Women, War and the Struggle for Change in Mozambique*, New York: Monthly Review Press.

Verluise, P. (1995), *Armenia in Crisis: The 1988 Earthquake*, tr. L. Chorbajian, Detroit: Wayne State University Press.

Vickers, J. (1993), *Women and War*, London: Zed.

Vogel, U. (1994), 'Marriage and the boundaries of citizenship', in B. van Steenbergen (ed.), *The Condition of Citizenship*, London: Sage, pp. 76–89.

Vorotnikov, V. (1995), *A bylo eto tak*, Moscow: SI-MAR.

Wade, R. (1990), *Governing the Market: Economic Theory and the Rise of the Market in East Asian Industrialization*, Princeton, NJ: Princeton University Press.

Wade, R. (1996), 'Globalisation and its limits: reports of the death of the national economy are greatly exaggerated', in S. Berger and R. Dore (eds.), *National Diversity and Global Capitalism*, Ithaca, NY: Cornell University Press.

Walby, S. (1989), 'Woman and nation', in A. D. Smith (ed.), *Ethnicity and Nationalism*, New York: E. J. Brill, pp. 81–99.

Waldron, J. (1999), 'What is cosmopolitan?', *Journal of Political Philosophy*, 8:2, 227–43.

Wallace, W. (1999), 'The sharing of sovereignty: the European paradox', *Political Studies*, 47:3.

Wallerstein, I. (1974), *The Modern World-System, vol. 1: Capitalist Agriculture and the Origins of the European World-Economy in the Sixteenth Century*, New York: Academic Press.

Wallerstein, I. (1991), 'Does India exist?', in I. Wallerstein, *Unthinking Social Science: The Limits of Nineteenth-Century Paradigms*, Cambridge: Polity Press, pp. 130–4.

Walvin, J. (1987), 'Symbols of moral superiority: slavery, sport and the changing world order 1900–1940', in J. A. Mangan and J. Walvin (eds), *Manliness and Morality: Middle-Class Masculinity in Britain and America 1800–1940*, Manchester: Manchester University Press, pp. 242–60.

Walzer, M. (1983), *Spheres of Justice: A Defense of Pluralism and Equality*, New York: Basic Books.

Warren, A. (1986), 'Citizens of the Empire, Baden-Powell, Scouts, Guides, and an imperial ideal', in J. M. MacKenzie (ed.), *Imperialism and Popular Culture*, Manchester: Manchester University Press, pp. 232–56.

Warren, A. (1987), 'Popular manliness: Baden-Powell, scouting, and the development of manly character', in J. A. Mangan and J. Walvin (eds), *Manliness and Morality: Middle-Class Masculinity in Britain and America 1800–1940*, Manchester: Manchester University Press, pp. 199–219.

Waylen, G. (1996), 'Democratization, feminism, and the state in Chile: the establishment of SERNAM', in S. M. Rai and G. Lievesley (eds), *Women and the State: International Perspectives*, London: Taylor and Francis, pp. 103–17.

Weber, E. (1976), *Peasants into Frenchmen: The Modernization of Rural France 1870–1914*, Palo Alto, CA: Stanford University Press.

Weber, E. (1977), *Peasants into Frenchmen: The Modernisation of Rural France 1870–1914*, London: Chatto and Windus.

Weber, E. (1979), *Peasants into Frenchmen: The Modernisation of Rural France, 1870–1914*, pbk ed., London: Chatto and Windus.

Weber, M. (1948), 'The social psychology of the world religions', in H. H. Gerth and C. Mills (trs and eds), *From Max Weber: Essays in Sociology*, New York: Oxford University Press.

Weber, M. (1978), *Economy and Society: An Outline of Interpretive Sociology, vol. 1*, ed. G. Roth and C. Wittich, Berkeley and Los Angeles: University of California Press.

Weil, P. (1996), 'Nationalities and citizenships: the lessons of the French experience for Germany and Europe', in D. Cesarani and M. Fulbrooke (eds), *Citizenship, Nationality and Identity in Europe*, London: Routledge.

Weiss, L. (1995), 'Governed interdependence: rethinking the government-business relationship in East Asia', *Pacific Review*, 8.

Weiss, L. and Hobson, J. (1995), *States and Economic Development: A Comparative Historical Analysis*, Cambridge: Polity Press.

West, L. (1997), *Feminist Nationalism*, New York: Routledge.

Wiberg, H. (1983), 'Self-determination as international issue', in I. Lewis (ed.), *Nationalism and Self-Determination in the Horn of Africa*, London, Ithaca Press.

Williams, R. (1976), *Keywords*, London: Flamingo.

Wihtol de Wenden, C. (1988), *Les Immigrés et la politique: Cent-cinquante ans d'évolution*, Paris: Presses de la FNSP.

Wihtol de Wenden, C. (1994), 'Immigration, nationality and citizenship in France', in R. Baubock (ed.), *From Aliens to Citizens: Redefining the Status of Immigrants in Europe*, Aldershot: Avebury.

Wihtol de Wenden, C. (1995), 'Generational change and political participation in French suburbs', *New Community*, 21:1, 69–78.

Wilson, W. (1987), *The Truly Disadvantaged: The Inner City, the Underclass and Public Policy*, Chicago: University of Chicago Press.

Wilson, W. (1994), 'Citizenship and the inner-city ghetto poor', in B. van Steenbergen (ed.), *The Condition of Citizenship*, London: Sage, pp. 49–65.

Witt, L., Paget, K. and Matthews, G. (1994), *Running as a Woman: Gender and Power in American Politics*, New York: Free Press.

Woolf, S. (ed.) (1996), *Nationalism in Europe 1815 to the Present*, London: Routledge.

Woolf, V. (1977), *Three Guineas*, Harmondsworth: Penguin.

Yatani, C. and Bramel, D. (1989), 'Trends and patterns in Americans' attitude toward the Soviet Union', *Journal of Social Issues*, 45, 13–32.

Young, I. (1989), 'Polity and group difference: a critique of the ideal of universal citizenship', *Ethics*, 99, 250–74.

Young, M. (1993), *The Rising Tide of Cultural Pluralism: The Nation-State at Bay?*, Madison: University of Wisconsin Press.

Youssef, I. (1994), 'Bareheaded women slain in Algiers: killings following Islamic threats', *New York Times*, 31 March, p. A3.

Yuval-Davis, N. (1981), *Israeli Women and Men: Divisions behind the Unity*, London: Change International Reports.

Yuval-Davis, N. (1993), 'Gender and nation', *Ethnic and Racial Studies*, 16:4, 621–32.

Yuval-Davis, N. and Anthias, F. (1989), *Woman-Nation-State*, London: Macmillan.

Zavalloni, M. (1993a), 'Ascribed identities and the social identity space; an ego/ ecological analysis', paper delivered at Changing European Identities Conference, Farnham, Surrey, April.

Zavalloni, M. (1993b), 'Identity and hyperidentities: the representational foundation of self and culture', *Papers on Social Representations*, 2, 218–35.

Zetterholm, Z. (1994), *National Cultures and European Integration*, Oxford: Berg.

Ziegler, P. (1977), *Crown and People*, London: Collins.

Zolberg, A. (1972), 'Moments of madness', *Politics and Society*, 2, 183–207.

COPYRIGHT ACKNOWLEDGEMENTS

Grateful acknowledgement is made to the following sources for permission to reproduce material in this book previously published elsewhere. Every effort has been made to trace copyright holders, but if any have been inadvertently overlooked the publisher will be pleased to make the necessary arrangement at the first opportunity.

1. '"Ethno-symbolism" and the Study of Nationalism' from *Myths and Memories of the Nation* by Anthony D. Smith, Oxford University Press, 1999. Reproduced by permission of Oxford University Press.
2. 'The Nation and Nationalism' from *The Construction of Nationhood: Ethnicity, Religion and Nationalism* by Adrian Hastings, Cambridge University Press, 1997. © Cambridge University Press, reproduced with the permission of the publisher and author's literary estate.
3. 'The Industrial and Industrialising World' and 'Do nations have navels?' from *Nationalism* by Ernest Gellner, Weidenfeld and Nicolson, an imprint of the Orion Group, 1997. Reproduced with the permission of the publisher.
4. 'Introduction', 'Cultural Roots' and 'The Origins of National Consciousness' from *Imagined Communities: Reflections on the Origin and Spread of Nationalism* by Benedict Anderson, Verso, 1991. Reproduced with the permission of the publisher.
5. Extracts from *Nationalism and the State, Second Edition* by John Breuilly, Manchester University Press, Manchester, UK, 1993 and the University of Chicago Press, 1994. Reproduced with the permission of Manchester University Press and the University of Chicago Press.
6. 'Liberal Nationalism: An Irresponsible Compound?' by Andrew Vincent from *Political Studies*, Vol. 45, No. 2 1997, Blackwell Publishing. Reproduced with the permission of the publisher.
7. 'Explaining Nationalism' from *Really Existing Nationalisms: A Post-Communist View from Marx and Engels* by Erica Benner, Oxford University Press, 1995. Reproduced by permission of Oxford University Press.

8. 'Masculinity and Nationalism: Gender and Sexuality in the Making of Nations' by Joane Nagel from *Ethnic and Racial Studies*, Vol. 21, No. 2 (1998), Routledge. Reproduced with the permission of Taylor & Francis Ltd and the author. http://www.tandf.co.uk/journals

9. Extracts from *Ethnicity and Nationalism: Anthropological Perspectives, Second Edition* by Thomas Eriksen, Pluto, 2002. Reproduced with the permission of the publisher.

10. Extracts from *Between Camps: Nations, Cultures and the Allure of Race* by Paul Gilroy, Allen Lane, 2000 (published as *Against Race: Imagining Political Culture Beyond the Color Line* by Paul Gilroy, Cambridge, MA: The Belknap Press of Harvard University Press, 2000). © Paul Gilroy 2000 & 2004. Reproduced with the permission of the author and The Belknap Press of Harvard University Press.

11. 'Racism and Nationalism' by Etienne Balibar from *Race, Nation, Class: Ambiguous Identities* edited by Etienne Balibar and I. Wallerstein, Verso, 1991. Reproduced with the permission of the publisher.

12. 'National and Other Identities' from *National Identity* by Anthony D. Smith, pp. 8–15. © Penguin Books, 1991 and the University of Nevada Press, 1993. Reproduced with the permission of Penguin Books Ltd and the University of Nevada Press.

13. 'Remembering Banal Nationalism' reprinted with the permission of Sage Publications Ltd from *Banal Nationalism* by Michael Billig. © Sage Publications Ltd, 1995.

14. 'Good and Bad Nationalism' reprinted with the permission of Sage Publications Ltd from *Nationalism: A Critical Introduction* by Philip Spencer and Howard Wollman. © Sage Publications Ltd, 2002.

15. 'On National Self-Determination' by Margaret Moore from *Political Studies*, Vol. 45, No. 5 (1997), Blackwell Publishing. Reproduced with the permission of the publisher.

16. 'Whose Imagined Community?' from *The Nation and Its Fragments: Colonial and Postcolonial Histories* by Partha Chatterjee. © 1993 Princeton University Press. Reprinted with the permission of Princeton University Press.

17. 'Constructing National and Cultural Identities in Sub-Saharan Francophone Africa' by Dominic Thomas from *Not On Any Map: Essays on Postcoloniality and Cultural Nationalism* edited by Stuart Murray, University of Exeter Press, 1997.

18. 'How Nationalisms Spread: Eastern Europe Adrift the Tides and Cycles of Nationalist Contention,' by Mark R. Beissinger from Social Research, Vol. 63, No. 1 (Spring 1996) edited by Arien Mack, New York: New School University. Reproduced with the permission of the publisher and the author.

19. 'Has globalization ended the rise and rise of the nation-state?' by Michael Mann from *Review of International Political Economy*, Vol. 4, No. 3 (1997), Routledge. Reproduced with the permission of Taylor & Francis Ltd and the author. http://www.tandf.co.uk/journals

20. 'Citizenship and the Other in the Age of Migration' reprinted with the permission of Sage Publications Ltd from *Ethnicity and Globalization: From Migrant Worker to Transnational Citizen* by Stephen Castles. © Sage Publications Ltd, 2000.

21. 'Culture and Political Community: National, Global and Cosmopolitan' by David Held from *Conceiving Cosmopolitanism: Theory, Context, and Practice* edited by S. Vertovec and R. Cohen. Oxford University Press, 2002. Reproduced by permission of Oxford University Press.

INDEX

Note: The index uses word-by-word alphabetical order. Page references in **bold** type indicate major treatment of central topics. Page references in *italics* indicate tables.